Credit to the Community

MAXINE GOODMAN LEVIN
COLLEGE OF URBAN AFFAIRS

Cleveland State University

Cities and Contemporary Society

Series Editors: Richard D. Bingham and Larry C. Ledebur,
Cleveland State University

Sponsored by the
Maxine Goodman Levin College of Urban Affairs
Cleveland State University

This new series focuses on key topics and emerging trends in urban
policy. Each volume is specially prepared for academic use, as well as for
specialists in the field.

SUBURBAN SPRAWL
Private Decisions and Public Policy
Wim Wiewel and Joseph J. Persky, Editors

THE INFRASTRUCTURE OF PLAY
Building the Tourist City in North America
Dennis R. Judd

THE ADAPTED CITY
Institutional Dynamics and Structural Change
H. George Frederickson, Gary A. Johnson, and Curtis H. Wood

CREDIT TO THE COMMUNITY
Community Reinvestment and Fair Lending Policy
in the United States
Dan Immergluck

Credit to the
Community

Community Reinvestment and Fair Lending Policy in the United States

Dan Immergluck

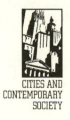

CITIES AND
CONTEMPORARY
SOCIETY

M.E.Sharpe
Armonk, New York
London, England

Library of Congress Cataloging-in-Publication Data

Immergluck, Daniel.
  Credit to the community : community reinvestment and fair lending policy in the United
States / by Dan Immergluck.
      p. cm. — (Cities and contemporary society)
  Includes bibliographical references and index.
  ISBN 0-7656-1258-5 (cloth : alk. paper)
  1. Bank loans—United States. 2. Mortgage loans—United States. 3. Community
development—United States. 4. Discrimination in mortgage loans—United States.
5. Discrimination in consumer credit—United States. I. Title. II. Series.
HG1642.U5 I46 2004
332.7′08′0973—dc22

                                                                            2003023978

Printed in the United States of America

The paper used in this publication meets the minimum requirements of
American National Standard for Information Sciences
Permanence of Paper for Printed Library Materials,
ANSI Z 39.48-1984.

MV   (c)   10   9   8   7   6   5   4   3   2   1

Contents

List of Tables and Figures vii

Acknowledgments ix

List of Acronyms xi

1. Introduction 3
2. The Visible Hand of Government in U.S. Credit Markets 19
3. Discrimination, Redlining, and Financial Restructuring in Business Credit Markets 52
4. A Brief History of Mortgage-Lending Discrimination and Redlining 87
5. From Fair Access to Credit to Access to Fair Credit 109
6. Mobilizing for Credit: Community Activism, Policy Adoption, and Implementation Through 1987 133
7. Community Reinvestment from 1988 to the End of the Twentieth Century: Struggles for Bank and Regulator Accountability 168
8. The Predatory Lending Policy Debate 211
9. The Community Reinvestment Act and Fair Lending Policy in the Twenty-first Century 236

Notes 271

Bibliography 281

Index 297

List of Tables and Figures

Tables

3.1 CRA-Reported Small Business Loans, 1997   71

3.2 Loans to Firms with Less than $1 Million in Sales in Residential Central-City Neighborhoods, 1997   72

3.3 Small Business Lending by Racial Composition of Census Tract in Nine-County Philadelphia Area, 1998   73

3.4 Regression Explaining Small Business Lending Flows   74

5.1 Increase in Subprime Lenders' Refinance Loans, 1993–1998, United States   112

5.2 Lenders with the Most Refinance Applications in Predominantly *White* Neighborhoods in the Chicago Area, 1998   115

5.3 Lenders with the Most Refinance Applications in Predominantly *Black* Neighborhoods in the Chicago Area, 1998   116

5.4 Regression of Subprime Lenders' Market Share in Chicago Census Tracts, 1998   117

5.5 A Sample of Predatory Lending Practices and Loan Terms   123

6.1 CRA Assessment Factors Used by Regulators, 1978–1995   156

6.2 CRA Examination Ratings of Federal Reserve Member Banks, 1980   160

7.1 Numerical Equivalents of Component Test Ratings   210

Figures

3.1 The Small Business Lending Process   70

4.1 The Home Mortgage Lending Process   101

5.1 The Growth in Subprime Mortgage Lending in the
     United States   111

5.2 Growth in Refinance Loans by Subprime Lenders by Race
     of Neighborhood, Chicago Area, 1993–1998   113

5.3 Home Equity Asset-Backed Securities, 1995–2002   128

6.1 Number of Formal CRA Challenges Received by the FRB,
     1977–1987   164

7.1 CRA Ratings, 1990–2002   179

7.2 Outstanding CRA Ratings by Regulator, 1990–2002   180

7.3 Outstanding CRA Ratings by Asset Size of Institution,
     1990–2002   182

7.4 Needs-to-Improve and Substantial Noncompliance Ratings,
     1990–2002   184

7.5 Factors and Processes Affecting Banks' Choice to Engage
     in a CRA Agreement   186

7.6 CRA Commitment Activity, 1979–2000: Agreements
     vs. Pledges   188

7.7 Cumulative Dollar Amount of CRA Commitments,
     1990–2000   189

7.8 Fannie Mae and Freddie Mac Performance vs. Low-
     and Moderate-Income Housing Goals, 1993–2001   200

8.1 Changes in Unemployment Over the CRC Study Periods
     in North Carolina and Adjacent States   231

Acknowledgments

I never feel up to the task of thanking people adequately. And because this book is partly a manifestation of a good deal of my professional work over the last ten or more years, it is something that I will not be able to do very well here. I have had the pleasure of working with so many energetic, committed, and genuinely good people on issues discussed in this book that I could never name all those whose impact is reflected in these pages. But I have to mention some of them. I begin with Malcolm Bush, the best colleague I have ever had. My nine years of working with Malcolm allowed me to recognize and develop newfound energies and passions. In addition to supporting my work at the Woodstock Institute for almost a decade and entrusting me with so many critical projects, Malcolm has always been the best of intellectual colleagues. People who know Malcolm have witnessed his leadership and insight on community reinvestment policy and research; they understand what a tremendous stroke of luck it was when he was recruited to join the Woodstock Institute in the early 1990s. Malcolm read a draft of the book and gave me helpful comments.

Greg Squires and Allen Fishbein also read a draft copy and offered very useful suggestions. Greg, in my view, is a role model for academics who seek to contribute to the social and political world in real, tangible ways while maintaining their commitment to scholarship and teaching. I asked Allen to read the book because of his long and widely respected history as a leading and thoughtful advocate for sound reinvestment and fair lending policies. Unfortunately, I was not able to follow up on all the suggestions made by Malcolm, Greg, or Allen. Moreover, in cases where I attempted to address their concerns, I am sure my efforts were not always as strong as they could have been.

Katy Jacob, a good friend and colleague, proofread and edited the entire book before I submitted it to the publisher, demonstrating once again her remarkable skills in that arena. Some of the work in this book is a direct result of joint undertakings with Marti Wiles and Geoff Smith, both of whom have been excellent collaborators on research projects over the years. I also appreciate the support I received from all the staff members at the Woodstock Institute with whom I worked during my time there. At Grand Valley State University, I want to thank Dan Balfour, director of the public administration program, for supporting my scholarly activities, and Sherry Moyer for her help on all sorts of things. In addition, I had the excellent research assistance of several graduate students, including Daniel Szmytkowski, Irvin Chikoti, and Alexandra Pruszewicz. The librarians at Grand Valley, especially Aram Snyder and Ben Hayes, were also extremely helpful and always accommodating of my many requests. At M.E. Sharpe, I want to thank Harry Briggs, Elizabeth Granda, and Susan Rescigno for their help with editing and the entire publication process. Dick Bingham, editor of the Cities and Contemporary Society series, was also of great assistance.

This book is a product of the last fifteen years of my working life, which has included on-the-ground work in community and economic development as well as later advocacy and research. I trace my interest in urban and community affairs and public policy to my parents, who gently, even subtly, instilled in me a commitment to social justice. They recently celebrated their fiftieth wedding anniversary, and I would like them to think of this book as partly a return on their investment in teaching me that being good means doing good.

Most of all, I want to thank my wife and daughters. In the year or so that I worked on this book, we underwent some significant changes: We moved from Chicago to Grand Rapids—a major cultural shift—my wife and I both started new jobs, and we had a new baby. Was it the best time to write a book? Probably not. But my wife, Lilly, encouraged me at every step of the way, and Kate and Anna gave me so much fun and joy when I had no time for any other form of amusement. They were enough. More than enough.

List of Acronyms

ACORN	Association of Community Organizations for Reform Now
ACRA	Atlanta Community Reinvestment Alliance
AFSA	American Financial Services Association
AMTPA	Alternative Mortgage Transaction Parity Act
APR	annual percentage rate
BHC	bank holding company
CDBG	Community Development Block Grant
CDFI	community development financial institution
CRA	Community Reinvestment Act
CRC	Credit Research Center
CRL	Center for Responsible Lending
DIDMCA	Depository Institutions Deregulation and Monetary Control Act
ECOA	Equal Credit Opportunity Act
EOL	Emergency Opportunity Loan
FaHA	Fair Housing Act
FDIC	Federal Deposit Insurance Corporation
FHA	Federal Housing Administration
FHC	finance holding company
FIRREA	Financial Institutions Reform Recovery and Enforcement Act
FRB	Federal Reserve Board
GAO	General Accounting Office
GLBA	Gramm-Leach-Bliley Act
GSE	government-sponsored enterprise
HMDA	Home Mortgage Disclosure Act
HOEPA	Home Ownership and Equity Protection Act
HOLA	Home Owners Loan Act
HOLC	Home Owners Loan Corporation
HUD	Department of Housing and Urban Development
LIM	low-income or minority
MAHA	Metropolitan Area Housing Alliance
MBS	mortgage-backed securities

MSA	metropolitan statistical area
NAACP	National Association for the Advancement of Colored People
NCCF	National Commission on Consumer Finance
NCO	Northwest Community Organization
NCRC	National Community Reinvestment Coalition
NHS	Neighborhood Housing Services
NPA	National People's Action
NSSBF	National Survey of Small Business Finances
OBA	Organization for a Better Austin
OCC	Office of the Comptroller of the Currency
O.N.E.	Organization for the North East
OTS	Office of Thrift Supervision
PSSA	primary savings service area
S&Ls	savings and loans
SBA	Small Business Administration
SBIC	small business investment company
SMSA	standard metropolitan statistical area
SPCI	single premium credit insurance
VA	Veterans Administration

Credit to the Community

MAXINE GOODMAN LEVIN
COLLEGE OF URBAN AFFAIRS

Cleveland State University

CHAPTER 1

Introduction

Public utility is more truly the object of public banks, than private profit. And it is the business of government to constitute them on such principles, that while the latter will result, in a sufficient degree, to afford competent motives to engage in them, the former be not made subservient to it.
 —Alexander Hamilton, Secretary of the Treasury, Report on a National Bank, December 13, 1790.[1]

The regulators seem to think we're all living in Lake Wobegon. Like the children of the fictional village, U.S. lenders are all above average. Almost all get high ratings year after year and almost none is ever held back.
 —Senator William Proxmire, 1988.[2]

Full responsibility for CRA enforcement has always been the job of people in the neighborhoods.
 —Gale Cincotta, National People's Action, 1999.[3]

This book is about access to credit and basic financial services in the United States. It focuses on how public policy has—and sometimes has not—worked to improve such access for households and small businesses in lower-income and minority communities. For many middle- and upper-income white Americans, access to reasonably priced credit has become so ubiquitous that it may be hard to understand why there would be much concern about these issues. In lower-income and minority communities, however, poor access to fairly priced credit remains a key concern and a major barrier to economic security and neighborhood stability. The Community Reinvestment Act (CRA), the Home Mortgage Disclosure Act (HMDA), the Fair Housing Act (FaHA), the Equal Credit Opportunity Act (ECOA), and their hundreds of pages of attendant regulations and guidance are little known to the average

3

citizen. Yet these policies have played important roles—ones that I will argue have been positive but far below their potential—in enabling working-class families of all ethnic and racial backgrounds to fare better in improving and maintaining their economic status. Beyond the impact on families and small businesses, these laws have worked to slow, and in some cases have been a key force in the reversal of, neighborhood decline.

At the turn of the twenty-first century, public confidence in the ability of federal policy to make a positive contribution to society (particularly in modest-income urban neighborhoods) may be at an all-time low. The trend over the last twenty-five years has largely been to reduce the federal role in business regulation, as well as in issues of social and economic justice. Those favoring such reductions sometimes argue that the declining confidence in the efficacy of these efforts justifies the policy pullback. Weak arguments— rarely supported by empirical evidence—have often won the day politically. Some have pointed to the persistence of urban poverty and decline in many cities to argue that policies such as CRA have not been successful. These arguments ignore the forces—from both the private and public sectors—that have typically dwarfed the scale of federal efforts supporting urban neighborhoods. They fail to recognize how much worse things would be without CRA and other pro-urban policies. They also ignore the substantial investments in many lower-income neighborhoods throughout the country that have been bolstered by CRA, as well as the significant reductions in concentrated poverty that occurred in the 1990s when CRA was more aggressively enforced (Jargowsky 2003). Opponents of CRA and fair lending laws disregard the great missed potential of CRA and fair lending policies, that is, what these policies would have produced if they were more consistently and vigorously enforced over a substantial period of time. In the entire twenty-seven year history of CRA, for example, the law was enforced vigorously only during a couple of brief two- or three-year periods.

Another approach of critics of CRA and fair lending regulations is to rely on the gospel of neoclassical economic theory to argue that regulation and policy interventions result in more negative, unintended consequences than positive, intended ones. One of the purposes of this book is to provide wider access to evidence that can counter the arguments based in a knee-jerk, anti-government paradigm that gained steam in the 1970s and 1980s. Evidence of the positive, though limited, impacts of the CRA is strong and robust in favor of the law's improving access to credit.

At the same time, another purpose of the book is to alarm those concerned about cities and urban neighborhoods and about fair access to economic opportunity for minority and lower-income families. The potency of federal policy in this area has been waning for at least the last ten to fifteen years, and this decline has become steeper during the last five years. In the name of allowing what are now only nominally domestic financial institutions to be more competitive in the global financial marketplace, proponents of deregulation have effectively stymied any efforts to improve—or even maintain—the effectiveness of federal reinvestment and fair lending laws. Moreover, when states look to fill the void left by the absence of meaningful regulation by federal regulatory agencies and legislators, they are increasingly pre-empted by federal policymakers who seek to cater to the deregulatory desires of these global firms.

Why Care About Credit?

Access to fairly priced credit is a critical component of a community's economic infrastructure. For families to become and remain home owners, credit is needed at fair prices and terms. For small businesses to maximize their productivity, they need fair credit to convert receivables into capital for continued production and to invest in necessary equipment. Consumers need reasonably priced credit to purchase automobiles and other durable goods. Greater access to fairly priced credit improves the efficiency and productivity of local and national economies. It increases what economists call the "velocity" of money, which then circulates more throughout the economy, distributing and magnifying the benefits of trade and commerce.

Access to credit is more than a macroeconomic issue. It affects individual families and particular neighborhoods. In the 1950s and 1960s, when blacks in many cities had difficulty obtaining credit as they began to increase their incomes, they were forced to purchase homes from real estate speculators on a "land contract" basis (Bradford and Marino 1977; Helper 1969, 45). Speculators would purchase homes at fairly low prices—sometimes obtained via blockbusting real estate techniques in which speculators would scare white home owners by warning of rapid racial change—and then sell houses, typically to black buyers, at inflated prices. These homes were financed not with formal mortgages but with abusive land contracts, under which the buyer would make monthly payments to the speculator/owner. These contracts did not allow for the buyer to build up owner equity in the home as he made monthly payments. Only after every scheduled payment over the life of the contract was paid did he obtain ownership. If a family missed just one, even one of the last payments, ownership could revert to the speculator.

Though many situations—including the ability of minorities to get home purchase loans—have improved due to fair lending laws and CRA, a new set of access-to-credit problems has arisen forty years later. Many of these patterns are the result of an explosion of new high-cost, high-risk, "fringe" lenders. In 2003, in a lower-income neighborhood on the South Side of Chicago known as "Back of the Yards," Neighborhood Housing Services (NHS) of Chicago, a nonprofit community development lender, was working to save a community from what had become a foreclosure epidemic—one that has been repeated in many communities across the country. In NHS's Back of the Yards target area, more than one in ten homes began the foreclosure process in 2002 alone (Neighborhood Reinvestment Corporation 2003). Approximately one-half of these home owners were expected to lose their homes through foreclosure. And in neighborhoods like this one, foreclosures often result in abandoned, boarded-up homes that lead to lower property values and increased crime. The bulk of these foreclosures were due to high-cost "subprime" loans, which are loans priced at higher rates and generally intended for borrowers with blemished credit. Significant numbers of subprime loans carry abusive terms and conditions.

Credit access also plays a crucial role in neighborhood economic development. Poor access to credit remains a significant barrier to small business development and growth among minority-owned firms and businesses located in modest-income urban neighborhoods. Bates (1993) has shown that levels of credit and capital are key determinants of business viability for small, young firms. Yet, even after controlling for a wide variety of firm and owner characteristics, including credit history, black firms are denied small business loans at twice the rate as white-owned firms (Bostic and Lampani 1999; Cavalluzzo, Cavalluzzo, and Wolken 1999). And firms located in black neighborhoods receive fewer loans than those in white neighborhoods, even after controlling for a variety of neighborhood characteristics, including the credit scores of local firms (Immergluck 2002).

The Urban Context for Community Reinvestment and Fair Lending

The economic and social conditions of many lower-income and minority urban neighborhoods in the United States deteriorated during the middle and later parts of the twentieth century (Jargowsky 1997; Zielenbach 2000). Many communities lost substantial amounts of population and jobs and saw poverty increase. One of the causes of these problems was industrial restructuring—changes in the technologies, methods, and locations of industry. In the first half of the twentieth century, growing or at least steady demand for industrial labor, combined with a strong union movement, provided a sellers' market in industrial labor across the nation's cities. This meant that even those with weaker connections to unions and job networks could often find living-wage jobs that would support their families and provide the income on which their neighborhoods depended. The emergence of international competition, the flight of jobs overseas, and changes in production technologies took their toll on lower-skilled and, particularly, minority workers. This economic restructuring was accompanied by a spatial restructuring of urban areas, with employers fleeing central-city locations for green-grass sites in far-off suburbs.

While deindustrialization and the suburbanization of employment were accelerating, residential suburbanization was also taking its toll on central-city neighborhoods. Suburbanization was not a new phenomenon in the post–World War II era, but it accelerated in many places (Jackson 1985). White flight out of older central-city neighborhoods was strong as blacks migrated into northern and Midwestern industrial cities (Lemann 1992). Blockbusting by real estate agents, redlining by banks and mortgage companies, and other forms of discrimination in real estate markets hastened the racial and economic polarization of metropolitan areas (Abrams 1955; Massey and Denton 1993).

Urban researchers and historians have argued about the importance of various causes of urban decline. Some argue that global and national economic forces, including shifts from manufacturing to service employment, international competition, and the demand for suburban space by homeowners and businesses, have been the primary drivers of urban decline (Wilson 1996). Others have argued that discrimination in housing and mortgage markets has been a larger factor (Massey and Denton 1993). Still others have pointed to public policy, especially federal policy, as a key promoter of suburban development and institutionalized redlining that were forces of urban decline (Jackson 1985).

Much has been made of the arguments between these different factions. However, the complexity of cities and the likely interactive and cumulative causation involved with urban problems will tend to preclude any strong consensus over which factors have been the most important. Once we examine any one cause of urban decline, we tend to find it related to at least two or three other causes. For example, it is very difficult to isolate a "demand" for outer suburban locations by manufacturers from a desire by discriminatory employers to avoid minority workers. Moreover, the debates over whether highway construction was in response to a demand by employers and new suburban residents or a cause of such development will rest primarily on one's view of government's role and responsibilities. Acknowledging the importance of economic restructuring on urban decline does not preclude the argument that a public policy significantly exacerbated urban decline or, in other cases, slowed it. Scholars often lack the humility to acknowledge that they cannot precisely measure the various contributions of different factors. In addition, many research methodologies work to model highly complex systems in reductionary ways, thereby constraining the potential findings in the research design itself.

Flows of private-sector credit have been important factors in shaping the vitality and prospects of urban communities. Disparities in access to credit and capital have played a key, but not always independent, role in urban decline, and efforts to reduce these disparities have had some significant positive impacts. While community reinvestment and fair lending are ingredients to a more complex recipe for urban revitalization, policies in this area have had demonstrable impacts.

In the face of daunting and complex urban problems and the political obstacles to their solutions, some may suggest that low- and moderate-income urban neighborhoods and their residents should be abandoned. But others are working to counter these trends, to spur investment and jobs for residents of central cities, and to rebuild communities. They recognize that policies that work to maintain or increase the social and economic isolation of these neighborhoods carry grave short- and long-term costs to entire metropolitan regions. In the short term, the lack of access to economic opportunity means more poorly educated workers, more crime, and greater tensions between those with resources and those without. In the long term, this isolation and the continuous fleeing of people and businesses with resources away from lower-income areas cannot be sustained either environmentally or economically. The residents of these communities provide the labor on which regional economies depend, and, to a large degree, these neighborhoods will provide the future middle-class consumers and home owners that will sustain the economy of tomorrow. But if these communities continue to be neglected, they will not constitute a strong labor force or have the ability to improve their economic status. The persistence of these economic inefficiencies and inequities creates a drag on regional economies and the entire nation.

While attacking these problems requires multiple and mixed approaches, one strategy that needs to be pursued more vigorously is improving access to fairly priced credit and financial services for home owners, home buyers, and small businesses in lower-income and minority communities. This will require reshaping the tools provided under CRA and fair lending laws and enforcing these regulations more aggressively.

The Politics of Banking and Deregulationist Ideology

Contrary to what many might assume, the history of banking and formal credit markets in the United States is filled with interesting stories of highly charged public policy debates and political struggles. Some of these struggles involved fundamental notions of societal organization, states' rights versus centralized government, civil rights, and the appropriate power of the corporation. In many ways, access to credit has always been a controversial topic in the United States, from colonial-era arguments about the need for a central bank to current debates over predatory mortgage lending. The nature and specific subjects of the debates have changed, but the role of credit is such a powerful determinant of the life chances and economic opportunity of individuals and communities that, by their very nature, credit markets and their structure will always be politically contested. In her history of banking policy, Susan Hoffman argues that

> Public policy has made banks. . . . The banking process is political. Banks . . . decide where credit will flow throughout society and thus what human initiatives will flourish and which will wither. People, ventures, regions win and lose. This is the stuff of high politics, not calculus. (Hoffman 2001, 2, 3)

Credit is so political in large part because it is a key and necessary instrument to accessing economic opportunity, generating income, and building wealth. It is instrumental and necessary for acquiring what the philosopher John Rawls referred to as "primary" economic goods (Rawls 1971, 90–95). Moreover, access to credit means more than access to current resources. It helps to determine future access to primary goods such as income, wealth, and a home. Credit is a potent signal of one's life chances and the life chances of one's children. In the twenty-first century, as credit history is increasingly used to determine everything from the price of auto insurance to the ability to rent an apartment or gain employment, and is distilled into one numerical score, credit access has become a sort of an economic opportunity rating. It is a label that can work to restrict one's opportunities in all sorts of markets.

Credit is also the subject of political debate and social construction because its provision is so lucrative to banks, finance companies, and other suppliers. Political decisions regarding financial services regulation have driven the industrial structure of financial markets. At every stage in the historical development of U.S. financial markets, different types of firms have seen the prospects of great gain or great loss in public policy, and have waged correspondingly intense lobbying battles. Regulation has not just been a matter of an industry bearing the "cost" of consumer protection regulation. Rather, finance generally has been a highly public matter, with large doses of public-sector involvement in the design, regulation, and even management of the operations of banks and credit providers. Moreover,

the close involvement of government in financial services has greatly benefited the sector. Banking and securities markets were nurtured by state and
federal government throughout much of U.S. history because policymakers
recognized how important these industries were to local and national economic development and opportunity.

Certainly, there have always been entrepreneurial responses in financial
markets in the United States that have not been provoked by government
action. That is a clear component of the mixed economy in U.S. financial
services history. In the last three decades, however, there has been a deliberate and organized movement, aggressively promoted by the financial services sector, Congress, and many federal regulators, to reduce the public-sector
oversight of the financial services sector. Those "deregulationists" arguing
in favor of this shift suggest that such a system benefits from the efficiencies
of freer markets.[4] They apply the logic of a market for doughnuts or buttons
to the market for home loans or small business credit. Less government
involvement is almost always seen as a superior model for any form of
interpersonal exchange. This is the neoclassical paradigm that has dominated
so much of federal policy in the last thirty years, beginning with the strong
deregulatory moves in the late 1970s and 1980s.

The recent shift to deregulationist ideology has been at least as political as
any other phase of financial services history in the United States Some argue
that the recent victory of deregulationist forces is related, both as a cause and
as a result, to the increasing concentration of wealth in the United States. In
a vicious circle, those owners of capital served well by deregulation push for
even more deregulation. But Hays (1995), Hoffman (2001), and Stone (2001)
argue that public policies are shaped by more than a simple competition of
interests; they are shaped by the competition of ideas. I believe both interests
and ideas are at work. Campaign finance and the dominance of corporate
lobbyists have clearly been important in moving in this direction, especially
in the increasingly concentrated and converging financial services sector.
For example, the 1999 Gramm-Leach-Bliley Act (GLBA), which rolled back
the 1933 Glass-Steagall Act's barriers between banking and nonbanking financial services, involved more than twenty years of lobbying fights between different segments of the financial services sector and has been called
the most heavily funded legislation in U.S. history.

The brute force of financial industry lobbying, however, has not been the
only factor supporting deregulation. The ideology of free-market advocates
and a corresponding gospel of deregulation have been accepted even by
many who do not have clear financial interests in a laissez-faire financial
system. Many university graduates have been taught just enough economics
to be dangerous. The standard "principles of economics" courses provide a

one-size-fits-all, theory-over-evidence view of the inherent benefits of markets over government, rather than an empirically based, more sophisticated understanding of the real workings of markets and society. Such understanding requires more than a set of unrealistic assumptions and some elementary mathematical models. By the late twentieth century, the typical policymaker at both the federal and the state level had developed what social scientists call "priors" that include a strong antiregulatory posture. Regulation is now frequently seen as ineffective and often counterproductive. Those holding such views rarely rely on evidence for such claims, however.

For most of the history of the United States, the deregulationist ideology did not dominate policy thinking as it does today. Nineteenth-century state government, for example, was heavily involved in licensing and regulating occupations, enforcing health requirements, and constraining trade (Novak 1996). It is true that the regulatory agencies were much less present in earlier eras, when regulation occurred more through legislative action. But, with some possible exceptions, the strongest moves toward a vision of "unfettered" free markets, particularly in the area of financial services, occurred in the last decades of the twentieth century.

One thing that the recent devotion to free markets has done is conceal the highly political nature of banking and credit markets. It has served to mask the extent to which our current economic success was derived from a long history of government action and involvement in financial markets. To hear many modern conservative analysts describe financial developments, one would gather that private entrepreneurs and inventors of technological innovations have been responsible for the birth and development of U.S. financial markets. In fact, government agencies and actions created, subsidized, and institutionalized most of the fundamental infrastructure of today's credit markets. This includes the long-term fully amortizing mortgage; the secondary markets that make mortgages cheaper and more plentiful; the mortgage-backed security, which has enabled the growth of entirely new lending industries; and all sorts of standardization and discipline that have enhanced the stability of the financial services industry. The prime rate, the term loan, the adjustable-rate mortgage, the junk bond, and other financial devices came into existence only after legislation was passed allowing these concepts to become reality (Geisst 1990, xvi). It is true that some government-induced or -supported lending practices facilitated urban decline and lending discrimination. (See chapter 4 for further discussion.) But the point remains that federal and state government nurtured, supported, structured, and secured the mainstream providers of credit in the United States from the earliest days of this nation and throughout the nineteenth and twentieth centuries.

Acknowledging the special role of government in supporting the development of the U.S. financial systems—not just banking and mortgage lending but areas like securities and insurance markets—is key to moving beyond the myopic and naive arguments that work in favor of continually deregulating the financial services sector and, in particular, restricting the scope of laws such as the CRA. The act represents a social contract between the banking industry and the broader public. Banks owe their existence to a wider financial infrastructure that was—and in most cases still is—operated by, or dependent on, government in fundamental ways. In the same way, mortgage companies and securities firms depend on regulation and government action for their effective operations. This is not the day of the voluntary, isolated building and loan association where borrowers pool their own funds to fund their own mortgages. The complexity of the financial system depends on government regulation and owes many of its innovations to government sponsorship and, frequently, to outright subsidy. Just because some of the more explicit subsidies no longer continue does not suggest that the social contract is no longer valid. The U.S. market for financial services is as robust as it is today precisely because of a strong government role in supporting and regulating its development. Moreover, the regulatory infrastructure that is needed to provide the public confidence in the financial system is ongoing, as are a variety of explicit and implicit subsidies and guarantees.

Key Themes

With topics as broad as community reinvestment and fair lending, it is impossible to cover all policy concerns. This book focuses primarily on issues of fair access to credit for home buyers, home owners, and small businesses and, to a lesser extent, on issues of basic banking account services. Access to small consumer loans, equity financing for small businesses, and other closely related issues are not given substantial attention, due only to a lack of time and expertise on the author's part. In terms of public policies, the focus is on CRA and the federal fair lending laws. Some attention is also given to the HMDA and the Federal Housing Administration (FHA). Other policies and programs that have direct implications for access to credit and capital include the Community Development Financial Institutions Fund, Small Business Administration loan programs, and the New Markets Tax Credit, among others. Again, time, energy, and expertise kept me from addressing these policies.

There are four related themes in this book. The first theme is that financial markets have benefited from government support and regulation throughout U.S. history. Access to credit and financial services has generally been viewed as a public policy issue and an area appropriate for government intervention. The strong historical relationship between government and the financial services industry provides ample justification for the expansion of the CRA social contract to the entire spectrum of financial services firms, especially those serving households and small firms. The view that unfettered markets should be given free rein has not been dominant, although the last twenty-five years have seen a shift in that direction among policy elites. During this more recent period, deregulationists have been successful at portraying financial products as just another set of widgets and have often convinced policymakers that consumers are best served by unfettered markets and the removal of social contracts, especially CRA. Moreover, U.S. housing policy also became increasingly dominated by advocates of less government involvement in housing markets, thus buttressing the efforts of financial deregulationists (Hays 1995).

The book's second theme is that credit markets have always been, and continue to be, rife with problems of discrimination and market failure. Contrary to notions popularized in some academic literature, the federal government did not invent lending discrimination or redlining. The federal Home Owners Loan Corporation may have supported redlining by banks by developing its neighborhood-risk rating system (Hillier 2003a). But similar systems were already being used by some mortgage lenders, and others discriminated without the need for such systematic approaches. As opposed to the arguments of some doctrinaire neoclassical economists, discrimination and redlining are persistent and, in some ways, inherent features of credit markets. It is important to note that some forms of credit market discrimination have declined. Some significant progress has been made, particularly as a result of CRA and fair lending laws. However, despite technological changes in mortgage and small business lending, problems of disparate treatment and disparate impact continue to plague these markets. The nature of some problems may have changed, but technology has generally not eliminated or drastically reduced disparities. In some cases, technological developments have given rise to increased disparities or new problems to which regulators have been slow to respond.

In mortgage lending, the problem of a lack of access to formal credit has been transformed into a problem of a lack of access to fairly priced credit and a problem of unsustainable credit promoted by abusive lenders. In small business lending, credit scoring and the decline of relationship lending may bring some benefits to the strongest firms in lower-income areas. However, these trends make it more difficult for the firms at the margin to obtain credit at advantageous terms. Moreover, the segmentation of bank customers by income, account size, and marginal profitability has moved banks to charge higher fees for holders of small accounts.

A related sub-theme is that lending discrimination and redlining problems have never been confined to the housing sector. Small business lending discrimination, while less studied, is no less real. The failure of regulators to address this issue represents their dismissal of the problem and a failure to carry out their responsibilities under CRA and the ECOA, both of which apply to small business lending. Because public and community pressure have focused more on housing issues, regulators have given short shrift to business lending problems.

A third major theme of the book is that regulators have generally done a poor job of implementing reinvestment and fair lending laws. It has been pressure from community and consumer groups, together with the accompanying media and congressional attention, that has pushed regulators to enforce laws that some of them had previously argued against. Banking regulators are easily captured by industry interests. Brief periods have existed where the key leadership at a regulatory agency has been able to get the agency to more aggressively enforce CRA, but they have been the exception. These exceptions illustrate the power that political will can have in affecting the implementation of the law.

The CRA, in particular, has been called a form of "regulation from below" because community and public interest groups have played a key role in its implementation (McCluskey 1983). They play a major role by negotiating "CRA agreements" with banks to increase lending in lower-income and minority communities and by protesting mergers based on CRA grounds. These have been critical functions of community groups in CRA's implementation. The role that community and public interest groups have played in highlighting the continuing problems of lending discrimination and redlining has been even more important. Beyond shining a spotlight on credit access problems, community and consumer groups have been the key advocates for strengthening implementation of CRA and fair lending laws and have regularly drawn attention to the weak performance of regulators in enforcing these policies.

The CRA and fair lending laws have been only as successful as regulators have allowed them to be. The effectiveness of CRA was most pronounced from 1989 to about 1992, after Congress chastised regulators for failing to enforce the law and passed important amendments to CRA and HMDA. In the middle to late 1990s, improvements to CRA regulations and more aggressive prosecutions of fair lending violations by the Department of Justice also had some positive impacts. However, by the end of the decade, regulators generally had moved back to a mode of weak enforcement. This trend was partly due to a congressional attack on CRA that peaked in 1999 under the leadership of Senate Banking Committee Chairman Phil

Gramm. Advocates of CRA were forced into a defensive posture, simply trying to minimize rollbacks to the law while sweeping changes to bank regulation were occurring. Instead of being able to exploit such legislation to enact improvements to CRA, as was done with the savings and loan bail-out bill in 1989, advocates had to fight furiously to avoid the effective evis-ceration of the law.

A final theme is that, despite limited enforcement, the evidence shows that CRA and fair lending laws have had a positive impact on access to credit for lower-income and minority communities. Related to this point, however, is the argument that with some "modernization" to keep pace with changes in financial markets and more aggressive enforcement, these laws could be much more effective. There is little doubt that CRA has had impacts in other areas, including the growth of community development financial institu-tions and the maintenance of some bank branches in lower-income neigh-borhoods, systematic data and research in these areas have been scarcer. Moreover, the limits to CRA and fair lending laws and their vacillating en-forcement by federal regulators mean that these policies have a great deal more promise than is evidenced by their performance thus far. Much could be done to increase the impact of CRA and fair lending laws through changes in administrative regulations and commitments by the regulators to stronger enforcement. In some cases, legislative improvements to the coverage of CRA are needed also.

One example of how regulators could move to make the law more effec-tive is by changing the methods that banks can use to define so-called CRA "assessment areas." Currently banks are allowed to define these areas only around physical branch locations. In the early days of locally capitalized savings and loans in the nineteenth century, such a definition may have made sense. But at least as far back as the early twentieth century—and increas-ingly since then—credit markets have involved flows of funds across the country and between nations. Today, even if the bulk of a bank's lending or service activities are located far away from their brick-and-mortar facilities, the bank can choose a small assessment area surrounding its physical loca-tions. One example is Charles Schwab Bank, N.A., an affiliate of the large retail investment company. The bank has included only the Reno, Nevada, metropolitan area as constituting its assessment area despite its intentions to market lending and deposit products to Charles Schwab's 8 million custom-ers across the country. Other examples of such evasions of CRA via restric-tive assessment areas include current and future banking giants such as American Express Centurion Bank, State Farm Federal Savings Bank, and E-Trade Bank. Regulators cite the statute's language and legislative history in permitting such highly restrictive definitions, but chapter 6 of this book demonstrates that a thorough reading of the legislative and early regulatory history of CRA does not provide such a defense. In numerous other instances, regulators have chosen to implement CRA in ways that reduced its effectiveness. Some of these are outlined in chapter 9 of this book.

As this book goes to press, the prospects for improvements to CRA are not terribly strong. Regulators tend to be more concerned about keeping the banks they currently regulate from changing their charters and thus shifting to a different regulator. In 2004, they have begun to move further in the direction of weakening CRA. The agencies derive their revenues from fees imposed on the banks they regulate, providing a perverse incentive against strong regulation. Congress, in general, hardly seems concerned with issues of fair lending. Even with all the attention that the predatory lending issue has received in recent years, Congress appears more prone to preempt state antipredatory lending regulations than to pass any substantive protections of its own. But reinvestment advocates have not sat still. They continue to push for antipredatory lending policies at the state level, as well as work against lender-supported proposals in the opposite direction. Just as importantly, on the predatory lending issue, at least, they have developed additional tools that do not rely on policymakers at all. Community and public interest groups have used the power of reputational risk as a tool to encourage lenders to reform their lending practices. Highly publicized campaigns against Citigroup during and after its purchase of the Associates and against Household Finance both produced demonstrable, if not entirely satisfying, results. Both lenders pledged to stop offering single-premium credit life insurance, a notoriously predatory loan product, in 2000. They also made other reforms in controls over broker abuses and other practices. Beyond the specific gains, these advocacy efforts showed that, even without regulatory support, well-organized community campaigns can influence the behavior of major lenders. With the growing dominance of the top twenty mortgage lenders in the United States, this is an increasingly attractive approach. Community organizers and advocates do not have the resources to wage lending-reform campaigns against scores of lenders. But by taking on the largest and worst of the lenders, these groups can achieve substantial victories and demonstrate that responsible reinvestment is a viable alternative to dual markets and predatory lending.

None of this is to say that policy advocacy efforts are misplaced at this time. In the long run, policy changes are needed to provide sustainable improvements in credit markets. However, given the current political climate, a mixed strategy is needed to provide some realistic prospects for near-term improvements in lending markets while still working on policy issues. Efforts utilizing reputational risk should be expanded to other areas of reinvestment, including expanding prime mortgage-lending activity in minority communities and improving access to small business loans and basic banking services. More state and local governments can choose to do business with responsible banks that provide loans to underserved markets and can publicize these efforts widely. Local and national community groups need more support to develop "CRA scorecards" that rank lenders on how well they serve local credit and banking needs. Given the complexities of modern financial markets these days, these scorecards need to be carefully constructed so that predatory financial service providers are not rewarded by such measures.

The Organization of the Book

Chapter 2 begins with a summary of the history of commercial banking and mortgage lending in the United States. Some of the key policy arguments in the book are related to the role that government has played in the development and regulation of banking and financial markets in the United States. Federal and state government were key players in the establishment and development of banks and financial markets from the nation's earliest days. Moreover, since the 1930s, government has always been a critical source of innovation and standardization in mortgage markets and can be largely credited with creating a nation where a majority of households are home owners. Chapter 2 also presents a critique of the deregulationist ideology used to argue against bank regulation and CRA. This ideology stands in contrast to the mixed-economy concepts of banking and lending markets that were dominant throughout most of U.S. history. It is important to understand the deregulationist perspective because it has grown increasingly influential among policymakers and regulators in recent decades.

Chapter 3 reviews both historical and current evidence of discrimination in small business lending. It also discusses recent changes in banking and lending that impact small businesses, especially those in lower-income and minority neighborhoods. Chapters 4 and 5 discuss home lending markets. Chapter 4 reviews the history of mortgage lending discrimination, as well as the role of the FHA in redlining and discrimination. The continuing evidence on the persistence of mortgage lending discrimination is also covered. Chapter 5 turns to the issues of subprime and predatory lending that rose high on the fair lending and reinvestment policy agenda in the late 1990s.

Chapter 6 discusses the early history of the Fair Housing Act and the Equal Credit Opportunity Act, as well as HMDA and CRA. It describes early CRA-type activism, the growth of the CRA movement, and the legislative history of the HMDA and CRA. It also covers CRA policy and action through the middle-to-late 1980s, when CRA was very weakly enforced. Chapter 7 picks up with the activism and national attention that fair lending issues received in the late 1980s and the legislative victories to improve CRA and HMDA. It also covers the CRA reform process in the middle 1990s and changes in CRA agreements between banks and community groups during the decade. Other issues discussed include the increased enforcement of fair lending policies in the middle part of the 1990s, the push for accountability at the government-sponsored secondary mortgage market agencies (Fannie Mae and Freddie Mac), and the fight over CRA during the adoption of the 1999 GLBA.

Chapter 8 describes the efforts to increase regulation of high-cost subprime lending at the state and federal levels. Beginning in the late 1990s, advocates for regulation looked to the states due to inaction by federal regulators. Only after states began making moves and the media began covering the problem extensively did regulators make even small, marginal moves to improve regulations. As a result of federal inaction, advocates for responsible lending have continued to push for state regulation. Chapter 8 also reviews recent studies that have been conducted on the nation's first state antipredatory lending law, which was adopted by North Carolina in 1999. Chapter 9 first reviews the evidence on the impacts of CRA. It then considers key areas of CRA policy where improved enforcement, changes in regulations, or, occasionally, legislative changes are needed. It also includes recommendations for community action to improve access to fairly priced, responsible credit.

As this book goes to press, the prospects are weak for public policies that promote access to fairly priced financial services for those who are often excluded from mainstream markets. Congressional support for such policies is tepid at best. Federal regulatory agencies, often regardless of whether the top official is a Democratic or Republican appointee, are generally complacent about or even hostile to consumer and community issues. Advocates for community reinvestment and fair lending face continual efforts to roll back gains they have made in the past. Without more support and a broadening of its coalition, the reinvestment movement will have great difficulty preserving CRA and fair lending policies or making them relevant to the twenty-first-century financial marketplace. However, the achievements in the past have also been in the face of significant adversity. These victories were enabled in large part by the forging of loose coalitions, principally among civil rights, consumer rights, and neighborhood organizing groups. New allies are needed now as well. Without them, deregulationist forces will eat away at consumer protections, community reinvestment, and fair lending laws until they are mere footnotes in regulators' procedural manuals.

CHAPTER 2

The Visible Hand of Government in U.S. Credit Markets

The Public Policy–Financial Services Nexus

Throughout much of the history of the United States, stimulating credit flows and providing access to credit to particular economic sectors or communities was seen as an important function of government at both the federal and state levels. At the same time, there have always been debates about the proper role of government in financial markets. In the eighteenth century, Alexander Hamilton, both before and during his tenure as George Washington's secretary of the treasury, envisioned a strong national bank as a crucial element in building a strong nation (Hoffman 2001; Wright 2001). While Hamilton did not want to see a central bank that was a direct branch of the federal government, he did envision the United States as the designer, developer, and subsidizer of the central bank. As the architect of the First Bank of the United States, Hamilton saw the institution as primarily a supporter and stimulator of economic development in the nation. He did not take a laissez-faire view of national economic development, but saw that a central bank that could finance both private and public projects would be needed.

Banking and credit have also been seen as tools to encourage a variety of other public-interest goals beyond economic development. Building and loans, savings banks, and, later, credit unions were designed and promoted by public policy in large part to encourage savings and thrift. Installment lending and fully amortizing, equal payment loans were promoted and standardized in part to encourage thrift and financial discipline (Calder 1999). Installment credit fostered financial discipline by helping borrowers to budget consumption over time. Building and loans, the predecessor to savings and loans or what we now call thrifts, were also designed to enable and support home ownership. While the earliest small building and loan associations were not necessarily dependent on public action, by the end of the nineteenth century, building and loans were often started and run by the business and civic community in some collective form to facilitate housing and economic development. Most of these associations were nonprofit in structure and were often led by what political scientists of the twentieth century would call local "growth coalitions." Thus, they were much closer to semiformal public action than to private action.

The growth of building and loans was later supported by licensing, regulation, and, in the twentieth century, the subsidization and creation of public or quasi-public supportive institutions like the Federal Home Loan Banks. Complementary to building and loans were savings banks, which were principally created and supported for encouraging saving and thrift rather than home ownership. However, by investing savings in mortgages, they supported access to more affordable housing finance.

More than building and loans, many early commercial banks were largely creatures of the state. While there were "private banks" that existed outside of much state or federal regulation, these were less influential than the state and later federally chartered banks. Until well into the nineteenth century, state-chartered banks—and many corporations as well—were granted charters by individual acts of the legislature. Bank charters were not justified primarily on the right of a group of entrepreneurs to enter the credit market, but rather on the notion of some public need for a certain type of credit or financial service. A bank charter might be awarded for a bank that was designed to provide credit for farmers, and another to provide credit for heavy manufacturers.

The scarcity of money in the late eighteenth and much of the nineteenth centuries meant that citizens were aware of the power of banks to "make money." Banks would issue their own currency to merchants and others based on "bills of exchange" that represented current debts owed them. This would put the banks, rather than the merchant, in charge of converting the bills of exchange into specie or gold. In this way, banks created liquidity, increasing the ability of merchants and firms to turn their business activity into a medium that they could spend. This process, in turn, increased the multiplier effect—or velocity—of the firms' revenues. The more liquid the bills of exchange became, the more spending was allowed in the community. Up through the early twentieth century, commercial banks were not very involved in providing longer-term credit. The "real bills" doctrine, which was relied upon by industry and regulators alike, argued that commercial banks should only finance "current" assets, primarily a company's accounts receivable that were due within thirty to ninety days. Longer-term lending was not seen as an appropriate activity for banks. So providing liquidity meant turning short-term loans (or "discounts," as they were called) into bank notes and later U.S. currency, but did not include selling long-term loans on a secondary market.

In the same way, access to credit today is critical to the true supply of money in the economy. As credit becomes more available or more affordable, individuals, households, and businesses are able to purchase goods and services previously unavailable to them. When interest rates are lowered, money becomes more plentiful, and purchasing and investment generally increase. In the same way, restricting credit can slow an economy. In fact, the federal government deliberately worked to reduce consumer credit access during World War II. This action depressed the demand for durable consumer items such as automobiles to encourage automakers and other firms to shift to military production (Geisst 1990, 59–60).

Promoters of the neoclassical ideology that is so ever present today tend to suggest that there is an "efficient" level of credit availability that is best determined by eliminating government influence in credit markets and letting suppliers and consumers of credit set the price and quantity. However, in dealing with an instrumental, primary good that is necessary and critical to the production of so many other goods and is such a strong determinant of the life chances of different individuals and groups, the laissez-faire approach is fraught with difficulties and faces many fundamental challenges. Even from within the neoclassical paradigm, we must deal with the issues of the provision of public goods, quasi-public goods, and positive and negative spillover effects. Alexander Hamilton realized that a financial infrastructure that would provide for short-term credit and a more standardized currency was, in effect, a public good. It entailed substantial fixed costs and was best made operational by a centralized entity that had standard-making powers. Access to credit would bring all sorts of positive externalities to society. Economies need a ready supply of money to grow and a financial network to facilitate exchange. Much later in the early 1930s, President Herbert Hoover—hardly a radical—recognized that financial markets, left on their own, would not provide for socially optimum levels of home ownership. Home ownership has all sorts of positive benefits that accrue not just to the home owner but also to her neighbors and wider community (McCarthy, Van Zandt, and Rohe 2001).

The neoclassical view that the public interest is best served by the near complete deregulation of credit markets is also vulnerable to criticism from outside the free market perspective. Because they do not view access to credit in the same way as they view access to doughnuts or buttons, modern progressives argue that distributional issues take on paramount importance in examining policy alternatives and market structures. Even if one agrees that deregulation may result in a greater total amount of credit and a higher gross utility among consumers in the United States, the benefits of a deregulatory action may not be deemed to be worth the costs—including possible heavy concentrations of losses among a small minority of households. The ability of the average homeowner to save $2 per month on her mortgage due to some major deregulatory policy, for example, may be seen as less important than enabling a modest share of families to gain or maintain home ownership. Regulation may be judged socially beneficial even if the simple sum of the benefits to a segment of the population do not outweigh the widely distributed costs to the many. Moreover, because access to credit means access to future economic opportunity, the denial of credit to members of certain communities—whether demarcated by geography or race—means more than losses to a set of random individuals. It means that a community can be held back and that the prospects of economic advancement for that community will be diminished. As Stone (2001) argues, the neoclassical paradigm does not deal well with notions of community, always reducing everything to the level of the individual. But in the real world, community matters, and notions of public interest typically consider how different groups are treated as well as how individuals fare.

The Role of Commercial Banking in Early U.S. Economic Development

The history of U.S. banking can be broken down in a number of ways. One approach is the identification of four periods, demarcated by major policy shifts and differing notions of the role of government in banking and the relations between the two sectors. The formative period of U.S. banking began in approximately 1781, when the Bank of North America—the nation's first real bank—was authorized by the Confederation Congress. It lasted until around 1832, when Andrew Jackson successfully fought to extinguish the Second Bank of the United States, the country's second central bank (and one of the predecessors to the Federal Reserve). The second phase of U.S. banking history might be said to have covered the period from 1832 to approximately 1913, when the Federal Reserve was founded. During this period, state banks grew at substantial speed and general state banking laws were established. The modern era of banking is generally said to run from 1913 to the present. However, the modern era can be further divided into the periods before and after 1980, when major financial services deregulation had clearly gotten up a head of steam with the Depository Institutions Deregulation and Monetary Control Act. From 1980 to the present, financial deregulation continued at a swift pace, and banking and other financial services industries converged through holding company arrangements. This trend culminated in the 1999 Gramm-Leach-Bliley Financial Modernization Act (GLBA).

During the formative period of U.S. banking, government played the lead role in developing a financial infrastructure in the new country. Hamilton recognized that to be productive, a new nation needed to encourage a common currency and to standardize and make more secure methods for merchants and businesses to increase their liquidity, thus enabling them to reinvest and grow their businesses. This period corresponds with the early economic development of the new nation, which occurred at great speed. Hamilton saw the need to involve government in banking rather than rely on a purely free market approach. Colonial America was serviced primarily by British banks and financiers, and with the Revolutionary War, the United States experienced both a demand for credit (especially in the form of massive state debts) and a loss of supply from British sources.

At the end of the preconstitutional Confederation in the middle-1780s, there were just three organized formal financial intermediaries that served primarily local markets in Philadelphia, New York, and Boston (Rousseau and Sylla 1999). The three banks issued their own notes. However, these notes were of varying quality, so the availability of a reliable uniform currency, other than gold or silver specie, was very limited (Wright 2001, 112). States issued their own paper monies, but the rates of exchange among them varied. Much like the drive for a common currency in Europe in the late twentieth century, the lack of a common currency was seen as an impediment to interstate and interregional commerce and development. The first bank, the Bank of North America based in Philadelphia, was clearly a creature of the Confederation. It was initially "chartered" by the Confederation (although it was unclear whether the Confederation had such power), and the Confederation initially owned more than 600 of its 1,000 shares of stock (Hammond 1957, 51).

There were a number of reasons that banks were needed to stimulate the U.S. economy. First, banks provided cash, an accepted medium of ready exchange. Banknotes were the primary form of money used in New York and Pennsylvania from the 1790s to the 1820s. While notes issued by different banks did not offer the maximum fluidity of currency that a single currency would, the notes of major banks provided a good deal of security and allowed for increased commerce. At first, banknotes were viewed simply as promissory notes by the bank. They had to be carefully tracked and catalogued to ensure value. As a bank's notes became more established and viewed as secure in value, they began to function more as cash instruments (Wright 2001, 111–13).

Another way that banks fueled economic development was through providing businesses with the liquidity they needed to buy new inventory, invest in new equipment, and generally fuel their operations. Banks would finance working capital through lending based on what were termed "bills of exchange," the accounts receivable that businesses had derived from goods and services it had sold. An example of such a loan, known as a commercial paper loan, might involve an artisan or manufacturer bringing the bill of exchange from a customer merchant to the bank, adding his endorsement to it, and providing it as collateral for the loan. The bank would then collect from the merchant, rather than the borrowing manufacturer. Thus, banks also served as collection agencies on bills of exchange, something like what we would call "factors" today. They also initiated lawsuits to recover debts and formalized credit, taking it from more of a moral obligation to more of a business transaction (Wright 2001, 84; Lamoreaux 1994, 2). Without this short-term credit, businesses would be forced to keep a great deal of working capital on hand in the form of specie, thereby tying up the firms' capital.

Related to this use of bank credit, the liquidity provided by short-term credit could be used by the firm to diversify its business, providing the capital needed to create a new product or offer a new service. Banks also provided what were called "accommodation" loans to firms that were not secured by bills of exchange or other collateral but relied on outside guarantors. These loans, although technically short term, were often renewed—thus looking something like what a modern bank might call an "evergreen" line of credit. Banks also provided investment opportunities for entrepreneurs and wealthier individuals. Average dividends on bank stock in the nation's early days ran from 9 to 12 percent, and banks were one of the largest components of early stock markets (Sylla 1998).

One major difference between commercial lenders in the early history of the nation and lenders today was the lack of readily available and standardized financial statements and credit history information. Due to this lack of financial information, small firms were even more "opaque" than they are today. This situation gave local lenders with strong personal or particular knowledge of firms a great advantage. It also meant that entrance into social and personal networks was inextricably tied to successful access to capital and credit. New England had the most active banking sector by the middle 1930s, with local banks in most small towns and 300 banks overall. The notion of economic development as part of the mission of banks also meant that insider lending (the lending to stockholders and associates of stockholders) was often not seen as a bad thing but rather was accepted, at least by those with access to credit, as the method for creating local community as well as individual wealth. Lamoreaux (1994) argues that the close ties and commonalities between bank owners and borrowers were widely understood and also a key factor in making banks a vital force in regional economic development.

While insider lending and cooperation between the state and bank owners was likely beneficial to local and regional aggregate economic development, it did not benefit all citizens to the same degree. As early as the 1830s, for example, Democrats in Massachusetts organized for "a bank of moderate capital becoming men of moderate means" (Lamoreaux 1994, 55). They argued that that the steep initial capital requirements for chartering a bank in the state supported the development of banks by the wealthy for the wealthy. They had some success and were able to get banks chartered for well under the usual $500,000 minimum capital requirement. Lamoreaux argues that the insider lending allowed in the first era of U.S. banking in New England enabled even middle-income entrepreneurs to band together to form banks and gain the capital necessary for economic mobility.

Rousseau and Sylla (1999) have shown that the emergence of a "modern" financial structure predated the development of canals, railroads, water systems, and steam-powered machinery in the early United States by three or four decades. By the mid-1790s, the nation had restructured its war debts, formed a national bank system with branches, and established networked securities markets in several cities. Hamilton had established his First Bank of the United States by 1792. The new central bank permitted the retirement of state currencies. The creation of a national bank—a true "public-private" partnership led by the federal government and with significant federal ownership—was the key step toward the development of stable and universal financial structure for the young country.

Hamilton's First Bank facilitated and supported a significant growth in local banks chartered by states to serve particular economic development needs. The number of state-chartered banks grew from three banks in 1789 to approximately thirty in the 1790s and then to more than a hundred by 1810 (Fenstermaker 1965, 13). By 1825, the United States had approximately 2.4 times the banking capital of England and Wales even though its population was smaller (Sylla 1998). Through the middle 1830s, state banks generally continued to grow.

In the early years of the nation, banks financed projects for reasons beyond simply maximizing profits. They would often be more motivated by ties of family or friendship, politics, or some policy or social goal. In New England, early banks routinely practiced insider lending, awarding more than half of their loans to directors, large stockholders, business partners, friends, and family (Lamoreaux 1994). Moreover, pricing of loans would sometimes be adjusted to stimulate economic development in new areas or for some social purpose. This was especially the case when land speculators were trying to get settlers on their tracts quickly by offering low rates to prospective buyers (Wright 2001, 33). Businessmen made their way onto bank boards to assist with their own access to capital or that of their industry. Many started banks for this purpose. State charters generally focused on economic and social needs. Again, bank laws in the formative period of U.S. banking were institution-specific; general banking laws came later.

The ties between government and banking in the formative stage of the development of U.S. financial services were strong. During the credit crunch of the 1790s, small businesses were cut out of the credit market to a significant degree. Small businessmen organized politically in New York and Pennsylvania, and banks were forced by law to extend commercial credit to artisans and mechanics (Wright 2001, 126). States began demanding routine reporting of financial information from banks in the early nineteenth century, although the rigor and quality of this regulation appears to have been severely lacking (Klebaner 1990, 43). Under its 1829 Safety Fund Act, New York established a bank supervisory authority, which investigated every bank's affairs at least four times annually. Within a decade, every state in New England had followed suit. Again, however, the power and efficacy of these agencies was limited, especially given that agencies were loath to spark fear among depositors by suggesting that a bank's management was questionable.

States were active investors in banks in the late eighteenth and early nineteenth centuries. By the early 1800s, a majority of state governments owned at least some bank stock (Klebaner 1990, 41). Massachusetts owned one-eighth of all the bank stock in the state by 1812. Eight states organized wholly government-owned banks. The state-owned banks often had explicit economic development or social infrastructure purposes. Ten states appointed directors to bank boards (Klebaner 1990, 43). State legislatures used banks explicitly to support economic development. They recognized that banks were different from other firms because they provided an important financial infrastructure for other companies. States made decisions about the distribution and—by controlling supply through chartering—the cost of credit to different parts of their economies and societies. Some specified various proportions of lending for different purposes or sectors. Banking was highly localized because standardized financial information was nonexistent and banks lent almost entirely based on intimate and local knowledge. Therefore, states were able to control the geographic distribution of credit through branching requirements, chartering new local banks, or actually allocating credit by county (Hoffman 2001, 77–81). In Louisiana, for example, the chartering of each new bank during the 1830s created a battle in the state legislature. Each rural district wanted a branch. The New Orleans legislators fought the decentralization of banking, because it created competition for city banks as well as for nonbank factoring companies, which provided much of the farmers' liquidity (Green 1972, 221–23).

Some states chartered their own central banks to regulate and steer banking activity in the state. Some of these banks, in turn, actually handled state finances and spending. New York even created an insurance fund for state banks in 1829, through the New York Safety Fund law. Banks were required to pay 0.5 percent of their capital into a safety fund each year for six years. The fund would pay off the note-holders of any bank that could not redeem its currency.

The Contested Terrain of Government Involvement in Banking and Finance in the Nineteenth Century

Hoffman (2001) has argued that competing ideologies have always played a role in the history of U.S. banking and financial development and regulation, with different ideologies dominating during different eras of U.S. history. In the formative period of U.S. banking, from the 1780s to 1832, Hamilton's vision of a quasi-governmental central bank supporting the growing, interconnected national economy won out over Jefferson's anticorporate vision of a strict separation of government and banking (and commerce more generally). At the same time, state chartered banks grew, and state power in banking was substantial. But banks were not seen as separate from the state. They were, to a large extent, creatures of the state. In some cases they would even be agents of the state, although most involved some substantial level of private control.

The second era of banking is marked by Andrew Jackson's veto of the charter of the Second Bank of the United States in 1832. Congress had allowed the charter of the First Bank of the United States to die in 1811. The end of the First Bank had led to a dramatic rise in the number of state banks from 118 in 1811 to 232 in 816 (Hoffman 2001, 45). This result led to a proliferation of bank-specific notes with different values in various places, creating a barrier to easy trade and commerce. The Second Bank of the United States was created in large part to remedy this situation and provide for a uniform currency. But there was also a need to regulate this new, larger set of state-chartered banks and the paper money they issued. The Second Bank, unlike the first, was explicitly designed to be a regulator of other banks as well as a bank itself.

The Second Bank had significant difficulties after its initiation in 1817, but was strengthened and reformed in the 1820s. Seemingly ignoring these reforms, Jackson was always dead-set against the concept of a central bank and worked successfully to get rid of it. Jackson followed Jefferson's anticorporate classical liberal ideology, believing that banking belonged entirely in the private sector and that the intermingling of public and private control was improper. Jackson had a good deal of success in convincing the public, or at least policymakers, that government should not be involved significantly with banking. Ironically, he was helped by the Panic of 1837, after which the number of state-chartered banks plummeted until stabilizing in the early 1840s (Rousseau and Sylla 1999). President Van Buren and the Democrats blamed the overissue of bank credit as causing the crisis, saying that it was due to state involvement with banking. Hoffman (2001) has argued that it was more likely due to the rapid expansion of banks that resulted from the closure of the Second Bank of the United States.

The mood against public-sector involvement in banking in turn facilitated the trend among state legislatures to adopt "free banking" legislation, under which banks were seen as private, profit-driven ventures with no particular social purpose. Free banking involved establishing general chartering laws in the mid-nineteenth century rather than public-purpose chartering of specific institutions (Hoffman 2001, 83–87). A growing populist movement saw institution-specific chartering as monopolistic. The movement believed the policy provided benefits to wealthy charter-seekers who curried favor with legislators. The shift to free banking meant that the notion of banks serving a public purpose was severely diminished. Banks were less likely to be given monopolistic power by the state in a certain specialty lending or finance area. Competition increased, and banks were freer to determine the direction of their operations, the geographic areas of business in which to specialize, etc. Some supporters of the banks were motivated by neoclassical notions of greater efficiency through the "unfettering" of markets, and others saw opportunities for greater profits. But the more important force was a resurgence in Jacksonian notions of separating government from business out of principle and out of a fear of government's unduly favoring concentrated financial interests.

The free banking experience illustrated the dangers of rapid deregulation. In New York, Wisconsin, Indiana, and Minnesota, four states with good historical records, bank failure has been conservatively calculated at 15 percent from 1837 to 1863 (Rolnick and Weber 1983). Coggins (1998, 44) has argued that the actual rate of failure was probably substantially higher than this. Due to this level of problems, states tended to restore many of the same regulatory controls that were used with individually chartered banks. Problems were mitigated to some degree because free bank currencies were often backed by bonds that states held as security. Moreover, during this first period of free banking, free banks operated in conjunction with many existing individually chartered banks.

Gradually, states began taking a stronger role in regulating banks. By the end of the nineteenth century, fifteen states had distinct banking departments (Klebaner 1990, 99). More commonly, officials with other functions were responsible for supervising banks. But things began to change in the early twentieth century. The National Association of Supervisors of State Banks was founded to foster and professionalize state banking supervision, and by 1913, there were twenty-nine state banking departments. Because public confidence was typically enhanced by state regulation, banks often called for regular supervision or regulation, albeit of limited scope.

This second period of banking history includes what some call "National Banking Era," from the 1864 National Bank Act to 1913. This latter part of the century was a period of rapid economic growth, both created by and resulting in an explosion in the number of commercial banks in the United States from fewer than 500 in 1864 to more than 21,000 in 1913 (White 1998). Banks were prohibited from investing in securities and governed in different senses by the "real bills doctrine," which stated that they were to avoid all but short-term loans. The National Bank Act supported the move to less direct government involvement in banking, while maintaining a regulatory role aimed primarily at safety and soundness. The act did not call for any central bank, but created uniform government-printed bank notes and the first official federal bank regulator—the Office of the Comptroller of the Currency (OCC). National banks outside of New York and eighteen other "reserve" cities were required to maintain reserves equal to 25 percent of their deposits and note circulation (Sylla 1972, 249–57). The reserve system moved funds from every part of the economy and concentrated them in leading financial centers and facilitated the flow of funds out of rural countrysides and into industrializing cities. In the New York money market, the balances of thousands of scattered bank reserves were used to fund industrial development. This practice helped make capital very plentiful and inexpensive, thus supporting railroad construction, manufacturing, and other postbellum nineteenth-century growth industries.

Therefore, largely precipitated by the philosophy and influence of Andrew Jackson, the second phase of banking development in the United States began with an increased separation between banking and government. However, by the latter part of the century, the National Bank Act had created a new federal regulatory infrastructure, and states began creating regulatory infrastructures of their own. Compared to the earlier phase of U.S. banking, though, banks were seen more as private entities rather than as creatures of legislatures (Hoffman 2001, 93–95). The classical ideologies of Jefferson and then Jackson moved the country toward a more free-market system, though still subject to significant regulation. It would take the establishment of a new central bank, and later the Great Depression of the 1930s, to move the balance back toward a system of more extensive—and more specifically designed—public intervention in financial markets.

The Federal Reserve, the Federal Deposit Insurance Corporation, and Modern Bank Regulation

The modern era of U.S. banking history began with the establishment of the Federal Reserve in 1913. The Panic of 1907 led to the Aldrich-Vreeland Act of 1908, which created the National Monetary Commission. The commission in turn recommended the creation of a central bank to influence the money supply. Though directed primarily by current and former bankers, the vision for the bank was still of a quasi-governmental entity that would play a strong role in the economy. The commission rejected the notion of the "real bills" theory as a form of self-regulating natural law (Hoffman 2001, 116–19). The establishment of the Federal Reserve was guided by a mix of the early-twentieth-century Progressivism of Woodrow Wilson and the more utilitarian perspective of the banking elite. Wilson valued the expertise of bankers as key to a central bank, and Paul Warburg, the lead architect of the bank, valued government intervention in the economy to stimulate or restrain growth as called for by the times. Thus, the commission and the Federal Reserve Act represented a return to more federal involvement in the banking and credit markets.

In 1927, the McFadden Act began allowing banks to branch within cities, as long as state-chartered banks in their state had similar powers. But it also allowed states to block out-of-state banks from establishing branches within their borders. The next major piece of policy was the 1933 Glass-Steagall Banking Act, which had two major components. First, it created the Federal Deposit Insurance Corporation (FDIC) to insure bank deposits and instill consumer confidence in the banking system. Second, the act established a boundary between banking and securities activities. The involvement of banks in securities had not been common until after the Federal Reserve Act, but grew more intense in the 1920s. The 1927 McFadden Act allowed banks to invest in bonds, and in the same year the OCC allowed national banks to invest in stocks. Banks became more involved in margin lending, i.e., providing loans to speculators in the securities market, and losses on such activity caused many bank failures following the 1929 crash. Following Glass-Steagall, the 1935 Bank Act strengthened the role of the Federal Reserve Board and gave it much more discretionary authority, confirming the shift to a utilitarian/progressive ideology.

At the same time that the nation moved to a more active government role in banking, the industry encountered a fundamental challenge to their primary competitive advantage. Commercial lending had been the primary domain of banks, due in large part to its special knowledge of local markets and ability to obtain information on business customers that was not so easily available to others. However, with the advance of "managerial capitalism" and "scientific management," financial and credit information become more readily available. This meant that regional or national-scale nonbank financial institutions could enter the market for commercial lending much more easily. These advances also enabled somewhat larger firms to issue commercial paper more easily, reducing their reliance on banks. One way that banks responded to this new competition was to offer larger businesses term loans, which enabled them to lend to businesses over a period of more than one year (Geisst 1990, 54–56). Regulators obliged and allowed banks to offer such a product. There were significant complaints, however, that banks were doing little to help small businesses. At the same time, the Industrial Revolution had created a more consumer-oriented society with increased demands for consumer durable goods that required financing. Banks were eager to find new markets and began to court consumers. Moreover, the availability of FDIC insurance provided the banks with the perfect tool to attract new customers. From 1933 to 1935, bank deposits rose from \$38.6 billion to \$48.9 billion (Geisst 1990, 54–55).

The next major development in modern banking policy occurred with the 1956 Bank Holding Company (BHC) Act. BHCs are parent corporations that control one or more banks. The 1956 act, however, required only BHCs owning the stock of two or more banks to register with the Federal Reserve. BHCs owning just a single bank, but perhaps other nonbank financial firms, did not have to register. The BHC was originally designed to allow only banking activities to be conducted under the BHC umbrella, consistent with Glass-Steagall prohibitions and concerns for safety and soundness. The act was amended to allow the Federal Reserve to approve mergers and acquisitions through holding companies that might reduce competition as long as the public benefit was deemed to outweigh the costs (Geisst 1990, 60–62).

At the same time, single-bank holding companies remained exempt from registration with the Federal Reserve. Banks frequently reorganized into single-bank holding companies to avoid Federal Reserve oversight and allow for entry into nonbanking lines of business via the BHC. These lines of business originally included activities far removed from banking. Banks also used BHCs to expand the geographic reach of their banking activities. By creating a mortgage company affiliate, for example, a bank could get around McFadden Act restrictions and essentially expand its mortgage lending across state lines. In 1970, Congress passed an amendment to the BHC Act to require Federal Reserve oversight of single-bank holding companies. If expansion was deemed inequitable or uncompetitive, it could be rejected. This time, banks were allowed to acquire only businesses that were "closely related" to the business of banking.

The BHC was used, for example, to allow banks to enter the credit card business. Credit cards had been instituted first by Western Union and later by Diners Club in 1950 (Geisst 1990, 60–63). American Express followed in 1958. Due to their local nature in the 1950s, banks did not have natural advantages in this large-scale business at first. Credit card operations also needed access to broader sources of funding than banks' deposit bases. The BHC allowed banks to raise money by issuing commercial paper for their credit card operations. The BHC also reduced the regulation that banks would encounter if they offered cards directly through the depository.

The BHC is a very important development from the standpoint of consumer regulation and community reinvestment. While often viewed as a way for regulators to segregate the deposit base of a financial institution from its other activities to preserve the safety of the deposit base, the BHC and— since the 1999 GLBA—the financial holding company (FHC) represent very convenient ways for financial institutions to restrict and minimize regulatory oversight over their lending activities. Depositories are held to higher standards in terms of safety and soundness for somewhat obvious reasons, although how fireproof the "firewalls" separating the depository parts of a FHC from the nondepository parts are is certainly debatable. But depositories are also subject to a higher level of legalized and de facto regulation in consumer protection, fair lending, and community reinvestment arenas than are their nondepository affiliates.

In the area of Community Reinvestment Act (CRA) policy, nondepository affiliates are essentially not covered by the law, at least as regulators currently interpret it.[1] In the areas of consumer protection and fair lending, nonbank lenders also benefit from de facto differences in regulation. A sizable regulatory infrastructure has been developed by the federal government to regulate depositories. This is not true for nonbank lenders such as mortgage and finance companies. A key period within the modern banking era was the late 1970s when state bank branching regulations began to fall. Most states traditionally had restricted intrastate bank branching, and not all states allowed interstate branching. This was a long tradition in state banking regulation. In 1982, the Garn-St. Germain Act amended the BHC Act to allow failed banks and thrifts to be acquired by any bank holding company, including interstate acquisitions. Also in the 1980s, most states entered into multistate agreements that allowed mergers between banks in participating states. This went on for over a decade before Congress passed the 1994 Riegle-Neal Interstate Banking and Branching Efficiency Act, which made interstate branching through merger and acquisition nearly universal. Only Texas and Montana took advantage of the ability to opt out of these provisions. The interstate branching compacts accelerated merger activity in the late 1980s.

Merger activity again picked up in the late 1990s following the adoption of the Riegle-Neal Act. Consumer advocates and others were able to include some minimal safeguards in the Riegle-Neal Act. For example, no one banking organization is allowed to control more than 10 percent of nationwide deposits or more than 30 percent of deposits in a single state.

The History of Residential Mortgage Finance Through the Twentieth Century

The history of the home mortgage is not closely related to that of the commercial bank. In fact, during many parts of U.S. history, many commercial banks were not even legally permitted to make mortgages. During other eras, banking orthodoxy relied on the real bills doctrine. This meant that banks would not even make any loans over a few months in duration. They focused on financing commercial paper or essentially personal revolving lines of credit known as accommodation paper. The history of financial intermediaries in the United States up until very recently has been dominated by different forms of lenders being created for different purposes. Banks were essentially created to provide liquidity to firms and, in many cases, to increase the supply of paper money in the economy. Building and loans (later called "savings and loans"), insurance companies, and mortgage companies have been the primary providers of mortgage credit. After the 1930s, banks became much more active in mortgage lending, and in recent decades have expanded their presence through establishing and purchasing mortgage companies.

Throughout the last seventy-five years, the federal government has been a major initiator and supporter of mortgage markets, using a variety of tools and interventions to support access to credit, primarily for middle-income homebuyers and homeowners. From at least the mid-nineteenth century up until the 1980s, the primary provider of mortgage credit in the United States had been the building and loan, later called the savings and loan, and now known, together with savings banks, as "thrifts." Other forms of lenders were significant providers of residential credit, including individuals, life insurance companies, mortgage companies, and later banks. But the savings and loan was the dominant provider for many decades. Michael Lea (1996) has defined three periods in the history of mortgage markets in the United States. The "Origins" period went from 1831 with the formation of the first known building and loan to 1931 with the beginning of strong depression-induced federal interventions in the housing market. The Capra-esque "Wonderful Life" period began in 1932 and lasted until 1981 when government-sponsored secondary markets and securitization began to dominate. Finally, the "Brave New World" period began in 1982.

The Oxford Provident Building Association, established in 1831 in what is now Philadelphia, is generally considered to be the nation's first building and loan, or what came to be called "savings and loans" (S&Ls). The earliest building and loans were membership-based nonprofit associations, which served basically as home-buying savers clubs and were modeled on Britain's "Friendly Societies." The S&Ls would issue shares through regular contributions from members. As capital accumulated, it was offered to the member who agreed to pay the highest premium for it. Profits accumulated in the fund, which helped it grow more quickly. Loans had fixed rates and were generally fully amortizing. The earliest S&Ls were called "terminating societies." Once the original members each received a loan, the group was terminated. Later, permanent S&Ls were formed, which allowed savers to join even if they did not wish to borrow.

The primary purpose of savings and loans was not profit motive, but home ownership. It is true that many local merchants and businessmen helped organize them in order to stimulate residential and economic development. At the same time, many participants and organizers saw the promotion of savings and loans, and the resulting home ownership, as the development of a movement more than an industry (Lea 1996). Building and loans were local institutions, with members all living in the same area and many of them knowing each other. This social and geographic cohesiveness gave them an informational advantage that kept underwriting costs and defaults low.

Time deposits (what are commonly called "certificates of deposit") were introduced by S&Ls in the late nineteenth century. S&Ls offered them at fixed terms, which created greater funding and liquidity in the mortgage system and allowed for pooling of risk. Borrowers and savers benefited from economies of scale as the organizations grew. Yet, once S&Ls began offering deposit services to nonborrowers, they lost some of their inherent peer-lending enforcement advantages. Depositors and borrowers were decoupled—so that losses from defaulting borrowers were spread over more depositors. By 1931, of the 12 million savings and loan members in 12,000 institutions, only 2 million had home loans (Hoffman 2001, 154). This outcome created the need for the S&Ls to act more like banks and rely more on staff to assess the quality of loans rather than rely primarily on peer pressure. Moreover, dividends became more important compared to the original goal of maximizing home ownership.

Mutual savings banks were similar in form to the S&Ls, except that they were organized primarily for the purpose of encouraging thrift and savings among those of modest means, not for making mortgages. They did, however, have a stimulating effect on mortgage lending because many of their assets were invested in mortgages even before they became direct lenders themselves. Mutual savings banks actually preceded S&Ls in the United States, with states chartering them as early as 1816 (Hoffman 2001, 152). Later, in the 1850s, they entered the mortgage market and soon became the largest source of mortgage funds until surpassed by S&Ls in the 1920s (Lea 1996).

Life insurance and mortgage companies were also important providers of mortgages in the late nineteenth century. These national-scale lenders utilized independent agents to originate loans. Mortgage companies issued mortgage bonds modeled after those in France and Germany to provide their capital (Lea 1996). These were general obligation bonds backed by pools of mortgage loans. Insurance companies from the United States and Europe were key investors in these bonds, thus evidencing a very early partial globalization of residential finance.

National S&Ls also arose in the late nineteenth century but operated more like national mortgage companies than local building and loans. They solicited deposits via the mail and door-to-door solicitations and made loans via external agents such as real estate brokers. Hoffman (2001, 158–60) has argued that they were designed more to benefit the promoters financially than to make many loans. They increased to 240 by 1893, but were wiped out by the recession that started that year. Both the national mortgage companies and the national building and loans were guilty of questionable appraisal and lending practices and both experienced significant industrial collapse. This development, in turn, led many states to begin imposing interstate lending restrictions and to begin regulating S&Ls more.

Supported by increased regulation, S&Ls grew significantly in the early twentieth century as providers of mortgage credit. Life insurance companies were also significant providers and managed to avoid many of the problems of other national-scale lenders. Commercial banks had been largely restricted from mortgage activity, both by the National Bank Act and by the power of the real bills doctrine. But state banks had begun entering the market, and the 1913 Federal Reserve Act allowed national banks to enter as well. By 1914, 25 percent of the loans and 15 percent of state-chartered bank assets were in real estate (Snowden 1994). However, the role of commercial banks in mortgage lending remained somewhat limited until at least the 1960s.

By 1930, S&Ls held about one-third of the outstanding home mortgages in the United States (Hoffman 2001, 155). Thrifts, including savings banks, comprised approximately 45 percent of mortgage debt. Despite the mix of suppliers of mortgage credit in the early twentieth century, some significant differences remained in the nature of credit provided by different sorts of lenders. S&Ls provided longer-term loans with higher loan-to-value ratios than banks or insurance companies. In the 1920s, the average term of mortgages was eleven years for those written by S&Ls, versus six to eight for those from insurance companies and two to three for those from commercial banks (Lea 1996). Average loan-to-value ratios were 60 percent for savings and loans and 50 percent for those from other lenders. Shorter term, lower-loan-to-value loans made by banks and insurance companies were known as "straight" mortgages. The lower loan-to-value ratios typically required the involvement of a substantial second mortgage. The lenders on these loans often charged very high additional fees (15–20 percent of principal) and high interest rates (Gries and Ford 1932, 28). They were offered by "marginal participants" in the financial industry and were often unregulated and operated in violation of state usury laws.

The 1930s marks the watershed of strong, direct federal involvement in U.S. mortgage markets. The massive failures of banks during the depression and the collapse of the housing and construction markets provided the context for the establishment of some very important agencies and programs. The policies and practices of these institutions had a tremendous impact on the mortgage and financial services landscape, an impact that continues to be felt today.

Many associate the initiation of the federal activism in the housing market with Roosevelt's New Deal. To be sure, the 1934 Housing Act, which created the Federal Housing Administration (FHA), was one of the most important pieces of housing legislation in the twentieth century. However, it followed the Federal Home Loan Bank Act of 1932, which President Hoover advocated and signed. This bill created the Home Loan Bank system to provide liquidity to savings and loans to increase their role in the mortgage market. Hoover and others saw the longer-term, higher loan-to-value mortgage provided by savings and loans as a key tool in promoting home ownership and stimulating the housing market (Hoffman 2001, 159–62). The law gave the federal government a much larger role in promoting and regulating the housing market. Government not only authorized, but also invested in, the creation of the new secondary market institutions. The federal government initially capitalized the Home Loan Banks, and the member institutions were required to purchase small amounts of stock to gradually become the owners of the banks.

By providing member institutions with access to additional capital for mortgages structured with longer maturities and higher loan-to-values, the Home Loan Banks fostered a new standardization and federal validation of the S&L-type loan. It was also the first direct government vehicle for dealing with the long-term/short-term liquidity mismatch that faced banks and institutions with short-term demand deposits. By allowing banks to "rediscount" their mortgage assets, the government was creating liquidity, thereby stimulating the mortgage and housing market. Beyond subsidizing and stimulating the longer-term S&L mortgage, the Home Loan Bank system responded to the credit allocation imbalances present in the S&L system. Because S&Ls were generally local institutions, imbalances could arise in terms of the supply and demand for credit across the country. Some areas, especially growing ones, might have an excess demand for mortgages, whereas older parts of the country might have an excess supply of savings and investment available to fund them. By providing for a system of routinized inter-S&L borrowing, the Home Loan Bank system allowed money to flow around the country through a new secondary market (Hoffman 2001, 163).

Like most government policy regarding financial markets, the Home Loan Bank bill was contested. Insurance companies and mortgage companies who viewed S&Ls as competition and did not currently provide the S&L form of loan argued against the bill. They claimed that the Home Loan Banks were unnecessary and encouraged unsound lending with overly long maturities and excessive loan-to-value ratios. The straight mortgage was proper finance. The Home Loan Banks, opponents argued, would encourage precisely the sort of overbuilding that helped create the depression in the first place.

When Franklin Roosevelt was elected, he pushed for even more aggressive interventions in the housing market. The Home Loan Banks really did nothing for home owners who were losing their homes through foreclosures, which were occurring at the rate of 1,000 per day. Moreover, because they were wholesale institutions, the banks were viewed as benefiting only the lenders and not the borrowers. In fact, they were vulnerable to this charge, in part because the act did call for direct lending, but the banks did not have any such capacity. Rather than merely reorganizing the Home Loan Banking System to suit the demands for more direct intervention, Roosevelt and Congress passed the Home Owners Loan Act (HOLA) of 1933. The main purpose of HOLA was to pull people out of foreclosure. It created the Home Owners Loan Corporation (HOLC), which purchased mortgages in default. It was capitalized and owned by the federal government and governed by the Federal Home Loan Bank Board. To enable homeowners to remain in their homes, HOLC used long-term federal bonds to buy the loans and extend the term of loans to lower monthly payments. Up to 80 percent of the loans were fully amortizing over fifteen years (Hoffman 2001, 168–70). HOLC was generally perceived as successful and made loans from 1933 to 1936.

HOLA also created the federal savings and loan charter in large part to provide a vehicle for the establishment of S&Ls in places where none existed. In addition, the federal government through the Home Loan Bank Board could invest in the establishment of new, federally chartered S&Ls. Up until the 1980s, these were required to be mutual, not-for-profit organizations. Hoffman (2001) has argued, however, that the establishment of the federal S&L charter increased the standardization and professionalization of S&Ls, shifting them in the direction of becoming an "industry" rather than a "movement" of community-based financial institutions. Originally S&Ls referred to deposits as "shares," much like the credit union movement still does. Later, the terminology changed to "savings accounts."

The next development in federal mortgage policy was the National Housing Act of 1934. The major content of the 1934 act was the creation of FHA mortgage insurance, which has had a major influence on mortgage lending practices and patterns since the 1930s. The FHA loan was created in large part to stimulate job creation in the construction industry. But the FHA was responsible for introducing a key credit enhancement that had a strong direct effect on credit availability and served as a model for the development of private mortgage insurance, which has proven to be a critical tool in the expansion of home ownership.

Beyond simply offering mortgage insurance, the FHA established the twenty- and later thirty-year, fully amortizing, fixed-rate mortgage with an 80 percent loan-to-value ratio as the dominant, standardized mortgage format for the rest of the twentieth century. The standardization of FHA loans increased standardization of mortgages generally, setting the stage for the eventual expansion of secondary market activity and securitization that dominated the last quarter of the twentieth century. FHA was a "market maker" in the standardization and commoditization of mortgage credit. These characteristics of the market, in turn, led to all sorts of technological developments and made possible increased automation in underwriting, processing, and servicing loans in later generations. This legacy of FHA is an excellent example of how government involvement and innovation in financial markets led so-called private-sector developments. In fact, it is hard to call almost any major development in mortgage markets wholly private; they were almost all initiated in some substantial way by public policies and programs. This is the nature of housing credit. It is not that the federal government "invented" the concept of mortgage insurance. In fact, mortgage insurance had been used as far back as the late nineteenth century by mortgage companies to improve the marketability of the loans that they sold to investors. Rather, it is the financial and institutionalizing power of the government and government-sponsored entities that makes their involvement in mortgage markets so influential and that leads to standardization.

FHA mortgage insurance increased the supply of mortgage credit and allowed for an expansion in demand by liberalizing underwriting criteria and making debt service more affordable. From the 1930s to the 1940s, the average term for mortgages made by S&Ls increased from eleven years to fifteen years, and S&Ls were not even major users of FHA insurance (Lea

1996). For insurance companies, which were larger FHA users, the average term increased from a range of six to eight years to twenty years. Overall, the average loan-to-value for mortgages increased from less than 60 percent to 75 percent, and the bulk of loans became fully amortizing.

The FHA also provided national risk diversification for local lenders, allowing them to compete more effectively with national lenders. It relied on a national pool of mortgages for its insurance. Most lenders in the 1930s were local. S&Ls and savings banks were still local by design and regulation. Insurance companies and mortgage companies had some advantage by being able to spread risks more geographically, thus being less susceptible to local economic downturns. Banks also suffered from geographic concentration, and FHA insurance allowed them to move more into the mortgage business, which they did steadily from 1934 through the late 1940s.

The impact of the FHA on the overall housing market was phenomenal. By 1937, FHA housing starts accounted for 45 percent of all housing starts in the United States (Jackson 1985, 326). During World War II, FHA activity declined even more than total housing starts, but by 1947, the agency again accounted for a significant portion of housing construction. In 1950, the agency accounted for 35 percent of starts. Together with the newer Veterans Administration (VA) loans, the two programs accounted for 48 percent of starts.

From 1935 to 1939, FHA-insured loans accounted for 23 percent of single-family lending (Vandell 1995). This share grew to 45 percent during 1940–1944. When the VA program was introduced after the war, the FHA share dropped sharply. The program gradually declined in significance, until the late 1960s when Congress authorized a substantial expansion of FHA activity, including a major subsidized loan component. In 1970, FHA loans still accounted for almost 30 percent of single-family loans.

While the FHA was generally initiated as a program to stimulate the construction industry, it was later modified to support various segments of the housing sector. During and after World War II, more specialized FHA programs were created to increase the supply of military housing, national defense housing, urban renewal housing, nursing homes, mobile home parks, and housing for the elderly, among others (Vandell 1995). As government-sponsored secondary markets expanded the conventional mortgage market, and S&Ls offered more long-term, fixed-rate mortgages, some of the demand for FHA, particularly among middle-income borrowers, declined. The fees charged by the FHA created an adverse selection problem in which only higher-risk borrowers were targeted by FHA lenders, creating a market more segmented by income and risk. To some, this segmentation seemed appropriate, as government intervention in the market for middle-income home buyers seemed unnecessary during the generally good economic times of the 1950s and 1960s. However, the FHA program was traditionally seen as "actuarially sound," which meant that it would be self-funding from its fees and premiums and not require outside funds from the U.S. Treasury.

Following the development of FHA loans, the federal government created the Federal National Mortgage Association (now known as Fannie Mae) in 1938 to create a secondary market in FHA-insured loans. Fannie Mae allowed a new form of intermediation between nondepository mortgage originators such as mortgage companies and investment capital from other sources. This meant that a new source of capital became available for the mortgage market, often benefiting from explicit and implicit guarantees from a government corporation. In 1968, Fannie Mae became a "government-sponsored enterprise" (GSE), meaning a privately owned corporation that is subject to significant federal oversight and receives various forms of federal subsidy. Fannie was able to raise capital through the sale of common stock to the public. Its mission also changed in that it became focused on providing a secondary market for non-FHA (or "conventional") mortgages to provide liquidity and support to the mortgage market by purchasing conventional loans.

Two major "circuits" for housing finance developed in the United States, both initiated by federal intervention (Lea 1996). First, the "thrift circuit" was supported by deposit insurance, and the Home Loan Banks provided a majority of funds. Second, insurance companies and commercial banks, supported by the FHA and Fannie Mae, and often acting through mortgage companies, provided a smaller share. The thrift circuit dominated until the 1980s and the explosion of the GSE secondary markets and securitization. In both circuits, the public sector has seeded, nurtured, and been largely responsible for the size and functioning of mortgage markets now and in the foreseeable future. Without federal involvement, we would today have far fewer home owners or potential home owners. Thus, the size of the home lending market today and for the foreseeable future rests on a federally initiated, supported, and sponsored infrastructure. Regardless of ongoing subsidies or guarantees, the federal role in mortgage markets will remain a lasting legacy.

Another major innovation in mortgage financing was the development of mortgage-backed securities (MBS), a tool that some view as a purely private-sector creation. It took a couple of decades for the impact of this development to be felt. Ginnie Mae, a federal agency designed to purchase FHA loans, issued the first mortgage-backed securities in 1970, guaranteeing interest and principal payments on pools of FHA- and VA–insured mortgages. In the middle 1970s, Ginnie Mae also spurred the use of MBS by directly subsidizing below-market-rate MBS so that investors would get market-rate returns (Geisst 1990, 91–93). MBS further increased the number and types of investors in the mortgage market, thereby also increasing the number of new lenders in the market. Also in 1970, the Emergency Home Finance Act created the Federal Home Loan Mortgage Corporation, now Freddie Mac, to provide secondary market capacity for the Home Loan Bank system members. The act also allowed Fannie Mae and Freddie Mac to perform secondary market operations for conventional mortgages.

Fannie Mae and Freddie Mac function as buyer-holders of loans in their portfolios as well as conduits of mortgage capital from investors to retail lenders. They assemble pools of mortgages and sell shares in these pools to investors, or issue bonds backed by repayment income from the mortgage pools. These securities offer several advantages to lenders. They provide greater diversity in underlying asset risk; they provide greater liquidity to lenders because these more diversified assets are more marketable than individual whole loans; and they redistribute credit supplies across regions and standardize the price of credit. By doing these things, they also allow lenders to improve the condition of their balance sheets.

One manifestation of the improved liquidity and increased competition made possible by the federally initiated innovations like mortgage insurance and secondary markets was the decreased cost of mortgage credit to homebuyers and homeowners. The development of secondary markets in the late 1960s corresponds to the "spread" between the price of mortgages and the cost of mortgage funds actually becoming negative for a short while (Lea 1996). At the same time, thrifts lost market share to mortgage companies as the mortgage companies gained access to cheaper funds and were able to offer long-term, fixed-rate mortgages at competitive interest rates. The national scope of mortgage companies and their lack of branches allowed them to benefit from economies of scale and specialization. S&Ls were still both savings and lending institutions and had depended on advantages of local knowledge, which were made irrelevant by the "commoditization" of residential credit. Secondary markets required and promoted the standardization of mortgage terms and underwriting requirements. This standarization was accompanied by an increased supply of standard credit information, reducing the benefit of local information. And the scale and inherent subsidies of the secondary markets meant that they offered lenders lower-cost capital for making mortgages. Thus, loans became more standardized and "one-size-fits-all." Mortgages increasingly resembled commodities rather than individualized products. The commoditization of mortgage credit and the increased role of secondary markets also meant that much more weakly capitalized companies could become substantial lenders in mortgage markets. Many of these lenders were subject to a great deal less routine regulatory examination than S&Ls or banks were. Some of the problems arising from this development will be discussed in chapter 5.

The last phase of modern mortgage lending began in the early 1980s. The Depository Institutions Deregulation and Monetary Control Act (DIDMCA) of 1980 phased in the general abolition of state usury limits on first mortgages (by 1986) as well as the elimination of Regulation Q, which limited the rates that depositories could pay on deposits. S&Ls were already under pressure to pay higher and higher returns on deposits, yet their assets were predominantly in fixed-rate loans. This created a mismatch between their cost and use of funds and drove down their profits. DIDMCA also allowed S&Ls to make commercial real estate loans, which would open a Pandora's box of new problems for the industry, while increasing deposit insurance from $40,000 to $100,000. Thus, lenders were given greater insurance yet allowed to enter into high-cost risky ventures. As Mayer (1998, 373) commented, "How did commercial mortgages, historically a high risk form of lending, solve the maturity mismatch? . . . The question answered itself—pretty quickly too." Congress was pressured by the industry to allow it to enter riskier enterprises. These amounted to desperate attempts to dig out of a hole that had been built by earlier deregulatory moves and government-supported competition from the GSE secondary markets.

In 1982, the Garn-St. Germain Act further loosened regulations on savings and loans, again due to political pressure from a contracting industry. Regulators also relaxed capital standards, so that S&Ls were allowed to have weaker balance sheets. What had been considered thrifts in need of shutting down were instantly reclassified as institutions having only manageable difficulties. A regulatory policy called Memorandum R-49 allowed S&Ls to sell their mortgages and invest in new high-risk securities that were being peddled by Wall Street investment houses (Mayer 1998, 379). Thus, S&Ls, which had being squeezed by new government-sponsored competition and a mismatch between assets and liabilities, were encouraged to invest in high-risk commercial real estate and securities products with the hope that these might pull the industry back from the brink of extinction. With increased deposit insurance and an increasingly hands-off regulatory structure, institutions were allowed to funnel depositors' money, backed by the federal government, into speculative investments. The result was the largest collapse of U.S. financial institutions since the depression. From 1986 to 1995, 1,043 thrifts with over $500 billion in assets failed. As of 1999, the crisis cost taxpayers an FDIC-estimated $124 billion and the industry another $29 billion (Curry and Shibut 2000). These estimates do not consider many tangible and intangible opportunity costs, however, such as the diversion of the bulk of the thrift regulatory infrastructure into the cleanup and the chilling effects that the crisis had on credit markets generally. Large-scale financial crises have contagion and legacy effects that make credit more difficult to get, even for creditworthy borrowers.

The Garn-St. Germain Act also allowed depositories to cross state lines to acquire failing institutions, providing the first major movement toward interstate banking. At the same time, depositories capitalized on the increasing failures of thrifts and banks to argue for eliminating limitations on intrastate bank branching.

It has been argued that the preemption of state usury limits by DIDMCA was critical to the growth of secondary mortgage markets in the 1980s. Certainly, the MBS market grew during the decade. MBS issued by Fannie Mae and Freddie Mac increased from $14 billion in 1982 to $160 billion in 1986 (Chinloy 1995). By the 1990s, Fannie Mae and Freddie Mac's purchases accounted for more than one-half of new mortgage originations. However, the growth in secondary markets was well under way by 1980, and state usury laws for first mortgages were not phased out until the mid-1980s. It is likely that the preemption of state usury limits increased the market for MBS by increasing the returns to investors (by increasing fees and rates paid by borrowers), but the MBS market was already well on its way to being a major source of mortgage capital prior to DIDMCA. Moreover, it can be argued that DIDMCA, by stoking the creation and growth of a new set of lenders, by removing deposit rate regulations favoring S&Ls, and by fostering the development of the mortgage brokerage industry, constituted the death knell for S&Ls. (I will discuss the important role of MBS in the later growth of subprime lending in chapter 5.)

In the late 1980s, more changes in bank regulation supported the growth of Fannie and Freddie and securitization. The 1989 Financial Institutions Reform Recovery and Enforcement Act—the S&L bailout bill—required thrifts to rid themselves of loans to improve their liquidity and lower their risks. Mortgages in portfolio received a 50 percent reserve requirement rating while MBS received only 20 percent. This created a strong incentive to hold as few mortgages in portfolio as possible. In turn, this effectively increased the cost to lenders of holding loans in portfolio and, therefore, of making loans that did not conform to secondary market standards. From 1988 to 1991, the share of all single-family mortgage holdings held by Fannie and Freddie increased from 21.8 percent to 29.4 percent while mortgage holdings of thrifts declined by 5.7 percentage points and MBS increased by 9 percentage points (McDonald 1995).

The commoditization of mortgage lending made possible by a federally supported financial infrastructure entered a penultimate phase in the last ten to fifteen years of the twentieth century with the proliferation of automated underwriting, or credit scoring. While credit scoring has been driven in part by advances in computer technology and innovation, it has also been heavily fostered by the GSEs and the move to securitization. Credit scoring benefits the largest-scale financial institutions the most due to the heavy fixed costs of establishing and maintaining a good credit scoring system and database. Smaller lenders do not reap as many rewards from automated systems. Credit scoring, which was in large part developed for the credit card market, allows lenders to underwrite loans much more quickly, especially those that conform to standard criteria. Applications that are unusual are likely to be either rejected or require much more time than the loans that conform to the credit scoring model. Credit scoring technology, however, can be and is used for much more than merely underwriting loan applications. The same technology can be combined with databases on consumers and homeowners to prescreen strong candidates for marketing purposes. In this way, lenders can preselect entire classes of borrowers and reduce search costs by not bothering to market to marginal candidates. Credit scoring is also being used increasingly in loan servicing, to maintain information on the credit position of existing borrowers (Lea 1996). (Chapter 4 discusses the distributional impacts of credit scoring and automated underwriting.)

Pretending the Visible Hand Was Not There—The New Dominance of Neoclassical Deregulationist Ideology

The history of U.S. financial institution policy illustrates a continual back and forth between those arguing for greater or lesser involvement of banking and government. In the formative decades of the nation, the debate was often about the degree to which government should invest in, stimulate, and be involved with the functions of banking and finance. The notion that financial institutions and financial markets should be wholly private or only very minimally regulated was not commonly accepted by policymakers during most of the nation's history. Even Adam Smith, the primary prophet for the ideology of unfettered markets, was a fan of the government-sponsored Bank of England and made an exception for banking and finance when he argued that some regulation or government involvement was appropriate:

> To restrain private people, it may be said, from receiving in payment the promissory notes of a banker, for any sum whether great or small, when they themselves are willing to receive them; or, to restrain a banker from issuing such notes, when all his neighbors are willing to accept of them, is a manifest violation of that natural liberty which it is the proper business of law, not to infringe, but to support. Such regulations may, no doubt, be

considered as in some respect a violation of natural liberty. But those exertions of the natural liberty of a few individuals, which might endanger the security of the whole society, are, and ought to be, restrained by the laws of all governments; of the most free, as well as of the most despotical. The obligation of building party walls, in order to prevent the communication of fire, is a violation of natural liberty, exactly of the same kind with the regulations of the banking trade which are here proposed. (Smith 1976, 324)

The Hamiltonian view in favor of proactive government involvement in banking was the dominant ideology until Jackson managed to kill the Second Bank of the United States and the Free Banking movement rose during the mid-nineteenth century. Gradually, with national banking, increased state regulation, and a series of federal interventions such as the Federal Reserve and FDIC insurance, the center of ideological gravity moved back toward more government involvement. But in the pre–World War II era, neoclassical orthodoxy began to take a firmer hold among academic economists. Franklin Roosevelt's activism in the economy and the domination of Keynesians in his administration and in subsequent ones kept the pure free-marketers at bay among policymaking circles. By the early 1960s, however, the rise of conservative monetarists, led by Milton Friedman, began to threaten the fiscal Keynesians.

In 1963, Friedman and Anna Schwartz published *A Monetary History of the United States, 1867–1960*. Friedman did the lecture circuit, preaching his monetarist and laissez-faire ideologies (Greider 1987, 87). He and his compatriots were set on a mission of resurrecting the classical Smithian faith in free markets and a crusade against government intrusion in markets. In some ways, Friedman was resurrecting Jefferson's and Jackson's classical liberal beliefs in the separation of government and markets. On the other hand, Friedman had no problem with the concept or reality of corporations or the protection they gave to capitalists.

Bruce Coggins (1998, 42–45) has linked the rise of the financial deregulationists to the rise of Friedman and his monetarist school. The deregulationists adopted Friedman's description of market mechanisms and his view that financial markets, when left to their own devices, are inherently robust and stable. According to Friedman, any periods of instability are short-lived and usually the result of exogenous forces like intervention by regulators. Coggins has pointed to the high rate of bank failures during the Free Banking era of the mid-nineteenth century as evidence that deregulated banking markets are generally not very stable. During what he describes as the postwar era of banking, from 1947 to 1989, during which banks operated mostly under the stronger regulatory structure developed in the 1930s and which includes the difficult banking period of the 1980s, the bank failure rate was only 0.2 percent. The S&L failure rate was higher, of course, but this is often attributed to the deregulation of interest rates (creating a mismatch between the low-rate loans of S&Ls and the higher rates they had to pay depositors), a deregulation of permissible S&L activities, and the government-subsidized growth of secondary mortgage markets.

Meanwhile, the Federal Reserve Bank of St. Louis became what William Greider calls a "guerrilla outpost" for monetarism with the Federal Reserve System (Greider 1987, 97). In a review of Nixon's Hunt Commission Report of 1971, which recommended major deregulation of banking and financial services, a St. Louis Federal Reserve economist criticized the commission as not going far enough and articulates the deregulationists' simple call for complete deregulation:

> Financial institutions . . . are subject to the same competitive forces as other firms . . . The most efficient firms survive and prosper . . . and the less efficient tend to drop out and are taken over by the survivors. . . . Such a system meets our demands for goods and services at the lowest per unit cost. (Luttrell 1972)

Luttrell's comments reveal the neoclassical ideologues' view of credit as no different from any other good or service.

The 1971 Hunt Commission (the President's Commission on Financial Structure and Regulation) articulated a new, stronger focus on the "competitive market principle" for recommending financial policy. The commission called for the phasing out of interest-rate ceilings on deposits, the allowance of different sorts of financial institutions to enter the product markets of other segments of the sector, some consolidation of the regulatory structure, a combination of deposit insurance sources, and the lifting of Glass-Steagall barriers between banking and securities (Hoffman 2001, 230). The Hunt Commission report provided an outline for the deregulationist agenda that was largely accomplished by the end of the century.

While the political interests of various segments of the financial services industry were certainly influential in advancing the deregulationist agenda, they were heavily aided by the increased dominance of laissez-faire ideology in academic and policy elite circles. According to Kuttner (1998, 5), Milton Friedman, "who had been marginal, became central" in scholarly economics. Following Nixon and Ford, the Carter administration continued the movements toward deregulation in a variety of industries, including airlines, telecommunications, and banking. In banking, there were additional factors supporting the deregulationist ideology. One very important one was the presence of a major institutional supplier of deregulationist ideology in the form of the Federal Reserve System. The Federal Reserve System is by far the single largest employer of economists in the United States, and a substantial portion of these economists focus on financial regulation.[2] Federal Reserve economists interact closely with academic economists and frequently move into university positions. Thus, the economics establishment, in general, came to generally adopt the deregulationist agenda.

Economists in academia, the Federal Reserve System, and industry increasingly adopted extremely strong predispositions against consumer protection regulations of almost any sort. Moskowitz (1987) argues that policymakers often seek to adopt policies on the basis of "policy maps," which are sets of key images and concepts that are linked to one another by their sense of causal relationships and processes. Thus, as deregulationists' view of how financial markets work and how regulation is often counterproductive became more dominant, these concepts become embedded in the policy maps on which legislators and policymakers rely. While money and the influence of competing parties can be important in determining the prospects for a legislative or regulatory proposal, these ideologically based policy maps are important. Through dominating the discussions and educational processes regarding the arcane, technically complex, and seemingly uninteresting (at least to many policymakers and much of the general public) issues of financial regulation, the deregulationists have had a great deal of impact on the policy maps of legislators and regulators. Many policymakers tend to react negatively to regulatory proposals or government involvement in credit markets because of a simplistic interpretation of what in actuality are highly complex theories of how markets work. In these policy maps, regulation tends to lead to scarcity, inefficiency, and economic stagnation. "Unintended consequences" are often of more concern than intended consequences. Evidence is less important, and rarely relied on, in the construction of such policy maps. These maps are often seeded by doctrinaire training in some introductory college economics course, and then are reintroduced again and again as policymakers encounter the machinery of financial services research and banking regulation.

One example of how ideological institutions can become political forces and work to shape policy dates back to a government body created in the late 1960s. Perhaps ironically, as it has turned out, the Consumer Protection Act of 1968 created the National Commission on Consumer Finance (NCCF), a nine-member body (three senators, three congressmen, and three appointees of the president) with a full-time staff and a group of outside academic contractors. The NCCF remained the "center of credit research for several years" after its official closure in 1972 (Durkin and Staten 2002). Its recommendations formed a central component of credit policy debates through the 1970s. Several authors of NCCF reports went on to establish strong deregulationist reputations.[3] After the demise of NCCF, a group of industry executives met with one of its former commissioners, an economist at Purdue University. Through "generous grants," the group established the Credit Research Center (CRC) at Purdue University in 1974 (Durkin and Staten 2002).

The CRC, now located at Georgetown University, has since published scores of studies on consumer credit markets and public policy, many of which have a clear deregulationist perspective. The CRC portrays its work as maintaining "integrity and objectivity as an unbiased resource for policymakers" (Credit Research Center 2003a). Its Web site states that its Research Committee "ensures that the Center's research product meets high academic standards. [The Research Committee] also serves as a 'firewall' between the Center's reliance on corporate funding and the conclusions of its policy-oriented research" (Credit Research Center 2003b). Yet the CRC Web site also lists the members of its Research Committee as including representatives from Experian and Trans Union (credit bureaus), MasterCard, Visa, MBNA (a major credit card bank), Household International, and Fair, Isaac and Company, Inc. (the primary provider of credit scoring services), as well as three economists from the Federal Reserve System and a number of academic economists. Its governing board included representatives from Discover Card, General Motors Acceptance Corporation, and Household International. No representatives of consumer groups of any kind are listed as being on either the board or the research committee.

A review of the CRC's recent work shows that not only does it make policy recommendations in its analysis, it proactively develops position papers on important pieces of federal policy, all of which seem to favor deregulationist or large financial service provider positions. For example, CRC staff have submitted testimony against the voluntary collection of racial data on small business loans (which had been prohibited until early 2003), and have testified in front of Congress in support of restricting consumers' access to bankruptcy protection. Also recently, CRC was commissioned by members of the American Financial Services Association, a lobby representing large finance companies, to analyze a database of a small sample of its lenders (nine firms) to estimate the effects of the nation's first state anti-predatory mortgage regulation, which was passed in North Carolina in 1999. From 2000 to 2002, the CRC issued two studies arguing that the law has had a large negative affect on mortgage availability to the detriment of North Carolina home owners. CRC has testified repeatedly against state and federal laws aimed at curbing predatory mortgage lending. Chapter 8 goes into the substance of CRC's work on this issue.

The dominance of deregulationist thinking in U.S. financial services policy has certainly grown in the last three decades. Regardless of the party in power in the White House, high-level appointments have primarily been advocates—or at least accommodators—of much of the deregulationist agenda. This was most recently seen in the strong advocacy and support for repeal of the Glass-Steagall Act with the passage of the 1999 GLBA. President Clinton's last appointee as comptroller of the currency, John D. Hawke, was himself a member of the deregulationist Shadow Financial Services Regulatory Committee, a group on record as opposing the CRA, prior to his service in the Treasury Department and then as comptroller.

Besides Coggins (1998), other observers of financial markets have taken issue with the agenda and assumptions of the deregulationists. Dymski (1993) argues that the financial services structure provides three functions for the economic system:

1. provides finance and other requisite services, such as transaction outlets, to support productive investment and consumption;
2. fosters economic opportunity by channeling financial resources to neglected, but potentially viable, areas and individuals within the economy; and
3. maintains a stable financial environment.

A financial system that does not provide all of these functions imposes social and private costs. Poor performance on any of the three functions may lead to deteriorating performance on the other two functions. For example, allowing highly speculative financing can cause instability, which can then lead to a retrenchment in overall credit availability, with likely disproportionate effects on smaller and disadvantaged borrowers.

The deregulationists begin with a premise that financial markets represent a real-world approximation of the model of perfect competition. This, then, leads to the argument that any firm or household deserving of credit will receive it at an appropriate price, and that public policy does not have a role in helping ensure that credit or capital are provided where they are needed. Lending discrimination, for example, will not persist because viable borrowers will attract lenders who capitalize on the underserved opportunity. Dymski (1993), however, argues that credit markets are far from perfect, and that discrimination and other barriers can and do persist. Moreover, as credit does not flow to certain types of communities, there is a negative spillover effect on the community. The availability of jobs and the values of homes depend on the availability of fairly priced credit and capital. If credit becomes unavailable, then this damages the collateral and creditworthiness of the neighborhood, potentially leading to a vicious circle in which any lender interested in venturing into such an area is forced to assume significantly higher risks. The abandonment of areas by conventional financial institutions then leads to social problems that choke off more investment and lending.

Another spillover problem caused by the lack of regular financial activity in an area is the notion of negative information externalities. If lenders as a whole make few loans in an area, any lender potentially interested in making loans there will have little information about how to evaluate applications from the area. Due to this incomplete information, lenders may avoid marketing to such communities or deny applications from them at higher rates than applications from other, higher-income communities. In this model, lending generates information, including data on property values and credit history—a public good beneficial to other lenders (Lang and Nakamura 1993).

A final extension of the financial spillover problem is the more recent problem of the proliferation of "fringe" financial institutions, including high-risk subprime mortgage lenders, payday loan outlets, and car-title lenders. High-risk lending, especially when accompanied by abusive loan terms, can result in negative spillovers by pushing borrowers into debt beyond their capacity to handle it. Loan terms, high-pressure marketing, and deceptive sales can trap people in escalating, unsustainable cycles of debt. If a disproportionate concentration of these lenders is active in a community, it is likely to lead to worsened credit histories of local residents and businesses, making them less attractive to mainstream financial institutions and accelerating the disinvestment cycle further.

Kuttner (1998, 21, 173) also questions the deregulationist view of banking and bank regulation. He notes that during the period from 1945 to 1973, when the banking system was "an effective hybrid of market and nonmarket forms of discipline," there were only 105 bank failures costing the deposit insurance agencies less than a billion dollars. For the decade after 1984, following quickly after DIDMCA and Garn-St. Germain, there were more than 100 failures every year. The costs of instability in the banking system are far-reaching because, after periods of major bank failures, lenders become excessively risk averse, constraining economic growth and development. Like others, Kuttner points to the rapid deregulatory moves of the early 1980s as the key cause of the S&L collapse. S&Ls were encouraged—by the deregulation of deposit rates—to become involved in a whole new set of speculative activities, many of which they were ill equipped to manage, but that would presumably allow them to pay their depositors' higher interest rates.

The ascendance of deregulationist thinking regarding financial services policy was accompanied by a growing anti-interventionist sentiment among federal housing policymakers. The economic problems and restructuring of the 1970s gave political conservatives ammunition to argue for less government spending on social programs—including housing programs. Conservatives attacked programs as ineffective and wasteful (Hays 1995, 49–50). The economic troubles of the 1970s also set the stage for a backlash against civil rights policies, as blue-collar whites were encouraged to blame programs aimed at assisting minorities for their problems. In 1973, President Nixon declared a moratorium on all new commitments for subsidized housing programs. Difficulties with public housing projects and FHA programs fed into conservative arguments against government involvement in housing markets. As will be discussed in chapter 6, this meant that advocates did not face a generally supportive political climate when they proposed stronger fair lending and community reinvestment policies in the middle to late 1970s. The larger shifts by policymakers toward deregulating financial services and toward less involvement in housing would make strong community reinvestment and fair lending policy proposals a tough sell. Three decades later, the ideological climate for such policies has only gotten worse.

The U.S. financial system has involved, and continues to involve, substantial interaction between public and private sectors. Ideological differences and disparate interests have always been important ingredients in the policy debate. In recent decades, however, the tide has clearly turned toward the deregulationist side, both through an ideological embeddedness among policy elites and through the raw political power provided by vastly greater lobbying and campaign finance resources. Advocates for regulation and a renewed social contract between the public and the financial services sector have their work cut out for them. Recent scandals and implosions in corporate finance provide evidence of the potential costs of strong deregulatory actions. Yet the attention to these problems has not yet translated into concern for the financial system's treatment of traditionally excluded and marginalized communities and groups. The Enron, WorldCom, and Tyco fiascos received so much attention in part because they directly affected middle-class, middle-American constituencies. Two key challenges for those seeking to preserve and expand community reinvestment and community development finance policies will be: (1) to forge real relationships with a broader set of interests and constituencies; and (2) to recast these issues as meaningful to a broad segment of the American public.

CHAPTER 3

Discrimination, Redlining, and Financial Restructuring in Business Credit Markets

Black Americans and Business Credit in U.S. History

> *Those (free blacks) who are shop keepers earn a moderate living but never expand their businesses beyond a certain point. The simple reason is that . . . the whites, who have the money, are not willing to lend to a Negro the capital necessary for a big commercial establishment. . . . If, then, Negroes here are limited to the small retail trade, let us not attribute it to their lack of ability but rather to the prejudices of the whites, who put obstacles in their way.*
> —J.P. Brissot de Warville, *Travels in the United States of America, 1788* (1964, 232)

The history of U.S. banking and credit markets is filled with systemic exclusion and segmentation based on race and geography. Minority entrepreneurs and households, as well as businesses and residents in lower-income and minority neighborhoods, have suffered from poor access to credit at reasonable prices and terms. This chapter first reviews the history of exclusion of black-owned businesses from adequate access to business credit in the United States. It also examines historical attempts to counter such exclusion by building black-owned banking institutions. Finally, it examines the recent evidence on lending discrimination and redlining in small business credit markets. It is important that the history of discrimination in credit markets not be viewed as a completed legacy. Rather, the evidence clearly indicates that, while the form and nature of discrimination have changed over time, segmented and discriminatory patterns in lending are still systemic and of a serious magnitude. There have been gains in some areas, but differential access to credit by race and space, in particular, is still holding back a large segment of society from access to economic opportunity. This condition continues to play a significant role in patterns of urban disinvestment.

From the earliest days of the nation, blacks were constrained in their efforts to develop businesses by a whole host of restrictions, poor access to credit being only one type of barrier. Certainly, some of the difficulties black businesses had in obtaining credit stemmed from the diminished prospects the businesses had due to their difficulties in serving white markets hostile to their success. Challenges in collecting bills (especially from white customers), restrictions on various forms of property ownership, and legal and quasi-legal barriers to participating in various markets were barriers to black business development. Some of these restrictions were directly enforced by state laws, such as the state of Maryland's 1852 law restricting black investment in depository institutions, or restrictions against blacks filing suit and similar actions key to enforcing loan covenants (Harris 1936, 22). Other barriers were the direct or indirect result of legal restrictions or of harassment by whites fearing the economic empowerment of blacks. The formidable barriers faced by blacks did not mean that they did not create and develop significant enterprises, for historical records show that even significant numbers of slaves were able to generate self-employment income. Free blacks in the North and South were able, to some limited extent, to establish businesses and farms of some size.

In addition, the nature of commercial lending involved a very heavy reliance on personal knowledge of the borrower by the banker. This was even truer in the earliest decades of the country when accommodation loans— those relying on the guarantee of the borrower and a co-endorser—were the major method of lending. When lending began to be based more on actual business assets, and later when standardized accounting was adopted and relied on by lenders, personal relationships were no longer the sole basis for underwriting decisions, although they remained important.

As argued in the previous chapter, access to credit and capital was a critical factor in the development of the U.S. economy. Economic development, especially in the early decades of the nation and following severe recessions or depressions, has been largely finance-driven. Moreover, government support for financial institutions, in different ways, has been critical to the development and resurrection of the nation's financial infrastructure throughout the country's history.

The history of black business development in the United States is inextricably linked to the history of social and economic development of blacks more generally in this country. Occupational, legal, and de facto segregation as well as slavery severely limited income and wealth generation for blacks. In fact, Walker (1998, xxiv–xxv) estimates that 3 percent of black slaves were self-employed as business proprietors who established general stores and craft and dressmaking and other enterprises around 1860. While laws technically prohibited business ownership by slaves, such laws were often not enforced because slave owners profited in various ways from the practice. The antebellum business ownership rate was higher among slaves than among free blacks due in part to poorer access to black markets and resistance from northern white customers and governments.

As early as 1788, Brissot de Warville (1964) observed the difficulty that black merchants had in obtaining credit from either banks or suppliers. Small artisans experienced somewhat less of a disadvantage. They would often require enough down payment to pay for their supplies. But merchants had difficulty obtaining stock for their stores. Blacks depended mainly on private individual moneylenders to obtain credit and capital for their businesses. In the North, there is some record of wealthy blacks investing in bank stock. Stephen Smith, one of the wealthiest antebellum northern blacks, sat on the board of Columbia Bank in the 1830s. It was said that he would have been president had it not been for his being black (Walker 1998, 87). In the South, however, blacks were banned from owning bank stock. However, a small number of more prosperous blacks, including barbers and slaveholders, provided private loans to other blacks.

There are numerous stories of free blacks having difficulty obtaining loans from commercial banks, all of which were white-owned. Of course, there are also successful examples of black businessmen who obtained bank credit on occasion, especially planters and slaveholders who had substantial collateral, some of whom in turn re-lent money to less affluent black entrepreneurs. At the same time, even some of the wealthiest blacks were described in credit reports as being poor credit risks. These reports spoke heavily of character and lacked the detailed financial information of today's credit reports (Walker 1998, 90–91). As in real estate markets, black businessmen were often compelled to utilize seller financing or promissory notes, which left them open to usurious and extractive prices and terms. The only real access to fairly priced finance for many blacks was from relatives and friends with excess capital, which was not terribly plentiful.

The response of the black business community to exclusion from mainstream financial institutions was typically to look to resources within the black community. The earliest black-owned financial institutions in the United States had their roots in mutual aid associations of various sorts. The mutual aid society was a strong model in the black community that had its roots in precolonial Africa. Various West African societies had somewhat formalized mutual savings associations where members were required to make regular payments into a common treasury, governed by a set of officers. Withdrawals from the funds were often used to pay for funeral expenses, ritual cloth, and other ceremonial costs (Walker 1998, 9). This tradition followed slaves to America, where mutual aid societies were some of the earliest forms of organizations among slaves and freedmen alike. Cotton Mather commented on the prevalence of mutual aid activities among blacks as early as 1693.

The first mutual aid society among blacks, the African Union Society, was established in Newport, Rhode Island, in 1780. Among other things, the society made loans to members and encouraged thrift and real estate investment. In 1810, the first known black insurance company in the United States, the African Insurance Company, was established in Philadelphia. Black-owned insurance companies preceded the development of black-owned banks and grew directly out of the development of black mutual aid associations and burial societies.

The persistent exclusion of blacks from commercial lending markets led to calls among the black community for the development of black-owned banks. Some blacks pooled funds to invest in real estate, as the New York African Society for Mutual Relief did in the early twentieth century. "A convention of colored people" met in New York in 1851 to "discuss plans for forming a bank" to assist home buyers and entrepreneurs (Harris 1936, 23). At the 1855 National Negro Convention, again in New York, the concept of a rotating credit association was advanced. Neither of these proposals was implemented. In California in 1859, however, blacks were able to establish a savings and loan, the Saving Fund and Land Association.

During the Civil War, the military established savings banks in New Orleans, South Carolina, and Virginia primarily for black soldiers who had few options for depositing their earnings (Walker 1998, 164). These banks were government institutions, providing for the security of deposits. The first military bank, called a "Free Labor Bank," was organized in New Orleans in 1864 by General N.P. Banks to serve his soldiers, freedmen who owned property in New Orleans, and the freedmen laborers who worked on plantations seized by the federal government.

Soon after the war, Congress established the National Freedmen's Savings and Trust Company in 1865. It had branches in twenty-five cities, but was a privately owned, nationally chartered institution. According to Harris (1936, 28–30), the bank was viewed by Congress as a "philanthropic" effort under the control of the "public-spirited" citizens who would safeguard depositors' savings and encourage thrift. The bank was controlled by "white friends of the Negro ostensibly for his benefit." Few blacks were employed at the bank. Moreover, restrictions on the bank's activities required it to invest in stocks, bonds, treasury notes, and other government securities, keeping it from providing credit to blacks themselves.

Due to the government ownership of the military banks, and the way the Freedmen's bank was advertised, blacks generally believed that their deposits in the Freedmen's bank had the guarantee of the federal government. The images of Lincoln, Grant, and others were on the passbooks issued by the bank, and the U.S. flag was draped over the bank's branches. The bank was run fairly successfully as a savings, but not a lending, institution out of its New York headquarters until 1870 when it moved to Washington, DC (Harris 1936, 28). Changes at that time in the bank's federal charter allowed it to enter into real estate lending and make changes in management. However, little of the new real estate lending went to blacks. Instead, white managers often misused funds, including borrowing funds from the bank and not repaying them (Walker 1998, 165). The bank was not regulated as a national bank, and officers and staff were, by law, not subject to penalties for wrongdoing until the bank was "virtually bankrupt" in 1874. The early 1870s were a period of rampant speculation and then crisis in 1873. According to Harris (1936, 33), "the persons who were responsible for the failure of the institution were irresponsible plunderers" typical of financial speculators who rose to ascendance in the country's economic life in the post–Civil War period. This was during the tail end of the unstable, unregulated Free-Banking period and the very early years of the National Bank Act of 1864.

After the fall of the Freedmen's bank, many black leaders then and later argued that its failure was damaging to the perception of black financial entrepreneurship. W.E.B. DuBois called the failure of the bank more damaging to the "throttle and thrift" of freedmen than "ten additional years of slavery" (DuBois 1996). However, beginning in the late 1880s, blacks began forming banks of their own in significant numbers. The first banks formed were the Savings Bank of the Grand Fountain United Order of True Reformers in Richmond, Virginia, in March 1888 and the Capital Savings Bank in Washington, DC, in October 1888 (Harris 1936, 46). At least twenty-eight banks were started by blacks between 1899 and 1905. The bulk of these were created to serve as banks in conjunction with fraternal insurance and burial societies. These groups, in turn, were closely tied to the black church. From 1888 to 1934, at least 134 black-owned banks were created, though not all of them chartered with the state and federal government. This is in addition to a considerable number of credit unions, savings and loans, and industrial loan associations.

Black businesses were allowed to serve the black community but generally not permitted to compete in the mainstream market. The rapid growth of the black business community and of black-owned banks was driven in part by the migration of blacks to urban areas following World War I. This movement led to increasing racial conflicts over housing and employment, exemplified by more than two dozen race riots in U.S. cities in 1919. The increasing racial tensions also led to an increased black solidarity movement and calls to "buy black" (Bates 1997, 145–47). Supported by growing access to capital from the rise in black banks, the black business community grew rapidly in the 1920s. In addition to banking, blacks were entering other financial industries such as insurance. Bates calls the 1920s the "golden years" for the urban black business community.

Black-owned banks were a response to the exclusion of blacks from credit markets as well as from mainstream business markets generally. In the late nineteenth and early twentieth centuries, a black self-help business movement arose. John Hope, a professor at Atlanta Baptist College, articulated much of the feeling of the self-help business movement in a speech before the Fourth Conference for the Study of Negro Problems held in Atlanta in 1899:

> We must take in some, if not all, of the wages, turn it into capital, hold it, increase it. This must be done as a means of employment for the thousands who cannot get work from old sources. . . . Negro capital will have to give an opportunity to Negro workmen who will be crowded out by white competition. . . . There is not much race independence for the race that cannot speak its mind through men whose capital can help or harm those who would bring oppression. We need capital to dictate terms. . . .
>
> . . . In fact we can have very few really learned professional men, until we do have some capital, for a professional man must have time and facilities for increasing his knowledge. These cannot be obtained without money. This money must come from Negroes. . . . More money diffused among the masses through Negro capital will alter this unfavorable state of things. . . .
>
> . . . without these factories, railroads, and banks, he cannot accomplish his highest aim. We are living among the so-called Anglo-Saxons and dealing with them. They are a conquering people who turn their conquests into their pockets. (Hope 1899, 57–58)

While Booker T. Washington is commonly recognized as a leader in promoting the notion of cooperative business development as a solution to the social and economic problems facing blacks at the turn of the century, W.E.B. DuBois and Marcus Garvey also argued for similar visions, though they frequently called for somewhat more aggressive tactics. Walker (1998, 222) has argued that all three promoted a separatist, cooperative business development as the sole salvation for blacks. They essentially argued for an independent black economy that would exist parallel to, but really separate from, the mainstream white economy. DuBois was known for his approach of organizing blacks to do business only with black firms, thus increasing or maintaining the market for such firms. Garvey came to the United States from Jamaica in 1916 and established the Universal Negro Improvement Association. He developed an economic development program of significant scale, although due to poor access to capital and limited business expertise, much of it eventually failed. It included a cooperative manufacturing enterprise to make uniforms and dolls for the black community. He also published the *Negro World*, a weekly newspaper with a circulation of 200,000. DuBois maintained his arguments for black economic separatism well into the twentieth century.

Harris (1936) argued against the separatist, bootstrap movement, including the strategy focusing largely on black-owned banks to provide access to credit and capital. He felt that the exclusion of blacks from more capital-intensive and sustainable industries, such as manufacturing, and from mainstream markets limited the growth potential and stability of black self-help approaches. Moreover, in a system in which blacks experienced severe legal, societal, and economic disadvantages, the future of black business was directly and indirectly constrained.

The noted sociologist E. Franklin Frazier also criticized black economic separatism or bootstrapism as not being a viable economic development strategy for blacks (Frazier 1957a, 139–40). He argued that such approaches had poor prospects due to the limited support that black businesses earn from black consumers. But Frazier went beyond this contention to question the capacity of blacks to run successful businesses in general. This was not because of difficulties due to discrimination in credit markets, which he seemed to dismiss in the face of evidence to the contrary. Rather, he argued that the poor prospects of blacks in business had more to do with the "lack of traditions in the field of business enterprise" (Frazier 1957b, 411). He made these comments after Myrdal (1944) had pointed to direct and indirect discriminatory barriers of various sorts. To support his argument, Frazier contrasted the apparent success of other "alien" groups, especially "Orientals," to the lack of success in business formation among blacks. Unfortunately, such arguments served to reinforce and support discriminatory attitudes toward black-owned firms, and have a legacy that has lasted to this day.

It took four decades for social science to respond with strong evidence on this point, and when it finally did, Frazier's arguments were largely repudiated. Walker (1998) rejects Frazier's "lack of tradition" argument by providing a comprehensive and detailed picture of the rich business tradition of blacks in U.S. history—typically in the face of discrimination and adversity—as well as that of precolonial Africans. Bates (1997) has confronted the perpetual habit of comparing black business formation to that of immigrant entrepreneurs and largely dismantled the myth of the miracle of immigrant entrepreneurship. He found that the Asian-immigrant entrepreneur to whom blacks are often compared is often an overqualified, underemployed person using small business as a transitional strategy due to limited options because of limited facility with English and few contacts in the business world. Over time, they tend to leave entrepreneurship to enter jobs that are more economically rewarding. Unfortunately, it is not clear whether the work of Bates or Walker has done much to change the acceptance of Frazier's indictment of black business capacity among the mainstream public, including the banking establishment.

It was American racism and discrimination—particularly in credit markets—that compelled blacks to rely on starting their own banks to provide for savings and credit facilities. This was a rational and reasonable effort. What was the black business community to do? There was little prospect for civil rights activism at all prior to World War II, and certainly not for policies addressing credit access. But the development of black-owned financial institutions was a problem in part for at least two reasons. First, as pointed out by Harris (1936), the concentration of black businesses in the first half of the twentieth century was largely in personal service businesses with little debt capacity and limited and highly vulnerable markets. Second, because banking benefits from significant economies of scale, the limits of investment capital and the size of black-owned banks stunted their ability to serve larger, creditworthy firms. Prudent financial management precludes small banks from making large loans that would constitute a sizable share of their asset base and lead to a lack of financial diversification. This meant that even if a black-owned manufacturer did request a loan, many black banks would not be able to offer such financing without jeopardizing the soundness of the bank and incurring problems with regulators. Thus, the small size of many black banks—dictated largely by the limited investment capital in the black community—meant that loans made by black banks would remain concentrated in credits to smaller, personal-service businesses and the like. In fact, a study of more recent black-owned banks found that their performance is related to bank size (Ziorklui 1994). Even today, larger black-owned banks perform better than similarly sized nonblack-owned banks. At the same time, the presence of black banks offered some excuse for discriminating mainstream institutions to claim that black businesses were served by black banks.

Following the 1929 crash, black banks fared very poorly. By 1934, only twelve remained. While the 1920s had seen some movement of blacks into nontraditional lines of business, black-owned firms remained heavily concentrated in personal-service and retail sectors. Black banks suffered even more than white-owned institutions during the depression due to the concentration of black businesses in personal-service businesses, including grocers, pharmacists, barbershops, beauty parlors, and funeral parlors (Harris 1936). These were described as "defensive enterprises" because they were fostered and yet limited by cultural, residential, and occupational segregation.

Unfortunately, similar to the chains of disinvestments described by Massey and Denton (1993) in their examination of the worsening of ghetto poverty in the later twentieth century, these concentrated patterns meant that as blacks were harmed disproportionately by the depression, their businesses were hurt disproportionately. As blacks were the "first fired," the retail and service establishments serving them were hit the hardest. This result in turn spilled over onto the balance sheets of the banks serving these businesses. Moreover, the loyalty of the black consumer to the black business was weakened by the hard times (Bates 1997, 149). Drake and Clayton (1962, 450–51) showed that, in the heart of Chicago's South Side black belt, nearly 90 percent of the retail stores were white owned by 1938, with blacks retaining niches only in beauty parlors, barber shops, and funeral parlors.

The evidence of black businesses having difficulty obtaining credit continued throughout the twentieth century. Myrdal, in his classic *An American Dilemma*, described how:

> The Negro businessman . . . encounters greater difficulties in securing credit. This is partly due to the marginal position of Negro business. It is also due to prejudiced opinion among the whites concerning the business ability and personal reliability of Negroes. In either case a vicious cycle is in operation keeping Negro business down. (Myrdal 1944, 308)

In a national study of black-owned businesses, Joseph Pierce (1947) concluded that lack of access to capital and credit was the "foremost obstacle" to the "progressive operation" of black firms. Blacks overwhelmingly relied on personal savings to start their firms. More than 90 percent relied on such savings, or on relatives, for capital. Only 3.3 percent of firms secured any credit from banks. Pierce did not attribute the small amount of bank debt completely to discrimination:

> The difficulties faced by Negro businessmen seeking bank credit are due in part to prejudice of the white bank officials, in part to the lines of business which many Negroes operate, and in part to the fact that adequate records are not kept by a large percentage of the businesses. The Negro business man finds it difficult to obtain credit from Negro banks because of the small number of these and their limited resources. (Pierce 1947, 188)

Pierce also noted that, at least in the South, black firms would typically need white endorsers to qualify for a bank loan if they were able to get credit at all.

Pierce provided an earlier articulation of what has been an ongoing debate in minority economic empowerment. That is, is self-help finance via minority or specialized financial institutions sufficient, or is a wider attack on the dual economy needed? Pierce argued that opening up credit markets—and not just promoting black-owned institutions—made sense as a strategic first move to break down what he called the black-white "caste" economic system:

> What is the answer to the problem of credit for Negro business? Does its future lie in combining community resources by organizing a number of relatively small corporations or by creating, out of the meager incomes of Negroes, lending agencies which will make credit easier for individuals and partnerships? In attempting to study these questions dispassionately, full value must be given to the fact that prospective Negro business men must try in some manner to find opportunities to profit by the experiences of the majority groups in the operations of organizing and manipulating corporate structures. Again, there appears the need for cracking the caste wall, at least in strategic places. (Pierce 1947, 22)

After decades of lying somewhat dormant, black nationalism reemerged in the 1960s. With it came the black capitalism movement, which sometimes took on highly bootstrapping, separatist connotations. While attention to the problems of gaining better access to white-owned banks was growing, there was also a growth in black-owned financial institutions. From 1963 to 1976, the number of black-owned banks grew from thirteen to fifty (Walker 1998, 313–15). Some of the growth in black-owned banks in the 1970s, however, utilized public policy that sought to reduce the limited connection of black institutions to the mainstream economy. Chief among these was the Minority Bank Deposit Program of the Department of the Treasury. The program was created in 1970 to increase the amount of deposits in minority-owned financial institutions and increase access to credit in inner-city neighborhoods. Between 1970 and 1973, federal funds in minority-owned financial institutions increased from $35 million to over $80 million (Rengert 2002). Over the same period, total deposits of minority-owned institutions increased from $400 million to over $1 billion. The Department of Energy also created a separate, additional federal deposit program.

The second emergence of black-owned institutions was quite a bit more successful than the early-twentieth-century movement. In part, this result reflected some diversification and growth in the nature of black-owned firms. However, programs like the Minority Bank Deposit Program and a parallel program in the Department of Energy and in several states likely played a role. Beyond their direct impacts, these programs spurred many larger corporations to deposit funds in minority-owned institutions as well as some local governments (Rengert 2002).

In Chicago, for example, Alvin Boutte, a drugstore owner, and George Johnson, of Johnson Products, started Independence Bank in 1964. Later, in 1988, Independence acquired Drexel National Bank, a white-owned institution. It became the largest black-owned banking organization in the country, although it still had less than $250 million in assets. Independence, like many black-owned banks, was criticized for not being an active lender, especially to small, black-owned firms. Most black-owned banks were even less active, however, in part due to their very small size. One exception was Seaway National Bank, which was started by real estate developer Dempsey Travis and others in 1965. Travis and other blacks had been excluded from membership in the white mortgage bankers association. Seaway went on to be, for a while, one of the largest Small Business Administration (SBA) lenders in Illinois. Both Independence and Seaway benefited over the years from public deposit programs, including those of the state of Illinois and the city of Chicago.

Access to Business Credit Since the 1960s

Discrimination in business credit markets can be a thorny policy problem. This is because the barriers faced by minorities in establishing and successfully operating businesses have not been limited to the lack of capital and credit. Blacks, for example, continue to face a wide variety of barriers and disadvantages in attempting to establish and grow businesses, especially when compared to whites. Bates (1993, 1997) argues that, until the 1960s, black businesses were severely constrained by pervasive and legal segregation in housing, occupations, and education. While segregation and discrimination persist in many areas, some gains have been made—perhaps less so in housing and education than in labor markets. The increased availability of SBA-guaranteed loans and some attention paid to small business lending under the Community Reinvestment Act (CRA) induced some banks to make loans to black-owned firms. Very large barriers still exist, but significant gains have occurred. Public policy to improve credit access to black-owned firms has been criticized significantly, particularly when attempts to improve access came at the expense of prudent and sound underwriting decisions (Bates 1973, 1993). It was precisely because blacks had suffered from discrimination in credit, housing, employment, and other markets that they had accumulated less capital, less education, and less business experience, on average, than whites.

To improve access to credit for a group that has been discriminated against, at least two strategies are required. First, meaningful laws aimed at punishing discrimination based on race must be adopted and enforced. Lenders should fear being caught and expect heavy costs when they are caught. Second, lenders should be given tools that mitigate the real and perceived risks of lending to a group that, on average, suffers from poorer access to capital, less business experience, and less collateral. "Perceived risks" may be simply another term for statistical discrimination, where lenders economize by using the *average* weaker position of black businesses as a screening tool and so avoid black firms. Such practices, while perhaps economical, are still illegal. However, credit enhancements, together with enforcement of anti-discrimination law, can be useful in reducing this form of discrimination.

The use of credit enhancements to induce lenders to make more loans to black-owned firms that really do pose greater underwriting risks—again largely due to previous discrimination of various forms—can be a challenging enterprise. Some would argue against such an approach and urge that enhancements should be used only to mitigate perceived risks. At the other end of the spectrum was Howard Samuels who, as newly appointed director of the SBA in 1968, espoused a philosophy of "compensatory capitalism" in which very high-risk loans were made to stimulate a substantial increase in credit flows to black-owned firms. As Bates (1973) has pointed out, the SBA faced a major challenge in operationalizing Samuel's vision because lenders had essentially no experience in dealing with black firms, most of which were located in or near urban ghettos. Moreover, the SBA greatly increased the role of the Emergency Opportunity Loan (EOL) program after 1968. From 1969 to 1973, two-thirds of the more than 36,000 SBA loans to minorities were EOLs (Bates 1997, 143–44). But the EOL program was designed to help low-income people to establish or expand businesses in traditional fields. High incomes or a history of successful business experience could actually be cause for denial of a loan.

An SBA loan program is not, by itself, able to overcome the problems encountered by start-up entrepreneurs with little business experience or other resources. Such programs are only effective to the degree that they encourage lenders to look harder at black firms as potential borrowers and perhaps to overlook one or two minor disadvantages in issues like collateral or net worth. Unfortunately, the EOL program did more harm than good, resulting in defaults of more than 70 percent in Boston, Chicago, and New York (Bates 1997, 144). More than that, the program corroborated the incorrect view that black business was inherently risky and Frazier's notion of blacks' having a weak inclination for successful business. Poorly designed programs like the SBA EOL only work to reinforce and perpetuate patterns of discrimination, not reduce them. They serve as excuses for banks that do not want to lend to minority firms or neighborhoods and as evidence, however misplaced, that CRA and similar laws will lead to high losses.

Despite some of the SBA's failures to improve blacks' access to business credit, some progress was made in the 1970s and 1980s in improving access to broader markets outside of traditional industries based in low-income neighborhoods. This progress was in large part due to the impact of CRA and the Equal Credit Opportunity Act (ECOA), and it, in turn, improved the position of some black firms as they sought additional capital. The rise of black political power at the municipal level and the development of affirmative action and set-aside programs at all levels of government gave blacks access to markets in fields such as construction and business services and in other areas. In the 1970s, the number of black city administrators rose substantially, especially in cities with black mayors such as Detroit and Atlanta. These officials helped provide the connections between municipal contracts and black business. Bates (1993) found that cities with black mayors had relatively stronger black-owned firms and stronger growth in new black-owned firms in the late 1970s and early 1980s. Yet, he also found that firms in these cities actually suffered from worse access to credit than firms in other cities, despite their larger size and greater success, suggesting that access to credit problems persisted.

The evidence from the last decades of the twentieth century shows that, while some improved access to credit may have occurred, minority-owned firms, especially black-owned businesses, continue to suffer from discrimination in credit markets. Moreover, there is significant evidence that geographic redlining has also persisted. The evidence in this regard grew significantly during the late 1980s and throughout the 1990s. Using a survey of 1,300 firms, Faith Ando (1988) found that black firms, on average, actually had lower debt-to-equity ratios than white-owned firms, which could impede their development. She also found that black-owned firms were denied bank loans at significantly higher rates than white-owned firms, after controlling for a variety of credit risk variables. Using data from the 1987 U.S. Census Bureau's Characteristics of Business Ownership database, Bates (1993) found that small, young black-owned firms were able to leverage only $.89 of debt for every dollar of owner equity, while small, young, white-owned firms were able to obtain $1.79 of debt per dollar of equity, even after controlling for owner age and management experience and firm characteristics. Bates also found that the location of a business was an even more important factor in access to credit than minority ownership status, with firms located in minority neighborhoods having inferior access to credit.

The evidence continued to grow during the 1990s. In 1993, a survey of small business owners in the Chicago area was conducted by Yankelovich Partners and sponsored by a consortium of large Chicago-based banks. The survey found that firms in modest-income census tracts, which tend to be largely minority, reported lack of access to credit to be a "very serious problem" almost twice as often as firms located in upper-income tracts (29 percent to 16 percent). Firms in minority tracts reported lack of access to credit as a very serious problem two-and-one-half times more often than firms in predominantly white tracts (38 percent to 15 percent). Yankelovich also found that, among respondents who had applied for bank loans, applicants from upper-income tracts received the full amount of their loan request at a 40 percent higher rate than applicants whose businesses were located in modest-income tracts (88 percent versus 63 percent). Moreover, small businesses in modest-income tracts were substantially less likely than those in upper-income tracts to have applied for a bank loan (76 percent versus 88 percent). In a survey of 448 firms in the Denver area, Ford (1996) found that black-owned firms were denied loans more than three times as often as white-owned firms. After screening out firms that did not meet minimum sales and net worth levels as well as those with less than three years of operating history, the denial rates for screened white firms dropped significantly, while denial rates for screened black firms did not.

Despite the growing evidence that discrimination against minority businesses was a problem in the credit market, federal regulators charged with enforcing ECOA were slow to act on these concerns. The primary implementer of ECOA is the Federal Reserve Board, which issues the corresponding regulations for the statute and has the power to change how the law is implemented. The board's interpretation of the statute had, until very recently, prohibited banks from even voluntarily collecting racial information on business loans. This meant that, unlike with mortgage loans, regulators had no information on the racial patterns of business lending by specific institutions. In the mortgage area, the Home Mortgage Disclosure Act (HMDA) dataset, while not sufficient to prove that an institution is unlawfully discriminating, is a powerful tool that can be used by regulators to identify lenders whose patterns warrant further investigation. Because lending discrimination investigations are costly and politically sensitive, regulators are reluctant to initiate an investigation without substantial suggestive evidence. HMDA data provide such a tool in mortgage antidiscrimination enforcement. No such tool exists for small business loans.

Facing the mounting evidence of a problem, the Federal Reserve agreed to "study" the problem more. In the spring of 1999, the board held a conference entitled "Business Access to Capital and Credit." In this conference, three papers were presented analyzing a new set of national data from the Federal Reserve's 1993 National Survey of Small Business Finances (NSSBF), a large survey of small firms in the U.S. (Blanchflower et al., 1998; Bostic and Lampani, 1999; and Cavalluzzo, Cavalluzzo, and Wolken, 1999). The NSSBF contains a large number of variables on firm finances, experience in obtaining credit, characteristics of the firm owner (including credit history), type and pricing of loan, etc. Two of these studies also utilized additional nonpublic data—including data on firm credit score—made available to Federal Reserve staff. All three studies found large disparities in denial rates between white- and black-owned firms, so that black-owned firms were approximately two- and one-half times as likely to be denied a loan as white-owned firms. Raw differences in denial rates were substantial at 27 percent and 66 percent for white- and black-owned firms, respectively. Some of this diffrence was due to differences in the financial capacity of firms, credit histories of firm owners, and other firm and owner characteristics, which the NSSBF data generally show were weaker among black-owned firms.

However, after controlling for a wide variety of firm and owner characteristics, all three papers found that black-owned firms were still about two times as likely to have their loan applications denied as similarly situated white-owned firms. Moreover, even after controlling for firm characteristics, including credit score, black-owned firms were 37 percent more likely than white-owned firms to avoid applying for loans due to fear that their applications would be rejected, while Hispanic-owned firms were 23 percent more likely than white-owned businesses to fear rejection (Cavalluzzo, Cavalluzzo, and Wolken 1999).

Despite the large differentials in access to credit between white- and black-owned firms, some have questioned whether even these studies, with over 100 control variables, adequately capture differences in firm finances (Avery 1999). Others, however, have found the evidence convincing. Bates, in reviewing these papers, argued that the "totality of the evidence points toward discriminatory treatment of black business owners" (Bates 1999) Even the skeptical Avery admitted that this evidence "can't be used to dismiss" discrimination (Avery 1999). Moreover, the denial rate disparities in these studies may be underestimates of actual differentials. They are likely to suffer from selection bias, because firms rejected for bank loans and no longer in business were not included in the surveys. In addition, Bates (1999) has argued that the omission of younger, smaller firms from the NSSBF database biases the estimates of differential credit access downward because it is the smaller, younger firms that are most likely to suffer from credit access problems.

Redlining: Geographic Discrimination in the Marketing and Making of Business Loans

Since at least the 1960s, there has been concern over the loss of jobs and businesses in lower-income and minority urban neighborhoods. One factor that contributes to the economic decline of lower-income and minority neighborhoods is poor access to credit by minority-owned or white-owned firms that are located, or wish to locate, in these areas. Of course, the higher presence of minority-owned firms in minority and lower-income neighborhoods suggests that race-based discrimination, all by itself, will result in some geographic differential in credit flows between minority and nonminority neighborhoods, and between lower-income and upper-income neighborhoods. But beyond these effects, lenders may avoid certain areas even if white-owned firms are located there, or may further penalize minority-owned firms when they are located in minority or lower-income neighborhoods.

Besides discrimination against minority-owned firms, various factors might be expected to lead to an inadequate supply of credit to firms in minority and lower-income neighborhoods. First, lenders might exhibit a form of pure redlining, where they choose to avoid making loans to firms in such areas because they have a taste for doing so. White loan officers, for example, might prefer not to call on firms in minority neighborhoods. Pure redlining may involve varying degrees of awareness on the part of the perpetrator. Alternatively, banks might redline through a sort of "statistical" geographic discrimination, using the race of the neighborhood or neighborhood income as a signal of borrower risk or risk-adjusted profit. Typically, statistical redliners are highly aware of their actions. One distinction from pure redlining lies in the motivation for the action. The statistical redliner seeks to minimize costs or risks by using neighborhood racial composition as a signal of credit risk or loan profitability. One problem with such a practice occurs if the average risk among firms in a geographic area is overestimated—perhaps due to stereotypes of the form fostered by E. Franklin Frazier. In such cases, a negative impact on credit access is clearly expected. However, even when lenders make accurate assessments of the *average* risk among firms in a certain type of neighborhood, statistical redlining is likely to result in poor credit access in minority or lower-income neighborhoods. If the true average risk of firms in a neighborhood exceeds the lender's tolerance for risk, then entire groups or geographic areas may be denied credit access, even though some firms are creditworthy. Regardless of whether redlining is "pure" or "statistical," it is inconsistent with CRA.

A third reason that lenders might avoid lending in certain types of neighborhoods involves the notion of information externalities in lending. Lang and

Nakamura (1993) provide a theory of redlining based on incomplete information. If lenders receive few applications from lower-income neighborhoods, they have little information about how to evaluate applications from these areas. Due to this incomplete information, lenders deny applications from these areas at higher rates than those from other, higher-income areas. In this model, lending generates information, including data on property values and borrower risk. This information is a public good that is beneficial to other lenders.

The bulk of the literature on redlining and lending discrimination has concerned residential mortgage lending, so it is important to look there to understand the methodology of lending discrimination research. Much of this research has used data collected under the federal HMDA and related regulations. The availability of HMDA data and the historic focus of CRA and fair lending regulations on mortgage activity have spurred substantial research on residential lending patterns. The empirical literature on mortgage redlining can be categorized into two basic types: studies focusing on an outcome-based definition of redlining; and those focused on a process-based definition concerned with the approval or denial of formal applications (Yinger 1995). Outcome-based studies of lending flows, which focus on lending rates to different types of neighborhoods, were the norm before 1990, when HMDA began to include application-level data on loan applications rather than only census tract summaries of originations.

More recently, the mortgage access literature has focused on the approval or denial of formally submitted mortgage applications, in large part because the newer, publicly available HMDA data have repeatedly shown large disparities in approval rates by race even after controlling for income. The bulk of this literature has focused on lending discrimination by race of applicant, and less on a process-based definition of redlining, where the effect of the geographic location on approval rates is examined.

Outcome-based studies of mortgage lending have frequently found evidence of redlining when controlling for neighborhood characteristics (Yinger 1995). The outcome-based studies are more difficult to model because they attempt to explain the results of a number of different current and historical processes. These include the marketing and screening procedures of lenders and realtors, anticipated discrimination by potential borrowers, and historical discrimination. The process-based studies, on the other hand, merely attempt to isolate discrimination or redlining in the approval of formal loan applications, which is only one part of the lending process. Although these studies are easier to implement, the findings may be quite limited. If redlining occurs primarily through lenders not marketing their services in certain areas, for example, a process-based study finding no redlining in the approval process may be of limited relevance.

Traditionally, most studies of mortgage-lending discrimination and redlining focused on the home purchase loan process. In this process, the borrower in some sense initiates the process after deciding to try to buy a home. In small business lending, however, the process is quite different. A loan can be initiated by the bank or the small business. Moreover, the bank has an altogether more involved and active role in the process. Figure 3.1 shows the various stages of the small business lending-borrowing process. Although many studies of small business lending focus on the underwriting or approval stage of the process, there are actually multiple steps at which a firm may exit the process, beginning with a failure of marketing and solicitation by lenders. Some steps in the process are driven by the lender and some by the borrower. However, even when a firm chooses not to inquire about or apply for a loan, it may be partly due to previous denials or experiences, including possibly discriminatory actions. Thus, discrimination in lending may have a feedback effect on the explicit demand for loans. Cavalluzzo, Cavalluzzo, and Wolken (1999) found, for example, that minority-owned firms were much more likely to avoid applying for loans due to fear of denial than white-owned firms, even after controlling for financial characteristics of the firms.

Newer Data on Small Business Lending Patterns

As will be discussed in chapter 7, the regulations implementing the Community Reinvestment Act were substantially revised in 1995. One of the major changes was the beginning of the collection of small business lending data from banks and thrifts on a census tract basis. While not nearly as detailed as HMDA data, the new CRA small business data do allow for the first systematic analyses of the geographic patterns of small business lending by depository institutions in the United States. The CRA regulations require banks with more than $250 million in assets to report the number and dollar amount of loans of less than $1 million made to firms (of any size) broken out by census tract. It also requires the separate reporting of loans by tract to firms with less than $1 million in annual sales.

Calculations based on research by the Federal Reserve on CRA data for 1997 show that banks and thrifts reported roughly the same number of loans per small business (less than $1 million in sales) in U.S. central cities compared to suburbs (Canner 1999; Immergluck and Smith 2001). The ratio was 0.28 in central cities and 0.29 in suburbs. However, Table 3.1 shows that when tracts were disaggregated by income level, low- and moderate-income tracts in both cities and suburbs fared poorly. The small business lending rate was 45 percent higher in upper-income suburban neighborhoods than in lower-income suburban neighborhoods, and 42 percent higher in upper-income central-city tracts than low-income central-city tracts.

70

Figure 3.1 **The Small Business Lending Process**

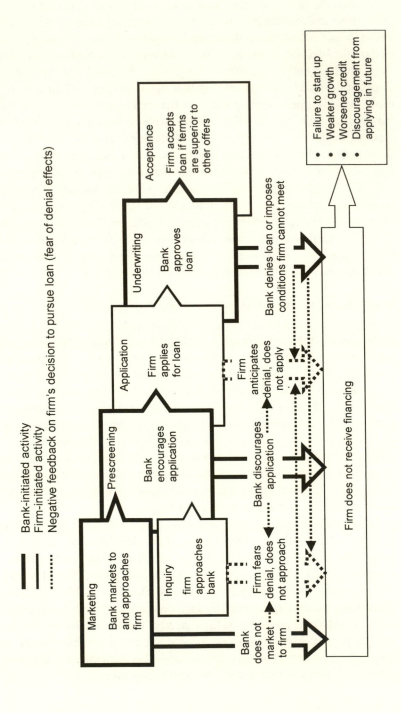

Table 3.1

CRA-Reported Small Business Loans, 1997

Type of metropolitan census tract	Number of loans	Firms	Loan-firm ratio
Low income			
Central city	106,704	453,900	0.24
Suburbs	7,704	35,600	0.22
Moderate income			
Central city	232,018	943,400	0.25
Suburbs	123,703	498,400	0.25
Middle income			
Central city	371,604	1,335,000	0.28
Suburbs	568,641	1,975,800	0.29
Upper income			
Central city	303,134	890,000	0.34
Suburbs	359,050	1,139,200	0.32
Total			
Central city	1,025,218	3,666,800	0.28
Suburbs	1,060,441	3,649,000	0.29

Source: Immergluck and Smith (2001), calculated from data in Canner (1999).

Many central-city loans are made in census tracts with a large number of businesses. Some of these tracts contain low-income residents but also contain parts of industrial or downtown business districts. While many businesses in central cities may be located in such places, most central-city neighborhoods are more residential in character. To control for this issue, Canner (1999) broke out central-city neighborhoods that were in the top quartile of tracts in each income group by the number of small and large businesses. When looking only at those tracts that do *not* fall into either of these two top quartiles (which is a large majority of central-city tracts), we can get a better idea of what the lending differentials are in lower- versus upper-income residential neighborhoods. Table 3.2 shows that, in such neighborhoods, the disparity in small business lending was much larger, with the lending rate in upper-income residential tracts being 136 percent higher than in low-income residential tracts. In a multiple regression analysis, Canner (1999) also found that minority tracts, after controlling for income, firm and residential population, industry, and regional location, receive fewer loans than white tracts.

Analyzing Small Business Lending Differentials Within a Metropolitan Area

To better understand factors that might affect business loan access among different neighborhoods, it is useful to look closely at one metropolitan area

Table 3.2

Loans to Firms with Less than $1 Million in Sales in Residential Central-City Neighborhoods, 1997

Central-city residential neighborhoods[a]	Number of loans	Firms[b]	Loan-firm ratio
Low income	10,114	92,297	0.11
Moderate income	30,341	230,742	0.13
Middle income	65,738	369,187	0.18
Upper income	59,417	230,742	0.26

Source: Immergluck and Smith (2001), calculated from data in Canner (1999).

[a]Residential neighborhoods are those that are *not* in the top quartile when ranking all tracts in income category by number of large (over $1 million in sales) or small (under $1 million in sales) firms. Figures are directly or imputed from Canner (1999).

[b]Number of firms with less than $1 million in sales are estimated from share figures in Canner.

and acquire more detailed data on the firms in this area. One key piece of data that is very useful in identifying credit access problems—and not widely available—is some measure of the credit history or condition of firms in different census tracts. I was able to obtain such data for the Philadelphia metropolitan area for 1998 and combined it with business and small business lending data for the same year to conduct a multivariate analysis of lending flows across Philadelphia-area neighborhoods.[1]

To identify differences in intrametropolitan business lending rates, I analyze loans to firms under $1 million in the nine-county, bi-state Philadelphia metropolitan statistical area (MSA) from the 1998 CRA data.[2] The Philadelphia area is economically diverse, with a broad distribution of neighborhood types and a diverse industrial mix. In the Philadelphia MSA during 1998, banks and thrifts made approximately 18,000 small business loans to firms with annual sales of $1,000,000 or less in census tracts with nonzero residential populations. Table 3.3 provides lending activity broken out by four race-of-neighborhood categories for the nine-county Philadelphia metropolitan area. The table breaks out the number of firms with sales of $1 million or less (as reported by Dun and Bradstreet) located in each type of tract in 1998. Also shown are aggregate loan-per-business rates in each of the four neighborhood income categories, as well as averages among each set of tracts for loan-per-business rates, median income, and Dun and Bradstreet credit score.

Table 3.3 shows that loan-per-firm rates are substantially higher in predominantly white tracts than in minority tracts. The average number of loans per 100 businesses for predominantly white tracts is more than 50 percent greater than the average for mixed-race tracts, more than two times that for

Table 3.3

Small Business Lending by Racial Composition of Census Tract in Nine-County Philadelphia Area, 1998

	Predominant race of tract			
	White	Mixed race	Hispanic	Black
Number of loans	14,761	2,248	62	419
Number of businesses	134,186	40,049	1,152	36,405
Loans per 100 businesses	11.00	5.61	5.38	1.15
Average loan per 100 businesses	14.10	8.95	6.69	3.38
Average credit score	30.82	29.55	26.38	29.50
Average median income of tracts	$49,665	$34,987	$12,799	$22,547
Number of tracts	828	237	13	119

Source: Immergluck (2002), from 1998 CRA data.

Notes: White = 85 percent or more white; mixed race = 16–74 percent minority, less than 50 percent Hispanic; Hispanic = 50 percent or more Hispanic; black = 75 percent or more black.

Hispanic tracts, and more than four times the average for black tracts. And the aggregate ratio of loans to businesses for all predominantly white tracts is almost 10 times the ratio for all black tracts.

Dun and Bradstreet data are expected to undercount firms, especially those with no credit experience or those operating primarily in the informal economy. However, in a comparison with other small-area data sources on small businesses, this data set is relatively comprehensive. Nonetheless, it might be expected that firms in minority neighborhoods, especially those that fear loan denial or operate in the informal economy, would be less likely than those in more affluent areas to be included in the Dun and Bradstreet data. If this is the case, then the differentials in loan-per-firm rates shown in Table 3.3 would underestimate the actual differentials.

Table 3.3 also shows that the average credit score of the firms varies over the four types of neighborhoods. Note that it is the Hispanic neighborhoods that have the lowest average credit scores, not the black neighborhoods, which have the lowest average loan-per-business rate. The Hispanic neighborhoods also have a substantially lower average income level than the black neighborhoods. Moreover, while the black neighborhoods as a group have almost as many firms as the mixed race neighborhoods (36,405 vs. 40,049), they see far fewer loans (419 vs. 2,248). Some of this may be due to differences in the strengths of the local market (e.g., median incomes and populations), although the magnitude of the difference is very large. To examine the role of neighborhood race further, multivariate analysis is needed.

The CRA data allow for a multivariate estimation of neighborhood lend-

Table 3.4

Regression Explaining Small Business Lending Flows

Variable	Coefficient (Standard error below)
Constant	−17.2379[a]
	3.3289
Spatial lag of loans	0.6876[a]
	0.0667
Number of small firms	0.0177[a]
	0.0014
Proportion of firms with five or more employees	21.0696[a]
	3.0276
Proportion of firms in manufacturing sector	8.1984
	6.9538
Proportion of firms in wholesaling	1.1303
	7.2432
Proportion of firms in retailing	−5.5642
	3.3948
Median family income of tract	1.48E-04[a]
	2.19E-05
Population of tract	0.0021[a]
	1.25E-04
Percent of residents who are black	−0.0681[a]
	0.0125
Percent of residents who are Hispanic	−0.0101
	0.0372
Average credit score of firms in tract	2.91E-05
	0.0898
Pseudo R^2	0.5490
Square correlation	0.4412

N = 1,197

Notes: Dependent variable is number of loans to small firms in census tract. Adjusted-white matrix requires use of z- and not t-tests for significance.
[a]Significant below 0.01; all others not significant at below 0.10.

ing activity, with the dependent variable equal to the number of loans made to small firms (those with sales under $1,000,000) in a census tract during 1998. Table 3.4 gives the results of a spatial regression of census tract–lending activity, in which a spatial lag variable is used to control for the amount of lending occurring in nearby neighborhoods.[3] All coefficients in the results have their expected signs, and most are significant. The number and size of small firms are both important determinants of small business loan flows. Greater population also increases the number of loans. The coefficients of the sectoral variables are not statistically significant. The credit-score variable is not significant either, although it does have the expected sign. Differences in credit scores do not account for a significant portion of the very large differences in lending rates between white and black tracts.

The demographic variables are the key concern here. Neighborhood income is highly significant, and the coefficient has a meaningful magnitude. A decrease in neighborhood median income of $20,000 (a bit more than a standard deviation) results in a decrease of about three loans. The percentage black variable is highly significant and very large in magnitude. Going from an all white neighborhood to an all-black neighborhood *with the same geographic context* (that is, surrounded by neighborhoods with similar lending volumes) results in a drop in the expected number of loans by 6.8, or almost one-half the mean of 14.6 loans. Of course, given the nature of residential segregation, the typical black tract is surrounded by a smaller number of loans than a typical white tract. A more common scenario involves black neighborhoods being surrounded by other black neighborhoods. So the scarcity of lending in such neighborhoods is even greater than indicated by the coefficient for the percentage black variable.

Black neighborhoods in Philadelphia suffer from lower lending rates than similarly situated white neighborhoods. This is true even after controlling for industrial mix, firm size, neighborhood income and population, firm population, and average credit score. Moreover, these findings are consistent with another study finding a geographic redlining effect using a different set of data and a firm-level methodology. In a firm-level study of credit approvals using the 1993 NSSBF, Bostic and Lampani (1999) found that, after first adding a variable on the minority composition of the neighborhood in which the firm is located, adding a variable describing the economic status of the neighborhood actually resulted in minority neighborhood location having a stronger negative effect on credit access. If a firm's location in a minority neighborhood dampened credit access because the market conditions in such a neighborhood were weaker due to lower neighborhood income, then adding the neighborhood income variable should reduce the coefficient on the minority composition variable. However, just the opposite occurred, suggesting a redlining effect.

Bank Branches and Small Business Lending

One of the factors that may reduce credit access to firms in lower-income and minority neighborhoods is the paucity of bank branches in such areas. A

good deal of small business lending—more than mortgage or consumer lending—is still significantly dependent on loan officers being present and active
in a community. As shown in Figure 3.1, the initiation of the small business
lending process depends critically on the marketing activities of the bank,
not just the inquiry of the business.

Branch locations may influence small business lending patterns for several reasons. Small business lending often involves loan officers making in-
person visits to firms. Loan officers often have distinct submetropolitan
market areas that may be partly determined by branch locations. At the same
time, small businesses may prefer to do business with an institution that is
conveniently located near them and where they can easily take and receive
cash or transact other business.

The difficulty of assessing small business creditworthiness (sometimes
referred to as the "opacity" of the small business) has traditionally required
lenders to be located relatively closely to their borrowers. This is especially
true for smaller, younger firms. Banks, in particular, have focused on opaque
borrowers (often smaller and younger firms) more so than finance companies have, in part due to their competitive advantage in having extensive
branch networks. These networks enable banks to maintain stronger relationships with borrowers. Traditionally, firms that borrowed from distant
lenders were only those with impeccable credit quality.

In a study of the small business lending of ninety-nine large banking organizations in six southern states, Frame, Padhi, and Woosley (2001) found that
the presence of branches in low- and moderate-income areas was a powerful
determinant of whether an institution lends in such areas. A large bank with a
branch in a typical low- or moderate-income census tract was 20 percent more
likely to make a small business loan in the tract than an otherwise similar
institution with branches in the same metropolitan area but not in the tract.
Immergluck and Wiles (2000a) found that lenders in the Chicago area that
devoted the highest shares of their small business lending to low- and moderate-income areas tended to be institutions with significant numbers of branches
located in or near such communities. Similarly, those with low percentages of
loans to low-to-moderate areas tended to have branches located farther from
such areas. Similar results have been found in Milwaukee (Squires and
O'Connor 2001). In an analysis of small business lending in Cook County,
Illinois, Immergluck and Smith (2001) found that the ten institutions making
the largest percentage of their loans to low-mod tracts (from 47 to 28 percent)
had 43 percent of their branches located in low- or moderate-income zip codes.
Conversely, the ten institutions making the lowest percentage of loans to low-
to-moderate tracts (from 3 to 11 percent) had only 11 percent of their branches
located in low- or moderate-income zip codes.

The continued problems of credit access for minority-owned firms and firms in minority and lower-income neighborhoods have important implications for both CRA and fair lending policies. Following the 1995 CRA regulations, examiners have been able to assess the geographic patterns of banks' small business and residential loans and compare them to those of other banks. The results above, and the available evidence on small business access to credit, suggest the need for regulators to take this charge seriously. Moreover, CRA regulation should consider lending patterns across differences in neighborhood race as well as income (more on this in chapter 9).

Under the ECOA, banks are prohibited from discriminating based on the race of the borrower. The Department of Housing and Urban Development, the Department of Justice, and federal bank regulators have investigated mortgage lenders for fair lending violations. Similar investigations, including the use of matched-pair testing, could be used to identify lenders that discriminate in small business lending. Such investigations are made more difficult, however, by the lack of racial and application information in the CRA data, which would enable investigators to identify banks that are more likely to be guilty of discrimination. Chapter 7 discusses the policy debate over changes to Regulation B, which implements ECOA, and which, until recently, actually prohibited banks from even voluntarily collecting race and gender data for small business loans. Unlike the situation with home loans, reporting of racial data for small business loans is still not required. Banks are now merely allowed to voluntarily collect such data without having to disclose the information to the public.

Recent Trends in Small Business Lending and Their Implications for Access to Credit by Urban Firms

The last twenty years have brought a great deal of change in the banking and financial services industries, and much of this change has had implications for small firms, especially those in lower-income and minority communities. Bank consolidation has led to the absorption of mid-sized and smaller banks into larger operations and the closing of bank branches, especially in lower-income neighborhoods. While consolidation appears to result in an increase in new, start-up banks, it is unclear whether these banks serve lower-income or minority neighborhoods at significant rates. Lending to small firms is no longer primarily the domain of the small community bank. The traditional form of small business loan—the highly customized loan based on a relationship with an individual loan officer—is increasingly giving way to a more commoditized "high-tech-low-touch" transaction. Finally, there has been some growth in the use of business credit cards for the purpose of providing working capital and equipment financing, as well as some changes in the presence of nonbank lenders in the small business market.

Bank Consolidation

One change in banking affecting small business lending in central cities and lower-income areas that has received a good deal of attention is the consolidation of the banking industry. Since 1980, the banking industry has experienced significant consolidation. Relaxations of state and then federal regulations on bank branching and structure have allowed merger and acquisition activity to reach all-time highs. Between 1980 and 1998, there were approximately 8,000 bank mergers involving roughly $2.4 trillion in acquired assets (Rhoades 2000). In this time period, the number of Federal Deposit Insurance Corporation–insured commercial banking institutions decreased by nearly 41 percent, from 14,434 to 8,581 (Immergluck and Smith 2001).

Between 1989 and 1999, the number of independent banking organizations (the sum of bank holding companies and independent banks) decreased from 9,500 to 6,800. The fifty largest banking organizations held 74 percent of all banking assets in 1999 compared to 55 percent in 1989, and the ten largest banking organizations controlled 49 percent of all assets in 1999 compared to 26 percent in 1989 (DeFerrari and Palmer 2001). Much of this top-end consolidation occurred in the latter part of the 1990s. The assets of the ten largest bank holding companies increased by 81 percent from March 1997 to December 2000, to top $3.6 trillion.

The effects of consolidation and changes in bank size on small business lending activity have been a common topic for research over the last decade. Most research has examined short- and long-run effects of mergers and acquisitions on the lending volume of the merging institutions or on overall small business lending volumes. No research has examined any explicit impacts on small business lending to central cities or lower-income areas. Moreover, as Dymski (1999) has pointed out, much of this research has focused only on the overall *volume* of lending and has failed to account for changes in the quality of this lending. Because larger banks have been shifting to higher volume credit-scoring techniques, the negative effects on lending volumes due to consolidation are being counterbalanced in some ways. However, focusing only on lending volumes may mask a decline in relationship-based loans to smaller firms of the sort that smaller banks specialize in.

There are a number of reasons to be concerned about the effects of consolidation on bank lending in central cities and modest-income suburbs. First, as discussed above, bank branch locations are an important determinant of intrametropolitan small business lending patterns. Because mergers and acquisitions affect branch locations, they are likely to influence the geographic distribution of small business lending. Mergers and acquisitions provide key opportunities for the spatial restructuring of bank branch operations. Larger banks, in particular, have often focused their acquisition strategies on growing their market share in more affluent markets and, hence, may avoid acquisitions with large central city branch presences.

Another concern regarding consolidation and access to small business credit is the effect on minority-owned firms. Cavalluzzo, Cavalluzzo, and Wolken (1999) found that black-owned small businesses were denied loans at substantially higher rates than white-owned firms after controlling for a wide variety of credit factors. Moreover, they found that the unexplained difference between white and black denial rates—essentially the level of discrimination—was larger in less competitive banking markets. Thus, consolidation can increase disparities in access to credit. The larger presence of minority-owned firms in minority neighborhoods means that this outcome will have a spatial as well as a racial effect.

The first study to directly measure the impact of mergers and acquisitions on small business lending in low- and moderate-income census tracts utilizes recent CRA small business lending data. Samolyk and Richardson (2001) found that small business lending growth rates in low- and moderate-income census tracts are smaller for banks involved in mergers. While growth rates of merging institutions in middle- and upper-income tracts are also smaller, the effect is somewhat smaller in magnitude. More importantly, the share of small business loans going to low- and moderate-income areas declines significantly for banks that have been involved in merger activity.

Start-up, or "De Novo," Banks

During the "megamerger" boom of the late 1990s, significant attention was paid to the phenomenon of new start-up banks, or "de novo" institutions. Industry commentators often argued that any loss in service due to consolidation would be compensated for by the establishment of new banks that would fill market gaps. Concerns over the effect of consolidation on small business lending were frequently addressed this way, in part because smaller banks are generally assumed to be more active small business lenders.

There were many more de novo commercial bank charters in the 1980s than the 1990s in the United States. There were over 190 new charters every year in the 1980s, with a high of 408 in 1984. One reason for the boom in de novos was the liberalization of charter policy beginning in the 1980s, when the Office of the Comptroller of the Currency began to pay less attention to the community's capacity to support an additional bank in granting national bank charters (Berger et al. 2000). State unit-banking laws, which limited instrastate branching, as well as stronger interstate banking restrictions, also played a role. After slowing in the late 1980s, the chartering of de novos picked up in the late 1990s about the time that merger activity reached its peak. New charters increased from only 50 in 1994 to more than 100 in 1995 and to almost 200 by 1998.

There is evidence that de novo institutions focus a substantially greater share of their activities on small business lending than do older banks. The portion of assets devoted to small business loans declines linearly with bank age for about the first twenty years of a bank's life, starting at more than 12 percent in early years to a minimum of 8 percent by year twenty (DeYoung, Goldberg, and White 1999). Thus, every five years, the portion of assets devoted to small business lending drops about one percentage point. In the first five years, this amounts to about an 8 percent decline (12 percent to 11 percent of assets) in small business lending. The effect of bank age on lending still holds after controlling for bank size, market concentration, and holding company affiliation.

There are a number of likely explanations for the emphasis of de novos on small business lending. First, young banks may find it easier to lend to small emerging firms than to steal larger business customers away from incumbent banks. The new banks may not offer the range of services demanded by larger firms. Also, smaller, younger banks may appear less intimidating to a young firm and may offer more intimate, personalized service. De novos are also likely to begin by concentrating on a small geographic area, so small businesses, many of which may prefer a nearby bank, are a logical target. Moreover, if de novos employ managers and loan officers displaced from a larger established institution, these personnel may be able to take some of their clients to the new bank. As a bank gets older, it is likely to lose some of the features that cause it to favor small firms. Some commercial customers may also outgrow the older, smaller bank. There is also the possibility that the culture of the bank will change, with management becoming less "hungry" for new business.

There are a number of questions regarding de novos that impinge on small business lending trends in central cities and modest-income suburbs. First, do de novo charters increase when mergers and consolidation increase in a local market? If so, does such activity compensate for a decline in small business lending by the merged institutions? Given the importance of branch locations to small business lending, it is important to understand where de novos tend to locate. Are they likely to compensate for the loss in lower-income branches due to mergers? Finally, what is the evidence on the lending of these de novos in lower-income areas?

Berger et al. (2000) found that mergers are responsible for more than one-fifth of de novo entry. In small metropolitan areas, the share of de novos due to mergers is even higher (30 percent), and larger effects are found in later years (1995–98) than in the 1980s and early 1990s. However, mergers do not appear to result in an increase in small business lending by de novo banks (Berger et al. 2000). A doubling of merger and acquisition activity from the mean level actually results in a small decrease in lending by small young banks and a very small increase by mature small banks.

As discussed above, branch locations have a substantial impact on the small business lending patterns of banks. Immergluck and Smith (2001) examined the office and branch locations of established banks and de novos in the Chicago metropolitan area.[4] The de novo locations were located far from the central city and in more affluent suburbs than branches overall. Of the 111 de novo locations, only 11 were in the city of Chicago, and 6 of those were in or near the city's large central business district. Only 8 de novo locations, or 7 percent of the 111, were in low- or moderate-income zip codes, compared to 14 percent of the offices of established institutions. Immergluck and Smith (2001) also examined the small business lending patterns of the de novo banks in comparison to those of established lenders. De novo banks made small business loans that comprised 1.00 percent of all loans in low- and moderate-income census tracts in the six-county Chicago area. At the same time, they comprised 1.22 percent of the small business loans made in middle- and upper-income tracts in the region. Thus, compared to other banks, the de novos focused 22 percent more on middle- and upper-income areas than on low- and moderate-income areas.

De novo institutions are unlikely to be a substantial source of small business lending in lower-income communities. They are likely to locate in newer and more affluent areas. The evidence does not suggest that de novos provide any compensatory response to declines in overall small business lending from bank mergers. Therefore, any rise in de novo banks is unlikely to significantly improve access to credit for small firms in lower-income and minority areas.

Credit Scoring

One of the major changes in small business lending in the last ten years has been the significant use of credit scoring for marketing and underwriting many small business loans. Once used primarily for consumer loans and then later for mortgages, there has been a major increase in the use of credit scoring in the small business arena. A lender may use credit scoring to automatically approve or reject certain types of loans, to enhance the approval process by giving lenders more information, to identify potential borrowers for solicitation, and/or to monitor existing borrowers. Larger banks have used credit scoring to increase the volume of smaller loans, especially those under $100,000.

Traditionally, small business lending has been heavily dependent on relationships between borrower and loan officer. Mortgages and consumer loans have generally been more transaction-driven and more easily commoditized. Relationships give lenders access to information on small firms from checking and savings accounts, other loans, or financial management experiences. As information on small businesses and their owners is increasingly made available through other means (credit bureaus and credit scores), the advantage of relationship-based information is diminished and relationships may become less important, at least to the lender.

In 1995, a survey by the *American Banker* of 150 U.S. banks showed that only 8 percent of smaller (less than $5 billion in assets) banks used credit scoring for small business loans, with 23 percent of larger banks using it (Mester 1999). Fair Isaacs, the dominant provider of credit scores for mortgage transactions, introduced its small business scorecard in 1995. By 1997, the Federal Reserve's Senior Loan Officer Survey showed 70 percent of large banks using credit scoring in small business lending, with 58 percent stating that they usually or always use it.

Frame, Srinivasan, and Woosley (2001) examined the use of credit scoring of 99 of the 200 largest banking organizations in the United States. As of January 1998, 63 percent of these institutions used credit scoring. All of these banks used scoring for all loans under $100,000, and 74 percent of them used it for all loans under $250,000. Only 21 percent of these banks used scoring for larger loans.

Banks use credit scoring in different ways and for different types of loans. While much has been discussed about the effect of credit scoring on the loan approval process, the technology has had a major effect on the marketing of small business loans. Credit scoring allows lenders, especially large ones, to mine small business databases and screen out strong borrower prospects over broad geographic areas. The Consumer Bankers Association survey found that a quarter of respondents had mailed preapproved small business applications in 1996, while almost none did this in 1992 (Feldman 1997).

In the approval process, credit scoring is sometimes used as the primary underwriting tool, so that loans may be automatically rejected or approved if certain low or high scores are attained. Frequently, loans with scores in a middle range are then subjected to review by a loan officer or committee. The Federal Reserve Bank of Atlanta survey of large banking organizations found that credit scoring was used for the automatic approval or rejection of loans by 42 percent of the scoring banks (Frame, Srinivasan, and Woosley 2001). Some banks, however, may use credit scoring only as a complementary tool to provide the loan officer or credit committee with additional, standardized information. Scoring can also be used to set interest rates or other loan terms. Of the banks in the Atlanta Federal Reserve survey that used scoring, 32 percent used it for such purposes.

A bank may hope to receive many benefits from using credit scoring. These include eliminating some documentation, reducing costs, improving loan performance, increasing volume and market share, making lending policies more uniform, controlling regulatory risks, extending geographic reach, reducing approval times, and improving customer service. Some of these benefits may stem from the use of technology in underwriting or processing applications while others may arise from using technology to help market products or monitor borrowers. Large banks are clearly a major beneficiary of credit scoring technology. Wells Fargo Bank, for example, was a large early user of scoring and was able to gain significant market share in locations far from its branch network. The cost advantages to large-volume lenders can be significant. A study by the Business Banking Board found that the traditional loan-approval process averages about 12.5 hours per small business loan and that lenders can take two or more weeks to process a loan. Credit scoring can reduce approval times to one hour or less (Allen 1995). Credit scoring has also been particularly attractive to large banks because implementing a system entails significant fixed costs.

Historically, the transaction costs of traditional relationship lending meant that making small loans—especially those of less than $50,000 to $75,000—did not meet the profitability targets of some large banks. Due to their wider variety of business options, larger banks were less likely to make very small loans to firms through traditional means. Conversely, small banks had a traditional informational advantage and were closer to the customer. Credit scoring for small business loans has turned this dynamic on its head. By lowering marketing or transaction costs dramatically, credit-scored small loans can be relatively profitable for a large bank. Because credit scoring is used for smaller loans, the increased adoption of it by larger banks has led to a rapid increase in the number of loans under $100,000 made by large institutions. The use of credit scoring is associated with an 8.4 percentage-point increase in the share of a bank's portfolio devoted to loans under $100,000 (Frame, Srinivasan, and Woosley 2001).

Loans of under $100,000 grew by almost 20 percent for banks with more than $5 billion in assets from 1996 to 1997, after adjusting for mergers (Immergluck and Smith 2001). Meanwhile, small banks saw these small loans grow at a slower rate than larger loans. This result suggests that large banks captured significant market share in the small loan market during this short period. Large-scale lenders may be more likely to use credit scoring to solicit customers, screen applications, and extend credit, while community banks may use the technology more to sort applicants or as one of several factors considered when making decisions.

Credit scoring may lower the overall absolute costs of small business lending to firms that are automatically approved by the scorecard. At the same time, it may greatly increase the *relative* costs of making loans to marginal firms that require more flexibility and loan officer attention. Borrowers requiring loan officer review entail higher costs than those able to be purely credit scored. This is especially true as the number of relationship-based nonscored loans decreases and as the fixed costs involved in such lending (including people) are spread out over fewer loans. It is possible that the absolute, and not just the relative, cost of relationship lending will increase with the continued adoption of credit scoring.

Credit scoring has implications for minority-owned firms and firms in lower-income and minority neighborhoods. However, whether credit scoring will benefit or harm such firms is not entirely clear. The answer depends partly on the nature and credit quality of the particular firms. If it is applied uniformly, it might be expected to improve access to credit for firms that were previously discriminated against and that are easily identified or approved by credit scoring methods. Thus, for black-owned firms and firms in minority areas that are very strong financially, credit scoring may well offer more credit opportunities. In a study of six southern states, Frame, Padhi, and Woosley (2001) show that the use of credit scoring has a modest positive impact on the volume of small loans (under $100,000) made by large banks in low- and moderate-income census tracts. A bank using credit scoring is expected to make 3.8 percent more small loans in a typical low- or moderate-income tract while making 1.7 percent more loans in middle- or upper-income tracts. This finding is consistent with the notion that credit scoring can increase the geographic reach of a lender. Since most large banks have more branches in middle- and upper-income tracts than in lower-income tracts, it is not surprising that credit scoring would enable them to improve their marketing and lending in lower-income areas. Moreover, if credit scoring reduces human decisions that result in discrimination, such an effect is expected.

At the same time, there are a number of causes for concern over the impacts of credit scoring on minority-owned firms and firms in lower income neighborhoods. The first concern is that of the possible disparate impact of the scoring models on smaller and less well capitalized firms. Chapter 4 goes into this more fully in the context of mortgage credit scoring. In addition to marketing and approvals, credit scoring is sometimes used by lenders to develop risk-based pricing, in which firms with weaker credit scores are given loans at higher interest rates. While this may be efficient from the lender's perspective, and may enable more higher-risk firms to receive loans, risk-based pricing can have negative impacts on higher-risk firms that were previously obtaining credit at lower, nonrisk-based rates. For financially strong borrowers needing smaller loans, credit scoring should prove a significant benefit. This benefit may be particularly important in lower-income and minority areas where relationship lenders may have discriminated against or ignored such firms. For firms with weaker financial standing, however, credit scoring may bring real costs. They will be seen as less attractive, more costly borrowers. To the extent that central cities and low- and moderate-income areas have more struggling firms, credit may become more expensive or scarce. Lenders who use credit scoring for marketing purposes are likely to avoid firms with marginal credit scores altogether because they want to minimize underwriting and transaction costs. Large lenders may choose to focus only on the easily approved, strongest borrowers, regardless of their location. If a community has more marginal firms that might be good credit risks but would require more than the automatic approval of a scoring system, it may find itself with fewer lenders marketing loans in the area.

So the credit-scoring trend works in both directions vis-à-vis lower-income and minority communities, in part because the market for small business credit is becoming segmented by credit score. One segment is reserved for high-volume, low-cost credit scored lending and one for traditional relationship credit. For firms that are in need of traditional, relationship-based credit, this segmentation of the market is likely to have negative effects.

Finance Companies, Credit Cards, and Minority-Owned Firms

Immergluck and Smith (2001) found that while finance companies did not gain appreciable market share from banks in the late 1980s and 1990s overall, they did gain share among minority-owned businesses. This would be consistent with concerns discussed earlier about bank branch declines in lower-income areas and about the possible disparate impacts of bank consolidation on minority-owned firms and communities. In 1987, 66 percent of loans to small minority-owned firms were made by banks, but by 1993 that share had dropped to 53 percent (Cole and Wolken 1996). Moreover, the proportion of black-owned firms using nondepository financial firms (for credit or other financial services) increased from 17 percent in 1993 to 29 percent by 1998

(Bitler, Robb, and Wolken 2001). While this increase in utilization is likely to be partly explained by the expanding economy, the growth was significantly faster than the increase in bank utilization by black-owned firms, which rose from 78 percent to 85 percent.

In terms of credit card use, business card use by black-owned firms has not increased as fast as it has among white-owned firms. From 1993 to 1998, black firms increased usage from 28 percent to 29 percent, while white firms increased usage from 28 percent to 34 percent (Bitler, Robb, and Wolken 2001). Conversely, black-owned firms increased usage faster for personal credit cards (from 34 percent to 44 percent for black firms versus 40 percent to 45 percent for white firms). Because personal cards are often priced at substantially higher rates than business cards, this is a significant cause for concern.

Barriers to credit for minority-owned firms and firms in lower-income and minority neighborhoods in the United States persist. Moreover, while some progress against the most overt discrimination has certainly been attained over the last thirty years, large disparities remain. Some of the substantial forces reshaping business lending markets do not necessarily bode well for businesses in these sectors. It will be difficult to make progress in this area without more meaningful application of CRA and ECOA to small business lending.

CHAPTER 4

A Brief History of Mortgage-Lending
Discrimination and Redlining

Origins of Mortgage Discrimination

Perhaps most well known among the discriminatory barriers in U.S. credit markets are those in mortgage markets. While lending discrimination and redlining became widely discussed federal policy topics in the 1960s and 1970s, the phenomenon had actually been recognized much earlier, although usually with different terminology. In 1917, the *Cleveland Advocate*, a black newspaper, reported that banks had refused to lend to blacks attempting to develop large-scale housing for blacks on Chicago's South Side, an area later to be called Black Metropolis ("Chicago Lays Plans" 1917). The local black merchants' association, a promoter of the plan, had to seek funding from individual wealthy black investors from Oklahoma and Kansas. The head of the association commented that "Chicago banks and capitalists thought they could prevent us buying property by refusing to lend us money or to renew mortgages on property we have purchased." In 1922, following the 1919 Chicago race riot, the Chicago Commission on Race Relations determined that blacks faced barriers in securing mortgages. Some lenders completely avoided areas where blacks lived (Hillier 2003b).

In the 1940s, Myrdal commented on the inability of blacks to get mortgages from mainstream financial institutions:

> The difficulties of Negroes who wanted to build their own homes and were almost entirely unable to get any assistance from white financial institutions was one of the main driving forces behind the foundation of Negro-managed building and loan associations. (Myrdal 1944, 315)

In 1955, in his seminal work on housing discrimination, *Forbidden Neighbors*, Charles Abrams described the problem in more detail:

> These mortgage lenders were conditioned by the same attitudes on the racial issue as were the realtors and home-builders. Their mortgage officers

87

read the same texts, swallowed the same myths. Their appraisers were generally allied with [the National Association of Real Estate Boards] or its affiliate, the American Institute of Real Estate Appraisers. And though there were men among the group who could do their own thinking, there was rarely any inclination to question the premises on which the hallowed practice rested. (Abrams 1955, 174)

And for those who might think the phenomenon of "predatory lending" is entirely a recent one, Abrams added:

. . . Mortgage loans (in New York City's Negro areas) are now made predominantly by individuals, with bonuses ranging up to 25 percent of the mortgage principal. (Abrams 1955, 175)

Banks, savings and loans (S&Ls), and mortgage companies generally made very few loans in black neighborhoods. Loans to black borrowers in white neighborhoods were even more rare. Abrams (1955, 176) called local S&Ls the "watchdogs of neighborhood purity" that would rate any areas where residents had resisted minority home-seekers as "out of bounds" for future loans. This left blacks wanting to build or buy homes with primarily two alternatives. They could borrow from a black financial institution or from an informal lender who would lend at exorbitant rates and under abusive conditions.

Black-owned S&Ls were the principal formal, regulated financial institution available for prospective black homeowners, but they were quite limited in number and lending capacity. While Myrdal dated black S&Ls back only to 1883, it appears that organized savings for real estate investment went back to the beginning of the nineteenth century. Formal S&Ls went back at least as far as the antebellum era. Blacks had pooled money for real estate purchases and investments as early as 1808 with the New York African Society for Mutual Relief Fund. Moreover, the first black building and loan in California, the Savings Fund and Land Association, dates back to at least 1859 (Walker 1998, 98–99). The postbellum period saw an increase in the formation of black S&Ls, including new institutions in North Carolina, Baltimore, and Nashville. In the 1880s and 1890s a few started in northern cities as well, especially in Pennsylvania and New York. However, the first three decades of the twentieth century saw the greatest growth in black S&Ls.

The depression hit many black S&Ls hard, reducing their number from seventy in 1930 to about fifty by 1938, with almost half of these concentrated in Pennsylvania (Myrdal 1944, 315). Moreover, white-owned institutions sometimes used the presence of black-owned banks to excuse their refusal to lend to blacks. When the federal government called a meeting of builders and S&Ls to prompt increase housing for blacks in Cook County, Illinois, a representative of one of the larger lenders said that this was the responsibility of black-owned lenders (Abrams 1955, 176). Even at their peak, the small number and small size of black-owned S&Ls were woefully inadequate to make a sizable contribution to financing black home buying. The result was that a good deal of home financing for blacks was done by informal lenders who tended to extract high rates of interest and up-front premiums, often on abusive terms.

In a study of real estate brokers and real estate practice in Chicago in 1955 and 1956, over half of the respondents in most parts of the city stated that a lending agency had prevented them from making sales to blacks (Helper 1969, 166–68). In most parts of the city, nearly two-thirds of respondents stated that few lending agencies in Chicago made loans to blacks. Many stated that, if lenders did make loans to blacks, they often involved higher up-front fees and interest, shorter amortization schedules, and larger payments. One respondent described the situation as follows:

> Darn few [make loans to blacks]. That's where your four percent commission comes in. In some cases it's ten percent. It depends on the buyer. Whereas in the white section it is one percent if any. (Helper 1969, 170)

The practice of redlining neighborhoods and discriminating against black buyers in the first half of the twentieth century is attributed to a variety of factors, including "pure discrimination," in which lenders have a distaste for lending to blacks or minority neighborhoods. One important factor supporting lending discrimination and redlining was a variety of academic and quasi-academic theories regarding neighborhood decline. At the same time that the mortgage industry was growing during the 1920s, the "social ecology" approach to urban sociology was being developed, principally at the University of Chicago (Bradford 1979). In the 1925 seminal work of Robert E. Park, Ernest W. Burgess, and Roderick D. McKenzie, *The City*, Burgess (1925) explained his theory of "succession," in which residents of lower-class neighborhoods closer to downtown extended their communities by the "invasion" of the next outer zone of more affluent neighborhoods. He explicitly drew this theory from plant ecology. He also drew from the metabolic processes of the body as a model for how cities function and change. By using a natural law approach, Burgess argued that the segregation of the poor into inner-ring neighborhoods close to the central business district is one that is appropriate and evolutionary. The excessive influx of lower-class populations was portrayed as a major cause of "social disorganization." He argued that the overcrowding of the lower-class inner ring causes the lower classes to spill into the adjacent middle-class ring of neighborhoods and then causes their decline. So Burgess combined an image of the foreign plant species invading native species with an image of an imbalance in the body that made it difficult to absorb or deal with an influx of a foreign substance. These organic metaphors are powerful. They fall into what Stone terms "natural order" arguments that liken inorganic systems to notions of nature and our bodies that make them very appealing (Stone 2002).

The plant ecology metaphors and use of terms like "succession" and, especially, "invasion" served to legitimize and support the practices of lenders that did not lend to blacks, and especially not to blacks moving into white neighborhoods. While some of the literature suggests that lenders' avoidance of lending in black neighborhoods was due to concerns primarily about the collateral value (and thus consistent with Burgess's view of neighborhood decline), the evidence on this theory is scarce. It is likely that many lenders and appraisers latched onto such theories and scholarly work as justification for their existing practices. What is clear is that these theories did have a strong impact on the formal education of appraisers and lenders in the 1920s and the 1930s and, later, in the formal regulations of the Federal Housing Administration (FHA). Such theories were used to reinforce and continue redlining and discriminatory practices among appraisers and lenders.

The reluctance of lenders to make loans to blacks, especially to blacks trying to buy in white neighborhoods, was directly linked, as Abrams (1955) pointed out, to the practices and codes of real estate agents. A year before *The City* was published, in 1924, Article 34 of Part III of the National Association of Real Estate Boards Code of Ethics read:

> A Realtor should never be instrumental in introducing into a neighborhood a character of property or occupancy, members of any race or nationalitity, or individuals whose preferences will clearly be detrimental to property values in that neighborhood. (Helper 1969, 201)

This provides more evidence that the notion of racial infiltration as detrimental to a community did not originate with the work of the Chicago social ecologists but was, rather, reinforced by it. The links between Park and Burgess and lending practices are made apparent by examining some of the language of real estate industry manuals. Frederick Babcock, who later authored the FHA's *Underwriting Manual*, was very influential in appraisal and lending markets via his 1932 book, *The Valuation of Real Estate*. Babcock worked in real estate in Chicago during the rise of the Chicago social ecologists. His book is perhaps the first clearly documented link between Park and Burgess and formal real estate practice. In it, he argued that land values depend partly on the racial heritage of local residents and implied that black inmigration would lower property values:

> Most of the variations and differences between people are slight and value declines are, as a result, gradual. But there is one difference in people, namely, race, which can result in a very rapid decline. (Babcock 1932, 91)

A year after Babcock's book came out, Homer Hoyt, who was a professor of real estate and a colleague of Park and Burgess, published his *One Hundred Years of Land Values in Chicago*. The book reinforced Babcock's work by arguing that "certain racial and national groups" inevitably lower property values due in part to their "greater deteriorating effect on property." Hoyt went so far as to rank races regarding their effects on property values. He ranked blacks as having the second most deleterious effects, just behind Mexicans (Hoyt 1933, 314–16). Then in 1935, the American Institute of Real Estate Appraisers came out with its first text, which warned against the adverse effects of the "infiltration of inharmonious social or racial groups" (Bradford 1979).

These models were also used by real estate agents who wanted to capitalize on the fears of white home owners who feared racial change. The use of biological and metabolic metaphors and terms like "invasion" helped agents convince whites that they should sell their homes before property values fell. According to Bradford (1979), the agents "peddled the appraisers' model to white neighborhood residents." The real estate agent could then purchase homes from fleeing whites, or work with speculators who would do so, and then sell them at heavily inflated prices to blacks, who had few housing options. A study by the Human Relations Commission of Chicago in 1962 found that in one changing community, real estate agents had sold homes via land contract to blacks at an average of 73 percent more than they paid for them.

Given that they were often unable to secure conventional financing, especially in white or integrated neighborhoods, the land contract was often the principal way for blacks to purchase homes. In the 1955–56 study of real estate agents, most considered the land contract to be a key source of financing for black buyers (Helper 1969). This was driven both by inadequate savings for down payments and by poor access to lending institutions. Oftentimes, however, the sellers were actually speculators—frequently real estate agents—who purchased the houses from home owners. Such speculators typically financed their activities with lines of credit from small S&Ls.

The speculators often repossessed the homes and then sold them again. The limited geographic markets where blacks were allowed to buy, combined with their narrow options for financing, proved a double penalty in many cases in terms of the effective prices they paid for the homes and the financing. The speculators were able to extract tremendous profits from the buyers. In one case in the early 1960s, a small S&L was found to have 25 percent of its assets invested in two contract sellers (Bradford and Marino 1977, 64–65).

In 1957, the U.S. Commission on Civil Rights was created and soon thereafter began conducting research and holding hearings on discrimination in a variety of arenas, including housing. In its 1961 Report on Housing, the Commission reported that it repeatedly heard of the "common policy of refusing to lend to Negroes who are the first purchasers in a white neighborhood" (U.S. Commission on Civil Rights 1961, 30). It also reported on practices where mortgages to blacks were made with short-term amortization schedules and high down payments, and simple pure redlining, in which a lender would simply not lend in an area.

The commission concluded that "little has been done by Government or the lending community to reduce or discourage discriminatory practices" (U.S. Commission on Civil Rights 1961, 30). It described the results from a 1959 Chicago survey of the 243 S&Ls in Cook County. Only twenty-one S&Ls made loans in a "heavily Negro-populated South Side area" during a one-year period, and only one white-owned S&L made a home purchase loan to a black family in a white neighborhood. The Civil Rights Commission also argued that bank and thrift regulators had the ability to reduce discrimination and redlining. For example, the commission report argued that the Office of the Comptroller of the Currency (OCC) had the "legal authority and the effective power to require the elimination of discriminatory mortgage lending practices by national banks" (U.S. Commission on Civil Rights 1961, 41).

Every Which Way but Right? The Role of the Federal Housing Administration in Minority and Changing Neighborhoods

As discussed in chapter 2, the history of stronger federal activism in housing markets began largely as a response to the foreclosure crisis of the late 1920s and early 1930s. It started with Hoover's creation of the Federal Home Loan Bank system, which was followed by the creation of the Home Owners Loan Corporation (HOLC), the federal S&L charter, and then the FHA and its loan insurance programs. There can be little doubt that these programs, especially in total, had a tremendously stimulating effect on home buying and home ownership throughout the country. They also represent the first time that the federal government consistently articulated a national goal of home ownership accessible to a wide spectrum of the public.

In 1932, President Hoover's Commission on Home Building and Home Ownership articulated the benefits and importance of home ownership and clearly presented high levels of home ownership as a national policy goal:

> Successful homeownership is worthy of every effort because it leads to an enriched family life and is evidence of proved habits of thrift and financial planning which usually place the family beyond a hand-to-mouth existence and in a position of relative security. . . . Every American family which so desires and is able financially should own their own home. (Gries and Ford 1932, 15)

Notwithstanding the important contributions of federal housing and credit-enhancement policies to U.S. housing and mortgage markets overall, blacks and many central-city neighborhoods were largely excluded from these benefits and adversely affected by many federal lending policies. Whether federal programs proactively initiated discriminatory policies is a matter of some contention, but there is little doubt that some of the programs helped institutionalize or subsidize such practices.

The degree to which federal agencies played leading, rather than supportive or reinforcing, roles in promulgating discriminatory underwriting and lending practices in the middle part of the century appears to vary by agency. The HOLC, which was established under President Roosevelt in 1934 by the Home Owners Loan Act, has been repeatedly accused of inventing and disseminating the mapping systems that rated neighborhoods as undesirable for lending *and* that were, to some degree, instrumental in causing lenders to avoid lending in minority neighborhood (Jackson 1985; Massey and Denton 1993). Recent evidence suggests, however, that HOLC's infamous risk-rating maps were not widely circulated to private-sector lenders and that private lenders were making their own maps independent of HOLC (Hillier 2003b). Some used their own maps before HOLC maps existed, and most lenders did not have access to HOLC maps. Moreover, in the surveys used to construct the maps, surveyors used the avoidance of an area by lenders as an input into rating an area as undesirable or risky, thus suggesting the maps' coding was a result rather than a cause of private-lender redlining. Finally, there is evidence that the FHA had developed a detailed rating system of its own even before the HOLC's was created.

There is much more consensus on the leading role that the FHA played in redlining. Over time, the agency provided a great deal of housing credit and also interacted more closely with the lending industry than the HOLC. With Homer Hoyt as its principal housing economist, the FHA constructed a methodology for making risk-rating maps and expected that its extensive collection of maps would help an appraiser "refresh his memory as to the danger points in a neighborhood" (Hillier 2003b). While the HOLC's maps may have influenced the FHA maps, the FHA had initiated much of its own work before the HOLC maps were completed. Moreover, the FHA influenced the HOLC maps as much as the other way around. The FHA also relied heavily upon industry expertise and input, and its own manuals and practices had a clear effect on the practice of private lenders.

The FHA institutionalized and supported redlining by categorizing loans according to risk levels and by directing appraisers and lenders to place considerable emphasis on racial composition and neighborhood change. The FHA used manuals and regulations more than maps to institutionalize and support redlining by FHA and non-FHA lenders. The FHA viewed itself as a standard setting agency and as a developer and disseminator of good underwriting practice. The participation of the FHA in redlining was recognized fairly early on, first by Myrdal (1944) and then more fully by Abrams (1955):

> But what could be expected in the formerly private fields now aided or entered by the public itself? What could be expected when entrepreneurs with their lower standards and their overruling drive for profit operated conjunctively with government? Which standard should government follow: the standard of the color-blind, moral government intended by the Constitution, or the devil-take-the-hindmost standard of the entrepreneur?
> ... Curiously the choice was never the moral approach. . . . In the Federal Housing Administration, representing the largest part of the federal housing program, discrimination and segregation were not only practiced but were openly exhorted. (Abrams 1955, 229)

Frederick Babcock, whose earlier work had argued that racial change hurt property values significantly, was involved in the earliest versions of the FHA's *Underwriting Manual* (Helper 1969, 202). He is credited with providing the FHA's risk-rating grid for neighborhood analysis that was used in the agency's manuals. The FHA actually encouraged restrictive covenants or written agreements not to sell to blacks until they were declared unconstitutional by the Supreme Court in 1948 (Bradford and Marino 1977, 48).

The 1935 FHA Underwriting Manual listed among the adverse influences on a neighborhood the "infiltration of inharmonious racial or nationality groups." It also stated that a neighborhood's appeal is enhanced by the "kind and social status of its inhabitants." The 1936 version of the manual included "racial occupancy" among adverse influences and stated that:

> The Valuator should investigate areas surrounding the location to determine whether or not incompatible racial and social groups are present, to the end that an intelligent prediction may be made regarding the possibility or probability of the location being invaded by such groups. . . . The protection offered against adverse changes should be found adequate before a high rating is given to the future. (Section 233 of the 1936 FHA *Underwriting Manual*, quoted in Abrams 1955, 231)

Jackson (1985, 206) has argued that FHA policies harmed minorities and the public not only by proactively furthering discriminatory lending practices but also by speeding the decline of urban neighborhoods by "stripping them of much of their middle-class constituency." FHA programs were liberalized in the 1940s so that maximum loan-to-values increased from 80 to 95 percent and finally as high as 97 percent. In some cases, only $200 down was required. Terms were extended from twenty to twenty-five years, and later to thirty years, with thirty-five years permitted in some situations (Vandell 1995). Thus, the major federal housing program made housing much more affordable primarily to those white buyers buying homes in racially pure and mostly suburban communities.

FHA insurance often went to newer developments on the edges of metropolitan areas. The agency and its programs favored the constriction of single-family over multifamily projects. It also provided more advantageous financing for purchase rather than repair or improvement. Beyond the explicit bias of FHA neighborhood evaluation systems, the agency adopted guidelines that included biases against higher-density neighborhoods or mixed uses of properties. The net result was that FHA lending overwhelmingly flowed to suburban areas. FHA financing often made it less expensive to build new homes in the suburbs than to rent homes in the central city. It did this by institutionalizing lower down payments and longer amortization schedules, Moreover, many of FHA's larger developer-based programs were only available to the sort of large-scale projects that would generally only be done in newer suburban areas.

Jackson (1985) found that more than 91 percent of FHA home purchase loans in the St. Louis area from 1935 to 1939 were for homes in the suburbs, and that more than half of home buyers had lived in the city prior to their purchase. This is despite the fact that, in the 1930s, more single-family homes were constructed in the city than in the suburbs (Jackson 1985, 209, 210). He found similar patterns in New Jersey and the Washington, DC, area.

The history of the FHA through at least 1949 was one of a major force in promoting and institutionalizing redlining. In May 1948, the U.S. Supreme Court ruled in *Shelley v. Kraemer* that restrictive covenants were in violation of the Fourteenth Amendment. The following year, the FHA ruled that it would not provide insurance for mortgages on property with restrictive covenants and that the racial composition of a neighborhood was not a consideration in determining loan eligibility. However, FHA made no substantial proactive move against private-sector patterns of redlining or discrimination. They merely allowed nondiscriminatory lenders to participate in their programs. The agency moved from an active promoter of redlining to a complicit subsidizer and facilitator.

Things began to change in the 1960s. The Housing Act of 1968 signaled a clear turnabout of the agency wherein it promoted the financing homes in minority neighborhoods. Policies had been put in place even earlier to foster this transition. However, while FHA programs were being redirected toward inner-city neighborhoods, conventional lenders were not. Despite the new Fair Housing Act, federal banking regulators paid little attention to the racial patterns of conventional lenders. (This will be discussed more in chapter 6.) The result was the development of a new form of dual financial market. Instead of minority buyers and buyers in integrating neighborhoods being forced to settle for abusive informal lenders or land contract financing, the FHA provided the primary source of financing. Unfortunately, FHA programs that worked fairly well when borrowers had options in the conventional lending market broke down in the dual finance system (Bradford 1979; Dane 1993). Moreover, FHA underwriting requirements were relaxed even though 100 percent insurance was provided. This created a "moral hazard" in which lenders were able to make loans to high-risk borrowers without bearing any of that risk. In addition, because foreclosures and abandoned homes negatively affected neighborhoods, the FHA did not bear all of the costs of default. Minority neighborhoods shared greatly in them.

Despite the new increased risks, the agency did not step up efforts to monitor lenders using the program for abuses. The FHA became a powerful new tool for block-busting real estate agents and speculators. Instead of having to rely on the scarcity of capital provided by marginal financial institutions backing their land-contract schemes, they could now use federally insured loans for the purpose. Mortgage companies specializing in FHA loans made increased fees from the rapid turnover of such properties, and the realtors made their commissions (Bradford and Marino 1977, 68–75).

Unfortunately, the FHA's history is frequently simplified into "the FHA tried to lend in minority neighborhoods, and see what happened." In fact, the story of the FHA says little about the wisdom of conventional lenders' making loans in minority neighborhoods. (The issue of CRA loan perfor-mance and profitability will be discussed more in chapter 9.) The picture is even more complicated than merely bad program design. While its social mission was being modified in the middle to late 1960s, changes in FHA structure and procedures were also occurring that had major negative impli-cations for lending operations. In addition, since the 1960s, the FHA has suffered from various forms of political and ideological hostility, often from within the executive branch, which further harmed its programs.

First, in 1969 and 1970, the FHA underwent a major reorganization. Secretary of the Department of Housing and Urban Development (HUD) George Romney was frustrated by the "entire Rube Goldberg structure" of housing and urban development policy. Vandell (1995) has argued that this reorganization backfired and had a devastating effect on the FHA. The FHA became less autonomous and more subject to interference and bureaucracy from HUD. The decentralization of HUD caused duplication and confusion at the local level. FHA functions were split among different HUD divisions. This resulted in less centralized control and efficiency in FHA underwriting, servicing, and property management. By the mid-1970s, the FHA had been "emasculated" (Vandell 1995). In May 1970, more than 90 percent of credit decisions were approved in less than three days. One year later, that ratio had dropped to 55 percent. Reserve funds suffered losses, and loss recoveries worsened. Vandell argues that "there is no doubt that FHA restructuring . . . contributed to the problems and bears part of the blame for their pervasive influence." Congress asserted that the Nixon administration had sabotaged the program to get rid of it, while the administration blamed Congress for not approving home ownership counseling programs.

In 1971, the president's Third Annual Report on National Housing Goals criticized the heavy supply-side focus of U.S. housing policy and argued that subsidized housing might be contributing to flight to the suburbs and urban disinvestment (Orlebeke 2000). This led to a January 1973 morato-rium on housing production programs, including the main FHA programs. FHA production had already slowed, largely as a result of the HUD reorga-nization. Credit approvals dropped from more than 15,000 per week in May 1971 to less than 11,000 in May 1972. The ratio of FHA to single-family lending dropped by almost 50 percent, from 29 percent in 1970 to 16 per-cent in 1972. After the moratorium, it dropped even further to under 8 percent, and did not consistently reach double digits until the late 1980s.

Vandell argues that the Reagan era brought a second major blow to the FHA:

Whereas the 1970s blow had been struck by well-intentioned reorganiza-tion efforts and perhaps less well-intentioned political reprioritizations, the blow of the early 1980s came in the form of explicit neglect combined with active hostility toward the aims of HUD. . . . Section 8 and other multifamily projects were routinely steered toward political cronies. Inadequate asset management and property disposition programs permitted losses . . . to increase substantially during the 1980s. Total budget authority at HUD dropped dramatically during the Reagan-Bush years from $33.4 billion in 1981 to $14.2 billion in 1989. . . . Lax underwriting and inadequate fiscal controls to prevent fraud and abuse began to permeate the FHA insurance programs. (Vandell 1995)

The 1980s were not a good time for FHA programs to experience such hostility, neglect, and abuse. Minority neighborhoods were already being disproportionately impacted by the Rust Belt recession of the early 1980s, deindustrialization, and generally widening income inequality. An agency that should have been of help to struggling communities was often a force in favor of neighborhood decline.

Continuing Problems with Access to Home Loans

Problems of lending discrimination and redlining continued to persist through the 1960s and into the 1970s. As will be discussed in greater detail in chapter 6, activism regarding these issues grew, first during the civil rights movement of the 1950s and 1960s and later as a key issue for the neighborhood organizing movement of the 1960s and 1970s. While there were some important smaller policies adopted earlier in the 1960s, the passage of Title VIII of the Civil Rights Act of 1968, known as the Fair Housing Act, was the first critical shift in federal policy with regard to the issue of access to mortgage credit. The Fair Housing Act explicitly prohibited mortgage lending discrimination by race and was later interpreted to prohibit redlining.

Later, after the neighborhood organizing movement got involved, two critical federal laws were enacted. First, in 1975, the Home Mortgage Disclosure Act (HMDA) was passed. It required federal bank and thrift regulators to begin collecting data on home mortgage lending by census tract for all depository institutions. Then, in 1977, the Community Reinvestment Act (CRA) was passed. CRA, which also deals with redlining, created an affirmative obligation for banks and thrifts to meet the credit needs of their communities. Moreover, CRA gave members of the community who were supposed to be served by a bank or thrift the ability to make comments on how well institutions were meeting the banking needs of their communities.

I argue later in this book that fair lending laws, HMDA, and CRA have had a substantial impact on the availability of mortgage credit for minorities and in minority and lower-income neighborhoods. However, these laws have been modified over time—sometimes strengthened and sometimes weakened—and their implementation has varied tremendously. CRA, in particular, is heavily dependent upon rules enacted by the federal bank and thrift regulators: the Federal Reserve, the Office of the Comptroller of the Currency, the Federal Deposit Insurance Corporation, and the Office of Thrift Supervision. The CRA statute itself is quite brief and leaves much to the promulgation of regulations. Moreover, even after regulations are adopted, the vigor with which these regulations are implemented has varied. Similar implementation issues arise in the case of fair lending and HMDA as well.

Notwithstanding the variability of these laws since they were adopted, I conclude in chapter 9 that they have had a good deal of positive impact on access to mortgage credit. However, this is not to say that very severe problems in mortgage markets do not remain. Rather, while the progress is very significant, substantial gaps due to race and neighborhood location still persist. Moreover, changing credit and financial markets have led to a new set of problems that have not been addressed adequately by the agencies responsible for implementing these laws and, in some cases, may require new legislative initiatives. My goal here is to review the current evidence on discrimination and redlining in the market for home purchase loans. Then, in chapter 5, I will focus more on an area of home financing of particular concern in recent years—the market for refinance loans.

It is not an exaggeration to say that hundreds of studies of mortgage-lending discrimination have been conducted since the middle 1970s. One thing that has challenged researchers has been the continual battle to gain access to larger and richer datasets that have more explanatory power in assessing why some people get loans and others do not. Another question that is less frequently asked, however, is whether all of the various sorts, sources, and types of discrimination are addressed in most studies. Many studies focus on only a narrow picture of discrimination. It is in the interest of those who wish to find no evidence of discrimination to define it as narrowly as possible. This lowers the probability of obtaining a significant measure of discrimination. There are a variety of parameters on which the definition of discrimination or redlining might be narrowed or widened. The first question is whether discrimination is measured only by the rejection or approval of formal loan applications or whether it includes differences in the pricing or terms and conditions of loans that are not explained by differences in risk. This aspect of lending discrimination has gotten much greater attention in recent years as the number of specialized subprime lenders has mushroomed. This issue will be dealt with in more depth later in chapter 5.

The second parameter on which studies vary in formulating research questions concerns which stages of the lending process are considered. Are stages before or after the formal underwriting and approval stage examined? The focus of most studies has been on whether formal loan applications are rejected or denied. These studies ignore many key parts of the overall access to credit process. What about marketing? Who markets to whom? What about differences in whether applicants are encouraged or discouraged to formally apply? What about differences on the servicing, collection, and foreclosure end?

Ross and Yinger (2002, 28–30) describe the stages of the mortgage transaction. Their effort is an important contribution to understanding the number of stages involved in the process of accessing credit. Even though their sketch of the steps involved in obtaining a loan indicate many of the complexities in analyzing credit access, their schematic description of the process remains significantly oversimplified, especially in the case of home equity and refinance lending. Figure 4.1 is an expansion of Ross and Yinger's schematic diagram for the mortgage process. Ross and Yinger's flow chart begins with the household deciding that it wants a mortgage. Figure 4.1 goes further and shows that a particular loan application may begin with the decision of a household that it wants a mortgage or, as is more common in the home equity lending markets, the process may originate in the marketing activity of a lender or mortgage broker. (The market for subprime refinance lending, as discussed more in chapter 5, is one in which marketing and sales play especially powerful roles in credit access and allocation.) Even when a specific loan inquiry appears to be originated by the home buyer or home owner, the choice of which lender to approach can be heavily influenced by the marketing and sales activities of the lender. In the case of banks and thrifts, this might include whether the institution has branches in or near the neighborhood of the prospective applicant. The presence of a local branch, and the active servicing of community credit needs through that branch, signals to the household that the institution is interested in doing business in the area and with local residents. Moreover, lenders utilize targeted marketing via direct mail, telephone marketing, and, increasingly, the Internet.

The growth of mortgage companies in the past twenty years has led to a corresponding increase in independent mortgage brokers. Because most mortgage companies—especially independent mortgage companies not affiliated with banks or thrifts—do not rely on branches, they often utilize mortgage brokers as their sales and application-taking agents. Mortgage brokers make their revenue from up-front fees on the loan. They also often earn "yield spread premiums" paid to them by the lender in exchange for selling a loan at an interest rate above the minimum rate demanded by the lender.

Figure 4.1 **The Home Mortgage Lending Process**

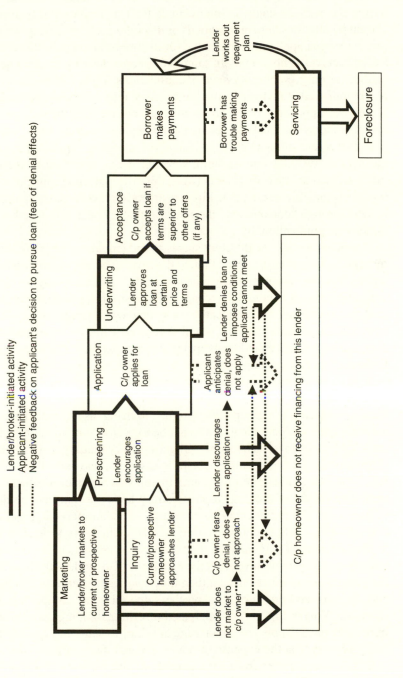

As Ross and Yinger (2002) note, the behavior of lenders and borrowers during the various stages is interrelated. First, if lenders fail to market to certain populations or neighborhoods or discourage certain groups from submitting formal applications, then the set of formal loan applications that the lender receives is not a random sample of people desiring credit. The applications are only a subset of *potential* applications, a subset that is more likely to be approved. Lenders, in particular, may rely on mortgage brokers to screen out applicants or do some sort of prescreening themselves. Other times, lenders may establish relationships with community-based organizations that screen out potential applicants. Prescreening applicants can reduce the overall rejection rate of the lender, but it can also tend to reduce the measured denial-rate disparities between minority and white applicants. While this can be an efficient relationship, it also tends to mask the true behavior of lenders through "outsourcing" their discriminatory behavior, whether intentionally or unintentionally.

Another way that the different stages of the lending process are related is through feedback effects over time and across different institutions. By rejecting loans for discriminatory reasons, lenders will discourage households from applying for another loan—especially at similar types of institutions—in the future. Figure 4.1 indicates some of these interactions or feedback effects through the use of horizontal dotted gray lines. These feedback effects are sometimes called "anticipated discrimination" effects and result in the reduction of future applications.

Similar to the problem caused by prescreening or differential marketing, anticipated discrimination increases the full impact of discriminatory practices and policies. If a group is accustomed to being discriminated against by a certain type of lender, they should not be expected to continually approach such lenders for loans. The word will get out very quickly that such lenders discriminate or are difficult to obtain loans from, and potential applicants will look elsewhere. Therefore, anticipated discrimination effects are an important legacy of previous discriminatory behavior that may be difficult to overcome. This may entail some sort of remedial marketing and education efforts as well as demonstrating a clear willingness to lend in the affected communities. If minority homebuyers or homeowners go to certain lenders because they have directly experienced or indirectly heard about discrimination by other lenders, then they may pay additional search costs, and may not end up with loans on the same terms as comparable whites (Ross and Yinger 2002, 91). Anticipated discrimination may convince some minorities not to apply for a mortgage at all, or to settle too quickly for the "easy approval" at the expense of not receiving a fairly priced loan.

If minorities suffer from long periods of discrimination by banks and thrifts, for example, they may be much more likely to apply for a loan at a mortgage company and to respond more favorably to sales pitches by mortgage brokers. Yinger (1995) estimates that 21 percent of potential moves by minority households are discouraged by discrimination in housing and mortgage markets, with most of this effect due to mortgage discrimination.

Marketing and sales are often neglected sources for potential lending discrimination and redlining. Formal studies, especially since the famous Boston Federal Reserve Bank Study of 1992, have focused primarily on the approval or rejection of formal loan applications. The large number of studies spurred by this report has drawn attention away from concerns over lenders' marketing and application-taking behavior. Lenders that prefer not to lend in a neighborhood or to a group are unlikely to market to such areas or groups. This issue is of even greater concern today as lenders and brokers have greater access to information and technology to select borrower groups to avoid. Mortgage brokers or lenders can, for example, gain access to sophisticated databases that include information on credit history, debt status, foreclosure experience, income and other demographics, etc. (Chapter 5 discusses this issue in more depth.) Depository institutions, of course, have information on savings account usage. Automated underwriting technologies, which include credit history and property information, can be used to identify "preferred" targets for lending products.

The evidence continues to show that, even in the formal approval stage of the process, lending discrimination exists. A substantial number of mortgage-lending studies in the last ten years have focused on reviewing or reanalyzing the results of the 1992 Boston Federal Reserve study. The Boston Fed study has received so much attention for at least three reasons:

1. It provided rigorous evidence of lending discrimination;
2. It was conducted by a Federal Reserve Bank, a source generally seen as sympathetic to the banking industry; and
3. It utilized a uniquely rich set of data that included credit history information on loan applicants and lender classifications that other datasets generally do not include.

The original study was published as a Federal Reserve Working Paper in 1992 but was revised and published in the prestigious *American Economic Review* in 1996 (Munnell et al. 1996). Previous studies had utilized more limited datasets and generally had found evidence of racial discrimination in loan approval and lending activity.

The Boston Fed study examined a sample of approximately 3,000 loan applications for conventional home purchase mortgages in the Boston area in 1990. The data supplemented the HMDA data with thirty-eight additional variables based on what the authors and lenders thought should be significant factors in explaining lending patterns. These variables included housing expense-to-income-ratio, debt-payments-to-income, net wealth, both consumer and mortgage credit histories, employment data, loan-to-value information, and other data. This study represented a dramatic increase in data on applicant characteristics compared to earlier studies. Munnell et al. (1996) found that the probability of loan denial was 8.2 percentage points higher for blacks and Hispanics than it was for whites, controlling for other variables, and that this difference was highly significant statistically. This was also a substantial effect in magnitude. The denial rate for whites was 10 percent, so that the 18.2 percent denial rate for minorities was 82 percent higher than for comparable white applicants. The authors also tested a variety of alternative specifications of their multivariate model and found that they had little impact on the results.

The Boston Fed study generated a tremendous amount of attention when it was released in 1992. Some economists—including many aligned with the deregulationists discussed in chapter 2—were highly skeptical of the study's findings. Many critics of the study relied principally on the theoretical labor market discrimination work of University of Chicago economist Gary Becker, who essentially argued that competitive forces would preclude discrimination from persisting. As Dymski (1995) relates the Becker theory, "if bigots leave $500 bills in the street, non-bigots will surely pick them up." Once again, the deregulationalists and others see little difference between the market for mortgage credit and the market for cotton candy. Even many economists who recognize differences markets for candy and markets for credit do not seriously entertain the notion of persistent discrimination in lending markets. Such rejections of discrimination in lending tend to be based on theoretical conceptions of markets and not on empirical evidence (Nesiba 1996). First, the definition of discrimination used by many traditional neoclassical economists tends to be quite narrow. It is often restricted to one where an individual engages in an intentional, irrational, not profit-maximizing, act.

In reality, credit markets are fundamentally different from a market for candy or widgets. To begin with, even many neoclassical economists acknowledge that credit markets do not involve simultaneous exchange, do involve incomplete and asymmetric information, and are affected by adverse selection and incentive effects (Nesiba 1996). But lending markets also have important spillover or externality effects, especially in the mortgage market. The costs of foreclosure, for example, extend far outside of the lender-borrower relationship and can affect the property values and safety of neighbors (when abandoned properties result), a community's tax base, and other issues. Home ownership can bring benefits to entire communities—either geographic or ethnic—and so decreased access to it has implications beyond that of the individual.

Some economists do pay attention to some spillover benefits of lending activity in a neighborhood. For example, Lang and Nakamura (1993) argue that if lenders do not make loans in a neighborhood, there will be weaker information on the value of homes in the area due to less sales activity. This will result in lower-quality appraisals that will then constrain lending by other lenders. Moreover, Nesiba goes further by arguing that redlining practices have a sort of contagion effect on other lenders:

> For instance, assume you are a banker and you know that the biggest lender in the area racially discriminates and will not finance loans in a particular community. Assume further that your bank alone is too small to stop the decline in home values caused by the big bank's redlining behavior (as homes become less marketable). You would be irrational, in an individual profit-maximizing sense, if you chose to make loans in that area. (Nesiba 1996)

In this way, discrimination by one lender in an area can influence the behavior of other lenders, and discrimination or redlining can become institutionalized. Rather than other lenders rushing in to capitalize on the great business opportunity, many may avoid the area. Moreover, those that do venture into the community may find it rational to require a substantial risk premium to do so. This means that the borrower will suffer from higher borrowing costs brought about by lending discrimination.

Not all the criticisms of the Boston Fed Study have relied completely on theoretical arguments. Some have actually utilized empirical analysis, often reanalyzing the same data using different assumptions and models (Horne 1997). Ross and Yinger (2002) responded to those empirical critiques of the Boston Fed study that argue that no discrimination exists. They directly reviewed these studies and reexamined the Boston Fed data. They found that "the large differences in loan approval between minority and white applicants that are identified by Munnell et al. cannot be explained by data errors, omitted variables, or the endogeneity of loan terms" (Ross and Yinger 2002, 163).

Despite the continuing importance of the Boston Fed Study, a perhaps more important policy issue with respect to the study is the age of the underlying data. The data were collected in 1990, predating sizable gains to minority home buyers in the early to middle 1990s. There is substantial evidence that improved enforcement of fair lending laws during that period as well as greater attention to the CRA, together with a favorable interest rate environment and growing economy, contributed to these gains. However, during the 1990s there was also a substantial increase in the role that specialized high-risk lenders played in the mortgage market. While this latter trend may have contributed to the number of minority home buyers, it appears that discrimination has shifted, to some degree, from a question of simple access to one of access to fairly priced loans.

Credit Scoring, Automated Underwriting, and Lending Discrimination

Automated underwriting systems had been widely used in credit card lending in the 1970s and 1980s. In the 1990s, the use of credit scoring and automated underwriting mushroomed, especially in mortgage lending. As discussed in chapter 3, it also increased significantly in the small business lending arena. The providers of credit scoring systems and the developers and users of automated underwriting systems, including Fannie Mae and Freddie Mac, have argued that, because race is not used as a variable, such systems do not discriminate. They have also argued that these systems approve minority applicants at higher rates than traditional nonautomated underwriting. The second argument may be true, but given the high levels of discrimination found in the 1992 Boston Fed study, this is hardly a reassuring finding. Are we not to question the construction and performance of automated systems simply because they discriminate less than the highly discriminatory patterns of the past?

A number of mortgage market observers have expressed concern about the impact of credit scoring (Bradford 2000; Silver 2002) on minority borrowers and neighborhoods. Ross and Yinger (2002) discuss the potential discriminatory impact of automated underwriting systems extensively. They argue that, while automated systems themselves do not involve disparate treatment discrimination (though the ways that lenders implement them may involve disparate treatment), the econometric models used in the systems may result in disparate impact discrimination. Unfortunately, since researchers have not had access to these proprietary systems, it is difficult to determine the extent of any problem. There is good reason to expect some level of disparate impact discrimination that fails the "business necessity" test, which permits an activity that entails disparate impact discrimination only when lenders can show a business necessity for the practice.

Ross and Yinger (2002) begin with the assumption that, while controlling for all *available* loan characteristics, loans to minorities will perform worse than loans to whites. The available data are unlikely to capture all factors affecting loan performance. Given the legacies of discrimination in credit, employment, and housing markets, this is not an unreasonable assumption. For example, we know that blacks are much more likely to have subprime loans than whites and so be subjected to predatory lending practices at higher rates. These loans themselves can induce credit difficulties. Automated systems do not have good information on the extent of abusive debt held by applicants.

If lenders were to include the race of the borrower as an explanatory variable in the scoring model, they would be clearly guilty of disparate treatment discrimination. This sort of discrimination, if it were legal, would allow lenders to use minority status as a proxy for the unobserved characteristics that predict worse loan performance. Now, if the designer of an automated system merely omits race, he also creates a problem by omitting factors for which race was serving as a proxy. This means that other variables in the model that are correlated with race will now appear more important in determining higher defaults. This will increase the "weights applied to variables on which minority applicants rank relatively poorly, on average, and decreases the weights applied to variables on which minority applicants rank relatively well" (Ross and Yinger 2002, 284). This means that such a system will result in disparate impact discrimination. The simple elimination of the race variable will result in changes in the coefficients of other variables correlated with race. This means that while race appears to be eliminated, other variables are now serving, in combination, as a proxy for it. They are essentially "instruments" of the race variable. Thus, due to the econometric details, while appearing race-neutral, this technique "serves to approximate the outcome of disparate-treatment discrimination, not to obtain a better prediction of loan profitability based on observable loan characteristics other than group membership, which is what the law calls for" (Ross and Yinger 2002, 285).

Other concerns about credit scoring are based on the issues of inconsistent overrides or second reviews and on the uses of credit scoring and related technologies for marketing and sales. In the case of overrides, if lenders override lower credit scores more easily for some groups than others, they are guilty of disparate impact discrimination. Credit scoring and related technologies can be used to identify marketing targets as well as to approve and price loans. The use of data mining and credit-score-based technologies make lending to marginal borrowers much more expensive relative to lending to those who easily qualify via the automated technology. In most applications of credit scoring, only those with very strong or very weak scores are easily approved. Those with borderline scores often still need additional review.

Thus, a lender looking to earn revenue based on high volumes and low transaction costs may find it advantageous to market only to consumers or businesses with very strong scores. These "high-tech-low-touch" lenders are then able to cream off the best borrowers, leaving smaller and traditional lenders with a pool of applicants with higher average risk levels. Mainstream lenders then become less interested in these markets, leaving room for high-cost lenders to move in.

The problems of discrimination in access to mortgage credit persist but have changed in many ways. Access to formal mortgage credit of any sort has become more available, but access to credit at reasonable terms has become more of an issue in the last decade. Moreover, in some cases, access to credit has become too available. That is, there has been an increase in excessively risky home loans. These loans can carry serious consequences not just for the directly affected home owners but also for their neighborhoods and communities. The next chapter focuses on the recent surge in the problem of predatory mortgage lending and the hypersegmentation of home equity and refinance loan markets by race.

CHAPTER 5

From Fair Access to Credit
to Access to Fair Credit

The Rise of Subprime and Predatory Lending

Though the term "predatory lending" has become much more recognized by the general public and policymakers in recent years, high-cost, abusive lending is not an inherently new phenomenon. Abusive lenders, either informal or formal, have been operating in residential-, consumer-, and business-lending markets since the earliest days of the nation's history. Deregulationist defenders of unfettered credit markets argue that regulating providers of such loans is generally ineffective or detrimental to those seeking credit. But, at least since the early twentieth century, there have been various attempts to rein in such lenders, some with significant success. For example, in the early twentieth century, the Russell Sage Foundation waged an extensive campaign to promote standardized state regulation of high-cost small consumer loan outfits throughout the country. The foundation also promoted credit unions as a model for responsibly meeting the consumer credit needs of working-class populations (Carruthers and Guinnane 2002). The Russell Sage model small loan law was widely adopted and had positive impacts on reducing abuses in the market for consumer loans. More recently, consumer activists and public interest and legal aid law operations have worked, at least since the early 1990s, on improving regulations on home equity loans. In fact, the 1994 Home Ownership and Equity Protection Act (HOEPA), which offers some limited consumer protections for high-cost mortgages, was largely the result of such activism.

During the middle 1990s, however, a major shift occurred in concerns regarding access to mortgage credit in the United States, especially in minority and lower-income communities. Many mortgage-lending analysts began to notice a significant increase in the activity and number of a newer set of mortgage lenders. These newer lenders were mortgage companies, and they were very active in minority communities. Moreover, most of them made many more refinance than home purchase loans. Soon afterward, local legal aid offices in cities across the country began reporting increased cases of high-cost mortgages with abusive terms and conditions, with clients coming mostly from predominantly minority communities. In many cases, the same borrower was being repeatedly victimized, and in most cases, the loans involved these new lenders, known as "subprime" lenders.

Subprime loans are intended for borrowers with significant credit history problems. Risk ratings in mortgage loans have traditionally been classified as "A," meaning prime, "A–," a sort of near-prime, and then "B," "C," and "D" grades. Grades are based on delinquency and default history, court judgments, and bankruptcies. Lenders who specialize in lending to such borrowers are called "subprime lenders." The Department of Housing and Urban Development (HUD) has classified lenders who claim to make at least half of their loans to subprime borrowers as subprime lenders (Scheessele 1999). Subprime loans are made by specialized subprime lenders and by some "prime" lenders that make mostly prime but also some subprime loans. In the middle to late 1990s, the volume of subprime lending exploded. Figure 5.1 shows the total dollar volume of subprime loans from 1994 to 2001, according to a leading industry research firm.

Refinance and home equity loans account for the bulk of the growth among subprime lenders. According to research by the HUD on data reported under the Home Mortgage Disclosure Act (HMDA), refinance loans by subprime lenders increased by more than 700,000 loans from 1993 to 1998, an increase of almost four times the rate for subprime home purchase loans. Moreover, refinance loans by subprime lenders increased by 890 percent from 1983 to 1998, even though refinances by prime lenders grew by only 2.5 percent (Scheessele 1999). Table 5.1 shows the growth in subprime lender refinances from 1993 to 1998 broken out by race and ethnicity of the borrowers. The first thing to note is the very large increase—both by number and by percentage—in HMDA loans where race is not reported. Unfortunately, HMDA data have had significant loopholes allowing lenders to avoid comprehensive reporting.[1] In fact, subprime lenders fail to report race at substantially higher rates than prime lenders. Loans with no race information increased by more than twenty-five times from 1993 to 1998 and, by 1998, comprised 31 percent of subprime lender loans. In 2000, 35 percent of refinance loans by subprime lenders had missing race data compared to 19 percent of loans by prime lenders (Bradford 2002). In twenty-one metropolitan areas in the United States, subprime lenders failed to report race on more than 50 percent of their refinance loans, and this rate went as high as 67 percent. Wyly and Holloway (2002) found that cities with higher subprime activity had higher nonreporting rates. In examining Atlanta data more closely, they also found that nonreporting rates for refinance applications were much

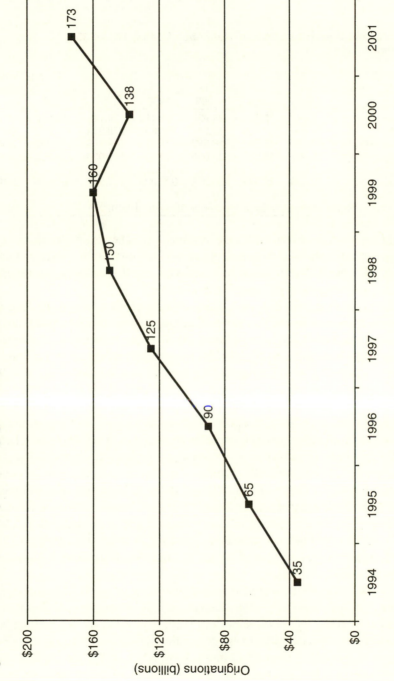

Figure 5.1 The Growth in Subprime Mortgage Lending in the United States

Source: Departments of Treasury and Housing and Urban Development (2000) and Scheessele (2002).

Table 5.1

Increase in Subprime Lenders' Refinance Loans, 1993–1998, United States

Borrower race	1993	1994	1995	1996	1997	1998	1993–1998 Increase (%)
Black	9,747	19,174	24,925	45,419	74,145	99,560	921
White	48,763	72,606	82,511	163,653	278,234	374,572	668
Other minority	11,682	16,069	16,863	31,213	49,983	71,762	514
Race missing	9,501	18,927	34,096	79,954	149,034	243,802	2,466
Total	79,693	126,776	158,395	320,239	551,396	789,696	891

Source: Home Mortgage Disclosure Act; Scheessele (1999).

higher in black neighborhoods than in white ones. They estimated that blacks were overrepresented among missing-race loans, constituting over one-third of all 2000 HMDA unreported records.[2] This result was likely substantially higher for the records of subprime lenders.

The reporting problem, the spatial concentration of subprime lending, and the disproportionate incidence of failure to report race in black neighborhoods suggest that a disproportionate share of the "race missing" subprime loans were made to black households. Thus, the growth in subprime loans to blacks was probably much higher than the 921 percent shown in Table 5.1.

One way to complement the race-of-borrower analysis that does not suffer from the missing data problem is to examine the racial composition of the census tracts in which the loans were made. Census tract reporting does not suffer from substantial missing data problems in the HMDA data. Looking at racial composition of neighborhood shows that refinance lending grew much faster in predominantly black neighborhoods than in white neighborhoods. Figure 5.2 illustrates the different 1993–1998 growth rates for neighborhoods of different racial composition in the Chicago metropolitan area.[3] It shows that the number of refinance loans made in predominantly black (75–100 percent black) census tracks grew by 29 times from 1993 to 1998, while subprime lending in predominantly white (90–100 percent white) tracts grew by only 2.3 times.

In 2000, the HUD analyzed lending patterns in the United States and more closely in five large cities (Department of Housing and Urban Development 2000a). By 1998, subprime lenders dominated black neighborhoods across the country. In predominantly black neighborhoods, those where 75 percent or more of residents were black, subprime lenders made 51 percent of refinance loans compared to only 9 percent in predominantly

Figure 5.2 **Growth in Refinance Loans by Subprime Lenders by Race of Neighborhood, Chicago Area, 1993–1998**

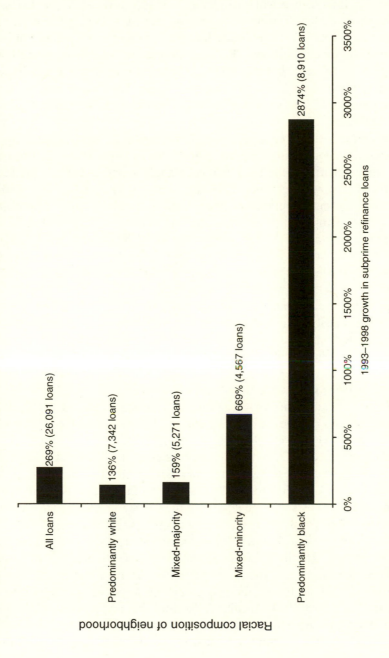

Source: Immergluck and Wiles (1999); calculations from HMDA data.

white neighborhoods. Moreover, the same study found that home owners in predominantly black neighborhoods were more than twice as likely as home owners in low-income white neighborhoods to receive subprime loans. In upper-income black census tracts, 39 percent of refinance borrowers received their loans from subprime lenders versus only 18 percent in low-income white neighborhoods. Refinance borrowers in upper-income black neighborhoods were six times more likely than borrowers in upper-income white neighborhoods to receive subprime loans. These same basic patterns were found in HUD's studies of Atlanta, Philadelphia, New York, Chicago, and Baltimore.

In Chicago, subprime lenders took 74 percent of all refinance loan applications in predominantly black neighborhoods in 1998. Table 5.2 illustrates the lenders that took the most refinance applications in 1998 in predominantly white census tracts in the Chicago area, and Table 5.3 lists the lenders that took the most applications in predominantly black tracts. Application volume is a strong indicator of a lender's marketing efforts. In white neighborhoods, eighteen of the top twenty refinance lenders were prime lenders. In black neighborhoods, precisely the opposite is the case. Eighteen of the top twenty top lenders were subprime lenders. This is a classic manifestation of a dual market, with prime lenders targeting white—or at least nonblack—neighborhoods, and subprime lenders targeting black and minority census tracts. Later analyses have documented similarly hypersegmented markets in cities throughout the country (Bradford 2002). These patterns have generally persisted since 1998. Bradford (2002) reported that in 2000, 67 percent of black borrowers lived in neighborhoods where more than half of the refinance loans were made by subprime borrowers.

From this simple analysis, race certainly appears to be a powerful determinant of who receives subprime refinance loans. A more detailed, multivariate analysis can shed light on the independent affect of race, while holding income, property value, and other variables constant. Table 5.4 presents the results of an ordinary least squares regression estimating the relationships between some key neighborhood variables and the proportion of refinance loans originated by subprime lenders in the Chicago metropolitan area. Because the subprime share of refinancing fluctuates widely in tracts with very few refinance loans, tracts with fewer than twenty loans were excluded from the regression. The independent variables include the number of owner-occupied housing units, median home value, average real estate debt for households with such debt, the age of housing stock (measured by the percentage built after 1984), median household income, resident educational attainment (measured by the percentage of adults with a high school education), and whether the tract is located in the city of Chicago.[4] Also, three

Table 5.2

**Lenders with the Most Refinance Applications in Predominantly *White*
Neighborhoods in the Chicago Area, 1998**

Lender	Number of applications in black tracts	Share of applications in black tracts (%)	Share of applications in white tracts (%)	Black-white tract disparity
First Chicago NBD Mortgage Co.	7,602	4.37	1.13	0.26
Norwest Mortgage	7,225	4.15	0.34	0.08
Countrywide Home Loans	5,833	3.35	1.88	0.56
Chase Manhattan Mortgage Corp.	5,504	3.16	0.74	0.23
Harris Trust And Savings Bank	4,776	2.74	0.24	0.09
Washington Mutual Bank	4,118	2.37	0.45	0.19
LaSalle Bank FSB	3,694	2.12	0.97	0.46
Ameriquest Mortgage Co.	3,622	2.08	5.68	2.73
Mid America FSB	3,505	2.01	0.05	0.02
Citibank	2,917	1.68	1.15	0.69
The Money Store	2,790	1.60	7.94	4.95
Standard Federal Bank	2,765	1.59	0.16	0.10
Old Kent Mortgage Co.	2,667	1.53	0.40	0.26
Bank of America	2,504	1.44	0.17	0.12
North American Mortgage Co.	2,407	1.38	0.46	0.33
Fleet Mortgage Corp.	2,292	1.32	0.22	0.17
Ohio Savings Bank	2,229	1.28	0.12	0.09
Fidelity Mortgage Inc.	2,177	1.25	0.91	0.73
Firstar Home Mortgage Corp.	1,986	1.14	0.07	0.06
Bank One	1,985	1.14	1.42	1.24

Source: Immergluck and Wiles (1999); calculations from Home Mortgage Disclosure Act data.

Note: Department of Housing and Urban Development-designated subprime lenders shown in ***bold italics***.

dummy variables are included to indicate whether the neighborhood is mixed-majority, mixed-minority, or predominantly black.

Of the variables in the regression, all are statistically significant except for the number of owner-occupied housing units and average real estate debt. The magnitudes of the standardized coefficients in the third column indicate which of these variables explain more of the variation in the share of loans made by subprime lenders. Thus, whether a neighborhood is predominantly black explains the greatest amount of variation in subprime lending, followed by educational attainment, median home value, and whether a neighborhood is mixed-minority. Holding median home value, income, and other variables constant, the results show that going from an all-white to an all-black neighborhood increases the share of refinance loans made by subprime firms by 40 percentage points. Higher education levels, as

Table 5.3

**Lenders with the Most Refinance Applications in Predominantly *Black*
Neighborhoods in the Chicago Area, 1998**

Lender	Number of applications in black tracts	Share of applications in black tracts (%)	Share of applications in white tracts (%)	Black-white tract disparity
The Money Store	3,733	7.94	1.60	4.96
Ameriquest Mortgage Co.	2,674	5.68	2.08	2.73
Equicredit Corp. of America	1,501	3.19	0.25	12.76
Advanta National Bank	1,462	3.11	0.70	4.44
New Century Mortgage Corp.	1,196	2.54	0.85	2.99
WMC Mortgage Corp.	1,132	2.41	0.54	4.46
Option One Mortgage Corp.	1,075	2.29	0.39	5.86
IMC Mortgage Co.	952	2.02	0.31	6.53
Parkway Mortgage	935	1.99	0.21	9.46
Countrywide Home Loans	885	1.88	3.35	0.56
Pan American Financial Service	881	1.87	0.04	46.82
Superior Bank	857	1.82	0.29	6.28
BNC Mortgage	840	1.79	0.33	5.41
Pinnfund	834	1.77	0.10	17.73
First Franklin Financial Corp.	832	1.77	0.86	2.06
Banc One Financial Services	814	1.73	1.08	1.60
Delta Funding Corp.	753	1.60	0.08	20.01
Mortgage Lenders Network USA	741	1.58	0.20	7.88
Corewest Banc	674	1.43	0.28	5.12
Bank One	666	1.42	1.14	1.24

Source: Immergluck and Wiles (1999); calculations of Home Mortgage Disclosure Act
data.
    Note: Subprime lenders shown in ***bold italics***.

might be expected, do have a negative effect on subprime lending, but the
effect is not very large, especially compared to the race variable. A 20
percentage-point increase in the proportion of residents finishing high
school—a sizable increase—results in less than a 4 percentage-point decrease in the subprime share. The next most important determinant of
subprime lending is median home value. A negative effect of higher home
values on subprime activity is expected because prime lenders may compete more heavily in segments of the market with larger home values where
their interest and fee revenues are higher even at conventional rates. Holding race, income, and other variables constant, a $100,000 increase in
median home value decreases the portion of refinance loans made by
subprime lenders by only 2.8 percentage points. Thus, while lower home
values explain some of the increased presence of subprime firms, race
again has a much stronger independent impact.

Table 5.4

Regression of Subprime Lenders' Market Share in Chicago Census Tracts, 1998

Variable	Coefficient	Standard error	Standardized coefficient	Significance level
Constant	0.301	0.023	0.000	0.094
Owner-occupied units	5.91E-06	0.000	0.027	**0.000**
Median home value	-2.79E-07	0.000	-0.158	**0.000**
Average real estate debt	-4.40E-07	0.000	-0.037	0.180
Percent of housing units built after 1984 (0.0 to 1.0)	-8.56E-02	0.016	-0.076	**0.000**
Median household income	6.41E-07	0.000	0.103	**0.000**
Percent of adults with high school education (0.0 to 1.0)	-0.188	0.025	-0.166	**0.000**
Predominantly black (0 or 1)	0.395	0.009	0.782	**0.000**
Mixed-minority (0 or 1)	6.75E-02	0.008	0.149	**0.000**
Mixed-majority (0 or 1)	1.56E-02	0.006	0.040	**0.005**
City (0 or 1)	-1.13E-02	0.006	-0.031	**0.047**

Notes: $R^2 = 0.802$; N = 1,478 (only tracts with twenty or more refinance loans are included); **bold** variables are significant at the 0.05 level or below.

Once race and home value are held constant, higher neighborhood incomes are actually associated with somewhat higher subprime lending shares, but the magnitude of the effect is small. It is important to be careful in interpreting this analysis. Since property values usually rise and minority populations fall as incomes increase, it is not accurate to say that higher-income neighborhoods are expected to have higher subprime lending shares. This is not the case because the typical higher-income neighborhood also has a smaller percentage of minority residents. However, after holding race and property values constant, lower incomes will not increase the level of subprime lending, so that race, not income, is the stronger determinant of subprime patterns. Scheessele (2002) conducted a similar analysis for census tracts throughout the country and obtained similar results, with race having a strong effect on the subprime lenders' share even after controlling for a variety of neighborhood characteristics.

The shortcoming in this analysis, as with most examinations of lending patterns, is the lack of credit history data. The authors of two later studies were able to obtain and incorporate credit history data in their work. In an analysis of subprime lending in Chicago and Philadelphia, Calem, Gillen, and Wachter (2002) found that, after controlling for education, income, and housing stock characteristics, black neighborhoods still had much higher levels of subprime lending than white neighborhoods. For refinance loans, an all-black neighborhood was expected to have a subprime share that was 24 percentage points higher than an otherwise equivalent white neighborhood, even after controlling for the credit history of neighborhood residents.

Silver (2003) analyzed the lending in six additional cities—Baltimore, Detroit, Houston, Atlanta, Milwaukee, and Cleveland—and again found similar results. Even after controlling for housing turnover, age of housing stock, median income, percent of residents aged sixty-five and older, and the percent of residents with high risk credit scores, the percentage of residents who were black was a consistently strong determinant of subprime lending activity. In all six cities, the percent of residents in a census tract who were black had a highly significant effect on the proportion of refinance loans made by subprime lenders. In every city, going from an all-white neighborhood to an otherwise equivalent all-black neighborhood resulted in the proportion of subprime lending increasing by at least 11 percentage points (Baltimore). The effect was typically closer to 20 to 25 percentage points and exceeded 40 percentage points in Houston. Moreover, in four of the six cities, the percentage of residents over age sixty-five had a significant and positive effect on subprime refinance lending.

The Problems with Hypersegmented Home Loan Markets

There are at least three reasons why we should care about the growth and geographic concentration of subprime lenders from a public policy perspective. First, if the market for home equity loans is excessively segmented by race, so that minority communities are served primarily by subprime lenders, homeowners in such communities may be effectively steered toward higher-cost products, some of which contain more restrictive terms. If minority communities are targets of higher-cost lenders and receive little attention from prime lenders, the odds of minority borrowers with good credit receiving higher-cost loans will be higher than those of white borrowers with good credit.

Various sources of data indicate that a substantial portion of subprime loans are priced in excess of what is merited by the risk involved. A study using an industry survey of mortgages priced as subprime found that almost 29 percent of subprime loans had credit scores above 640, generally considered the point at which prime lenders become quite comfortable with loans (Phillips-Patrick, Jones, and LaRocca 2000). In examining 15,000 subprime mortgages originated by four financial institutions, Freddie Mac found that between 10 and 35 percent of borrowers who obtained mortgages in the subprime market could have qualified for a conventional loan (Freddie Mac 1996). Freddie Mac also estimated that subprime borrowers who would have qualified for conventional loans paid mortgage rates on the order of 1 to 2.5 percentage points higher that they would have paid in the prime market. However, this does not take into account the higher up-front fees on most subprime loans. It is the fees, rather than the excessive interest rates, that tend to be the source of a good deal of overcharging.

A study of home purchase loans conducted by an affiliate of the Mortgage Bankers Association of America found that the probability of a home purchase borrower's receiving a subprime loan, controlling for credit history, location, and other variables, increased by approximately one-third, from 0.8 percent to 2.5 percent, if the borrower was black (Pennington-Cross, Yezer, and Nichols 2000). The loan sample in this study had relatively few subprime loans in it, but the increase was relatively substantial and statistically significant. Given the larger race-based differentials in the refinance market compared to the home purchase market, this finding of race-based pricing differentials in purchase loans certainly supports concerns about racially discriminatory pricing in refinance markets.

This dual market, including the resistance of prime lenders to marketing and making loans in minority communities, can create a sense of futility among minority homeowners in considering banks and other prime lenders as potential lenders. In Fannie Mae's 2001 National Housing Survey, only 34 percent of credit-impaired respondents were confident that they got the lowest cost mortgage available, compared to 68 percent of all homeowners surveyed (Fannie Mae 2001). Thirty-two percent of credit-impaired homeowners did not care whether they got the lowest cost mortgage, they were "just happy to be approved," compared to only 10 percent of all respondents. Moreover, more subprime respondents reported not knowing anything about their credit rating.

The second reason to be concerned about hypersegmented refinance markets is that the growth of subprime lending has been associated with a simultaneous rise in foreclosures. Subprime loans lead to delinquency and foreclosure at relatively high rates, especially among the higher-risk segment of the industry. An industry survey of twenty-seven larger subprime lenders indicates that ninety-day delinquency rates for C- and D-grade loans were 10 percent and 22 percent, respectively, compared to a rate of 0.25 percent for prime refinance loans (Phillips-Patrick, Jones, and LaRocca 2000). Even Federal Housing Administration (FHA) loans, which have been persistently tied to foreclosure and blight problems in minority communities, had ninety-day delinquency rates of less than 2 percent for refinance loans over the same period. The foreclosure rate for all subprime loans in this sample (including the 55 percent that were A– grade) was more than four times the FHA rate. The foreclosure rate for C and D loans is expected to be much higher. In this voluntary survey, almost 20 percent of subprime loans were C and D grade. However, the source of these data appears to be biased toward substantially underrepresenting higher-risk loans. Of even more concern is the fact that problems among subprime loans worsened considerably beginning in 2000. Seriously delinquent rates for subprime loans (of all grades) increased from less than 5 percent in early 2000 to more than 8 percent by late 2001. Prime loan delinquencies were almost constant over this period, at around 1 percent, and FHA loans rose much more slowly from about 3.5 to about 4.5 percent (Crews-Cutts 2003).

Because subprime lending—especially the higher-risk segments known as B, C, or D lending—is highly concentrated in certain types of neighborhoods, these neighborhoods bear a disproportionate share of subprime foreclosures. Moreover, many of the subprime lenders exhibiting the highest foreclosure rates are concentrated in certain areas, so that these areas are hit especially hard. The nature of residential sorting and the experience of the FHA program suggest that a lender may have a substantial but not unreasonable foreclosure rate nationally, and still have a foreclosure rate in certain neighborhoods that is exorbitant. Lenders may be able to tolerate foreclosure rates of 5 percent nationally and still be successful raising capital. These same lenders may have foreclosure rates of more than 10 to 15 percent in specific communities.

Foreclosures—particularly those leading to abandonment and blight—often have negative spillover effects, or externalities, that can be a key source of market failure. Because the negative social costs of these spatially concentrated foreclosures (abandonment, blight, crime, and lower neighborhood property values) are not captured in market transactions, the level of credit will be excessive even from an efficiency perspective. It is important to add that foreclosures in struggling, low- or moderate-income and minority neighborhoods may have more negative impacts than those in middle- and upper-income areas. In the latter case, the foreclosures are less likely to lead to abandoned buildings, blight, and crime.

At least three recent studies have explored the link between subprime lending and foreclosures (Greunstein and Herbert 2000; National Training and Information Center 1999; Department of Housing and Urban Development 2000b). In Baltimore, while the subprime share of mortgages in the city was 21 percent in 1998 (presumably higher than in previous years), 45 percent of foreclosure petitions in that year were tied to subprime loans. Subprime foreclosures accounted for 57 percent of all foreclosures in black Baltimore neighborhoods. In Atlanta, a study by Abt and Associates found that foreclosures attributed to subprime lenders accounted for 36 percent of all foreclosures in predominantly minority neighborhoods in 1999, while their share of loan originations was between 26 and 31 percent in the preceding three years. In the case of the Atlanta study, at least, the results tend to underestimate the proportion of foreclosures due to subprime originators and overestimate the proportion due to prime originators. Many subprime loans are sold to financial institutions identified by HUD as "prime" or are held in trusts at prime lending institutions (usually banks). The reverse does not tend to be the case; subprime lenders do not often buy loans from prime lenders and generally do not have trust capacity. In the Chicago study, some loan pricing data was analyzed. Foreclosures on loans with interest rates above comparable Treasury rates plus 4 percentage points (clearly subprime-priced loans) increased by 500 percent from 1993 to 1998 (National Training and Information Center 1999). Many of these foreclosures were concentrated in minority neighborhoods.

The third concern over the growth and distribution of subprime lending is the rise of abusive or predatory lending that has been associated with the subprime industry. Many major subprime lenders active in minority neighborhoods have been implicated in at least some instances of abusive lending. One former Chicago legal aid attorney recalled that, when looking at a list of the top fourteen subprime refinance lenders in black Chicago neighborhoods, he noticed that his agency had identified specific cases of predatory lending involving each of them (Rheingold, Fitzpatrick, and Hofeld 2001). A variety of loan terms and lending practices have been described as predatory or abusive, especially when employed in high-cost or subprime loans.[5] Some of these practices, particularly loan terms such as prepayment penalties, are used in the prime market often without any detriment to the borrower. However, the use of such terms and practices in the subprime market is largely inappropriate. For example, debt-to-income ratios above 40–45 percent may be appropriate in some cases in the prime market, especially for borrowers with high incomes. A 50 percent debt-to-income ratio leaves 50 percent of income available for nonmortgage expenses, which is generally sufficient for high-income households (although perhaps not always wise). But for most households with credit history troubles, stretching the debt capacity to this degree is not generally considered responsible lending. Another example is a short-term (e.g., five-year) balloon payment, in which payments may be reduced in the near term, but then a very large payment comes due at the five-year maturity. A balloon payment for someone who can be expected to obtain refinancing rather easily in the foreseeable future may be appropriate. But for most subprime borrowers, using a balloon payment to lower monthly payments to the point of "affordability" will leave a balloon or escalating principal that the borrower will have great difficulty repaying.

Table 5.5 provides a typology of these terms and practices together with several examples of each. Testimony at the federal, state, and local levels, research reports, and media accounts have provided hundreds of examples of the employment of these practices.[6] An instance of predatory lending could involve just one of these practices. More commonly, though, a number of practices occur simultaneously. For example, high-pressure or "push" marketing may be most effectively employed when targeting homeowners in vulnerable situations, including those with high levels of health-related or credit-card debt. Those not in immediate financial distress are less susceptible to pressure tactics and are more likely to "shop around" for better alternatives.

The proportion of loans made by subprime lenders that contain abusive practices is the subject of some debate, but it is rare to find a case of a predatory lending that does not involve a subprime lender. Some evidence suggests that the proportion of subprime loans with at least one problematic feature may be quite large (Ernst, Farris, and Stein 2002). For example, estimates of the number of subprime loans containing prepayment penalties range from 43 percent to 80 percent, while estimates of the share of prime loans containing prepayment penalties are much lower—between 2 and 11 percent (Fannie Mae 2001; Department of the Treasury and Department of Housing and Urban Development 2000).

Table 5.5

A Sample of Predatory Lending Practices and Loan Terms

Type of predatory behavior	Examples
Sales and marketing	• High-pressure telephone and door-to-door sales • Targeting vulnerable populations (e.g., those with health debts, elderly, less educated) • Steering to higher-cost loans despite borrower qualifying for lower-cost credit, often rewarded by "yield spread" premiums paid to brokers • Flipping—excessive refinancing, with additional fees extracted at each refinancing • Home improvement scams, in which contractors act as loan brokers and receive kickbacks • Targeted marketing based on "vulnerability targeting"; searching for those in financial distress (e.g., hospital bills), in foreclosure, age, race, etc.
Excessive fees	• "Packing" loans with unnecessary fees, including credit life or disability insurance • Padded closing costs or third-party fees • Excessively high points or origination fees • High broker fees and yield spread premiums
Terms that trap borrowers into unaffordable financing or lead to difficulty in repayment	• Balloon payments, which conceal the true cost of financing and may force repeated refinancing or foreclosure • Negative amortization, in which payments are less than interest, resulting in an increasing principal balance and decreasing owner equity • Prepayment penalties, especially those equaling more than 1–2 percent of the loan amount • "Asset-based" lending, where the repayment amount is more than 40–50 percent of income of the borrower's income
Other fraudulent, deceptive, or abusive practices	• Reporting inflated income figures • Forgeries • Insufficient or improperly timed disclosures • Inflated appraisals • Mandatory arbitration provisions, limiting borrowers' access to the courts

A couple of recent local studies have surveyed recipients of subprime loans to understand the incidence of various predatory lending practices (Stein and Libby 2001; Stock 2001). In a study of 255 very high-cost loans in Dayton, Ohio, 75 percent were found to have prepayment penalties and 24 percent had balloon payments. The researchers also interviewed subprime borrowers who were in the process of foreclosure as well as those who were not. Thirty-nine percent of respondents in foreclosure and 33 percent of respondents not in foreclosure stated that the initial contact with the lender was initiated by the lender via phone or mail. Forty-five percent of foreclosure respondents and 24 percent of other respondents said that their loans' terms at closing were different from what had been discussed. Eighty-six percent of foreclosure respondents and 68 percent of the respondents who noted a difference in terms accepted the difference, perhaps due to pressure at the closing from the lender. And, finally, 19 percent of nonforeclosure respondents and 42 percent of foreclosure respondents were encouraged to borrow more than they had intended. In California, Stein and Libby (2001) interviewed 125 subprime borrowers and found that 39 percent of subprime respondents said that the idea to take out a home-secured loan came from the lender-broker. They also found that 64 percent of respondents had refinanced their homes six times. Forty percent of the refinances had taken place within two years of the prior loan, a strong indicator of flipping. The researchers found that 38 percent of the subprime borrowers fit a "worst-case scenario" characterized by a combination of onerous loan terms, high costs, and aggressive sales tactics.

What Explains the Growth and Concentration of Subprime Lending?

The explanation for why subprime lending grew so much in the 1990s involves the confluence and interaction of a number of economic and social conditions and policy changes. Overall, the growth of subprime activity is a manifestation of increasingly specialized and segmented financial services markets. Financial institutions have found larger corporate services less lucrative, due in part to the increased access of larger firms to alternative and more direct sources of credit and capital. Therefore, they have sought to more aggressively market credit products to consumer markets and to maximize profits through what is termed "price discrimination." This is the practice of segmenting markets in ways that allow lenders to extract the maximum price from borrowers. Borrowers who are willing to pay more, due perhaps to their inferior understanding of financial products, desperate financial situations, or other conditions, are identified and offered higher costs and less advantageous products. Borrowers who are expected to shop more for financial products and are actively courted by mainstream financial institutions are offered lower prices and better terms. This trend creates a perverse cross-subsidization, where borrowers in financial difficulty are generally targeted by higher-cost providers, and the strong profits in those sectors may compensate the more competitively priced business of the financial conglomerate.

The dual market in mortgage credit is too conveniently facilitated by a system of dual consumer financial regulation. Banks and thrifts are subject to CRA, fair lending, and consumer compliance regulation implemented by a cadre of thousands of well-trained bank examiners in the four federal bank regulatory agencies. But mortgage and finance companies undergo no regular examinations by federal regulators, and state regulators are much less well staffed than federal bank regulators. The Federal Trade Commission and a few other federal agencies have some minimal resources to address nondepository lenders, but the states are the principal source of regularory oversight, to the extent that it exists at all.

Other policies that have contributed to the rise in subprime lending include the federal preemption of state usury laws and other regulations through the Depository Institutions Deregulation and Monetary Control Act (DIDMCA) of 1980, the Alternative Mortgage Transaction Parity Act (AMTPA) of 1982, and the 1986 Tax Reform Act. DIDMCA generally overrode state-level usury ceilings on first-lien mortgages. The intent of Congress was generally to preempt state rate ceilings on home purchase loans, but it has been interpreted by the courts to include refinance loans as well. At the same time, second mortgages were not covered by the law, and state usury ceilings often still apply. This has given subprime lenders a clear incentive to shift to refinance lending, which is now generally unregulated. AMTPA was passed to accomodate lenders' claims that state regulations on alternative mortgages (e.g., adjustable rate mortgages) were impeding access to such products. AMTPA was a major deterrent to increased state regulation of subprime lending. It allowed state-regulated lenders like mortgage companies to avoid state regulations by allowing them to choose to be regulated under less stringent federal consumer protection laws.

The 1986 Tax Reform Act changed tax law to permit the deduction of interest paid only for mortgages on a principal residence and a second home. Interest on credit card or other consumer debt was no longer deductible. This created a direct incentive for homeowners to shift debt to home-secured sources, by either refinancing or taking out home equity or home improvement loans. The act gave a boost to the home equity and refinance markets overall, especially the prime markets. However, by stimulating the home equity sector overall, the tax law primed the pump for an expanded infrastructure for refinance and home equity lending. When interest rates began to rise in 1993 and 1994 after the refinancing rush of 1991 and 1992, mortgage lenders and brokers were left with a great deal of excess capacity, some of which was quickly redeployed to encourage subprime borrowers to refinance.

Other factors have also stoked the rise in subprime lending, on both the supply and the demand sides of the market. However, many of the factors that might be termed "demand-side" are clearly stimulated by supply-side activities, especially targeted marketing. One "demand-side" factor was the growth in the elderly population, including some relatively isolated homeowners who were unfamilar with formal mortgage products. Seniors in minority neighborhoods are often especially isolated and, due to a legacy of discrimination and redlining, not well acquainted with mortgage terms and practices. As discussed in chapter 4, many older blacks purchased their homes in an era where formal financial institutions were not at all interested in making loans to them. Many had little choice but to purchase their homes through abusive land contracts.

Elderly homeowners tend to have substantial equity in their homes. It is the low level of debt on the home that makes homeowners ideal targets for lenders wishing to extract large amounts of fees via "equity stripping" practices. If homeowners have little equity in their homes, it is difficult for predatory lenders to structure loans with large amounts of up-front or deferred fees financed into the loan.[7] In 1993, 78 percent of U.S. homeowners aged sixty-five to seventy-five had no housing debt, and 90 percent of those over seventy-five had no mortgage debt (AARP 1997). Walters and Hermanson (2001) found that mortgage borrowers sixty-five years or older were three times more likely to hold a subprime mortgage than borrowers less than thirty-five years old. Moreover, the survey found that 45 percent of subprime loans were held by older female borrowers but only 28 percent of prime loans were held by older women. Health bills are also a major determinant of credit problems and bankruptcy, spurring demand for debt by homeowners in desperate situations. This problem has been aggravated by high numbers of uninsured families.

Another key demand-side factor is the increase in income and wealth inequality in the United States, generally in the latter decades of the 1990s. Squires (2003b) points out that, between 1967 and 2001, the share of income going to the top 5 percent of U.S. households grew from 17.5 percent to 22.5 percent. Moreover, much of the growing inequality has manifested itself spatially. The poverty rate in central cities increased from 12.6 percent in 1970 to over 20 percent by 1995.

Notwithstanding demand-side forces, changes in the supply of capital and the delivery of credit have been very important in explaining the growth of subprime lenders. The growth of the mortgage- and asset-backed securities industries that fund high-risk mortgage lending operations fueled the rise of subprime lenders. Mortgage companies bundle loans in a large pool and obtain a rating on the security, often after it is enhanced by insurance. Oftentimes a "trustee" or some other special-purpose entity is employed that actually retains legal possession of the loans. These securities are then frequently subdivided into "tranches" by investment banking firms that sell the securities to institutional investors, such as insurance companies or pension funds. Tranches are rated from higher to lower risk and provide differing rates of return. The lower-risk tranches typically have a higher claim on payments and collateral from the mortgage pool. Figure 5.3 shows the tremendous growth in home equity asset-backed securities during the late 1990s. Outstanding asset-backed securities tripled from $33 billion in 1995 to $90 billion 1997 and grew to $286 billion by 2002, for an annual growth rate of 36 percent. Much of the lending funded by these securities is subprime in nature (Canner, Durkin, and Luckett 1998). By 2000, about 42 percent of outstanding subprime mortgages were securitized (Landerman 2001). Given the rapid increase in securitization, the percentage of recently originated loans that have been securitized is no doubt subtantially higher.

Subprime credit markets build on each other. Aggressive marketing and lax underwriting of subprime credit cards resulted in heavy debt loads, credit history problems, and increased bankruptcies. This, in turn, helped build the demand for subprime refinance loans, which were increasingly used to pay off such debt. Federal Reserve figures show that outstanding nonmortgage consumer debt increased from $840 billion in 1993 to $1.3 trillion in 1998. Manning (2000) has detailed the explosion in credit card debt in the 1980s and the 1990s, as well as the related explosion in bankruptcies, which grew from a rate of around 300,000 annually from 1980 to 1984 to between 700,000 and 900,000 from 1991 to 1995. Bankruptices then rose further to more than 1.2 million annually from 1997 to 2000. Moreoever, the onslaught of credit card soliciations in the 1980s and 1990s pushed people into having poor credit ratings. Hyperaggressive credit card solicitations hit minority communities particularly hard. Working-class families that were suffering from economic restructuring in the 1980s could not be expected to turn down all the numerous offers of easily available credit that were arriving in their mailboxes. In 1990, before the major rise of subprime lending, a researcher at the Federal Reserve Bank of Atlanta argued that "high levels of consumer debt are seriously undermining the ability of many of Atlanta's low- and moderate-income residents to qualify for home mortgage loans" (Cowell and Hagler 1992).

The explosion of credit card debt created a perfect market for subprime home equity lenders. Credit card banks created a mountain of unsecured debt, and mortgage lenders knew how to turn it into secured debt and make a tidy profit on the transactions. They only needed higher-risk sources of capital than traditional banks, savings and loans, and the government-sponsored secondary markets. They found that source in private securitization. If needed, they could segment the collateral and revenue streams to raise

Figure 5.3 **Home Equity Asset-Backed Securities, 1995–2002**

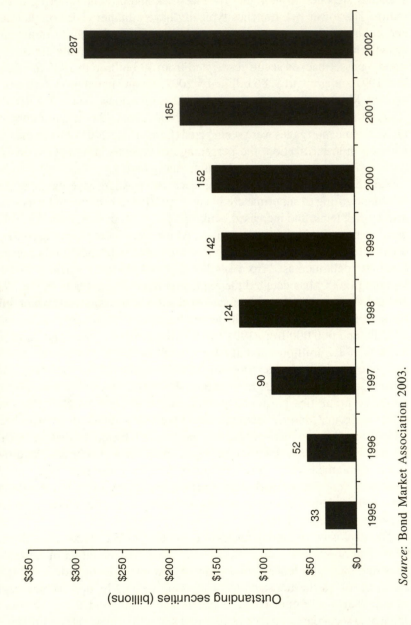

Source: Bond Market Association 2003.

money from lower-risk (and lower-cost) sources, as well as higher-risk (and higher-cost) sources. So, credit card debt, pushed by the financial services industry, created a demand for a new segment of the industry—subprime mortgage lending. Subprime lenders disproportionately make refinance loans for "cash-out" purposes, meaning the new loan is larger than the existing loan, so that the borrower removes or converts her equity to cash—often to pay off credit cards. In a survey of subprime mortgage lenders, Morgan Stanley researchers found that cash-out and debt-consolidation loans represented 58 percent of subprime lenders' activity, compared to only 25 percent of prime lenders' activities (Posner and Meehan 2002). Thus, homeowners are increasingly using their home equity to finance current consumption well before retirement, something that was not done at high rates before the 1980s.

Another critical and complementary factor in the explosion of subprime lending has been the large growth in the number of independent mortgage brokers over the last ten to twenty years. From 1991 to 1998, the number of brokers grew at an annual rate of 14 percent (Kim-Sung and Hermanson 2003). In 2000, 30,000 mortgage brokerage firms employed an estimated 240,000 workers and accounted for approximately 55 percent of all mortgage originations. Moreover, broker-originated loans are twice as likely to be subprime as lender-originated loans. Among older borrowers, brokers are also more likely to lend to divorced, female, and nonwhite borrowers. Sixty-two percent of older nonwhite borrowers received loans via brokers, while only 38 percent of white borrowers did.

Brokers are heavily associated with aggressive "push marketing." In their study of older borrowers, Kim-Sung and Hermanson (2003) found that 56 percent of borrowers with brokered loans reported that contact was initiated by the broker, while other borrowers reported that lenders initiated contact only 24 percent of the time. More than twice as many borrowers using brokers received loans with prepayment penalties (26 percent versus 12 percent), and significantly more brokered loans involved refinancing two or more times over a three-year period. Borrowers with brokered loans were generally less satisfied with their loans and were less likely to feel that they received honest information. Brokers are generally regulated only by state regulators, and the degree of such regulation tends to vary from minimal to nonexistent.

Increasing market segmentation has been facilitated by advances in information technology that have enabled banks and prime mortgage lenders to mine sophisticated databases in an effort to identify higher-income segments of the market. This plays out by race and geography, especially for banks, which continue to expand branch operations in white, affluent neighborhoods (Avery et al. 1997). As banks and prime mortgage firms compete more furiously for more affluent customers, they leave the minority and lower-income neighborhoods ripe for penetration by subprime lenders. And because the marketing and sales efforts of prime lenders are often tied to branch locations and mail solicitations, segmentation takes on a particularly geographic nature.

Gale (2001) has identified four innovations in mortgage banking technology that have supported the hypersegmentation of refinance lending markets:

1. Geodemographic marketing tools;
2. Data warehousing and mining;
3. Internet usage between wholesale lenders and brokers; and
4. Credit scoring and automated underwriting.

These innovations have worked, both individually and in combination, to provide a new set of tools for those seeking to segment mortgage customers in all sorts of ways.

Geodemographic marketing tools permit lenders to identify clusters of potential borrowers by income, age, home value, and race and ethnicity (proxied perhaps by neighborhood location). Claritas Inc., a marketing technology firm, uses neighborhood classification systems such as "Upper Crust" and "Trying Rural Times" (Gale 2001). Other firms such as Experian, Insource, PerformanceData, and A.C. Nielsen provide similar services. Zip codes and tracts are classified according to racial and ethnic characteristics.

Recently, the city of Milwaukee launched a campaign to criticize such characterization and segmentation, arguing that it stereotyped neighborhoods and impeded neighborhood sustainability and revitalization (City of Milwaukee 2003; Pawasarat and Quinn 2001). It found that CACI, a competitor of Claritas, described the residents of a category called "Distressed Neighborhoods" as follows: "They splurge on fast food, cable TV, and lottery tickets" and "unemployment is high; those who do work only have part-time jobs." Another segment is described in the following manner: "Eat at fast food chicken restaurants, smoke menthol cigarettes, and shop at Lady Footlocker." The city also found examples of significant bias in Claritas and CACI population and income projections against central-city and minority neighborhoods. These firms' segmentation models have served to legitimize neighborhood stereotypes, which are then likely to result in the segmented marketing of high- and low-cost financial products.

Data mining and warehousing involve the creation of elaborate datasets on current and potential customers. This process has been enabled by faster computers and the ability to store larger and larger quantities of data, as well as advances in data-mining algorithms and programming (Gale 2001). Lenders can now extract highly detailed data and utilize statistical models to sort "good" and "bad" prospects. Banks are leading investors in and users of data-mining operations, principally to segment customers and potential customers. In 1999, a bank research firm estimated that about half of banks with more than $1 billion in deposits used profit data to make customer decisions. According to industry analysts, banks spent an estimated $500 million in the late 1990s on software and consultants, with spending to grow at least $500 million per year in the near future (Brooks 1999). Banks use these systems to charge less lucrative customers more for specific services, and then waive fees for more affluent customers. Computer technologies inform tellers and loan officers of the "status" of different customers and allow them to provide preferential treatment for some customers over others. "Preferred" customers are also likely to get more responsive reactions when complaining about costs, terms, or services.

A variety of more specialized real estate data firms have developed targeted marketing data systems specifically for the mortgage industry, and these are widely accessible via the Internet to even the smallest mortgage brokers. But the Internet has also assisted small independent brokers in gaining access to highly sophisticated data-mining and warehouse operations maintained and sold by firms like First American Real Estate Solutions and DataQuick.[8] As of 2001, First American argued that industry-data repositories captured 85 percent of real estate transactions (Livermore 2001). Some firms provide Internet-based subscription services that allow brokers and lenders to gain access to highly customized and targeted prospect lists, using searches based on five- or nine-digit zip codes, age of borrower, recent property transactions and mortgage activity, the identity and type (subprime/prime) of the current lender, whether the loan is an FHA or Veteran's Administration loan, current cumulative loan-to-value ratio, an estimate of "available equity," other property details (e.g., current estimated market value, presence of swimming pool), as well as address and phone number. At least one firm marketing its services on the Internet explicitly states that it can provide data on "ethnicity" of homeowners.[9] Some firms offer data on pre-foreclosure filings. Such homeowners are particularly susceptible to predatory lenders who may flip them into a new loan, preventing foreclosure in the short run, but often not for very long. Moreover, while lists of borrowers with subprime loans may assist in marketing lower-cost loans to such borrowers, they may also be used to signal homeowners who are vulnerable to repeated high-cost and predatory practices. One firm, SMR Research, publishes a regular study detailing the concentrations of subprime borrowers across the country. According to its Web site, "If your company does subprime real estate lending—or wants to—the one thing you *must* know is: Where are the customers?" Thus subprime lending leads, via highly customized data systems, to more subprime marketing to the same communities and the same borrowers (SMR Research 2002).

The increased accessibility and ubiquity of the Internet has also facilitated the broker's role in the mortgage-lending process. Often, observers tend to think of the Internet as providing more direct access to mortgages to savvy, intensive rate-shoppers, and that is certainly happening to some degree. Such borrowers are likely to be disproportionately young, white, prime borrowers, thus potentially exacerbating race- and age-based lending disparities. But what has generally been ignored is the important boon that the Internet provides to mortgage brokers. Brokers can now obtain approvals from a variety of lenders in a matter of hours or even minutes via Internet connectivity. The broker has become the "Internet-enabled" link between the borrower and the lender (Gale 2001).

The problems of discrimination and redlining in mortgage markets have changed. While issues about disparities in loan approval, especially at prime lenders, remain an issue, the price and terms at which loans are made available has become a more central concern. Moreover, a hypersegmentation of borrowers, by race, age, and neighborhood, has been facilitated by technology and regulation. Rather than encouraging uniform access to all sorts of credit by all sorts of homeowners and homebuyers, the regulatory infrastructure has followed, and in some cases led, the formation of dual markets. Chapters 8 and 9 will discuss policy remedies for this situation. Some of these remedies involve legislation at state and federal levels, while others merely require the political will of regulators to implement and enforce existing laws in more effective ways.

CHAPTER 6

Mobilizing for Credit

Community Activism, Policy Adoption, and Implementation Through 1987

Cracks in the Wall

Previous chapters described historical and continuing problems in access to credit for small businesses and mortgage seekers in minority and low-income communities. While access to fair credit remains a serious problem, a stronger set of policy tools does exist today for addressing these problems compared to what existed prior to the 1970s.

This chapter focuses on the emergence of efforts by civil rights organizations, community activists, and other public interest groups to create public policies that would work to reduce discrimination and redlining in credit markets and support reinvestment in lower-income and minority neighborhoods.[1] It then goes on to detail some of the political history and policy debates involved in the creation and evolution of reinvestment and fair lending policy, including the critical role of banking regulators.

The focus of most descriptions of the history of the antiredlining or antidiscrimination campaigns around credit issues is on the early to middle 1970s, during which neighborhood activists and public interest groups played critical roles in the drafting and passage of the Home Mortgage Disclosure Act (HMDA) and the Community Reinvestment Act (CRA) (Bradford and Cincotta 1992; Squires 1992; Sidney 2003). Indeed, this period was the most critical in the formation of community reinvestment policy and had a strong impact on the implementation of fair lending law. However, the origin of activism around access to credit and fair lending issues certainly went back further than the late 1960s and early 1970s. As seen in earlier chapters, the recognition of lending discrimination goes back well into the nineteenth and even eighteenth centuries in the United States. However, well-organized advocacy on this topic did not become common until the post–World War II era and was directly influenced by the civil rights movement of the 1950s and 1960s.

Occasional policy actions on these issues occurred much earlier than the 1970s. As early as 1946, the U.S. Department of Justice filed a complaint in New York against the Mortgage Conference of New York and twenty-eight of the city's leading financial institutions.[2] The suit charged them with causing the "exclusion of certain minority racial and national groups from certain areas" by the denial of mortgage loans. The suit alleged that they "prepared, published . . . and distributed maps of each section of New York City showing blocks on which Negroes and Spanish-speaking persons resided" and refused to lend to such areas. The defendants did not contest the case and settled in 1948 (Abrams 1955, 165).

Studies of social movements in the United States point to the cold war as having a profound effect on the civil rights movement (Fisher 1994). Groups like the National Association for the Advancement of Colored People (NAACP) had been fighting housing discrimination since the 1920s, but with little success. The advent of the cold war made institutionalized racism and legalized segregation more of an international embarrassment to the United States. President Truman warned that "those with competing philosophies . . . have tried to prove our democracy an empty fraud, and our nation a consistent oppressor of underprivileged people" (Fisher 1994, 85). The NAACP was quick to capitalize on this opportunity. At the same time, a new wave of black migration was putting severe housing pressures on the already segregated cities in northern states. Local neighborhood improvement associations had successfully defended racially restrictive covenants, which kept housing inaccessible to blacks, in state courts. But in 1948, in *Shelley v. Kraemer*, the U.S. Supreme Court held that such covenants were not enforceable. The national civil rights groups had more power at the federal level than the neighborhood improvement groups, and now they had the support of an increasing number of federal policymakers.

Shelley v. Kraemer made a crack in the wall of institutionalized and legalized housing segregation in the United States. It gave civil rights groups a clear victory on which to build and sent a signal to the real estate industry that other barriers might begin to fall. The victory had a heartening effect on the civil rights community, and in particular enshrined fair housing as a part of the larger movement. One early example of protest led by civil rights activists against redlining practices by banks occurred in Harlem in 1955. Congressmen Adam Clayton Powell, a leading early civil rights figure, organized a boycott of white-owned banks in Harlem due to the "refusal of these banks in the Harlem area to lend any money for mortgages and improvement of property in this area" (Walker 1998, 313, 314). Powell's church, Abyssinian Baptist, had withdrawn funds from the banks, and he urged others to do the same and to deposit those funds in Harlem's black-owned Carver

Federal. Five years earlier, the local NAACP had produced evidence of disparate small business lending patterns at Harlem's white-owned banks, showing that they had made essentially no loans to Harlem businesses.

The First Step—The Fair Housing Act

Abrams's seminal work on housing discrimination, *Forbidden Neighbors*, was published in 1955. The book led to a great deal more attention to the problems of housing discrimination generally, including lending discrimination and redlining. Two years later, the U.S. Commission on Civil Rights was created, and it began looking into discrimination in various sectors, including housing. The commission was charged with a number of duties. A key one was to "appraise the laws and policies of the Federal Government with respect to equal protection of the laws under the Constitution" (U.S. Commission on Civil Rights 1961, xi). In 1959 the commission found that "housing . . . seems to be the one commodity in the American market that is not freely available on equal terms to everyone who can afford to pay" (U.S. Commission on Civil Rights 1961, 1). The commission held public hearings on housing and other issues in San Francisco, Los Angeles, and Detroit in 1960. These hearings included testimony on redlining and lending discrimination and provided substantial media attention on these issues. In 1962, a year after the U.S. Commission on Civil Rights report, President Kennedy issued Executive Order 11063, which prohibited discrimination in the use of federally funded or managed housing programs, including Federal Housing Administration and Veterans Administration loans.

Following race riots and urban unrest in cities across the country from 1965 to 1968, Congress passed the Civil Rights Act in 1968. The legislative history of the act shows that Congress and the National Advisory Commission on Civil Disorders, better known as the Kerner Commission, found that residential segregation and "slum formation" were major causes of urban unrest (Massey and Denton 1993; Nier 1999). Title VIII of the Civil Rights Act, known as the Fair Housing Act (FaHA), called for the prohibition of discrimination in home lending. However, exactly which forms of discrimination were covered by the new law was left up to the courts for interpretation. The courts, at least for the first years of the act, generally were quite restrictive over what constituted lending discrimination under the law. Even though the law was intended to prohibit discrimination in access to credit, it was interpreted by the courts to cover primarily the denial of formal loan applications, not marketing or sales practices. The affected party had to demonstrate that she attempted to obtain a loan and that she met all the relevant qualifications. The borrower also had to show that the lender continued to make loans to similarly qualified applicants after the denial of her loan (Walter 1995).

In a 1976 case, *Laufman v. Oakley*, the courts ruled that the FaHA extended to redlining. However, the courts defined redlining as the practice of "denying loans" for housing in certain neighborhoods, even if the applicants were creditworthy. Again, redlining was not defined to include the exclusion of certain neighborhoods in marketing or outreach efforts. It is important to understand the severe limitations of the Fair Housing Act in preventing discrimination or redlining in home lending, especially as it was originally written and then interpreted by the courts. The courts held that plaintiffs must be able to show that the lender acted with "discriminatory animus" due to the race or location of the applicant (Nier 1999). Thus, if a lender had a policy, such as minimum loan amount, that only had the "effect" of rejecting black applicants or applicants from lower-income neighborhoods, it was not guilty of discrimination. Of course, this begged the question of whether such lending policies were merely "cover" for racial bias and whether, regardless of the motivation, such practices should be covered by the law.

There were other problems with using the FaHA as a tool for fighting lending discrimination and redlining (Dane 1993; Massey and Denton 1993). Before some 1988 amendments to the law, the act had little teeth. The Department of Housing and Urban Development (HUD), the enforcing agency, was only allowed to engage in "conference, conciliation, and persuasion" as the means of enforcing the law. It could refer a case to the Justice Department, but the attorney general was generally authorized to act only if there was evidence of a "pattern and practice" of discrimination. Only 10 percent of the cases that HUD could not conciliate were referred to the attorney general, and a very small number of these were pursued (Massey and Denton 1993).

In 1988, after Democrats took control of the Senate, several amendments to the Fair Housing Act were passed. The amendments permitted court costs to be recovered by plaintiffs if they were victorious, created a process for trying cases before an administrative law judge in HUD, and empowered these judges to compensate victims for damages as well as levy substantial fines. The amendments also permitted the secretary of HUD to initiate fair housing investigations, rather than merely respond to complaints. Notwithstanding these improvements to the law, the FaHA remained a far-from-perfect tool for fighting lending discrimination and redlining.

First, the act generally relies on the victim of discrimination to recognize that she has been discriminated against. The history of discrimination and redlining has made many minorities "accustomed" to rejection and less likely to question or contest it. In addition, even if a victim does feel that discrimination has occurred, it is highly likely that she will not pursue the matter. In a national survey in 2001, almost a quarter of blacks and Latinos reported that they had been victims of housing discrimination (Abravanel and Cunningham 2002). Of those saying they had been discriminated against, 83 percent did nothing about it. Only 3 percent reported that they sought help from a fair housing group, only 1 percent filed a formal complaint with a government agency, and only 1 percent talked to a lawyer. Many felt that filing complaints would be futile.

Only rarely are financial institutions successfully sued for fair lending violations by individual borrowers, and even more rarely are they seriously disciplined for such actions. Moreover, HUD, which has primary responsibility for handling FaHA complaints, has generally not been adequately funded to handle even the complaints that it receives. Squires (2002) adds that the "predominant problem is trying to use individual, case-by-case complaint processing to respond to what is in fact a set of structural and institutional problems." Galster (1999) argues that relying on complaints or responses from victims of housing discrimination is a fundamental flaw in the FaHA and that more proactive measures, including matched-pair testing, are needed. The FaHA does not require any collection or reporting of lending data. Under 1989 changes to the HMDA, data on the race of loan applicants was collected from most mortgage lenders. But this did not resolve the fundamental limitations of the Fair Housing Act.

Beyond the FaHA's fundamental design flaws as a tool to fight lending discrimination and redlining, there was also the question of implementation by regulators. The FaHA's was the first clear indication that federal bank and thrift regulators were not very supportive of policies that attempted to address discrimination and redlining. In 1971, after seeing no signs that bank regulators were taking any actions to enforce the FaHA's, a group of eleven civil rights organizations, the National Urban League, and twelve other civil rights and public interest groups petitioned bank regulators to develop and issue fair lending regulations (Goering and Wienk 1996, 401). By the middle 1970s, other agencies, including the Office of Management and Budget and the Department of Justice, called for action by the regulators. By 1976, only one regulator (the Federal Home Loan Bank Board) had issued final regulations, and those fell far short of what advocates had requested. The other regulators only proposed requiring banks to adopt nondiscrimination policies and display equal opportunity posters in their lobbies.

In 1974, the four bank regulators agreed to a pilot study involving collecting mortgage application data in eighteen metropolitan areas (Goering and Wienk 1996, 402). Even after controlling for income and other factors, the data showed that minority applicants were rejected for loans at rates significantly higher than whites. Despite this evidence, the regulators continued to drag their feet on larger-scale data collection regulations. Advocates fought hard to push regulators to collect and analyze data on a regular basis. Then, in 1976, the Urban League sued the agencies. Settlement agreements were reached with all but the Federal Reserve Board (FRB), which remained recalcitrant. The Office of the Comptroller of the Currency (OCC), for example, established a significant data collection and analysis effort, although it was seriously limited in its ability to detect discrimination (Goering and Wienk 1996).

In 1976, as the Urban League was settling its suit with three of the regulators, the agencies testified before the Senate that they were reluctant to create enforcement measures except those that were designed to address previously known violations of the act. Examinations of lending data or testing procedures were not being used. Furthermore, the FRB declared that it would not analyze data HMDA data to detect possible fair lending violations (Bradford and Marino 1977). (Chapter 7 discusses more recent developments in fair lending enforcement, including a period of increased enforcement in the middle 1990s and the activities of nonprofit fair housing groups.)

As bank regulators limped along in their implementation of the FaHA, the overall issue of fair access to credit—not just in housing—was beginning to receive more attention. In 1972, the National Commission on Consumer Finance held hearings on women's access to credit. The commission heard a large amount of what it termed "anecdotal evidence" that single women had more trouble obtaining credit than single men did (Smith 1977). It also heard testimony that women were often required to reapply for credit after getting married, and that lenders were frequently unwilling to consider a married woman's income when a couple applied for a loan. Although the commission did not recommend any federal action on the issue, the House of Representatives soon held hearings regarding access to credit among women. By late October 1974, the Equal Credit Opportunity Act (ECOA) was signed into law by President Ford. In 1976, ECOA was amended to prohibit lending discrimination by race and age as well as gender.

In some ways, ECOA was a stronger, more robust law than the Fair Housing Act. It covered lending discrimination in nonhousing areas, including small business and consumer lending. Also, the legislative history of the ECOA demonstrated that Congress intended for the law to cover more than "disparate treatment" in the making of loans but also something termed "disparate impact."[3] Disparate treatment is when lenders explicitly use race as a factor to treat potential borrowers differently. Disparate impact occurs when individuals or businesses receive equivalent treatment but a lending policy tends to have a disparate, adverse impact on members of a minority group or another protected class. Even if a lender applies a certain policy universally, if it tends to adversely affect minority borrowers, then it can be justified only if there is a "business necessity" for such a policy. A common example of a policy with disparate impact is the use of a minimum loan amount. Since minority homebuyers tend to buy less expensive homes than white buyers, on average, a minimum loan size can have a disparate impact on minority applicants.

ECOA has advantages in that it clearly covers a variety of participants in the credit process. For example, it includes those purchasers of loans who participate in the decision to extend credit and those who "arrange" credit, including mortgage brokers. It also requires lenders to provide rejected applicants with an explanation of why their loans were denied. On the other hand, like the FaHA, ECOA does not call for any data collection or reporting. Moreover, at least twelve federal agencies have enforcement authority under ECOA, including five over mortgage transactions alone (Dane 1993). This can lead to confusion among victims and sometimes a passing of the buck by regulators.

Neighborhood Organizing—A New Force in the Fight for Fair Credit

While federal fair lending laws were being implemented—or not being implemented in some cases—the neighborhood organizing movement across the United States had built up substantial capacity. A movement that in many respects operated both parallel to and separate from the civil rights movement, neighborhood organizing in the 1960s frequently involved mobilizing citizens of urban neighborhoods to confront government in order to block highway and urban renewal projects that they felt were harming their communities. One observer estimates that, in 1970 alone, there were approximately 400 ongoing community struggles just against highway construction plans (Fisher 1994, 137).

Neighborhood organizing in the United States dates back to at least the late nineteenth century, when settlement house movements, such as Jane Addams's Hull House, began working in poor neighborhoods for the betterment of low-income immigrants. Settlement houses were often dominated by altruistic members of the societal elite. This "social welfare" model of organizing *for* low-income residents was soon challenged by those who believed that residents should be trained and empowered to work for their own betterment. In the 1930s, a young organizer named Saul Alinsky invented a new form of organizing built on local empowerment rather than outside benevolence. Ironically, Alinsky studied under E. W. Burgess in sociology at the University of Chicago and so was well acquainted with the ecological theories of social disorganization emanating from Burgess and Robert Park (Horwitt 1989). But he also worked with Clifford Shaw of the Chicago Area Project, who in some ways originated the concept of helping lower-income communities strengthen themselves. Alinsky extended Shaw's work by joining economic justice issues and direct-action advocacy methods to confront city government and other forces outside the neighborhood. He understood the importance of higher-level resources and power. His organizing in Chicago neighborhoods such as Back of the Yards and Woodlawn laid a blueprint for neighborhood groups all over the country to organize for political and economic power. He developed a set of strategies and tactics focused on building power and using it forcefully. He advocated for the use of high-profile confrontation with those who had the power to change policies. Unfortunately, while Alinsky himself rejected racism, some of the organizations he founded evolved into neighborhood-protection, racist organizations. Moreover, some of his tactics were adopted by such groups around the country.

Neighborhood organizations of the 1940s and 1950s were typically reactionary and focused on maintaining neighborhood homogeneity and property values by fighting "infiltration" by minorities (Fisher 1994; Sugrue 1996). In the early 1960s, radical left-wing organizers had tried, generally with little success, to use neighborhood organizing as a strategy for building political power. The most successful neighborhood organizing groups in the 1960s were fighting not to overturn the capitalist system but against concrete problems in their neighborhoods and specific processes that they viewed as unjust and harmful to their communities.

The growing acknowledgment of bank redlining and its tie to blockbusting and other real estate problems gave neighborhood activists a new target. Some Alinsky followers argued that banking and lending were too complex to be good subjects for neighborhood action, but others were undeterred (Bradford and Cincotta 1992). Organizing against redlining and bank disinvestment began before HMDA and CRA were enacted. Neighborhood groups looked to the financial institutions themselves first, sometimes using confrontational approaches and at other times employing more collaborative tactics. An early documented case of community-based reaction to bank disinvestment occurred in Milwaukee in 1964. Park State Bank announced that it was closing its west side branch. Four years later, community organizations convinced the parent holding company of Park State Bank to establish a new bank in the neighborhood (Glabere 1992). Soon after that, the local NAACP and other black organizations helped establish a black-owned bank, the North Milwaukee State Bank, in the city. Glabere has suggested that these actions had a formative influence on Senator William Proxmire's later attention to issues of redlining and reinvestment.

In Pittsburgh, the first "public private neighborhood reinvestment initiative" began in 1957 with the creation of the Allegheny Council to Improve Our Neighborhoods–Housing, or ACTION-Housing (Metzger 1992). ACTION-Housing approached local banks to finance new and rehabilitated housing for moderate-income households in Pittsburgh neighborhoods. Later, in 1968, ACTION-Housing worked with other neighborhood groups and thirteen local banks and savings and loans to help create the nation's first Neighborhood Housing Services (NHS) program on the city's central north side as a response to redlining. NHS later expanded to many other cities and remains a successful model of a community development financial institution.

While there was undoubtedly some community reinvestment organizing of various sorts going on in the late 1950s and 1960s in cities throughout the country, most longtime observers of CRA activism point to Chicago as the birthplace of larger-scale, and often more confrontational, CRA organizing. Chicago, after all, was Alinsky's hometown, and by 1970 there were scores of Alinsky-style neighborhood groups in the city. Many of these groups had leaders who were veterans of organizing battles involving urban renewal and similar fights with powerful opponents. In 1969, Gale Cincotta, a resident of the west side Austin neighborhood and president of the Organization for a Better Austin (OBA), joined with other organizations to form the West Side Coalition (Pogge 1992; Christiano 1995). OBA had been organized in part by Tom Gaudette, an Alinsky disciple and leader in the "new populist" neighborhood organizing movement.

Mariano (2003) describes how in 1971, two people walked into the offices of the Northwest Community Organization (NCO), a strong Alinsky-style group on the city's near northwest side, after being turned down for loans at a local bank. An NCO committee visited the bank to discuss its lending policy and was told that the bank was an active lender in the community. When pressed, the bank told the group that it declined the loans because of their locations. After a variety of tactics aimed at getting the bank to change its lending policies failed, the group started what it called a "bank-in." Fifty to sixty community group members showed up with hundreds of pennies each "asking the bank tellers to count them, or asking for withdrawals in pennies." This action won the group a meeting with the bank's board of directors that same afternoon, and they soon negotiated a $4 million agreement under which the bank pledged to increase its lending in the community (Bradford and Cincotta 1992). Afterward, other groups in Chicago were asking NCO how to do "bank-ins." NCO was at the time run by Shel Trapp, an organizer who had worked with Gale Cincotta at OBA, and Trapp had been involved in the West Side Coalition. In March of the next year, Cincotta and Trapp organized the National Housing Conference to discuss housing issues. Soon afterward, Cincotta and Trapp started the Housing Training and Information Center (later the National Training and Information Center) and the national network now known as National People's Action (NPA).

In 1971, the Center for Community Change issued a report examining housing abandonment in New York City and found that redlining was a critical factor in the deterioration of apartment buildings there (Christiano 1995). In 1972, a community organization called the South Shore Commission led a coalition of community groups in challenging the application of the South Shore National Bank that had petitioned the OCC to relocate from the South Shore neighborhood on Chicago's South Side to downtown (Woodstock Institute 1978). The coalition argued that the bank should not be able to leave the neighborhood without a bank. The OCC denied the application, commenting that the bank had not sufficiently responded to the harm that the move would do to the community. The bank was subsequently sold to new owners who turned it into what is now the internationally recognized Shorebank, the largest community development bank in the United States.

After the first NCO bank-in, the Metropolitan Area Housing Alliance (MAHA) in Chicago began confronting more financial institutions about their lack of lending in certain neighborhoods. MAHA then convinced the Federal Home Loan Bank Board to survey banks on their lending and reported the findings by zip code. The analysis showed substantial disparities across zip codes (Squires 1992). Then, in 1974, the Organization for the North East (O.N.E.), a coalition of residents and neighborhood institutions on Chicago's far north lakefront, negotiated a formal, written "understanding" with the Bank of Chicago, a local community bank. The purpose of the agreement was to implement policies "of reciprocal positive support between the bank and the surrounding community residents, businesses, and institutions" (Pogge 1992). The Bank of Chicago agreement did not include specific dollar amount goals for lending, but the bank agreed to prioritize loans to depositors and residents in targeted areas and to report on the geographical distribution of its loans. O.N.E., in turn, agreed to designate the bank as "community responsive," to help the bank in seeking public-sector deposits, and to promote the bank in the community. O.N.E. then launched similar negotiations with other local banks and, by the end of 1974, had reached agreement with three more community banks. The ability of community organizations to negotiate with banks in the absence of HMDA or CRA, as O.N.E. had done, was rare. But O.N.E. was a powerful organization, including a number of strong churches and neighborhood institutions, and was located in a neighborhood known for its activism and attention to the concerns of low-income residents.

Grassroots community organizations were used to fighting against city hall, and sometimes against the state legislature, but they often had little experience in Washington. This helps explain why some states and cities took action against redlining and lending discrimination before the federal government did. California passed a law in 1964 that required state-chartered savings and loans to submit a range of data on lending patterns to the savings and loan commissioner. In Chicago in 1974, the city council passed an ordinance requiring all banks accepting municipal deposits to disclose neighborhood-level data on lending and deposit activity. The state of Illinois then passed two antiredlining laws, including a disclosure bill and an antidiscrimination statute. Other cities, including Minneapolis, Cleveland, and Los Angeles, also enacted various antiredlining or fair lending ordinances.

First the Home Mortgage Disclosure Act, Then the Community Reinvestment Act

Supporters of federal antiredlining policies did not begin with CRA. The notion of pushing through a statute that obligated banks to serve their local communities, and to penalize those that did not, was seen as a politically unfeasible first step. Instead, in the spring of 1974, community activists, led by Cincotta's NPA, met with Ken McLean, a staffer from Senator William Proxmire of Wisconsin, the number two Democrat on the Senate Committee on Banking, Housing, and Urban Affairs. McLean had grown up on Chicago's southwest side, a part of town threatened with decline. He had discussed issues of neighborhood decay with Proxmire in the past and arranged a meeting with the senator for NPA. The next year, Proxmire became chair of the banking committee and offered to introduce a bill calling for data collection and disclosure on savings and lending patterns by banks and thrifts. Proxmire was an ideal sponsor. He was a former journalist and publishing executive with a knack for dealing with the media. When he became chair of the banking committee, McLean became its staff director and hired Robert Kuttner, who became point person for the bill. The legislation was introduced the day after the release of an OCC survey of six cities showing that minorities were rejected for loans at twice the rate of whites of similar income levels (Hallahan 1992).

Community groups originally wanted a bill covering small business as well as housing loans, but that was not feasible at the time (Bradford and Cincotta 1992). Proxmire introduced a bill to require the collection and disclosure of data on home mortgage loans on a loan-by-loan level as well as data on deposit accounts. In the House, Fernand St. Germain, the Democratic chair of the Subcommittee on Financial Institution Regulation, sponsored a similar bill. A larger part of the justification for these bills was to inform consumers of their banks' lending patterns so they could choose where to bank. Thus, HMDA was pitched as a consumer right-to-know bill, in part due to the growing congressional popularity of consumer-lending regulations in the 1970s, which were often based on disclosure (Moskowitz 1987).

HMDA was a highly contested piece of legislation.[4] Studies demonstrating uneven lending patterns were presented from Chicago, Baltimore, Milwaukee, and other cities. Gale Cincotta testified in favor the bill, as did representatives from the National Committee Against Discrimination in Housing and other advocacy groups.

Industry interests were quickly represented by a coalition opposing the bill led by Senator Jake Garn, a Utah Republican, and Representative John Rousselot, a California Republican. Very early on, the bill was changed to call only for the disclosure of data aggregated at the census tract level, with no race or gender information.

Proxmire took the lead in pushing HMDA but soon ran into difficulties in his own committee. A Democratic senator from New Hampshire was concerned about the impact of the bill on banks in his state, and a Republican from Massachusetts was sympathetic to industry arguments that the costs would be too high. Proxmire agreed to exclude savings data to reduce concerns about the costs to industry. He also limited coverage to metropolitan areas, which effectively eliminated almost all of New Hampshire from the act's impact. These two issues helped to reduce opposition by making the defeat of the bill a lower priority for the banking industry. The removal of rural areas made the bill of little interest to thousands of small banks. In exchange for giving up these items, Proxmire was able to change the reporting geography from zip code to census tract, which allowed for more precise disclosure.

While industry interests, the FRB, and HUD opposed HMDA, the bill had a good deal of public appeal. Proxmire and his allies were successful in making a strong connection between redlining and neighborhood decline in Senate hearings. After many close votes and bargaining, the Senate and House bills went to conference. The success of the bill in the Senate especially relied heavily on the role of ideologically centrist Democrats and Republicans, often from northern states, who drove much of the compromise (Moskowitz 1987). In the House, less bargaining occurred, but St. Germain used logrolling and distraction measures to win HMDA. HMDA was Title III of St. Germain's Depository Institutions Amendments Act, which contained some high-priority issues for thrifts in particular. Another part of the larger bill permitted the nationwide offering of Negotiable Orders of Withdrawal accounts—checking accounts that paid interest—by savings and loans. This focused the resources of the American Bankers Association on this provision and away from HMDA. The larger bill also included an extension of Regulation Q, which capped savings deposit rates for banks at a lower rate than for thrifts, giving thrifts a clear competitive advantage in the deposit market.

After passage of HMDA in 1975, community activists and public interest groups kept up the pressure for moving beyond HMDA. While HMDA is appropriately considered largely a creature of grassroots consumer activism, the advocacy and political organizing involved in the passage of CRA involved a stronger role for Washington-based public interest groups and other allies. These included civil rights groups, Ralph Nader's operation, and mayors from around the country.

CRA was introduced in the Senate by Senator Proxmire in January of 1977. It was debated in the full Senate but not in the House and was reported out of conference committee in September 1977. It was signed by President Carter in October as Title VIII of the 1977 Housing and Community Development Act. The fight for CRA was eased in many respects by the groundwork laid by the victory on HMDA. The HMDA congressional debate had already placed redlining and disinvestment on the federal agenda (Dennis 1978; Sidney 2003). It had also effectively tied redlining to neighborhood decline.

The political environment in the mid-to-late 1970s is important to keep in mind when considering the design of the CRA bill. Unlike in the late 1960s, social and racial justice was not high on the policy agendas of Congress or the executive branch. Two clear trends had taken hold in Washington policymaking that were relevant to the CRA debate. One was the growing power of advocates for deregulation in all sorts of historically regulated industries, including airlines, telecommunications, and banking. As discussed in chapter 2, Keynesian economists who dominated federal policymaking from the middle 1930s through the 1960s had moved into disfavor. Led by Milton Friedman, monetarist and deregulationist ideology had ascended as the new dominant force in regulatory policymaking. Even the Democrats' economists, such as Charles Schultze and Alfred Kahn, pushed deregulatory initiatives in a wide variety of regulated industries. The economists at the Federal Reserve had traditionally been skeptical of regulation and became more so in the 1960s and 1970s. Despite the movement in Congress for increased consumer protection policies in credit markets in the 1970s, the Federal Reserve and other regulators were generally resistant. They were much more supportive of deregulatory moves like the Depository Institutions Deregulation and Monetary Control Act (DIDMCA) of 1980, the granting of interstate branching requests, and the relaxation of separations between banking and securities businesses.

The second characteristic of the political environment in the middle-to-late 1970s was some level of negative public reaction to the Great Society programs of the 1960s and the civil rights movement. More and more, conservatives were effectively and pejoratively describing the social and racial justice movements as just additional "special interests." The climate was not very good for programs seen as primarily benefiting minority homebuyers or minority small businesses. On top of this, the Nixon administration had moved away from federally mandated solutions in urban and housing policy toward local decisionmaking and "public-private" partnerships (Hays 1995; Orlebeke 2000). The Carter administration continued this trend by supporting moves to block grants. Carter also favored neighborhood-based initiatives over traditional federally directed urban programs.

Those crafting and working for CRA recognized these trends, especially the hostility to race-based policies and strong regulation. Some CRA advocates were even sympathetic to some of these perspectives. Two of the leaders in the early community reinvestment movement described it as "conservative, both in its opposition to big government and its reliance on the private sector. It is American in its fundamental support for the free enterprise system with its focus on the engine of private capital" (Bradford and Cincotta 1992, 230).[5] Supporters of the CRA bill were very cognizant of the more conservative environment of the late 1970s, and they designed and adapted the policy proposal to accommodate the situation (Sidney 2003). Congressional supporters portrayed the bill as a minor clarification or adjustment to an existing framework governing the industry. Since 1935, federal banking law had held that banks were chartered to meet the "convenience and needs of their communities." Proxmire portrayed CRA in the legislative debate as clarifying and strengthening this statement:

> . . . unfortunately many bankers and bank regulators have forgotten the meaning of those words . . . convenience and needs does not just mean drive-in teller windows and Christmas Club accounts. . . . It means loans. (Proxmire quoted in Sidney 2003)

In fact, regulators, especially the FRB, publicly opposed CRA on the stated grounds that they already had the authority to assess credit flows. The board even claimed that it already did so. In many ways, supporters portrayed CRA as a law aimed more at regulators than at banks. It was a forceful command to regulators to do their jobs and pay attention to redlining issues. The regulators had been taken to task in the HMDA hearings and elsewhere for poor enforcement of the Fair Housing Act. The legislative history suggests that CRA was in large part a "congressional rebuke" to the four bank and thrift regulators and a clear message for them to emphasize urban lending obligations as an important component of the public purpose for which they were chartered. Regulators did not employ "systematic, affirmative" programs to encourage lenders to evaluate how well banks served their communities (Dennis 1978). Yet regulators could have been doing this and could have used their authority in approving charter changes to encourage banks to meet community credit needs.

Many reinvestment advocates had been disappointed with the final version of HMDA, wishing that it had included more detailed data, including racial data and data on small business loans (Bradford and Cincotta 1992). Congressional supporters downplayed the role of community activists and organizers in CRA, fearing that it would incur more opposition from the banking industry and regulators. More importantly, perhaps, supporters avoided discussions of race in the CRA debate. On the Senate floor, race was mentioned only once (Sidney 2003, 62). CRA was described as being about neighborhoods, more about lower-income places, than about individuals. At the same time, the term "inner city" was used extensively to describe areas particularly affected by redlining, clearly signifying a concern with predominantly minority neighborhoods.

While the CRA was not as contested as HMDA, there was still significant opposition. Senator Garn, the leader of the anti-HMDA coalition in 1975, also worked against CRA. He argued the deregulationist line, and seemed to be ignorant of the strong history of public-sector involvement in banking and mortgage markets:

> I would like you to know there are some members of this committee who feel that it is the banking industry and savings and loan industry in this county who have been responsible for building this (country) and not government. Damn it to hell, we have had 200 years of the private sector building the greatest country.[6]

The senator's statement belied the history of Hamilton's First Bank of the United States, the highly active role of states in initiating and supporting banking, and the critical role of regulation, deposit insurance, and a wide variety of subsidies and supports to the financial services sector throughout the nation's history.

The basic justification used to argue for CRA was that banks and thrifts were given public charters in large part to serve the "convenience and needs" of their communities, and thus the public had a right to expect them to fulfill that obligation. As Proxmire put it, "a public charter conveys numerous economic benefits and in return it is legitimate for public policy and regulatory practice to require some public purpose." In another statement he said, "It is fair for the public to ask something in return."[7]

In reviewing the legislative history of CRA, Dennis (1978) argued that during the 1970s Congress took a broader view of the role of financial institutions in the economy and "enacted numerous consumer protection and civil rights measures which place affirmative responsibilities on depository institutions beyond the mere obligation to operate safely and soundly, and which give the financial regulatory agencies responsibility as 'enforcers' in the compliance scheme." Moreover, HMDA's preamble set the stage for CRA by declaring that "some depository institutions have sometimes contributed to the decline of certain geographic areas by their failure pursuant to their chartering responsibilities to provide adequate home financing to qualified applicants on reasonable terms and conditions."[8]

The legislative history demonstrated that the purpose of CRA was more than "stopping redlining" (Dennis 1978). The purpose was also to rebuild and revitalize inner-city and other struggling areas. One important discussion in the legislative debate was over the concern that regulators too often excused a lack of lending activity by the scarcity of "demand." This was consistent to some degree with the courts' interpretation of fair lending laws governing the approval of formal loan applications and placing the burden on borrowers to formally seek financing. Fair lending law, especially at this time, did not really cover disparities or unfairness in marketing. Ron Gryzwinski, a cofounder of Shorebank, the community development bank in Chicago, testified that demand often had to be stimulated in lower-income communities, especially those suffering from legacies of disinvestment and redlining. Proxmire put it succinctly:

> Demand in our economy is not a passive, fixed thing. It is manipulated and promoted. If a banker is willing to get out of the office he will find it. This bill will encourage him to do so.[9]

To make his case, Proxmire pointed to Shorebank, the Philadelphia Mortgage Plan, and other programs that had successfully made loans in lower-income and minority neighborhoods.

One common misperception is that the CRA legislation was intended to be aimed solely at access to mortgages. In fact, some banks have argued that regulators' review of small business lending is not authorized by the statute. While it is true that the legislative discussion emphasized housing lending, it also discussed small business loans. In opening the hearings on the Senate bill, Proxmire commented that a premise of the bill was that private financial institutions should play the "leading role" in providing capital for "local housing and economic development needs."[10] Proxmire also argued that banks should have "aggressive, affirmative programs of local housing and small business lending" in low- and moderate-income neighborhoods. Senator John Heinz (R-Pennsylvania) argued that the legislation would make lenders more sensitive "to the requirements of lending both to residential and small business entities."[11]

Regulators and congressional and financial industry opponents branded the bill "credit allocation." They argued that banks would be required to make a specific number of loans or portion of its loans in a certain community. One key opponent denounced the bill as a "foot in the door" toward mandatory credit allocation (McCluskey 1983). Arthur Burns, the chairman of the FRB, argued that the bill could lead to a regulatory nightmare as regulators tried to develop lending targets for thousands of communities across the country.

The CRA proposal went through three versions before it was enacted, and after each draft, the bill was moderated further. Enforcement mechanisms were based largely on the existing merger and branch approval process, with the examination procedure expanded to cover CRA concerns. To the chagrin of many community reinvestment advocates, who had seen regulators move slowly on fair lending law, the final bill also relied heavily on the discretion of the regulatory agencies. The bill left much of the CRA process to administrative regulation and, as a result of the rules that followed, to examiner judgment. The reliance on examiner discretion, especially in bank evaluations or examinations, was a strong tradition in bank regulation (Khademian 1996). Regulators reacted very negatively to the notion of any highly prescriptive legislation that might tell them how to evaluate the community reinvestment record of a bank or thrift (Dennis 1978).

Besides the skillful reading of the political environment in Congress by Proxmire and others, the bill benefited from at least three other factors. First, its insertion into the larger Housing and Community Development Act reduced some of the scrutiny that it might have otherwise received. That bill included changes to the Community Development Block Grant (CDBG) program, a major new local funding program that was only three years old. Legislators focus heavily on CDBG matters, and so the CRA portion received less attention by most congressmen (Sidney 2003). Second, the highly specialized and complex nature of banking regulation reduced the attention that CRA received from rank-and-file legislators. Congressmen often defer to committee heads or those with recognized expertise on more specialized, complex issues. By lining up Senator Proxmire as the key sponsor of the bill, CRA advocates achieved perhaps the critical step to the bill's passage. Finally, the bill received relatively minor attention from the organized banking lobbies such as the American Bankers Association. Some individual banks argued against the bill and the regulators opposed it. But other issues were more pressing to the bank lobbies. Again, this period was a formative one for major bank deregulation legislation, particularly the 1980 DIDMCA. Banks were focused on their own problems, such as financial disintermediation, in which depositors were pulling deposits out of banks and putting them in new money market mutual funds.

One very key change in the CRA bill that occurred during the legislative process was a change in the notion of what constituted the "community" of a financial institution. The legislative history suggests that some supporters of the bill had originally constructed a definition of redlining as dependent on a bank or thrift taking deposits from a neighborhood and then "exporting" those funds via loans to households and firms in some other, generally more affluent area. In this sense, banks were not strictly "reinvesting" the funds of neighborhood depositors in the neighborhoods from which they came. Despite the general lack of data on the balance between deposits and loans in low- and moderate-income neighborhoods, some activists appeared to have a notion that there was a surplus of deposits over loans in many if not most poorer neighborhoods. Underlying this notion was the concept of locally isolated financial and mortgage markets. It was perhaps a notion that was relevant for the early building and loan model, where savers would pool their funds and then invest those same funds in mortgages for members, who were usually living in the same small community. However, this model of reinvestment was antiquated.

Financial institutions, in the absence of discriminatory and redlining practices, functioned to redistribute funds across urban space. In fact, ideally, they would be expected to take surplus savings from capital-rich, often wealthier communities, and make it available for lending and investment in communities with less household wealth. If residents and businesses in lower-income neighborhoods could only draw on the savings of fellow residents, they would be at a severe disadvantage. The problem of redlining was not just that some banks were not reinvesting the deposits of residents of low-income neighborhoods back in those same neighborhoods, though that was part of the problem. Redlining meant that banks were not reinvesting the deposits of people in middle- and upper-income neighborhoods in lower-income neighborhoods. Using the former model of small-area, isolated reinvestment would severely limit the mortgage and loan money available in lower-income neighborhoods. This narrow concept of disinvestment, focusing only on the exportation of lower-income neighborhood deposits, was "naïve, or at least incomplete," and such a construction would be counterproductive in the long run because it "ignores the more important systematic aspects" of redlining and disinvestment (Dennis 1978).

It was the incomplete, narrower notion of redlining that was used in the original draft of the bill. Dennis (1978) argued that this may have been due to the "reinforcing affect of repetitious testimony by the same witnesses before the Senate Banking Committee on the issue of redlining." In particular, he pointed to community activists from Chicago who held to the narrow view of disinvestment. From the perspective of some community organizers, it was certainly easier to mobilize residents against redlining by describing redlining as a purely local issue, in which banks were taking "our money" and exporting it to somewhere else. Organizers, after all, are often trained to make issues concrete and simplify them to enable more grass-roots understanding. This was logical; avoiding the complex workings of larger-scale mortgage markets suited their organizing purposes. However, it also influenced their notion of how community reinvestment policy ought to be designed.

In fact, mortgage markets were already significantly delocalized by the middle 1970s. While some smaller savings and loans still relied heavily on deposits from nearby neighborhoods to fund their mortgage activity, many larger lenders drew on metropolitan deposit bases to do so. Banks had already begun establishing larger territories and crossing state lines. More importantly, since the Federal Home Loan Bank System was established in the 1930s, savings and loans could borrow from the system to fund lending activity. In this way, the system provided a way to redistribute mortgage capital from capital-surplus areas to capital-short areas. In fact, this was a major justification for the creation of the home loan bank system. For mortgage companies and banks, the secondary market agencies, while not as dominant as they are today, were already established and provided for additional mobility of mortgage capital throughout the country.

The incomplete, localized notion of disinvestments was operationalized in the original draft of the CRA bill by incorporating the concept of a "primary savings service area" (PSSA). The PSSA was to be a compact area contiguous to deposit facilities. Again, the narrow view of disinvestments held that depositors near the branches would see their deposits exported off to higher-income neighborhoods and perhaps to foreign countries. Yet, as Dennis (1978) argued, this version of the act would have hurt the revitalization process:

> The view . . . ignored the problem of institutions located in affluent areas which are in proximity to "disinvested" areas. By tying the responsibility to lend primarily to the source of deposits, the early version of the law would have sanctioned decisions of suburban institutions not to make

loans in adjoining urban areas. Further, this insular view of "redlining" did not adequately address the obligations of large city or state-wide institutions, or money center banks.

Ironically, it was some of the opponents of CRA who managed to successfully argue that the PSSA and the highly localized notion of disinvestment were inappropriate. (Some community reinvestment advocates apparently also made this argument.) The primary savings service area language was dropped in conference committee and replaced by the notion of "entire community." This was the key amendment in the conference process and, given what we now know about changes in banking and financial markets, made the act much more robust. The committee substituted the language "entire community, including its low and moderate income neighborhoods" for that of PSSA. Using an example, Senator Proxmire explained the problem of the earlier primary savings service area concept:

> Thus, a Los Angeles savings and loan wishing to branch into Beverly Hills could pledge to reinvest all of the money it took out of Beverly Hills and this wouldn't help the redlined areas. (Proxmire, quoted in Dennis 1978)

A related concern involves which activities help delineate the community whose "convenience and needs" a bank is to serve. Dennis took up this question also:

> By switching to "entire community," the CRA incorporates the general approaches to setting geographic boundary patterns used traditionally by each agency in defining service area or market area, and used by the courts for the same purpose. Generally it is the area defined by the institution itself for these purposes. By including the reference to "low and moderate income neighborhoods," Congress simply provided a safeguard against "gerrymandering" out all but the most affluent areas in defining community. . . . Generic rules of thumb are already in place at the four agencies and can be adept comfortably, keeping in mind the purpose of the inquiry and the emphasis on the needs of neighborhoods. (Dennis 1978)

The Federal Deposit Insurance Corporation (FDIC) had, for example, already been using the concept of "trade area" for its application process. And the Federal Home Loan Bank Board had been distinguishing between savings areas and lending areas, recognizing that the latter would be a larger area in most cases. As Dennis put it, the "principle of identifying different geographic markets for different purposes is not new in banking law." He then argued that, in the context of the legislative history, the definition of community should depend on where the banks offers a product and should be able to be varied by product.

> A rule of reason would dictate that large banks . . . should define community for CRA purposes in terms of the parameters of the metropolitan areas where they market their "retail" activities, seek deposits, are chartered, have their home offices and make most of their loans to individuals. . . . The CRA would impact these institutions most by imposing a legal obligation to meet credit needs in the low and moderate-income neighborhoods within this community. . . . The concept of community is flexible enough to permit the use of different criteria for the same institutions in different geographic areas. (Dennis 1978)

Thus, shortly after the law was passed, a banking attorney familiar with fair lending and CRA issues argued that bank regulators had a great deal of flexibility in determining the bases for what are now called CRA assessment areas. Despite the statute's flexibility on the issue, the history of banking law regarding trade and service areas, and the deliberate shift in the concept of community during the legislative process, bank regulators have continued to limit the basis for what are now called CRA "assessment areas." They have limited the basis for these areas to be the physical branch locations of the bank. As I will discuss in chapter 9, this interpretation not only ignores the legislative history and intent of CRA, it has facilitated disinvestment and severely limited the scope and impact of CRA.

Implementing the Statute—The First Regulations

The CRA statute directed the four federal financial institution regulators— the Federal Reserve, the OCC, the Federal Home Loan Bank Board, and the FDIC—to develop regulations and operations to carry out the purpose of the act. When CRA was passed, reinvestment advocates were concerned about the vague language of the bill. They had seen the bank regulators stall on the implementation of fair lending regulations under the 1968 FaHA. Regulators had admitted in Senate hearings that even before CRA was passed, they had the power to deny mergers based on banks' not meeting the "convenience and needs" of their communities. Regulators claimed that such needs included credit needs, but that they had only taken action once in their history—the case of the old South Shore National Bank in 1972. Activists had tried to get regulators to take such actions well before 1977 (Moskowitz 1987). Senator Paul Sarbanes (D-MD) echoed these concerns in the markup session in the Senate on CRA: "I think it's clear that the agencies who implement the regulation want to do far less than what was specifically in the bill."[12]

Regulators had more than a year to draft regulations for the bill, which became effective in November 1978. They immediately faced two key questions in generating the first set of regulations. First was the definition of community. The other was defining the "affirmative obligation" of financial institutions with respect to that community. The first issue was settled in favor of a fairly broad geographic approach consistent with the shift in the third version of the legislation from a concept of a "primary savings service area" to that of an "entire community." However, rather than developing a consistent, systematic approach that institutions would follow for each type of market (e.g., mortgage versus small business loans), the regulators opted to allow banks to delineate their community areas themselves with minimal oversight. Regulators suggested two possible approaches to delineating community, but left a third, wide-open option for banks:

1. the use of existing boundaries such as those of standard metropolitan statistical areas (SMSAs) or counties in which the bank's office or offices are located . . . a small bank may delineate those portions of SMSAs or counties it reasonably may be expected to serve.
2. may use its effective lending territory, which is defined as that local area or areas around each office or group of offices where it makes a substantial portion of its loans and all other areas equidistant from its offices as those areas.
3. may use any other reasonably delineated local area that meets the purposes of the CRA and does not exclude low- and moderate-income neighborhoods.[13]

The vagueness of the last option, including uncertainty over the meaning of "does not exclude low- and moderate-income neighborhoods," proved critical to the history of CRA. Also, over time, the language suggesting the construction of community areas around branch locations became more emphasized. Yet, this shift was not consistent with the statute's legislative history. It relied more on the earlier notion of "primary savings service areas" in the original version of Proxmire's bill, which was clearly rejected in the legislative process. This issue became more important, as banks and thrifts relied less on their branches for lending operations. By 2000, 25 percent of home purchase lending done by the twenty-five largest banking organizations was done outside of counties where they had branches (Joint Center for Housing Studies 2002). For some banks, this share exceeded 85 percent.

In terms of institutions meeting their "affirmative obligations," an issue that carried over from the legislative debate was whether the regulations would favor a system focusing on outcome measures—including measures of actual lending activity—or a system that would focus more on evaluating the processes—for example, marketing and outreach efforts—that the banks appeared to undertake to meet community credit and financial services needs. Reinvestment advocates argued for the outcome measure approach, which, as chapter 7 will discuss, became the favored approach when the regulations were revised in 1995. In 1978, however, the regulators chose to adopt a heavily process-based approach.

The final regulations required each bank or thrift to prepare and make publicly available a "Community Reinvestment Act Statement" for each of its local community areas. These were to include a delineation of the areas and a list of types of credit the bank was willing to offer in each community. Banks were required to maintain a public comment file and make it available for public examination. In these files, they had to include letters that they received criticizing their lending or services as well as their most recent CRA exams. Banks were also mandated to post a public notice in their lobbies that described the CRA and the rights of potential customers under the act. The regulators then developed a list of factors that they would consider to assess a bank's CRA performance. The twelve factors were then divided into five general performance categories as shown in Table 6.1.

The regulators also made another key policy decision regarding whether and how to account for lending and services activities of affiliates or subsidiaries of banks under their supervision. The Federal Reserve, the regulator of banking holding companies, declared that "at the request of an applicant, the Board will include in its consideration of an application the record of performance of nonbanking subsidiaries of bank holding companies in helping to meet the credit needs of the communities.[14] Thus, the regulators gave banks the option of including affiliate activity for consideration in their CRA exams. If an affiliate redlined lower-income communities, a bank would certainly choose not to have its activities included in its exam. If it happened to be an active lender in lower-income communities, the bank could, after the fact, earn a sort of "extra credit" by simply opting to include the affiliate's activities. This option actually created a loophole of sorts for banks and thrifts that wished to avoid CRA scrutiny. They could funnel their mortgages to upper-income neighborhoods through their mortgage companies and leave the programs geared to low- and moderate-income borrowers in the bank itself. This would make it look like a relatively large portion of a bank's lending was to low- and moderate-income populations. This option still stands in CRA regulation today and is discussed further in chapter 9.

Table 6.1

CRA Assessment Factors Used by Regulators, 1978–1995

Category	Assessment factors
Ascertaining credit needs	1. Activities to ascertain the credit needs of its community
	2. The extent of the bank's marketing and special credit-related programs
	3. The extent of participation by the board of directors in formulating the bank's policies and reviewing its performance
Geographic loan distribution	4. Any practices intended to discourage applications
	5. The geographic distribution of credit extensions, credit applications, and credit denials
Discrimination or other illegal credit practices	6. Evidence of prohibited discriminatory or other illegal credit practices
Geographic distribution of loans	7. The bank's record of opening and closing branches and providing services at offices
Community development	8. The member bank's participation, including investments, in local community development and redevelopment projects or programs
Types of credit offered	9. The bank's origination of residential mortgage loans, housing rehabilitation loans, home improvement loans, and small business or small farm loans within its community, or the purchase of such loans originated in its community
	10. The bank's participation in governmentally insured, guaranteed, or subsidized loan programs for housing, small business, or small farms
Community development	11. The bank's ability to meet various community credit needs based on its financial condition and size and legal impediments, local economic conditions, and other factors
	12. Other factors that reasonably bear upon the extent to which a bank is helping to meet the credit needs of its entire community

Early Regulator Enforcement

In the first few years of CRA's implementation, regulators appeared to go out of their way to send a message to banks that they did not want to influence the lending patterns of banks. In examination procedures issued soon after the regulations, the agencies stated that banks would not be required to document that they were actually extending the types of credit they had listed as available in their CRA statements (McCluskey 1983). Then, in January 1980, the FRB, perhaps considered the regulator most hostile to the CRA at the time, issued a "Community Reinvestment Act Information Statement." The statement assured the industry that the board would be highly understanding of explanations when banks made few loans in low- and moderate-income segments of their community:

> [The CRA] was not intended to establish a regulatory influence on the allocation of credit. . . . The Board has acted on the belief that banks are in the best position to assess the credit needs of their own local communities. . . .
> The Board believes that there are many reasons why a particular neighborhood may generate more deposits than loan requests, or more requests than deposits, and that disparity in a particular area . . . is not prima facie evidence of discrimination. (Federal Reserve Board 1980)

While it is not difficult to argue that simple geographic measures of lending volumes are insufficient to prove discrimination or redlining, it seems reasonable that at least large disparities in lending volumes, after accounting for neighborhood characteristics like single-family housing density and turnover, would prompt further investigations into possible discrimination or redlining. Yet, instead of signaling that this might occur, the regulators went in the other direction, almost to the point of coaching banks on how to explain away their poor lending records in lower-income communities.

Moreover, while the legislative debate made it clear that Congress did not want regulators to require all banks to lend some specific percentage of their assets in certain types of neighborhoods, the statute was certainly aimed at improving access to credit in lower-income neighborhoods and thereby increasing credit flows into such neighborhoods. Regulators, on the other hand, suggested that any impact on actual lending patterns by banks was evidence of "credit allocation," a term they used to describe antimarket schemes and to conjure up the legislative debate that used this language. In many ways, regulators and industry groups have over the years capitalized on the term "credit allocation" and have stretched its meaning. The term as used in the congressional debate described a highly formulaic, deterministic numerical system of regulator-enforced lending goals that would set hard floors on lending to lower-income neighborhoods. A bank might be told to make some specific percentage of its loans in low-income neighborhoods in its community area. Proxmire and many advocates disavowed this concept long ago. If, by "credit allocation," one meant efforts to improve lending performance in lower-income areas, then, yes, CRA proponents did want credit allocation. But this was not how the term was used in the legislative history. To guard against its much broader notion of credit allocation, the board warned banks and community organizations against any efforts that might favor lower-income communities:

> In particular, the Board does not endorse agreements to allocate credit . . . the Board will closely scrutinize any agreements to ascertain that they are not inconsistent with the safety and soundness of the bank involved, and do not establish a preference for credit extensions inconsistent with the evenhanded treatment of borrowers throughout the community. (Federal Reserve Board 1980)

Thus, the board transformed the phrase "credit allocation"—which has been used in congressional hearings to mean the systemwide, regulator-driven imposition of hard number lending quotas—to mean something much broader. A CRA agreement between a bank and a community group in which a bank agreed to try to increase lending by some numerical goal would be considered "credit allocation." This is despite the fact that the goal was likely the result of deliberation, discussion, and negotiation between the parties and not the output of some hard-and-fast deterministic hard-number rule. Regulators, especially the FRB, seemed more concerned about CRA-induced disparate treatment in favor of lower-income neighborhoods than about preexisting discrimination against such communities.

In 1982, FRB staff authored a paper titled "The Community Reinvestment Act and Credit Allocation," which analyzed the "degree to which credit allocation has arisen in private settlements of CRA disputes" (Canner 1982). The concern among the board and staff was that CRA agreements were actually affecting the distribution of credit. Yet this is precisely what CRA was intended to do. The 1982 paper examines the complaints of community organizations and repeatedly explains why the reasoning of the studies is flawed and how the banks might look better if the analysis were performed in a different way. The report accuses the "protestants" as demanding that "applicants allocate a particular fraction of their overall residential credit to the protestants' neighborhoods." The reader was led to believe that "credit allocation" in the congressional sense of the word had been at work. Yet, a closer look revealed that these fractions were often the result of negotiations between different perspectives on what a reasonable goal was for improved lending. The concern from the deregulationist camp, dominant in the Federal Reserve System, was that only the unfettered market should play any role in determining what lending levels should be and that these negotiations would lead only to inefficient credit flows. While the 1982 paper acknowledged that the CRA may have encouraged some banks to take positive steps to increase their lending to community groups and lower-income areas, it ended with a warning about the potential danger of "credit allocation" caused by CRA agreements:

> To date this credit allocation has not been of such magnitude nor has it imposed such severe constraints that it has threatened an institution's basic safety and soundness. Inasmuch as the geographic allocation of funds is often the primary goal of community-based protestants, negotiated CRA settlements in the future are likely to continue to involve some elements of geographic credit allocation. (Canner 1982)

Community reinvestment advocates, banks, and others waited to see how "tough" regulators would be with banks. Again, the expectation among community groups was not very high. They viewed the regulators as essentially "captured" by the industry. Regulators employed many former bankers and spent a great deal of time with bank staff and boards. Meanwhile, regulators rarely established relationships with community groups and often looked on community reinvestment activists as "troublemakers" (Sidney 2003). In congressional hearings in the late 1980s, it was revealed that the number of examiner hours devoted to consumer compliance responsibilities, including CRA, dropped by approximately 75 percent in the early 1980s (Fishbein 1992). This finding was due, in part, to a diversion of resources to the S&L and banking crises at the time.

The worst fears of the community reinvestment activists came to pass when regulators revealed early patterns of CRA grades. The Federal Reserve showed in late 1981 that it had rated only 3 percent of banks as less than satisfactory in 1980. (See Table 6.2.) The board adopted a policy of only requiring review at board-level those applications involving institutions with a rating of 5, representing only 0.2 percent of institutions and only two banks in 1980. Little appeared to change in this pattern through the 1980s. From 1985 to 1988, of the 26,000 CRA exams conducted by regulators, only 2.4 percent received less-than-satisfactory ratings (Fishbein 1993).

Another big question mark that awaited both banks and community groups after CRA was passed was the question of what actually would happen to banks found not to be fulfilling their CRA obligations. The law called for

Table 6.2

CRA Examination Ratings of Federal Reserve Member Banks, 1980

Rating	Number of banks	Percentage of banks
1	31	3.5
2	328	36.7
3	507	56.7
4	26	2.9
5	2	0.2
Total	894	100.0

Source: Canner (1981).

Note: 1 = highest rating, 5 = lowest rating; 4 and 5 are considered less than satisfactory.

regulators to take CRA performance into consideration when they consider applications by banks to merge with another bank, open a branch, or make other significant changes to their charter. What this would exactly mean was unclear. Would regulators actually reject important applications on CRA grounds?

As in most regulation, the risk-sanction calculation of the regulated bank is a key one. For regulations to be effective, banks must expect a reasonable likelihood of being "caught" when they do not comply with the law and must expect that they will pay a price for such behavior. In cases where very few firms are penalized, as is the case in many regulatory areas, the sanctions must be sizable and certain. With CRA, the sanctions are at least theoretically large, especially for banks that might consider merging, branching, or being acquired. Even the delay of a bank merger can be costly, and a denial can be devastating. Unfortunately, regulators left little doubt early on that, even if banks received poor CRA ratings or substantive community group challenges, outright application denials due to CRA would be exceedingly rare. Regulators even went so far as to publicly announce their "second chance" policy for poor CRA performers:

> In acting upon applications covered by CRA, the Board considers a bank's CRA record as part of the convenience and needs aspect. . . . Following its longstanding policy, the Board may in some circumstances give weight to commitments for future actions as part of its consideration. . . . Such commitments are not viewed as part of the CRA record but may be weighed with it. (Federal Reserve Board 1980).

The board went on to state that it would track such commitments and consider them in future application decisions. Regulators argued that providing these second chances could improve the impact of the law. However, such a strategy depends on follow-through and on heightening penalties for institutions not performing after being given their second chance. It is not clear if this happened very often. At least one case, involving the OCC, indicates that regulators did not follow through very vigorously on whether banks made good on their commitments. In 1980, the OCC approved an application for the Bank of Indiana based on conditions that they develop a CRA compliance plan. Over the following six years, the bank did not make a single mortgage loan in the city of Gary, within its community area (Bradford and Cincotta 1992). The OCC argued that there was a lack of demand in the area. However, after negotiating a reinvestment agreement with a community group, the bank began making loans.

Beyond allowing banks second—and maybe more—chances, regulators pointed out in various ways that, even if they found an institution's CRA record to be unsatisfactory, they were not compelled to act on that finding. The board stated that it "may approve the transaction even when the CRA record is unsatisfactory, if commitments or other convenience and needs considerations outweigh the negative aspects of the application" (Federal Reserve Board 1980). The board clearly took this prerogative seriously, because from December 1979 to August 1981, the Federal Reserve System reviewed twenty-six applications involving institutions with less-than-satisfactory ratings and approved all of them. Only one went to the board level for approval (Canner 1981). Moreover, the board did not actually deny a merger application until 1989, when it declined an acquisition by Continental Bank in Chicago, a bank that had sizable government ownership due to an earlier government bailout.

Among the four regulators, the board was the most resistant to affirmatively implementing CRA. The board had "disengaged" from the other three regulators over the use of the CRA and credit needs analysis as a regulatory tool (McCluskey 1983). In 1978, in its first opportunity to rule on a merger application contested on CRA grounds, the board made a clear policy statement. Commerce Bankshares Inc., a bank holding company, had been challenged by the community group Association of Community Organizations for Reform Now (ACORN) on the basis of a poor lending record in a neighborhood surrounding two of its subsidiaries. The board responded—with apparent irritation—to the challenge by stating:

> As the Board indicated to the Congress during its consideration of the CRA, the convenience and needs standard of the Bank Holding Company [BHC] Act already requires the Board to consider whether the institutions involved are helping to meet the credit needs of their community . . .

The Board finds nothing in the BHC Act that requires or authorizes the Board to dictate a bank's product mix . . . or to dictate what proportion or amount of an institution's funds must, or even should, be allocated to any particular credit need, borrower, or neighborhood. . . . The law permits each bank to choose how it should fulfill its responsibility to help meet the convenience and needs of its community. (Federal Reserve Board 1978)

In fact, it appears that the board could have easily dismissed the ACORN challenge by arguing the evidence of redlining in the case. The evidence against the bank was not very strong. Yet the board chose to argue policy and "belittle" the act, in McCluskey's words. Senator Proxmire apparently took some umbrage at the language of the decision, and wrote to the board that he felt that the board had misrepresented the "affirmative obligation" principle of the act (McCluskey 1983). McCluskey suggested that the hostility to the act by the board was "sending a message to the industry, and perhaps Congress, that the CRA would have no special impact on its evaluation philosophy." While other regulators were often seen as lacking in the vigor of their enforcement as well, the FDIC and the OCC did deny a few applications on CRA grounds in the early years.[15]

Community Reinvestment Act Organizing in the 1980s

Community and public interest groups responded to the CRA by challenging the applications of banks and thrifts to merge or establish new branches. The number of challenges was somewhat limited in the early years, in part because the regulatory process was unfolding and the basis on which to challenge banks was somewhat limited. Until regulators had articulated the regulations in 1978 and issued clarifying details, community expectations of banks were somewhat muted. On top of this, bank mergers and acquisitions were not occurring at a terribly fast rate in the late 1970s and early 1980s, so the number of challengeable opportunities was relatively small.

The FRB received challenges against one bank in 1977 (Commerce Bankshares, actually preceding the effective date of the act), one in 1978, ten in 1979, five in 1981, eight in 1982, and only three each in 1983 and 1984 (Cowell and Hagler 1992). None of these challenges prevented the approval of an application. Regulators often encouraged banks to meet with community challengers to resolve differences, and these meetings contributed to some of the "second chances" the regulators gave banks with poor performance.

Even though bank mergers were not occurring at a rapid rate in the first few years of CRA, community reinvestment advocates took advantage of the law to question banks' lending records. While CRA challenges to the FRB did not meet with success, consistent with the board's overall hostility to the law, petitions to other regulators were somewhat more successful. McCluskey (1983) commented that "other agencies have occasionally been more forceful in interpreting the 'affirmative obligation.'" In 1979, South Brooklyn Against Investment Discrimination challenged an application by Greater New York Savings Bank to open a branch office in Manhattan (Woodstock Institute 1978). The group maintained that the bank had failed to serve the credit needs of its existing Brooklyn community. This challenge resulted in the first denial of an application on CRA grounds. In Cleveland, community groups challenged an application by AmeriTrust on the grounds that the bank had engaged in lending discrimination and redlining. While the Federal Reserve approved the corresponding merger, it did impose some CRA-related conditions. In 1978, the Toledo Fair Housing Center challenged an application for a new branch by First Federal Savings and Loan to the Federal Home Loan Bank Board. Again, while the application was approved, the regulator required the savings and loans to establish a home improvement loan department, begin an affirmative marketing program, and conduct semiannual meetings with community groups. To make their challenges stronger, community groups making these challenges were aided by organizations such as the Center for Community Change and Ralph Nader's organization, which provided technical assistance and data analysis.

Interstate bank branching compacts between states increased in the early 1980s and were supported by a Supreme Court ruling in 1985. The opportunities for challenges increased and so did the number of challenges. Figure 6.1 shows that challenges at the Federal Reserve increased from three to seventeen from 1984 to 1985 and then increased to twenty and then thirty-six in 1986 and 1987, due in large part to increased merger and acquisition activity. The trend of increased challenges was consistent with a modest burst of interest by community groups in using CRA to challenge banks' lending records. The regulations were finalized in 1978, providing groups with more clarity regarding the decision-making process of the regulators. The initial spurt of activity would no doubt have been larger if more mergers had occurred in 1979. However, after the board demonstrated that these challenges would be rebuffed, some groups may have lost interest in challenges until the middle 1980s, when more and larger mergers began to occur. The complaint that bank regulators did not deny bank applications on CRA grounds continued through the 1980s. Only 8 of an estimated 40,000 expansion applications were denied on CRA grounds in the law's first ten years (Fishbein 1993).

The low rate of application denials based on CRA negatively affected

Figure 6.1 **Number of Formal CRA Challenges Received by the FRB, 1977–1987**

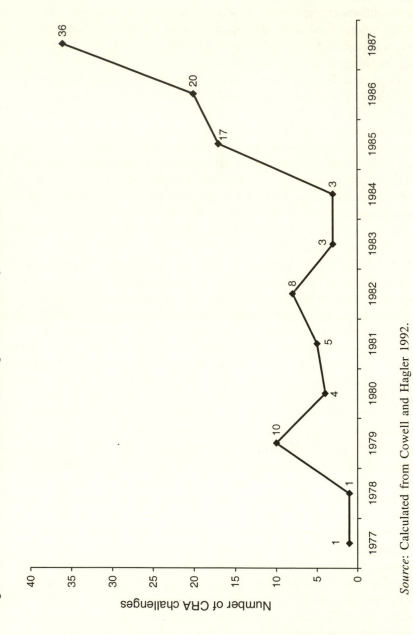

Source: Calculated from Cowell and Hagler 1992.

how seriously the new law was taken by banks and community groups. However, the statute still had significant impact. While denials send an important signal to financial institutions, from the perspective of the individual community organizations dealing with particular institutions, obtaining commitments from banks to work to improve their services in the community may be a preferable outcome. Ideally, there would be a mix of both outcomes. Certainly, some institutions may respond to the possibility of an application denial by working constructively with community groups. Others, however, may refuse. If there is no perceived threat of regulator sanction, the motivation for negotiating CRA agreements is diminished. CRA agreements are important tools for reinvestment. But they are more likely to be successful when more banks face a realistic threat of poor CRA ratings and/or a denied application.

When examining challenge activity, it is important to keep in mind that, for every formal CRA challenge, there were many CRA negotiations that resulted in CRA agreements or activity before any formal challenge was filed. In addition, CRA has prompted banks to proactively seek relationships with community-based organizations, including community development corporations and a variety of nonprofit intermediary loan funds. An early example of such an intermediary was NHS, which began in Pittsburgh but spread to become a national network of nonprofit housing lenders by the 1990s. NHS is a model in which bank funds are pooled in various ways, sometimes with public or philanthropic funds, to capitalize lending programs targeted to low- and moderate-income communities. The specific programs vary depending on the size, capacity, and needs in the local NHS community. As of 2003, the NHS of Chicago program, for example, includes programs to increase home ownership in targeted neighborhoods, to assist in the rehabilitation and repair of single-family homes, and to help refinance people out of abusive mortgages into loans with appropriate pricing and terms. CRA was a critical factor in supporting the growth and development of such programs during the 1980s. Whether via CRA agreements or not, banks would often commit not only to make loans, but also to invest in intermediary programs like NHS. Such investments are typically made with an eye to improving or maintaining a bank's CRA record.

Formal CRA agreements between community organizations and banks increased significantly in the late 1980s. The National Community Reinvestment Coalition, a coalition of community reinvestment groups that began in 1990, has compiled a database of CRA agreements dating back to the late 1970s. According to these data, the number of agreements increased from three per year in 1982 and 1983, to eleven and twelve in 1984 and 1985, and then to thirty-two and thirty-one in 1986 and 1987, respectively.[16] The size of the agreements also got much larger later in the decade. (Chapter 7 goes into CRA agreements in more detail.) As with CRA challenges, this was due to a number of factors, including an increasing number of bank mergers, but also due to an increased interest in CRA organizing and a wider understanding that federal regulators, by themselves, were not going to spur banks to improve to meet community credit needs. Community groups increasingly recognized that they had to "carry the burden of CRA and fair housing enforcement in the absence of responsible intervention by the financial regulatory agencies" (Bradford and Cincotta 1992).

One of the highest-profile series of CRA agreements during the 1980s occurred in Chicago in 1984. In the late summer of 1983, the First Chicago Corporation, the parent company of Chicago's flagship bank, the First National Bank of Chicago, announced that it intended to acquire American National Bank of Chicago, a leading middle-market bank. First National was the city's largest bank, and American National was among the largest in the region as well. The Woodstock Institute, a Chicago nonprofit, began researching the lending records of both banks, prepared briefing materials, and helped organize a communitywide meeting about the merger (Pogge 1992). A coalition of thirty-five neighborhood and citywide nonprofit organizations formed the Chicago Reinvestment Alliance, with key leadership including, among others, the National Training Information Center, the Woodstock Institute, the Chicago Association for Neighborhood Development Organizations, and the Chicago Rehab Network. The coalition met with key leadership at First National, including its CEO, and outlined credit needs in Chicago neighborhoods that were not being met by the bank. The negotiations involved a series of at least nine meetings with the bank. In February 1984, the alliance and the bank announced a five-year, $120 million agreement that initiated the "Neighborhood Investment and Revitalization Program." This program included lending targets for multifamily apartment building financing, single-family rehabilitation loans, small business loans, and other products. In the four months following the First National agreement, the alliance negotiated similar agreements with two other large Chicago banks, Harris Trust and Savings Bank and the Northern Trust Company. Because these banks were smaller than First National, the lending goals were also smaller. A study of the impacts of these agreements showed that the three banks had made almost $118 million in loans, including the production or maintenance of 5,000 housing units (Bradford 1990). Moreover, only one loan was delinquent at the time of the evaluation. What is more, the program led to the development of new loan products and to new partnerships between the banks and local nonprofits.

By the early 1990s, banks had negotiated at least $2.5 billion in formal

CRA agreements with community organizations, although this is certainly a substantial underestimate given that much of the data were compiled retrospectively (National Community Reinvestment Coalition 2002). Including unilateral commitments by lenders, the Center for Community Change estimated that at least $30 billion in CRA commitments had been made by the early 1990s (Fishbein 1992). Lawrence Lindsey, a member of the FRB, testified before Congress in early 1994 that "I suspect that the total impact of the CRA considerably exceeds the $30 billion estimate" (Lindsey 1994).

The rise of CRA agreements was forecast by McCluskey, who coined the term "regulation from below" in the CRA context (McCluskey 1983). The implicit standing given community groups provided them the opportunity to strengthen the implementation of the statute when regulators failed to do so themselves. Community activism forced regulators to create institutional processes such as public hearings and the consideration of CRA agreements in assessing CRA performance under the law. At the same time, the scale of CRA agreements, and of CRA activity more generally, was no doubt dampened in the 1980s by the very lax enforcement of the law and the extremely low rate of less than satisfactory ratings. In the late 1980s, pressure began building on the regulators to start enforcing CRA more vigorously. Chapter 7 picks up the story of CRA implementation and CRA reforms in the late 1980s and the 1990s and also discusses the ebbs and flows of CRA agreements and activism through the end of the century.

Community Reinvestment from 1988 to the End of the Twentieth Century

Struggles for Bank and Regulator Accountability

Activism, Media, and Policy Changes in the Late 1980s

As the last chapter described, the middle to late 1980s saw an increase in Community Reinvestment Act (CRA) agreements and organizing. This increased activism led to a renewed attention to problems of access to credit and a heightened focus on CRA and fair lending enforcement. The years 1988 and 1989 proved to be especially critical in the history of CRA. In 1986 and 1987, community-reinvestment organizing was on the upswing in many large cities. In early 1986, organizers held a workshop on CRA for local housing and community groups in Atlanta (Keating, Brazen, and Fitterman 1992). The groups at the workshop formed the Atlanta Community Reinvestment Alliance (ACRA) and began conducting reinvestment research and building a bigger coalition. After analyzing the lending patterns of banks and thrifts in the Atlanta area and finding low lending levels in lower-income and minority neighborhoods, the group approached the Federal Reserve Bank of Atlanta to discuss the problem. The head of the Federal Reserve Bank's supervision operations spurned ACRA's data and argued that lenders in the area did not redline. ACRA began organizing CRA strategies aimed at specific institutions and eventually challenged an application by SunTrust Bank to acquire another institution. The application was approved.

While ACRA continued its research and activism, the *Atlanta Journal/Constitution* hired Bill Dedman, an investigative reporter, to cover housing issues. Dedman began covering the redlining issue with a small article in late 1987. Then on May 1, 1988, after months of working with local and national researchers, the *Journal/Constitution* published a large front-page article, the first in a four-day series titled "The Color of Money" (Dedman

1988a). Dedman found that whites received five times as many home purchase loans from Atlanta's banks and thrifts as blacks with similar income levels. Even after controlling for home sales activity, banks and thrifts financed four times as many purchases in the white areas as in the black areas. Even lower-income white neighborhoods were better served by banks and thrifts than higher-income black areas. Dedman went on to expose the fact that 98 percent of banks and thrifts received CRA ratings of satisfactory or better and that regulators had denied just eight applications on CRA grounds since the act's passage (Dedman 1988b). In a story two months later, Dedman quoted a senior researcher at the Federal Reserve Board (FRB) as commenting on the Atlanta findings:

> Anybody who's familiar with it knows that what you found in Atlanta is similar to what we find in any city in the country. Atlanta isn't the worst and it isn't the best. It was somewhere in the middle. We've looked over the years at dozens of cities and dozens of cases. For us, the disparities are fairly well known. It might be news to the general public. (Dedman 1998c)

The Federal Reserve official based his comments on a study done in 1983 that was never released, not even to Dedman at the time of the series.

The "Color of Money" series had an immediate national impact, and its timing was critical. Senator William Proxmire, the original sponsor of CRA, was about to retire. The Senate Banking Committee had held hearings on the act's implementation six weeks before the series began, and he had questioned regulators' enforcement efforts then. The committee had heard from witnesses that CRA exams had become essentially impossible to fail.

Proxmire took advantage of the Dedman series to draw additional attention to regulators' weak enforcement of the law. He asked them to respond to the series and to report on their enforcement activities by the end of the summer. The increased public and congressional scrutiny of regulators had a clear effect of making weak regulator enforcement a much more prominent issue. At the time, CRA ratings were not publicly available, so the rating behavior of regulators, while known by those who followed CRA closely, was not widely recognized.

In late 1988, the *Boston Globe* began covering a controversy in Boston in which city housing officials and minority developers perceived that local banks were discriminating against projects in Roxbury, the city's major black neighborhood (Campen 1992). Officials at the Boston Redevelopment Authority proposed a study of mortgage lending similar to the Atlanta study and identified one of the researchers who worked with Dedman on the "Color of Money" series as their preferred contractor. But in December, the authority's board of directors voted against going ahead with the study. Then, in January

1989, the *Globe* obtained a copy of an unpublished report by researchers at the Federal Reserve Bank of Boston on home-lending patterns (Marantz 1989). The copy of the study obtained by the paper included a footnote indicating that it would be published in the May/June 1988 issue of the Federal Reserve Bank's *New England Economic Review*. The reporter quoted an anonymous source claiming that the decision to delay publication of the study had been made by the president of the Federal Reserve Bank.

The 1988 Boston Federal Reserve study used property transfer data to identify large lending disparities between white and minority neighborhoods in Boston. It found that if race were not a factor in lending in Boston, lending activity would more than double in Roxbury and Mattapan/Franklin, another minority neighborhood. Industry representatives attacked the report in various ways (Marantz and Hanafin 1989). Then in late summer of 1989, the Federal Reserve Bank released its revised version of the study. Using more sophisticated methods, the study still found that, even after controlling for differences in income, wealth, housing values, and other factors, black neighborhoods suffered from substantially lower lending activity when compared to white areas (Bradbury, Case, and Dunham 1989).

In January 1989, Bill Dedman published another study of mortgage lending, this time using loan data he obtained through a Freedom of Information Act request from the Federal Home Loan Bank Board. The data, collected by the agency for fair lending enforcement purposes, showed that black loan applicants were rejected about twice as often as white applicants, and at much higher rates in some cities (Dedman 1989).

The studies and media coverage in Atlanta, Boston, and other cities increased public and congressional scrutiny of the activities of CRA regulators. It was no coincidence that, in April 1989, regulators issued only their second CRA policy statement since the original regulations were promulgated (Garwood and Smith 1993). In it, the regulators emphasized that banks would be evaluated on their actual lending performance rather than simply on promises for improvements. The statement did not make tremendous changes in CRA regulation, but it was a clear signal that regulators were feeling some pressure. The statement encouraged banks to make CRA a more integral part of their day-to-day management planning, made it clear that CRA applied to wholesale banks (those not making loans to consumers or small businesses), and encouraged banks to expand their public CRA statements to include information on their actual CRA performance. For example, the statement suggested that an institution consider including in its CRA statement "a summary of the results of its internal CRA review and a summary of the documentation collected by the institution regarding its CRA performance."

The regulators' policy statement, however, was also somewhat defensive. It "strongly" encouraged community organizations to "bring comments regarding an institution's CRA performance to the attention of the institution and the appropriate supervisory agency at the earliest possible time. Interested persons are encouraged not to wait to present their comments through a protest to an application." In this way, the regulators were sending a signal that comments at the time of application would be held to a high standard if they were not brought to the attention of regulators earlier. Yet, community groups are generally severely resource-constrained and usually have difficulty tracking the activity of every bank and commenting on every concern with all institutions. Without access to the CRA exams themselves or an understanding of when examinations would occur, it was only natural for community organizations to focus on institutions when they made applications. Moreover, applications are an event in which community groups have clear, albeit implicit, standing (Fishbein 1993). It is difficult to mobilize resources, volunteers, community groups busy with other concerns, if no actionable event is taking place. By laying out their desire for earlier information from community groups, regulators were attempting to shift the burden to the community, so that they could effectively say, "You should have said something earlier."

The regulators also laid out a new, or at least newly articulated, expectation that banks were to document their CRA activities. They clarified their position on banks' commitments to improve CRA performance at the time of applications. They stated that commitments for future action would not be viewed as part of an institution's CRA record, but could be considered as an indicator of "potential for improvement." However, the regulators made no distinctions between commitments derived from negotiations with members of their community versus unilateral pledges developed without serious input from community groups. As banks got larger and interstate banking increased, banks began to turn to unilateral pledges as an "easier" and less accountable alternative to discussions with community groups. Rather than develop relationships and negotiate CRA agreements with groups in several cities, many larger banks began announcing unilateral reinvestment pledges when announcing a merger or acquisition plan. These banks have sought to essentially preempt any criticisms of their CRA record by obtaining a splash in the press with a commitment of tens of billions of dollars. When community groups have scrutinized these pledges, however, they have often found that they were very weak on details, often to the point where it was not clear the banks were committing to any increase in lending or services at all (Lee 2003; Taylor and Silver 2003).

In addition to the Joint Policy Statement, there were other signs that regulators were responding to criticisms over their enforcement performance. In the same month of the publication of the Joint Policy Statement, the FRB published its decision to deny an application by a large bank, Continental Bank of Illinois, to acquire a very small bank in Arizona. This was the board's first denial of a merger on CRA grounds. The denial sent "shock waves" throughout the industry (Fishbein 1992). One thing that was striking about the decision was that the board explained how the bank had devised a substantial CRA plan to remedy its poor performance, but it did not allow the acquisition on the basis of the remedial plan. The board commented, "Banking organizations should address their CRA responsibilities and implement the necessary programs before they file an application with the Board."[1] Real enforcement of the act appeared to be at work.

While clearly a reaction to the growing criticism of the regulators, the Joint Policy Statement and the denial of one merger were not enough to appease Congress. In 1989, allies of the reinvestment movement were able to make a number of changes to CRA and HMDA through the passage of the savings and loan bailout bill, the Financial Institutions Reform Recovery and Enforcement Act (FIRREA). These changes proved much more significant than the regulators' moves. FIRREA required the public disclosure of most aspects of CRA exams. This was a major step. Now community groups and others could identify how regulators had rated a bank's CRA performance. This served at least two purposes. First, it gave the public and community groups some information on the CRA performance of different banks. Foundations, churches, local governments, and even the American Bar Association began using CRA ratings as a screen for selecting their banks. But, more importantly, disclosure of CRA ratings made it possible for those dealing with banks more directly, either as CRA advocates or as potential community development partners, to understand how regulators viewed the banks' performance. A community group could look to target banks that had received satisfactory ratings when the group felt the banks deserved "needs to improve" or worse ratings. Some groups began providing information about banks to regulators and arguing that banks ought to be downgraded. FIRREA also changed the five-level, numerical CRA rating system to a four-level descriptive classification of "Outstanding," "Satisfactory," "Needs to Improve," and "Substantial Noncompliance."

The biggest impact FIRREA had on CRA, however, was not the changes to the statute itself but the changes it made regarding the Home Mortgage Disclosure Act (HMDA). The HMDA had been limited in its usefulness in two critical ways. First, it contained no information on the race or income of borrowers. Second, only originated loans were included, so no information on applications or denials was available. Under FIRREA, lenders had to report on each formal loan application, including the race, income, and gender of the applicant, the loan amount, the purpose of the loan, whether the loan was approved, denied, or withdrawn, and other information. These changes had a tremendous impact on the utility and power of the data. It is important to note that it was not simply the addition of racial information, but the shift to application-level disclosure that made HMDA so much more critical to the reinvestment and fair lending movements. FIRREA also required larger mortgage companies that were not affiliated with banks to report HMDA data for the first time. For loans sold on the secondary market, information was also required on whom loans were sold to.[2]

In November 1991, the Federal Reserve, after providing the banking industry with advance notice, released a national analysis of the first year (1990) of the new HMDA data. It showed that minorities were two to three times more likely to be rejected for home loans than whites of similar income levels (Canner and Smith 1991). Numerous studies soon followed, and the large differences in denial rates between minority and white loan applicants drew a great deal of media attention. The attention to race-based differentials in mortgage lending was arguably the single most important factor in improving access to home purchase loans in the early 1990s. Lending by mortgage companies also increased as the attention to racial disparities detailed by the new HMDA data led to better enforcement of fair lending laws. The large disparities between minority and white borrowers of similar incomes also led the Federal Reserve Bank of Boston to conduct another critical study, this time supplementing HMDA data with credit history information and other variables from actual loan files. The results of this study, now generally referred to as the "Boston Fed Study," were originally published in 1992 and then later in 1996 in a peer-reviewed economics journal.

The lending industry responded defensively to the new HMDA data. The American Bankers Association funded an academic economist to develop a critique of HMDA as a tool for detecting lending discrimination. Fishbein (1992) noted that, while the industry groups criticized the use of HMDA for not including credit history and other data, they had not proposed including such data when HMDA had been before Congress and had opposed a proposal to require lenders to report their reasons for rejecting loans.

The effect of increased scrutiny of regulators' enforcement of CRA was significant. The proportion of banks receiving a CRA rating of "less than satisfactory" rose significantly during the late 1980s and early 1990s. From 1985 to 1988, only 2.4 percent of institutions examined received less-than-satisfactory ratings (Fishbein 1992). From July 1990 through September 1991, about a quarter of all banks and thrifts were evaluated under the new disclosure law. The percentage receiving less-than-satisfactory ratings increased to

11.7 percent, a substantial increase. Only 8 percent of these new exams resulted in "outstanding" ratings. Certainly disclosure of exams may have had an effect on the ratings. However, the later return to "satisfactory" or better ratings of more than 97 percent suggests that other factors were also at work, including the increased scrutiny and criticism that the regulators underwent in the late 1980s.

The banking industry and its allies did not sit idly by while CRA enforcement was increasing. While efforts to repeal CRA had never gotten substantial support in Congress, by the late 1980s opponents were focused on more realistic strategies. These included measures to exempt small banks from CRA's coverage and to allow any bank with a satisfactory or better rating—which would amount to the bulk of banks and bank assets—a "safe harbor" from potential CRA challenges. That is, under such proposals, only the very few banks with less-than-satisfactory CRA ratings would be susceptible to CRA challenges.

One of the by-products of the late 1980s fights to protect CRA was the formation of a new coalition of community organizations and public interest groups. Many groups—local and national—with a history of waging policy battles on access to credit issues came together to form the National Community Reinvestment Coalition (NCRC). NCRC would become the leading voice in efforts to preserve and expand CRA in the 1990s. In the early 1990s, in order to fight a significant congressional threat to CRA, NCRC collected the signatures of more than 200 mayors and community leaders from across the country in support of the law (National Community Reinvestment Coalition 2003). As of 2003, NCRC had more than 800 members, including community organizations, community development corporations, and public interest groups from around the country.

Community Reinvestment Act Reform

In the early 1990s, the new HMDA data and public access to CRA exams helped create a revived interest in CRA among community groups, the media, and policymakers. On top of this, Bill Clinton made increasing CRA's impact a significant part of his urban policy campaign platform in the 1992 presidential election. CRA ratings, which were now public, had moved back up to extremely comfortable levels for banks. By 1993, the percentage of banks receiving less-than-satisfactory levels had dropped back down to less than 5 percent, from a level of about 12 percent in 1990. Community reinvestment advocates argued first to the Clinton campaign and then to the new administration that CRA, as it was being implemented and enforced, was not resulting in substantial improvements in reinvestment performance. Thus, in

1993, federal banking regulators proposed major revisions to CRA rules that promised to focus more on actual lending results and less on processes like demonstrating community contacts and advertising efforts. The administration, under its "reinventing government" efforts, also promised bankers less "paperwork." CRA reform was promoted as an attempt to make both sides happy.

In late 1993, the administration introduced its first version of CRA reform for public comment via a proposed regulation in the *Federal Register*. The proposal called for evaluating an institution's lending, in part, by comparing its market penetrations in low- and moderate-income neighborhoods within its assessment area to its penetrations in middle- and upper-income neighborhoods. The proposal did not identify a highly formulaic or deterministic approach, but did suggest this general use of market shares as a starting point. It did not call for any lending requirements per dollar of local deposit of the sort rejected in the original Senate CRA hearings. The market share approach was a commonly accepted method for measuring disparities in a wide variety of social science and business arenas, including employment discrimination and affirmative action set-aside programs. Many bankers and some regulators, however, opposed the move, again crying "credit allocation." The proposal also called for minimal collection of small business lending data. The proposal suggested an evaluation system focusing on three areas: direct lending; indirect "investments" in community development lenders of various sorts; and "services," including savings and checking accounts and branch distributions.

Community reinvestment advocates—in urban areas at least—were generally pleased with the original proposal, which was drafted mostly by the Office of the Comptroller of the Currency (OCC) under Eugene Ludwig, a Clinton appointee. However, some argued for a stronger emphasis on direct lending by banks, versus bank account services or indirect investments in intermediaries. Others wanted the law to require reporting and disclosure of race and gender data on small business loans in addition to geographic information. Also, many community groups argued against the proposal's two-tiered evaluation system, in which smaller banks were given much less scrutiny than large banks. Those in rural areas or smaller cities, where smaller banks were more important, were especially vocal about this.

While community and public interest groups generally supported CRA reform, they were outnumbered by banks in their responses to the regulatory proposal. Banks accounted for approximately 85 percent of the comments on the proposal (Woodstock Institute 1994). Banks were generally much less pleased with the proposed regulations. They argued most strongly against two core features of the proposed regulations. First, they were against any race and gender reporting on small business loans. Most opponents of small business loan reporting again argued that such data collection would impose a substantial burden. However, some banks and even some regulators were more forthright in their arguments on this issue. In particular, as comments were coming in from community groups calling for such data on small business loans, FRB member Lawrence Lindsey, the board's point board member on CRA, lobbied against race and gender data collection based on notions of "sensitivity" ("Lindsey Continues" 1994). Some banks argued that collecting such data would exacerbate discrimination. This was similar to arguments made in the debate over expanding HMDA a few years earlier. Bankers were also against the use of market share analysis in CRA exams. Again, they were well represented among the regulators by Lawrence Lindsey and others at the Federal Reserve. Any references to comparing market share numbers were removed in the final regulation.

In April 1995, after eighteen months of repeated public comments and debate, the four federal banking regulators—the Federal Reserve Board (FRB), the Office of the Comptroller of the Currency (OCC), the Federal Deposit Insurance Corporation (FDIC), and the Office of Thrift Supervision (OTS)—released new CRA regulations. The new rules replaced the twelve assessment factors in the previous regulations with an outcome-based evaluation system. This system was intended to assess how well institutions served their communities on lending, investments, and financial services, rather than on how well they conducted needs assessments and document community outreach.

While a shift from process to outcomes was the primary goal of the regulatory changes, there was also some attention given to "easing the regulatory burden" of banks, especially for smaller institutions. As a result, a two-tier evaluation system was established, with banks classified as "small" (less than $250 million in assets) having more limited evaluation procedures than "large" institutions. Another change that occurred was a shift in language from "entire community" to "assessment area." The regulators tied the assessment area more closely to the location of branch facilities, even though, as chapter 6 shows, the legislative history does not support such a tight connection.

Under the final new rules, which are in place today, CRA evaluations for large banks consist of three component tests: the Lending, Investment, and Service Tests. (See this chapter's Appendix for more details on the new regulations.) The Lending Test, which measures a bank's performance in direct lending primarily via mortgages and small business loans, accounts for 50 percent of the overall CRA rating. The Investment Test, which accounts for 25 percent of the overall CRA rating, considers banks' investment in community development activities such as investments in community development loan funds or minority-owned banks. The Service Test accounts for the remaining 25 percent of the overall score and is where banks are evaluated for branch locations and the provision of basic, affordable deposit services.

Wholesale or limited purpose banks, such as credit card banks, are evaluated based on a special "Community Development" test. Small banks are examined according to a less rigorous procedure that focuses on loan-to-deposit ratios and other very simple measures. Small banks are not evaluated for community-development lending or investments, although they may choose to have such activities considered in order to improve their ratings. The new regulations also call for the agencies to publish a list of banks that will be evaluated for CRA in the upcoming quarter in order to allow community organizations and others to comment on a bank's CRA performance at the time of the CRA exam.

All institutions receive an overall rating of "outstanding," "satisfactory," "needs to improve," or "substantial noncompliance." A bank examiner substantiates the rating in a written report. A public portion of the exam is published after the bank is informed of its rating. The final rules also call for the collection of small business lending by census tract, but not for any collection of race or gender information. For individual census tracts, the total amount of lending reported by all banks is made available. For individual banks, tables are disclosed indicating only the amount of lending in tracts of different income levels. This makes the data much less suitable for community groups who would like to identify how much lending a particular bank does in specific neighborhoods. However, they can identify which banks tend to make more loans to lower- vs. upper-income neighborhoods. The regulations also exempt "small" banks from having to report the data. In smaller cities and rural areas, this makes the data very incomplete.

Community Reinvestment Act Reform Makes Some Progress

CRA reform was an important improvement to CRA policy. It laid the groundwork for a meaningful evaluation process that focused more on actual reinvestment activity than on public relations and the distribution of "good will" philanthropy to groups unconnected to credit and development needs. Before CRA reform, banks tended to focus on documenting their marketing and outreach efforts, such as attending chambers of commerce meetings. However, despite the benefits of the 1995 changes, the evaluation process remained heavily dependent on the political will of the agencies and staff implementing the regulations. The new rules did very little to define acceptable performance. This was still in the hands of the agencies and the examiners. Most community-group observers of CRA were expecting, or at least hoping, that the 1995 regulations would lead to more appropriate CRA grades, at least more appropriate than the 98 percent satisfactory and outstanding ratings that were being awarded by 1995. Community reinvestment advocates supported CRA reform in large part because they believed that a shift to performance-based regulations would help reduce substantial "grade inflation" in CRA ratings that reached very high levels beginning in the late 1980s.

Figure 7.1 shows that by 1992, only three years after FIRREA, CRA "grade inflation" had resurfaced in the evaluation system. By 1993, the number of banks receiving outstanding ratings had increased to nearly 15 percent, and the number of those with needs-to-improve or substantial noncompliance ratings had declined from almost 10 percent in 1990 to 6 percent. By 1996, the year before CRA reform went into effect, outstanding ratings had reached their 1990s peak of 26.5 percent, and less-than-satisfactory ratings were back down to pre-FIRREA levels of less than 2 percent.

Beginning in 1997, the first real year of CRA reform, outstanding ratings began a steady decline, although needs-to-improve and substantial-noncompliance ratings remained at extremely low levels. The number of institutions receiving outstanding ratings, while usually not focused on by the media or even by some advocates, is important because an outstanding rating goes a long way toward giving a bank an effective "safe harbor" against the possible denial of an application. It is much more difficult to effectively criticize or challenge a bank with an outstanding rating. Moreover, for any grading system to be effective, the top grade must truly represent exemplary performance. Especially for the vast majority of larger banks, which typically have the greatest impact on lower-income communities, the realistic range of CRA grade in the current political climate is between satisfactory and outstanding. It is extremely rare for a large institution to receive a needs-to-improve or substantial-noncompliance rating.

Figure 7.2 breaks out the percentage of banks that receive outstanding ratings by which agency regulates them. It finds fairly consistent patterns among all four regulators. However, two differences stand out. First, the OCC, which tends to regulate large banks, experienced a particularly steep decline in outstanding ratings from 1995 to 1998, the initial implementation of CRA Reform.[3] The OCC was the agency that took the lead in drafting the revised CRA regulations and was seen as the regulator most supportive of outcome-based regulations. Leadership at the agency, including Comptroller Eugene Ludwig and his chief of compliance policy, Steve Cross, appeared to lead the charge toward outcome-based regulation. However, in April 1998,

Figure 7.1 **CRA Ratings, 1990–2002**

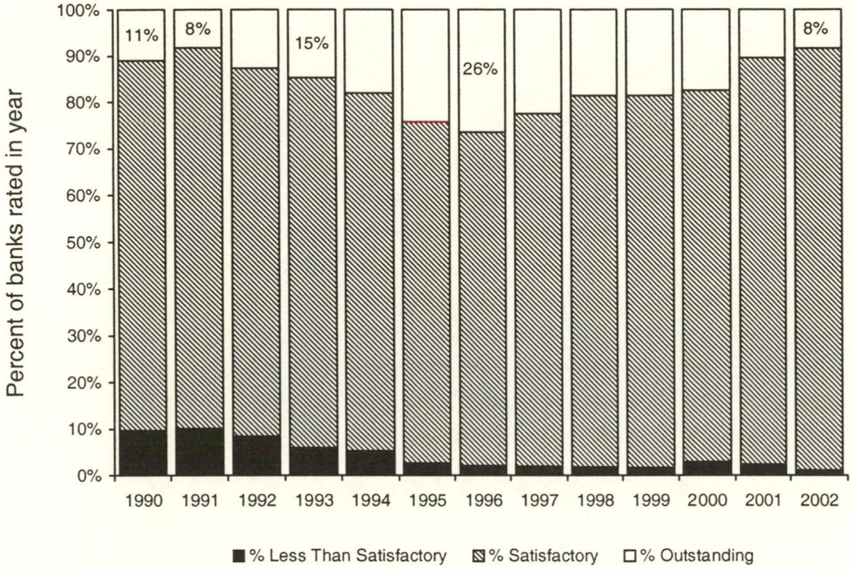

Source: Data from Federal Financial Institutions Examinations Council.

Ludwig left the agency and was replaced by John Hawke, a former banking attorney who had a long history of working closely with the industry. Hawke had been a member of the Shadow Financial Institutions Regulatory Committee, a group of deregulationists who had supported the abolition of CRA in the past (Shadow Financial Regulatory Committee 1994). Cross left the OCC for the FDIC soon afterward. The decline in outstanding ratings at the OCC and the OTS, the two executive agencies among the four regulators, began in 1996 and preceded the decline at the more "independent" FDIC and FRB. The decline at the OCC was particularly strong, going from more than 30 percent outstanding to just over 5 percent outstanding by 1998. However, there was a spike beginning in 1999, the year Deputy Comptroller Steve Cross left the agency, and ratings then closely matched those of the FRB and the OTS.

Since 1999, when Cross joined the FDIC to supervise compliance operations, the agency experienced a steep decline in ratings, so that by 2002 it was giving out fewer than 5 percent outstanding ratings. From 2000 to 2002, the FDIC, in particular, saw outstanding ratings decline to very modest levels. Before reading too much into the FDIC's apparent regulatory vigor in later years, it is important to control this analysis by size of institution. Large banks might be expected to have higher CRA ratings either because

180

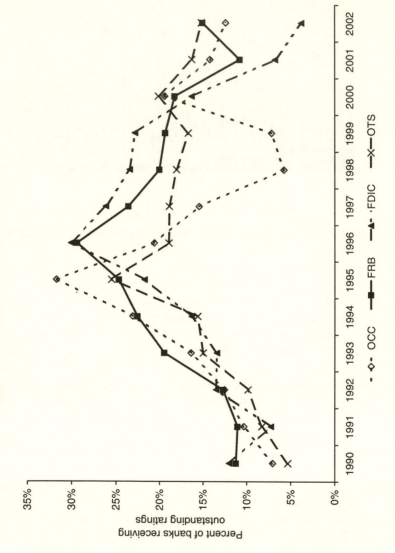

Figure 7.2 Outstanding CRA Ratings by Regulator, 1990–2002

Source: Data from Federal Financial Institutions Examinations Council.

they have been under more scrutiny by community groups and regulators or because regulators are more loath to give them poor ratings. Bank regulators are generally self-funded. They earn their revenues by levying fees on the banks they regulate. At the same time, most banks are able, if they choose, to reorganize their charters in a way that enables them to change their primary federal regulator. This means that if a regulator is "too hard" on a bank, it may simply switch regulators, thus costing the agency revenue. This is much less of a concern for agencies in the case of small banks, but is very important with larger banks, especially those with more than $5–10 billion in assets.

To control the effect of bank size on CRA ratings, Figure 7.3 breaks out CRA ratings by the asset size of institutions. Larger banks are much more likely to receive outstanding ratings. This is consistent with a multivariate analysis by Stegman, Cochran, and Faris (2002), which found that a $1 billion increase in asset level is associated with a 5 percent increase in the likelihood of a higher CRA rating. In fact, during the middle 1990s, more than 70 percent of banks with assets of more than $1 billion received outstanding CRA ratings. Other than a dip below 40 percent in 1998, outstanding ratings for the largest banks have remained well above 50 percent. Figure 7.3 also demonstrates that midsized and smaller banks, which account for the bulk of CRA evaluations, experienced much steeper declines in outstanding ratings. This size effect explains some of the lower ratings at the FDIC, which tends to regulate smaller banks than the other regulators. However, in 2001 and 2002, even when only considering banks with assets of under $250 million, the FDIC gave significantly fewer outstanding ratings than other regulators. In 2002, other regulators gave 10–14 percent of these small banks an outstanding rating while the FDIC gave only 1 percent of them an outstanding mark.

Again, while a variety of factors might account for this trend, it is worth noting that the former compliance policy chief at the OCC, Steve Cross, who was a key architect of CRA reform, moved to the FDIC in 1999 to take charge of compliance operations. Some may question the ability of one official to effect CRA ratings in such a substantial way, but the correlation between Cross's tenure at two different agencies and the rapid movement of OCC and FDIC ratings suggests otherwise. Moreover, Cross had earned a reputation as a conscientious regulator. Even Matthew Lee, an activist and perhaps the most outspoken critic of CRA regulators, said of Cross's move to the FDIC in 1999, "Increased CRA enforcement at the FDIC should be expected" (Lee 1999). Lee certainly appears to have been right. Whether this trend at the FDIC continues is questionable, given that Cross moved to the Federal Housing Finance Agency in 2002.

Figure 7.3 **Outstanding CRA Ratings by Asset Size of Institution, 1990–2002**

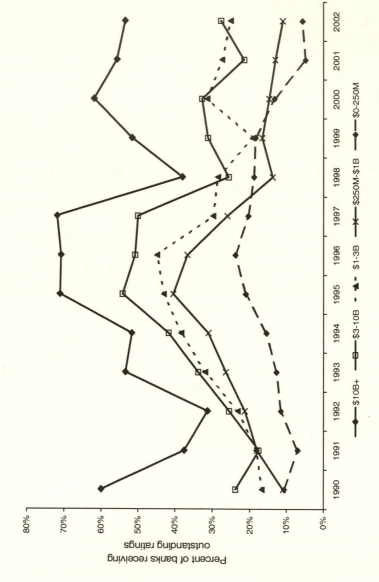

Percent of banks receiving outstanding ratings

◆ $10B+   □ $3-10B   ▲ $1-3B   × $250M-$1B   ◆ $0-250M

Source: Data from Federal Financial Institutions Examination Council.

The lesson of these significant changes in CRA ratings over relatively short periods of time is that, with leadership and political will, bank regulators can change the way they do things and create a more appropriate and sound CRA evaluation system. Any suggestions that CRA ratings are so high because examiners can find no flaws with bank performance is seriously undermined in the volatility of outstanding ratings during the 1990s. Different officials at regulatory agencies have clearly had different perspectives on what outstanding CRA performance means. Agency leadership has a choice of either exercising political will and regulatory independence or merely seeking to maintain budgets and allowing the agency to be become captive to industry interests.

Despite some of the positive developments in the late 1990s, post-reform CRA ratings did not signal a return to the highly aggressive CRA enforcement of the years immediately following FIRREA, when regulators increased less-than-satisfactory ratings to more than 10 percent of exams. Figure 7.4 shows that, whatever effect CRA reform might have had on strengthening the CRA evaluation process, it did not significantly increase the number of needs-to-improve and substantial noncompliance ratings. Within a few years of FIRREA, regulators returned to their practice of giving needs-to-improve and substantial noncompliance ratings only very rarely. All four agencies followed this trend, and CRA reform did not change this practice.

Another major continuing problem with CRA implementation is the persistent problem of large banks continuing to receive extremely high ratings. In the last five years of available data, 1997–2002, 46.5 percent of banks with assets of more than $3 billion—the sort of banks that dominate banking markets in midsized and larger cities—received outstanding ratings. With very rare exceptions, the remainder received satisfactory ratings. These ratings occur even in light of the continuing evidence of lending discrimination in mortgage and small business markets, the hypersegmentation of mortgage markets, predatory lending, and the large number of unbanked households.

From 1990 to 2002, one agency (the OCC) did not give the lowest rating, substantial noncompliance, to any bank with assets over $1 billion. The other three agencies did so only a total of six times. Over this same period, no regulator gave a bank with more than $3 billion in assets a rating of substantial noncompliance. Moreover, from 1998 to 2002, only one bank with assets of over $3 billion was given a needs-to-improve rating by any regulator.[4]

When looking at the very largest banks, those with $10 billion in assets or more, only three banks were given less than satisfactory ratings from 1990–2002. Figure 7.3 indicates that outstanding ratings for banks with more than $10 billion in assets are generally not as numerous as they were during their

Figure 7.4 **Needs-to-Improve and Substantial Noncompliance Ratings, 1990–2002**

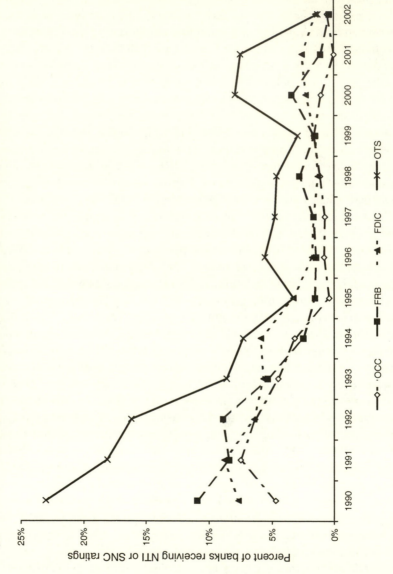

Source: Data from Federal Financial Institutions Examinations Council.

peak in the 1995–96 period. However, they remain at very high levels, with over 50 percent of the biggest banks receiving outstanding ratings.

Community Reinvestment Act Agreements in the 1990s

As discussed in chapter 6, CRA agreements have been an important tool in facilitating reinvestment in lower-income neighborhoods. However, they are more important than the specific dollars of reinvestment contained in their itemized goals. They represent an increased accountability of the banking industry to community interests. Increases in agreement activity suggests that CRA is being taken seriously by financial institutions and that regulators are actively enforcing the law. In an active CRA climate, regulators scrutinize bank lending, investments, and services closely, are discussing banks' performance with community organizations, and make CRA ratings more than perfunctory. As discussed earlier, the awarding of an outstanding rating (or its equivalent under the old system) has a good deal of significance. When institutions receive very high ratings, it is much harder to mount a meaningful challenge against them. While CRA technically offers no "safe harbor" from challenges from such institutions, the chance of an institution with an outstanding rating being denied or delayed during the application process on CRA grounds is very small. An institution with a satisfactory rating is much more likely to be concerned about a CRA challenge and about improving its performance.

Figure 7.5 illustrates some of the forces affecting banks' decisions to negotiate CRA agreements with community groups versus simply making unilateral CRA pledges or doing neither. Two critical factors affect the opportunities that community groups have to negotiate CRA mergers. First, as mergers increase, there are a larger number of important applications that involve CRA considerations. Second, these applications represent more significant opportunities for CRA agreements if the banks involved do not have outstanding ratings. If applications increase or outstanding ratings decline, community organizations are presented with more realistic opportunities for attempting to negotiate CRA agreements. At the same time, community organizations need to capitalize on these opportunities. A group's organizing and research capacity affects its ability to negotiate a CRA agreement. Another factor that affects CRA agreement activity is whether such agreements are considered favorably by regulators, especially compared to unilateral pledges by banks. These pledges entail very little scrutiny but can garner as much publicity as a CRA agreement. If regulators accept such pledges as the equivalent of CRA agreements that involve the serious input of community groups, banks are more likely to choose the unilateral pledge approach.

Figure 7.5 **Factors and Processes Affecting Banks' Choice to Engage in a CRA Agreement**

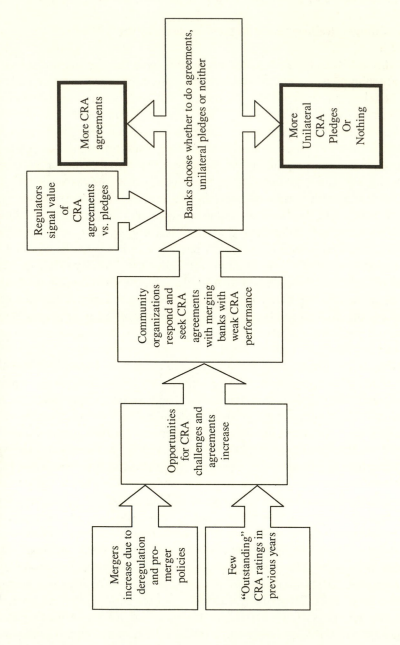

Figure 7.6 plots the number of CRA agreements and unilateral pledges involving banks from 1979 to 2000. The data were collected by the NCRC.` Also shown in the figure is the number of bank and thrift mergers in each year. There is a significant correspondence between the number of mergers and the number of CRA agreements, as expected. The figure also demonstrates that CRA pledges became more popular in the early 1990s.

As Figure 7.6 shows, the "heyday" of CRA agreement and pledge activity—at least as measured by the number of commitments—occurred from 1986 to 1994, with an average of twenty-nine CRA commitments per year. The peak in the number of CRA agreements occurred in 1990, the year following the FIRREA changes and the Joint Policy Statement on CRA by the regulators. What is different about the second half of the 1986–94 period, however, was the growth in the number of unilateral CRA pledges. While CRA agreements still outnumbered unilateral pledges, the pledges were on average much larger. Between 1991 and 1995, annual unilateral pledges averaged $12.5 billion versus only about $2.4 billion for CRA agreements. Figure 7.7 shows the cumulative amount of commitments of each type for the years 1990 to 2000. Pledges account for the majority of CRA commitment dollars in the 1990s.

By 1995, despite continuing high levels of merger activity, the number—but not the dollar amount—of CRA commitments began to wane. While mergers declined over the longer term, they did not fall significantly until 1999. One factor was the increase in outstanding ratings from 1992 to 1996. There is typically a significant lag in the effect of a CRA rating on a bank's predisposition to negotiate an agreement. When a bank files an application, its CRA rating is often over two years old. The FIRREA-induced correction of bank CRA ratings, from 1989 to 1992, to more reasonable levels had a very positive effect on CRA agreements, so that from 1992 to 1994, activists were much more likely to face banks with only satisfactory and not outstanding ratings. This made negotiation more feasible. However, from 1993 to 1996, banks had again benefited from extremely lax ratings, especially the larger institutions that were more likely to be involved in agreements. Thus, opportunities for agreements declined. More than 70 percent of the largest banks—those with more than $10 million in assets—now had outstanding CRA ratings, and many just simply ignored the criticisms and approaches of community groups. Regulators obliged by signaling that banks with outstanding ratings were unlikely to see a problem with the approval of applications.

Another factor played a role in the climate for CRA agreements. Banks were keeping an eye on the congressional debate over CRA, including how CRA agreements were viewed. The congressional climate was not supportive

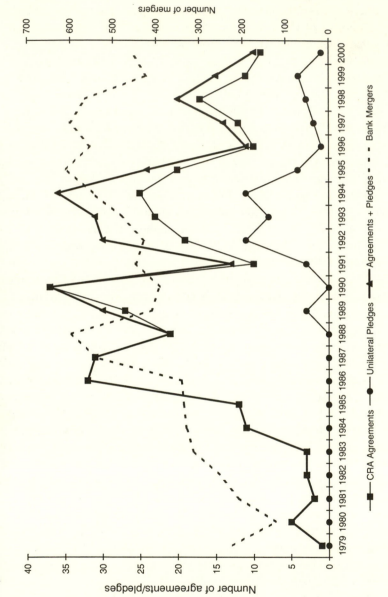

Figure 7.6 **CRA Commitment Activity, 1979–2000: Agreements vs. Pledges**

Source: Data from National Community Reinvestment Coalition 2002.

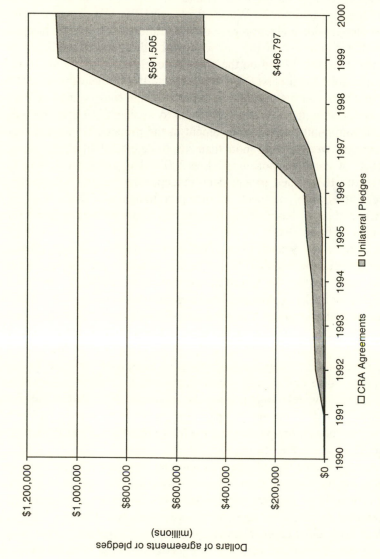

Figure 7.7 **Cumulative Dollar Amount of CRA Commitments, 1990–2000**

Source: Data from National Community Reinvestment Coalition 2002.

of community activism or CRA in the later half of the 1990s. Even if banks were not able to obtain outstanding ratings, in a CRA-hostile environment the likelihood of a merger denial or substantial delay was extremely small. Moreover, attacks on the motives and ethics of CRA activists diminished their standing and power. While attacks on CRA had occurred before, the 1994 congressional election gave the Republican Party, which has generally been less supportive of the law, control of both houses of Congress. The number two Republican on the committee, Senator Phil Gramm of Texas, was a vitriolic and tireless foe of CRA. In late 1998, when Alphonse D'Amato of New York lost his seat in the Senate, Gramm took control of the Senate Banking Committee. Gramm had set out to weaken CRA and, more directly, attack community group involvement in the process. He argued that CRA agreements were nothing more than corporate blackmail aimed at lining the pockets of greedy opportunists (Lee 2003). His office worked to develop stories of CRA-related arrangements that appeared, according to the senator's descriptions, highly suspect. Gramm's wrath against CRA was partly ideological and partly based on his historic ties to the politically powerful small bankers lobby in Texas.

In some ways, Senator Gramm's obsession with community activists may have diverted his attention from CRA evaluations and the regulators, who were implementing CRA reform and generally making it somewhat more difficult for banks to obtain outstanding ratings in the late 1990s. (The battle over the highly complex Gramm-Leach-Bliley Financial Modernization Act also occupied a great deal of his time and is discussed more below.) However, Gramm's efforts certainly undercut the ability of community groups to negotiate sound reinvestment agreements, especially for large, high-profile mergers. Some community groups were told by bankers with whom they had cooperative relationships that the senator's office had called the banks looking for "dirt" on the groups.[5] Groups were put on the defensive and forced to focus more on advocacy efforts aimed simply at protecting CRA from Gramm's efforts to gut the law.

Another factor that affected the number of CRA agreements in the late 1990s was the concentration of community groups' attention on a small number of very large mergers in 1998 and 1999. In some cases, groups focused substantial resources on negotiating agreements with the new "megabanks." But in many other cases, community groups were forced into the position of questioning the unilateral, nationwide pledges of these behemoth institutions. In 1998, when Nationsbank acquired Bank of America (and later took its name), it refused to negotiate agreements in local communities. It also refused to break down its $350 million unilateral community reinvestment pledge by region or city. Moreover, in this pledge it included $180 billion of small business loans that were not targeted to low- and moderate-income neighborhoods. Similarly, community groups criticized Citibank when it merged with The Travelers Group and announced a $115 billion CRA pledge, a large amount of which was credit card lending, which is generally not included in such pledges or considered in CRA evaluations (Lee 2003). In San Francisco, activists and local government pressed Nationsbank to disclose its plans for the former Bank of America headquarters and operations, as well as lending goals for California, but the bank refused (de Senerpont Domis 1998; Seiberg 1998). Bank One, which acquired First Chicago NBD in Chicago in 1998, also refused to negotiate local CRA agreements. Bank One made exceptions for Chicago and Detroit, where First Chicago NBD had agreements in place and where expectations among community groups for new agreements were high (Bush and Immergluck 2003).

After 1999, merger activity slowed down considerably. Therefore, even though there had been some decline in outstanding ratings in the late 1990s, there were fewer opportunities for agreements. In addition, the attention of activists had been drawn to two other critical issues: (1) protecting CRA from Senate Banking Committee Chair Gramm's attacks during and following the adoption of financial modernization legislation; and (2) increased advocacy and attention around the growing problem of predatory lending. The first issue will be addressed more below, and the second will be addressed in chapter 8.

Fair Lending in the 1990s—In Like a Lion, Out Like a Lamb

In addition to the varying attention given to CRA enforcement in the 1990s, fair lending laws also experienced large swings in how strongly they were enforced. Some of the factors that led to changes in CRA and HMDA also led to better fair lending law and enforcement. The improvement of HMDA to include race and gender information gave regulators and the Department of Justice a new tool to identify potential discrimination. Moreover, the release of the new HMDA data, the "Color of Money" series, the two Boston Federal Reserve studies, and the related congressional scrutiny all worked to push regulators toward paying much more attention to fair lending laws. Many of these factors were, in turn, the direct or indirect results of community organizing and activism. Even earlier, in 1988, changes to the Fair Housing Act (FaHA) gave authority to the Justice Department to seek monetary awards in fair lending suits. In 1991, the department was given similar powers under the Equal Credit Opportunity Act (ECOA). This increased the gravity of Justice Department actions, and, since the early 1990s, "every suit brought by the U.S. Department of Justice has been the focus of great interest, at least among lenders" (Walter 1995).

Fair lending law is important, not just because it specifically addresses discrimination against individuals, but because it includes enforcement mechanisms that CRA does not. These include civil fines and the consent decrees that force banks to change their processes and behavior. Moreover, fair lending law covers all mortgage and small business lenders, not just banks and thrifts. Given the growing market share of nonbank lenders, this has made fair lending law an increasingly important tool for improving access to credit.

Following the 1988 amendments to the Fair Housing Act, pressure mounted on the regulators to use match-paired testing to detect discrimination by lenders. In 1991, the Consumer Advisory Council of the FRB recommended that the board sponsor a systematic matched-pair testing study of mortgage lenders at the preapplications stage of the lending process. Unfortunately the board rejected this suggestion. Galster (1996) responded to the board's action by suggesting that "ignorance is bad public policy." In 1992, the Urban Institute proposed a five-city pilot study to all the bank regulators as well as Fannie Mae, Freddie Mac, and the Department of Justice. All the agencies rejected the proposal.

In the early 1990s, small amounts of federal funds began to made available for fair lending testing through the Fair Housing Initiatives Program, through which the Department of Housing and Urban Development (HUD) funds nonprofit fair housing groups to enforce fair housing laws. One of the earliest testing projects by fair housing groups was conducted in Chicago (Smith and Cloud 1996). The Chicago Area Fair Housing Alliance tested ten lenders and found some evidence of disparate treatment at seven of the ten institutions. This included black testers getting less help or less information from loan officers. Black testers also were told that the lender did not make loans under a certain amount, were referred to Federal Housing Authority (FHA) lenders, or were notified that the lender did not make loans to first-time homebuyers. In 1992, the Philadelphia Commission on Human Relations received HUD funding to conduct a testing study. It conducted more than 270 tests of 68 lenders. These tests resulted in eleven formal complaints to HUD. Five of these resulted in consent orders or settlement agreements, which included specific changes to lender practices. The presence of actual testing created a new climate in which discrimination carried substantially higher risks for institutions.

The Justice Department began its "fair lending initiative" in 1992 when the department and Decatur Federal Savings and Loan entered into a consent decree to settle the first suit alleging a pattern and practice of lending discrimination under ECOA and the FaHA. The Decatur suit followed directly from an investigation that used HMDA data and showed very large disparities in denial rates between minority and white borrowers of similar incomes. In this case and others like it, the Justice Department found evidence that bank employees were providing assistance to white applicants that they were not providing to black and Hispanic applicants (U.S. Department of Justice 2001). Soon afterward, the department announced its investigation of Shawmut Mortgage Company, an affiliate of Shawmut National Bank, for fair lending violations. Then, in the spring of 1993, the OCC issued a bulletin explaining that offering disparate levels of assistance to borrowers of different races and ethnicities was a form of discrimination. Later that year, the FRB denied Shawmut National Corporation's application to acquire a bank based on the Justice Department investigation. At the end of the year, the Justice Department entered into a consent decree with Shawmut. Then in the fall of 1994, HUD entered into a voluntary fair lending "best practices" agreement with the Mortgage Bankers Association.

A key policy event occurred in April 1994, when a federal Interagency Task Force on Fair Lending issued a joint policy statement (Interagency Task Force on Fair Lending 1994). One of the key points of the statement was a declaration that the agencies would follow the courts in considering disparate impact discrimination a violation of the law. In this statement, the regulators said that lenders that adopt lending policies having disproportionately negative effects on a protected class will be found to be discriminating under fair lending laws, unless they can show a business necessity for doing so. This meant that lenders could not easily use lending policies like large minimum loan sizes or compensating balance requirements to steer clear of lending to minority homeowners or businesses. The lending industry worked behind the scenes to undercut the new administration's efforts on fair lending. In 1995, for example, after Republicans gained control of Congress, Representative Bill McCollum, a Republican from Florida and longtime supporter of banking causes, proposed legislation to modify ECOA and the FaHA so that they would not cover disparate impact discrimination. The bill made it out of subcommittee but not out of the full House Banking Committee.

Another key step in fair lending enforcement was the move to consider discrimination not just in the approval of loans but also in marketing and sales. In August of 1994, Chevy Chase Federal Savings Bank entered into a consent decree with the Department of Justice to settle charges that the bank had failed to market its services in minority neighborhoods.[6] The Justice Department had found that the bank made very few loans in black neighborhoods in Washington, DC, and Prince Georges County, Maryland, and that it had very few branches in or near these areas. In the decree, the bank agreed to open branches in the affected neighborhoods. By 1995, 60 percent of the loans made by the bank were in black neighborhoods (Department of Justice 2001). The Chevy Chase case was a critical statement against not just discrimination but also redlining, and it considered disparate marketing and branch presences as a form of redlining.

In 1997, the Department sued Albank, a thrift in Albany, New York. Albank had made loans only through its branches until the middle 1980s, when it expanded its lending through mortgage brokers. It instructed its brokers that it would not take loans from certain cities in Connecticut (Department of Justice 2001). As it turned out, these cities were the only parts of Connecticut with significant minority populations. This lawsuit was another important move in that it extended the government's view of discrimination to policies and practices implemented via mortgage brokers. Thus, the government was suggesting that lenders would be liable in any attempts to "outsource" discriminatory practices. The bank entered into a consent decree in which it agreed to remove its geographic restrictions and make $55 million in loans at below-market rates to residents of the previously redlined areas.

The Justice Department depends partly on referrals from banking regulators and HUD to pursue fair lending cases. However, the department also initiates cases on its own. From 1992 through 2000, the department initiated sixteen major fair lending lawsuits, a record level, and obtained more than $63 million in relief for borrowers (Department of Justice 2001). Ten of these suits originated from referrals from bank regulators, and most dealt with home-purchase lending. Given their failure to enforce CRA and fair lending laws in the 1980s, the regulators were under a good deal of pressure to demonstrate a change in behavior. In the early 1990s, the regulators began using statistical, regression-based methods to help them identify lending discrimination, at least among larger lenders that made enough loans to use these techniques. Examiners could first use the regular HMDA data to spot large disparities and then pull samples of loan files to gather additional data on borrowers.

The Justice Department also filed a number of suits that had implications for recent developments in fair lending—predatory lending and credit scoring. First, the department filed three suits that addressed race-based differences in loan pricing. In suits against Huntington Mortgage and Fleet Mortgage Company in 1995 and 1996, the department found that the companies' loan officers were charging higher up-front fees for home loans for minority borrowers than for similarly situated white buyers. Then in 1996, the department sued a subprime lender, Long Beach Mortgage, later acquired by the thrift Washington Mutual, for allowing loan officers as well as independent mortgage brokers with whom it did business to charge borrowers up-front fees as high as 12 percent of the loan amount, and for charging minorities higher fees than whites. The department again argued that the lender was responsible for broker actions. In the settlement, Long Beach agreed to change its pricing policies and paid a total of $3 million to affected borrowers (Department of Justice 2001). In January 1998, the Federal Trade Commission filed an action against Capital City Mortgage, a lender in Washington, DC. The Department of Justice filed an amicus brief. The government argued that the company had engaged in reverse redlining by targeting minority neighborhoods for predatory home loans with high expectations of defaults.

Because mortgage lenders have increasingly turned to credit scoring and automated underwriting approaches, fair lending law enforcement has a new set of issues to address. One facet of credit scoring is the use of overrides, in which lenders approve loans that scoring systems alone would tend to reject. In 1999, the department filed a complaint against Deposit Guaranty National Bank in Mississippi. The department alleged that the lender allowed individual loan officers to override automated underwriting decisions in an inconsistent way. Black applicants were more than three times as likely to be rejected as similarly situated white applicants. The settlement called for 250 applicants to share in a $3 million fund and for the bank to tighten up its override procedures. But to this day, other than dealing with the override issue, neither the bank regulators nor the Department of Justice has made a serious attempt to investigate credit scoring or automated underwriting systems for possible discriminatory effects.

The vigor of federal fair lending enforcement by the banking regulators was not sustained past 1997. Fair lending referrals from regulators fell from twenty-seven in 1997 alone to only a total of twenty-nine for the years 1998 to 2001 combined. This finding appears particularly odd given the growth of subprime lending and the heightened public awareness to discrimination in the pricing and terms of mortgages. Also, in January 1999, the banking regulators issued new Interagency Fair Lending Examination Procedures. The procedures indicated a shift in regulator policy. First, they clearly deemphasized efforts to identify disparate impact discrimination. Exams were instead refocused primarily on disparate treatment. The procedures explicitly stated that "examiners should focus on possible disparate *treatment*" (emphasis is original) (Federal Financial Institutions Examination Council 1999, 27). In fact, any examination for disparate impact was categorized as "special analysis" and was discussed only in the appendix of the procedures.

Another problem with recent fair lending enforcement concerns the growing importance of credit scoring and automated underwriting. The 1999 procedures do not call for examining the issue of disparate impact in credit scoring systems or the use of credit scoring systems in highly segmented marketing practices. The procedures focus only on the override issue and the illegality of using protected class characteristics (or variables that are obviously proxies for such characteristics but that have no connection to lending criteria). As discussed in chapter 4, concerns over the discriminatory impact of these systems go well beyond these issues. Regulators should examine the detailed functioning of the underlying models. Moreover, given the historical and ongoing public sponsorship and subsidy of Freddie Mac and Fannie Mae, the public should have access to the detailed workings of their automated underwriting systems. The HUD, under some pressure from fair lending advocates, did undertake a review of government-sponsored enterprise (GSE) automated underwriting systems in the late 1990s. To date, no findings from this review have been released.

Overall, the vigor with which the federal government has pursued lending discrimination appears to have declined greatly since the middle-to-late 1990s. John Relman, a well-known attorney practicing in the fair lending field for many years, has been quoted as stating that the Bush administration had "deliberately put the brakes on fair lending investigations" by the Justice Department (Garver 2002). The department did investigate MAF Bancorp, a good-sized Chicago-based thrift, in 2002 and settled with them late that year. However, this investigation was difficult for the Justice Department to avoid initiating. The Chicago-based Woodstock Institute had analyzed the thrift's lending patterns in 2001 and found that the thrift's market share for home purchase loans among white borrowers was almost four times that among black borrowers (Woodstock Institute 2002). For refinance loans, the disparity was even worse, with MAF's share among white borrowers being more than seven times its share among blacks. The institute argued to the OTS that the thrift should not be allowed to acquire another local institution and that it should be investigated for fair lending violations. The institute later cited similar data in arguing to the FRB that the thrift's CRA assessment area arbitrarily excluded minority communities. The board required the thrift to expand the assessment area. The Justice Department investigation followed closely on the heels of the institute's analyses and appeals to regulators. In December 2002, the thrift agreed to, among other things, open or acquire two branch offices in minority areas, implement a targeted advertising campaign to increase minority lending, provide $10 million in benefits to borrowers through special financing programs of affected areas, and contribute $500,000 to home buyer education and counseling programs.

Fair Lending Policy and Small Business Credit

Another area that was the subject of a good deal of debate during the 1990s was the issue of fair lending policy in the small business arena. Until 2002, Regulation B, which implements the ECOA, actually prohibited banks from collecting data on the race and gender of small business borrowers, even though HMDA required them to do so for mortgage loans. As early as 1995, the FRB proposed changing Regulation B to allow, but not require, lenders to collect race and gender information about applicants for nonmortgage loans, including small business loans. But in 1996, the board pulled its proposal, arguing that it now felt that the issue was better dealt with in Congress. Then, as described in chapter 3, a series of new and compelling studies began to come out in the late 1990s documenting the existence and considerable magnitude of discrimination in small business lending. Several of these reports found that, after controlling for business and personal financial characteristics, black-owned firms were denied loans twice as often as white-owned firms. As the evidence mounted, the FRB issued an Advanced Notice of Proposed Rulemaking in 1998 questioning whether the board should change Regulation B to allow banks to voluntarily collect racial data on small business loans.[7] A year later the board followed with a Notice of Proposed Rulemaking, which indicated that it intended to make the change and allow voluntary data collection.[8]

While community groups, minority business advocates, and others desired mandatory small business data collection and disclosure of the sort required under HMDA, they recognized that this was not feasible in the political climate of the late 1990s. While some officially went on record as continuing to call for mandatory reporting and disclosure, they supported the voluntary collection proposal as a fallback position. In addition, the Departments of Justice and Treasury, as well as the OTS, the OCC, and the Small Business Administration, also supported the proposal. The Federal Reserve had had four years to consider this policy change, and now had ample evidence to argue that discrimination did exist in the small business credit market. However, the proposal faced considerable opposition from the banking industry and from Senator Phil Gramm, and Senator Richard Shelby, who later succeeded Gramm as chair. In a press release in late 1999, Shelby said, "The Federal Reserve has no business getting involved in social policy," in effect challenging the board's fundamental role in implementing the ECOA, or perhaps the act itself. Shelby, Gramm, and some other Senate Banking Committee members even made the curious argument in a letter to Federal Reserve Chairman Greenspan that "a creditor cannot discriminate against an applicant based on race . . . if the creditor never collects such data," as if to suggest that lenders were blindfolded when they made loans.[9] Opponents of the bill also reached out to conservative small business and privacy groups to garner additional opposition to the regulatory change. The result of the opposition was that the board delayed any decision on Regulation B until 2002, after Senator Gramm's retirement, when it finally ruled to allow voluntary data collection.

Unfortunately, while the change to Regulation B was an important first step, mandatory data are critical to adequately enforce fair lending laws in the small business market. Better bank-level data are needed to measure and explain business-lending activity in lower-income and minority neighborhoods, as well as lending to minority-owned firms in any location. Bank regulators need access to HMDA-like microdata on small business loan applications, including details such as denials, loan purpose, industry, and race of owner. These data would enable regulators to identify potential violators of CRA and fair lending laws in a much more efficient and effective manner than is currently possible. Moreover, public access to such data is needed to allow for the sort of activism and attention to small business lending that followed the FIRREA changes to HMDA in the early 1990s.

Neither the Department of Justice nor the bank regulators have been active in actually enforcing fair lending laws in the small business arena. In the middle 1990s, the Department of Justice clearly signaled that they would begin investigating potential small business lending discrimination. By the end of the decade, however, the department's annual reports did not indicate that any actual investigations had been initiated (Department of Justice 2001).

Fannie Mae and Freddie Mac: The Push for Accountability

As far back as the late 1970s, as community groups became more sophisticated in dealing with banks around CRA issues, they often ran up against the issue of secondary markets. Many banks would claim that they had difficulty making loans if Fannie Mae and Freddie Mac would not buy them. Regulators' risk-based capital standards require banks to hold larger reserves for loans that they hold in portfolio than for mortgage-backed securities or other assets. Thus, banks want to sell their loans to the GSEs in order to increase their liquidity and leverage. Moreover, independent mortgage companies, which typically have less direct access to capital than banks or bank-affiliated mortgage lenders, rely very heavily on Fannie and Freddie to replenish their capital for lending.

In the late 1980s and early 1990s, community and consumer groups focused more on the role of secondary-market GSEs.[10] In the tenth-anniversary hearings on CRA, held in March 1988, consumer and community groups, including ACORN, the Center for Community Change, the Woodstock Institute, and the National Training and Information Center, cited Fannie Mae and Freddie Mac underwriting policies, and the perception of those policies by lenders, as impediments to lending in lower-income and minority neighborhoods.[11] Critics of the agencies argued that their inflexible underwriting standards encouraged lending in middle- and upper-income areas. Reminiscent of criticisms of the FHA, the complaints focused on how the growing secondary market firms had created an unlevel playing field that worked to the detriment of more diverse, mixed-use urban neighborhoods.

Fannie Mae and Freddie Mac's charters required them to pay attention to the amount of their activities that benefited low- and moderate-income families. Since the 1970s, HUD had established a nonbinding goal that 30 percent of the mortgages purchased by Fannie Mae be for families with incomes below the metropolitan median income and that 30 percent be for homes located in central cities. However, Senate hearings had established that HUD had not monitored the agencies' progress toward these goals. In 1991, some consumer groups argued that Fannie and Freddie should be required to devote a portion of their earnings to low-income housing, similar to the approach used with the Federal Home Loan Bank system (Fishbein 2003). Others argued that somewhat stronger lending goals for lower-income households ought to be codified in a statute. A coalition of national consumer and housing groups met to develop a proposal and decided on the second approach. Their proposal called for a new, more targeted affordable housing goal in addition to the "30/30" goal that HUD had developed. This new goal was to count only housing for borrowers under 80 percent of the local area median income, with a portion directed at those with incomes below 60 percent of the median income. The GSEs supported a special affordable housing goal in legislative debate but opposed codifying the 30/30 goals. According to Fishbein (2003), the "compelling evidence of the GSE's weak performance in serving low income housing needs proved out." The 30/30 provision as well as the special affordable housing provision were enacted in the Federal Housing Enterprises Financial Safety and Soundness Act of 1992. The act gave HUD "mission" regulatory authority over the GSEs, directing it to set annual affordable housing purchase levels, collect data, and monitor compliance with fair lending laws.

Figure 7.8 illustrates the impact of the 1992 GSE Act on Fannie and Freddie penetration into lower-income lending markets. The GSE Act has led to an increase in the agencies' funding of loans to modest-income families.[12] Similar results are evident in the geographic targets. The percent of loans benefiting modest-income and minority tracts increased from 28 percent in 1996 to 32 percent for Fannie Mae and from 25 percent to 32 percent for Freddie Mac. The gains and goals grew more slowly for the geographic targets, in part because of the increasing mobility of modest-income households into suburban areas (Immergluck and Smith 2003).

As the secondary market GSEs made gains in serving lower-income households and neighborhoods, community and consumer groups began to hear reports of the agencies' forays into the subprime market. In 1997, Freddie Mac purchased over $200 million of subprime loans ("Freddie Mac Launches"

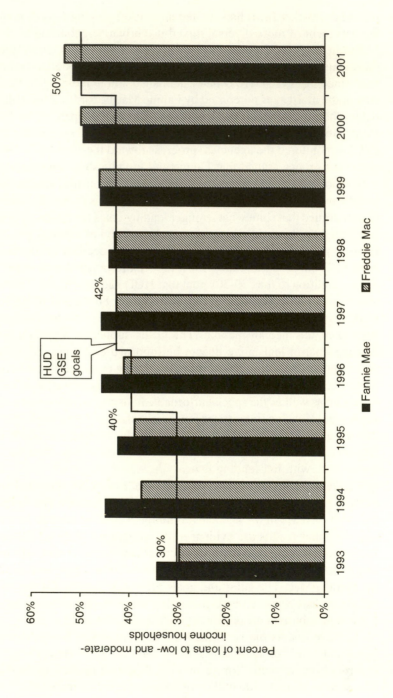

Figure 7.8   Fannie Mae and Freddie Mac Performance vs. Low- and Moderate-Income Housing Goals, 1993–2001

1997). In addition to purchasing mortgages, Freddie Mac also began guaranteeing securities packages backed by subprime mortgages. This process, known as "wrapping," enables subprime lenders to increase the marketability and profit on the sales of its loans. Freddie Mac had wrapped $8 billion of subprime securities through 1999, including substantial activity with specialized subprime lenders (Skillern 2000). Consumer groups became increasingly concerned that the GSEs would provide lower-cost capital to subprime lenders, enabling them to expand further with no reduction in predatory activity. At the same time, subprime lenders were generally opposed to the GSE's entering the subprime market, because this would expand the competition they would face. They had developed access to specialized high-risk capital sources through private securitizations. The entrance of the GSEs into the market would mean that more lenders could make subprime loans and do so at a potentially lower price. Consumer groups were concerned, however, that in many neighborhoods and market areas, competition would still be a minimal factor and that, if left to their own devices, subprime lenders would simply increase profits by obtaining lower-cost capital, enabling them to expand operations without passing on any cost savings to borrowers.

As a result of increasing community concerns over its growing role in the subprime market, Fannie Mae announced in April of 2000 that, in order to avoid funding predatory lenders, it would not purchase loans with a number of features. These features included single premium credit life insurance and fees exceeding 5 percent of the loan amount. Freddie Mac was compelled to follow suit, at least to some degree, and soon thereafter issued a statement saying it would not purchase loans with single premium credit insurance (Bailey 2000). However, community and consumer groups pushed for more. HUD was taking comments on revising the regulations implementing the 1992 GSE Act, and Fannie and Freddie's announcements were certainly aimed at winning the support of consumer groups during this process. But some consumer groups argued for more than voluntary pledges and little accountability. They argued that HUD should not count subprime loans toward the GSE housing goals unless they were screened for a much more complete set of predatory features. Some also argued that any loans that exhibit a more egregious set of predatory practices should be given substantial negative weight toward the goals.[13] While HUD did place some limits on what sort of loans they would count, it did not go nearly so far as these recommendations. In fact, Figure 7.8 shows that after performing worse than Fannie Mae for many years in terms of lending to lower-income households, Freddie Mac overtook Fannie Mae in 1999. This was most likely due to Freddie's more aggressive entrance into the subprime market. Moreover, while the regulations covered loan purchases by the agencies, they did not appear to restrict GSE involvement in guaranteeing and facilitating the securitization of subprime loans.

By the end of the decade, Fannie Mae and Freddie Mac were both significantly involved in the subprime market, although Freddie Mac remains the larger player thus far. In 2000, the GSEs purchased approximately 14 percent of subprime mortgages, but that portion could rise to 50 percent in the near future (Temkin, Johnson, and Levy 2002). In the first quarter of 2000 alone, Freddie Mac purchased approximately $2.5 billion of subprime mortgages and wrapped or otherwise participated in another $5.3 billion worth of subprime securitizations ("Freddie Mac Expecting" 2000). The growing role of the GSEs in the subprime market has the potential for reducing excessive pricing for subprime loans. However, the current HUD goals and voluntary restrictions by the GSEs are not enough to ensure that borrowers will benefit from secondary market involvement. Given the history of the GSEs and the fact that they were created by the federal government, received substantial initial federal funding, and continue to receive substantial explicit and implicit subsidies, the agencies should be held to much stronger standards of responsible lending. Moreover, these standards should cover all sorts of involvements—including any insuring or facilitating of subprime lending or securitization.

Financial Modernization Legislation and the Community Reinvestment Act

From the perspective of CRA advocates, the 1990s ended on a clearly defensive note. Since Republicans took control of Congress in the fall of 1994, there were a number of attempts to roll back CRA. In 1995, Senators Richard Shelby (R–AL) and Connie Mack (R–FL) and Representatives Doug Bereuter (R–NE) and Bill McCollum (R–FL) introduced bills that would exempt small banks from CRA and provide a "safe harbor" to institutions receiving satisfactory CRA ratings (Taylor 1995). The latter act would have preempted any CRA challenges for the 97 percent of banks receiving satisfactory or better ratings. McCollum, in particular, continued to pursue attempts to cut CRA back in succeeding years.

Even before Senator Phil Gramm took control of the Senate Banking Committee in November 1998, he sought to use financial modernization legislation—the name given to legislation that would roll back Glass-Steagall barriers between banking and other financial services activities—as a vehicle for weakening CRA (Taylor 1998). But when Gramm took over as chair of the committee, supporters of CRA knew they were in for a fight to save the law. Alfonse D'Amato, Gramm's predecessor, had not wanted any battle over CRA to derail the financial modernization bill. He was a pragmatist; Gramm was much more of an ideologue.

Gramm focused on three CRA policies that he wanted in the financial modernization bill. First, he wanted small banks exempted from CRA. Initially, the size threshold for exemption was under $250 million in assets, although that was reduced later to $100 million. Second, he wanted banks that had satisfactory CRA ratings to be given safe harbor from any CRA challenges. Finally, he wanted extensive oversight of community group–bank agreements and community group behavior, with criminal penalties for violations of new regulations.

Gramm was most vocal on, and received the greatest attention for, his aggressive attitude toward community groups. Gramm used terms like "bribery" and "extortion" to describe the actions of community groups negotiating CRA agreements with banks (Parks 1999). He pointed to anecdotes of groups that appeared to take money in exchange for not challenging banks' applications to regulators. He went further by implying that this was a common practice, effectively portraying all community groups involved in CRA agreements, as well as many involved in other sorts of bank partnerships, as "extortionists."

In response, community groups and coalitions argued that CRA agreements were not significantly about funding groups involved with the negotiations. NCRC, the leading association of such groups, analyzed its database of CRA agreements and found that, out of $1 trillion in CRA agreement commitments, only $160,000, or less than two thousandths of a percent, went to the advocacy groups involved in the agreements (Taylor 1999). Many groups that negotiated agreements did not accept any funds for themselves. Others tended to use the modest amount of funds from an agreement to operate programs that provided services directly supportive of the agreement, such as mortgage counseling. Moreover, the Treasury Department issued a report that found that fewer than 1 percent of applications were protested on CRA grounds, and of those, more than 90 percent were rejected by regulators (Fraser 1999).

Gramm's concerns about community groups' somehow abusing CRA were highly inconsistent with the power that community groups have relative to the banks themselves. Banks regularly request community development organizations that they fund at significant levels—often groups that are not likely to challenge a bank publicly—to provide testimony to the banks' community reinvestment performance. This may be in the form of letters that are put in banks' CRA public files or testimony at public hearings. For example, when the Federal Reserve held hearings on the Bank One–First Chicago NBD merger in 1998, Bank One was able to enlist a large number of groups that it funded to testify in favor of the merger.[14] Banks routinely use their philanthropic support as implicit or explicit leverage in such situations.

An anecdote is instructive here. In the late 1990s, a large bank developed its CRA Strategic Plan and, per the regulations, sought input from community organizations. The Strategic Plan is an alternative method of CRA regulation established by the 1995 CRA regulations in which banks can develop CRA goals themselves after seeking input from community groups. (For more on Strategic Plans, see the appendix to this chapter.) In this case, a few groups raised significant concerns in writing about the plan during the formal comment process. After receiving the comments, one member of the regulator's staff suggested to the bank that these comments were a potential obstacle to obtaining approval of the plan. The bank then contacted one of the groups, which it had been a contributor to, and asked the group to modify its comments. The group did so.[15] If there is any asymmetry in the bank-community group relationship, it certainly favors the bank.

While the major banking lobbies did not openly support Gramm's attacks on community reinvestment advocates, they certainly did not oppose them. A spokesperson for the American Bankers Association said, "We would not tell Senator Gramm to drop his concerns" (Parks 1999). In preparing for his committee's hearings on CRA, Gramm's staff approached major banks directly, asking them for copies of CRA agreements and correspondence with community groups. Despite substantial investigations, the committee failed to produce evidence of significant or systemic extortion in the CRA process.

In the meantime, the financial services industry was pushing Congress and the administration hard for a financial modernization bill. In the 1997–98 election cycle alone, banks, securities firms, and insurance companies made more than $87 million in contributions to federal parties and candidates, with the majority going to Republicans (Center for Responsive Politics 2000). In the final days of the debate, Citigroup, a major financial modernization supporter, hired former secretary of the treasury Robert Rubin, a key architect of the law, as cochairman of the company. The newsletter of the Independent Community Bankers of America commented, "The revolving door between high Treasury and White House officials and powerful financial firms is nothing new. But the timing of this one is particularly troublesome."

Due to opposition in the House Banking Committee and the White House, Gramm's proposals were weakened in negotiations. NCRC, its members, and other advocates worked extremely hard to demonstrate support for CRA across the country. They lobbied not only their legislators but also the Clinton administration. Their efforts resulted in editorials by major newspapers supporting the act and in mayors of major cities making public statements documenting CRA's importance to the vitality of their cities. Unfortunately, while advocates and their allies publicly argued that any modernization bill should extend CRA to the new financial conglomerates, including mortgage, securities, and insurance affiliates, most advocates recognized that they would be lucky to avoid a major elimination of CRA requirements even for banks themselves.

The final bill, the Financial Services Modernization Act of 1999, better known as the Gramm-Leach-Bliley Act (GLBA), damaged CRA in several ways. First, CRA was effectively weakened by allowing for the continuing convergence of banking and nonbank activities without extending CRA obligations to activities not directly carried out by the banks themselves. Under GLBA, even direct bank subsidiaries remain not covered by CRA. Banks can choose to have the activities of either subsidiaries or affiliates (through bank or financial holding companies) considered in a bank CRA exam, but this is at the discretion of the bank. This provides banks with a sort of "extra credit" option. If the affiliate or subsidiary detracts from the bank's performance, the bank is likely to opt not to have it considered. This also creates the ability to "game" the CRA regulations, by shifting lending to more affluent areas and borrowers to affiliates or subsidiaries, making the bank look like it focuses more on lower-income communities. GLBA did nothing to modernize CRA regulation as it modernized other forms of bank regulation. This was the largest single problem with the law from a CRA perspective.

Rather than eliminate CRA for small banks, GLBA rolled back the frequency of CRA exams for small institutions. It also imposed a new set of "sunshine" disclosure requirements on banks and community groups. The vast majority of community reinvestment advocates had no problem with making CRA agreements public, and many, if not most, already did. But the uncertainty over how burdensome the reporting would be and how it might affect advocacy—particularly among groups only occasionally engaged in advocacy—was a concern. For community reinvestment advocates who routinely worked with banks, such a statute was unlikely to affect their own direct activities. But many coalitions working on CRA issues include organizations for whom CRA negotiations are a small part of what they do. Such regulations, depending on how they were written, could push such groups to refrain from interacting with banks—hardly a desirable outcome.

The final version of GLBA also required that banks seeking to acquire affiliates through "financial holding companies" have and maintain CRA ratings of satisfactory or better. While this was certainly better than the safe harbor protections proposed by Gramm, it means little unless banks face a realistic, significant prospect of receiving a needs-to-improve or substantial-noncompliance rating. Moreover, earlier House versions of the bill would have required regulators to hold hearings in places where larger acquisitions or mergers might have significant impacts. The earlier House bill also included an application requirement for mergers between banks and nondepository institutions with assets of more than $40 billion. GLBA did not include these provisions.

Many view the GLBA CRA actions as moderately deleterious to the law, but not catastrophic. It is true that some larger bullets were dodged, including the complete exception of small banks from CRA and more aggressive attacks on community organizations. However, the bigger problem with GLBA was that it facilitated continued convergence within the financial services sector without requiring CRA obligations of these new diversified banking organizations. Unlike with FIRREA ten years earlier, CRA supporters were not able to use a major financial restructuring bill as leverage for preserving or expanding reinvestment policy.

APPENDIX

The Final 1995 Community Reinvestment Act Regulations

Lending Test

The Lending Test is an evaluation of a bank's lending activities, including the overall amount of lending and the distribution of loans by location and income of borrower. This part of the exam is the most heavily weighted portion in the calculation of the CRA rating, accounting for 50 percent of the overall score. It focuses primarily on direct lending to households and small businesses. Examiners consider residential, small business, and community development lending. Consumer lending is also considered if a bank chooses to include it or if consumer lending constitutes a substantial majority of the bank's business. Regulators examine the bank's lending performance according to the following criteria:

1. Lending activity—the number and dollar amount of loans.
2. Geographic distribution—whether the loans are within the bank's assessment area and the proportion of loans in low- and moderate-income census tracts.
3. Borrower characteristics—the income of homebuyers and the number of loans to small businesses/farms with less than $1 million in annual revenues.
4. Community development lending—additional loans with a primary purpose of community development.[16]
5. The use of innovative or flexible lending practices.

Community development lending includes loans that serve community development purposes and do not qualify as mortgage, small business, small farm, or consumer loans.[17] The loans must benefit the bank's assessment area or a broader area that includes the bank's assessment area. Examples of community development lending include loans for affordable housing, day care, education, and other social services. Credit is also given for debt provided to nonprofit or for-profit community development lenders who then re-lend the money for community development purposes.

The Investment Test

The second element of the exam is the Investment Test, an assessment of the bank's record of helping to meet the credit needs of its community through investments. The Investment Test accounts for 25 percent of the overall CRA rating. This was a new category in which the regulators delineate which types of investments are considered in evaluating a bank's CRA record. These "qualified investments" must benefit the institution's assessment area or a broader area including its assessment area, and they must be for the purpose of community development, as defined in the regulations. Investment activity is supposed to be judged for innovation, complexity, and responsiveness to community development needs as well as quantity. CRA-qualified investments include investments, deposits, membership shares, grants, and in-kind contributions in or to:

1. Financial intermediaries such as community development financial institutions or minority-owned banks;
2. Nonprofits serving community development needs, such as home ownership counseling or commercial development in low-income areas;
3. Other nonprofit organizations serving low- and moderate-income individuals in the bank's assessment area; and
4. Municipal revenue bonds targeted to lower-income areas; small business investment companies (not necessarily geographically targeted); low-income housing tax credits, and other qualified projects.

The Service Test

The Service Test is aimed primarily at examining a bank's retail banking services. It accounts for the remaining 25 percent of the overall CRA rating. Examiners are supposed to consider the distribution of branches among low-, moderate-, middle-, and upper-income areas, as well as the institution's branch openings and closings, especially those affecting low- to moderate-income areas or individuals. Also taken into account are alternative systems of service delivery (ATMs, bank-by-phone, loan production offices) and the range of services offered.

The regulations require an examination of an institution's community development services. These are services that promote credit availability, small business development, or affordable housing, or which provide technical assistance in the financial services field to organizations, working to meet the credit needs of low- to moderate-income communities or individuals. Community development services include seminars and bank-at-school programs aimed at providing financial literacy and education to lower-income households.

The Composite Community Reinvestment Act Rating

The overall CRA rating is the weighted sum of the three component test scores. An institution may receive any of five possible scores on each component test: outstanding, high satisfactory, low satisfactory, needs to improve, or substantial noncompliance. Table 7.1 indicates how points are assigned for different component scores. These component scores are then summed to arrive at a composite score that corresponds to an overall rating. A composite score of 20 or more yields an outstanding rating; 11–19 yields a satisfactory; 5–10 yields a needs to improve; and 0–4 yields a substantial noncompliance. In addition, to give additional emphasis to the lending test, an institution must receive at least a low-satisfactory on the lending test to attain an overall satisfactory rating. This scheme also means that any institution receiving an outstanding on the lending test is assured an overall satisfactory, even if it receives substantial noncompliance on the other two components.

The Strategic Plan Option

In CRA reform, regulators offered banks an alternative to the conventional large bank examination process. An institution may choose to be evaluated under the "strategic plan" option of the CRA regulations. The strategic plan option allows an institution to define its own community reinvestment objectives for lending, investments, and services, in a multiyear plan. Regulators give relatively little guidance to banks regarding what the plans should contain or what the nature or scale of the objectives should look like.[18] Moreover, banks may ask to be regulated based on their strategic plan only if they receive a satisfactory or outstanding rating. They are able to revert to the conventional evaluation if they do not meet their basic goals.

A bank pursuing the strategic plan option must publish a notice in a newspaper that it is formulating a plan and must give the public the opportunity to comment on the plan prior to submitting it for regulator approval. (Although regulators can review a plan for responsiveness to public comments, banks are not necessarily obliged to incorporate changes to the plan recommended in such comments.) Once the plan is approved, regulators have much less discretion in determining the bank's rating than in the case of conventional regulation. For strategic plan banks, the key intervention point for community development organizations is during the plan's comment period. Because plans can cover a period as long as five years, the opportunity to comment on a plan is an important one.

Table 7.1

Numerical Equivalents of Component Test Ratings

Component test rating	Lending	Investment	Service
Outstanding	12	6	6
High satisfactory	9	4	4
Low satisfactory	6	3	3
Needs to improve	3	1	1
Substantial noncompliance	0	0	0

Wholesale and Limited Purpose Banks

The 1995 regulations allow a financial institution to apply to its regulator to be designated either as a "wholesale" or "limited-purpose" bank. These types of institutions are regulated differently from conventional, full-service banks or thrifts. Wholesale banks are those that are not in the business of routinely extending home mortgage, small business, small farm, or consumer loans to retail customers. A bank serving only large businesses, for example, might apply to be classified as a wholesale bank. Limited-purpose banks are those that offer only a narrow product line, such as credit card or motor vehicle loans, to a regional or broader market.[19]

Wholesale or limited-purpose banks are regulated according to a "community development" test, which consists of an evaluation of an institution's community development lending, qualified investments, and community development services. These banks are not evaluated for direct residential or small business lending activities. Thus, investments and community development lending are especially important activities for such institutions.

CHAPTER 8

The Predatory Lending Policy Debate

Turning to Cities and States: The Fight Against Predatory Lending

In the late 1990s, as the predatory lending problem exploded, community and consumer groups around the country became increasingly focused on the issue. In the late 1980s and early 1990s, most of the advocacy for stronger regulation of subprime lending—which was a relatively small industry at the time—was being waged by national, Washington, DC–based organizations. These included the National Consumer Law Center, the National Association of Consumer Advocates, and other organizations tied more to the consumer rights movement rather than the community reinvestment and fair lending movements. This earlier phase of advocacy was largely responsible for the Home Ownership and Equity Protection Act (HOEPA) of 1994, which established a framework for regulation of "high-cost" mortgages, which were generally the highest-risk segment of subprime loans. HOEPA established a threshold of loan pricing. Mortgages priced over this threshold became subject to special disclosures and a few prohibitions of certain loan practices and terms. Advocates argued for stronger restrictions on high-cost loans, but were only successful at obtaining what was primarily a bill aimed at increasing disclosures to borrowers.

As shown in chapter 6, HOEPA clearly did not restrain the subprime market in any meaningful way.[1] Besides the focus on using additional disclosures to borrowers as the fundamental way to protect borrowers, HOEPA is generally faulted for having thresholds or "triggers" that are much too high. The subprime market continued to explode after 1994, especially for refinance lending, the primary target of HOEPA. With the explosion of the subprime market came the growth of predatory lending and, soon, an increase in defaults and foreclosures as well.

As subprime lending reached a critical mass, the disproportionate concentration of the most abusive loans in city urban neighborhoods began to be felt more acutely, especially in the form of foreclosures and abandoned housing. For many years, community groups around the country experienced problems caused by foreclosures and abandonment, particularly beginning in the late 1960s as Federal Housing Administration foreclosure problems began to worsen in central city neighborhoods. In the middle 1990s, as the boom in subprime loans aged a couple of years and began to go into foreclosure at high rates, community reinvestment advocates became more involved. Subprime and predatory lending became not just a consumer issue but also a neighborhood issue. Foreclosures impacted entire neighborhoods and communities, adding to the unfairness of the loss of homes to individual families.

Similar to the earliest action against redlining in the 1970s, advocates for stronger regulation found success first at the state and local levels. In North Carolina, a state with a long history of reinvestment activism, a number of organizations became involved in the issue. These included the country's largest community development credit union, the Center for Self-Help, as well as the Community Reinvestment Association of North Carolina and the North Carolina Fair Housing Center. This group formed the hub of the Coalition for Responsible Lending, which was able to gain the support of a major statewide elected official, the attorney general, who played a significant role in the legislative campaign. The legislature's black caucus was also supportive.

Traditionally, banks and financial services lobby groups have had a great deal of influence on state legislatures regarding mortgage and banking laws. While some states have passed consumer protection legislation, most state-level banking and mortgage policy is dominated by financial institution lobbyists and trade associations. Federal banking laws put pressure on state legislatures to accommodate banking interests. Federal law allows banks to "export" interest rate and fee regulations from their "home state." As a result, banks aggressively lobby state legislatures for favorable regulations that they can then use to override regulations in other states. They will frequently use economic development as a major argument in such lobbying, agreeing to maintain facilities—or simply the "main office" location—in the home state in exchange for favorable regulations. Some states have gone so far as to pass laws aimed at encouraging bank locations and facilities by reducing regulations in exchange for economic development commitments by the institutions. Two states well known for wooing banks with offers of reduced regulation are South Dakota and Delaware, both of which specialize in attracting credit card banks. Delaware, for example, passed a law in 1981 that eliminated fee and rate restrictions on consumer loans and reduced income taxes in exchange for employing at least 100 people in the state. Other banks have worked to win regulatory concessions on mortgage regulations, which they can then export around the country. Bank One, for example, lobbied the Illinois legislature unsuccessfully in 2000 and 2001 to exempt it from essentially any regulations on fees for second mortgages, a freedom that it could then export to other states. The bank holding company was already located in Illinois and did not pledge to increase or maintain jobs in the state in its lobbying efforts, but argued that less tangible, long-run economic development would occur as a result of the move. The bank threatened to locate its new main charter in Ohio or another state if the deregulatory bill did not pass (Hinz 2001).

In North Carolina, advocates for increased regulation of subprime home loans developed a bill that would go far beyond HOEPA in limiting the practices that could be used in making high-cost loans. In the summer of 1999, the North Carolina legislature passed the first comprehensive antipredatory-lending state legislation in the country. The bill followed the threshold approach of HOEPA but set the triggers significantly lower so that the law would capture a substantial segment of subprime loans while avoiding prime loans. It then prohibited certain lending features that, in the case of high-cost lending, are often viewed as predatory, including many of the features listed in Table 5.1 in chapter 5. Surprisingly, especially in the light of later fierce battles in other states, the bill was supported by both the Mortgage Bankers Association of North Carolina and the North Carolina Association of Mortgage Brokers.

Soon thereafter, two states, New York and Massachusetts, issued regulations aimed at the predatory-lending problem, although these measures were much weaker than the North Carolina legislation. Other states began debating similar measures. On the local level, the city of Chicago and Cook County, Illinois, each introduced proposed local ordinances aimed at the problem in early 2000. Unlike the North Carolina legislation, the Chicago and Cook County ordinances did not call for regulating lenders.[2] Rather, the proposals relied on a significant history of local and state laws aimed at encouraging banks to be socially responsible by linking government financial business to responsible banking. Chicago had an ordinance dating back to 1974 that required banks accepting municipal deposits to disclose data on their lending in the city. A number of cities and states have attempted to use public banking business to encourage reinvestment (McLenighan and Bush 1994).

The original Chicago draft bill followed the definition of predatory lending in the North Carolina bill but was somewhat stronger. City officials who were drafting the bill met with both community groups and representatives of major local banks as they were preparing the bill. However, as soon as the bill was introduced, it was immediately opposed by statewide banking lobbyists and most of the large banks. Even though the city did not have the power to regulate mortgage lenders, they could choose to stop doing business with them or their affiliates, some of whom were doing considerable business with the city. For example, the largest subprime lender in the city, Equicredit, was owned by Bank of America, which did business with the city and had a large local branch. Moreover, Citigroup owned both Solomon Smith Barney, which issued bonds for the city's O'Hare Airport, and Citifinancial, a subprime lender. Most observers did not know at the time that Citigroup was also poised to purchase the Associates, one of the largest and most ill-reputed subprime lenders in the country. Large banks fighting the bill hired former Illinois governor James Thompson as well as two former chiefs of staff to Mayor Richard J. Daley to lobby to weaken the ordinance. After months of advocacy on both sides of the issue, community group representatives were invited to meet with agency heads and the lead alderman on the City Council, a key ally of the administration.[3] The city officials and the alderman asked the community group representatives if they would support the current version of the ordinance. By this point, the ordinance had been watered down in a number of ways, including the removal of a key practice—single premium credit insurance—from the list of predatory loan features. The alderman who ran the meeting asked community groups to support the bill. He stated that he had been approached by representatives of Citigroup to remove single premium insurance from the ordinance's list of predatory-lending practices. He also made it clear that the city did a great deal of business with Citigroup and that he did not want to pass a bill that effectively labeled the bank as a predatory lender. Some community groups ended up supporting the ordinance with this substantial change, but others did not.

The Chicago ordinance was approved in August 2000. It stimulated the introduction and passage of similar bills in cities across the country, including Oakland, Dayton, Cleveland, and Detroit. These bills were generally not attempts to regulate. They generally sought only to withdraw municipal business from firms engaged in predatory lending. They followed earlier municipal deposit ordinances aimed at encouraging banks to reinvest in urban neighborhoods. They also bore close resemblance to antiapartheid ordinances that many cities passed in the 1980s, in which cities refused to do business with firms that invested in South Africa. The industry responded quickly by appealing to state legislatures, where they had more lobbying experience and relationships, to override the local ordinances. Some of the local predatory-lending ordinances—including those in Detroit, Dayton, and Cleveland—were soon overridden by state legislation. By preempting these incentive ordinances, state legislatures told local governments that they did not have a right to choose the financial institutions with which they did business.

The Federal Reserve Moves Slowly

Meanwhile, local and state policy developments were putting pressure on federal regulators to act on the predatory-lending problem. Bills were introduced in Congress by both the consumer as well as the industry sides of the debate. The Department of Housing and Urban Development (HUD) and the Treasury Department created a Task Force to develop federal policy recommendations. The HUD-Treasury Task Force held hearings in five major cities in the spring of 2000 and issued a report in June containing a number of federal policy recommendations, including calling on the Federal Reserve Board (FRB) to use more of its authority under HOEPA to outlaw predatory practices. In May, the House Banking Committee held a hearing on predatory lending in which the FRB was chastised by Chairman Jim Leach (R–IA), for not using its authority to act on the issue. A joint Federal Reserve-HUD report in 1998 had made several significant recommendations, but the board never acted on them. Chairman Leach asked Federal Reserve Governor Gramlich, "If there is a problem out there, if Congress has given very strong authority to regulators and the Federal Reserve, our regulators, is the Federal Reserve AWOL? That is a question that I think demands a response."[4]

The House hearing, the HUD-Treasury report, and public and congressional concern over the issue led the board to hold hearings in four large cities in the summer and fall of 2000 on potential revisions to HOEPA regulations. The board's hearings added to the evidence provided in congressional and HUD-Treasury hearings. By the end of 2000, the board proposed some significant, albeit modest, changes to the HOEPA rules. The largest changes in the rules were to consider single premium credit insurance (SPCI) in the definition of fees under HOEPA and to lower the interest-rate threshold at which a loan would be classified as "high cost." The former meant that almost any loan with single premium credit insurance would be classified as a high-cost loan under HOEPA (because SPCI typically exceeds the 8-percentage-point fee trigger in the law), thereby increasing the disclosures and protections associated with the loan. The latter meant that more high-rate loans would be covered by HOEPA.

The most successful effort by consumer and community advocates was the push to effectively ban SPCI. Considered by many to be the single most egregious predatory practice, SPCI involves selling people insurance that covers loan payments should some calamity (e.g., death or disability) occur. However, SPCI is relatively unique among insurance products in that it is financed completely up-front into the loan. With SPCI, rather than pay the premiums monthly or some other periodic way, the borrower pays the entire five to ten years of insurance up-front via the premium being added onto the mortgage amount. The lump-sum premiums for such policies can easily amount to 15 percent of the principal amount of loan. This increases the loan amount and reduces borrower equity. Moreover, unlike with insurance that is paid monthly, if the borrower gets into trouble, she cannot stop paying the insurance portion of her monthly payment without defaulting on the mortgage. Consumer and community groups began focusing on problems with the product as a key focus of their antipredatory-lending campaigns. By the summer of 2000, consumer activism on SPCI, and the inherent problems with the product, compelled Fannie Mae and Freddie Mac to pledge not to purchase loans containing the product. Following this, the product was condemned in the HUD/Treasury Report, and later in 2000 the Federal Reserve recommended including SPCI in the HOEPA definition of points and fees. Then, by the summer of 2001, three large sellers of single premium credit insurance, who clearly saw "the writing on the wall," voluntarily announced that they would no longer offer it.[5] By the end of 2001, the Federal Reserve finalized its proposal to include SPCI in the definition of points and fees.[6]

Meanwhile, states continued to consider legislation and regulations to regulate subprime lending. However, many states have passed bills that do little to restrain abusive practices. For example, in 2003 the National Conference of State Legislatures listed more than thirty states as having passed predatory lending statutes since 1999 (National Conference of State Legislatures 2003). The vast majority of these, however, did not have comprehensive, substantive predatory lending laws on the books. Most so-called anti-predatory lending laws at the state level have been heavily influenced by state banking lobbyists so that the thresholds are often the same as the current, very high federal thresholds, and the restrictions on practices are very minimal. In several states, including Michigan, Ohio, and Pennsylvania, the laws contained provisions that preempt any local ordinances on the issue. As of 2003, consumer groups tend to recognize the original North Carolina bill as well as those in New Jersey, New York, Illinois, and New Mexico as among the most substantive legislative solutions.

The Battle to Modernize HMDA

In late 2000, following its HOEPA hearings, the FRB proposed enhancing the Home Mortgage Disclosure Act (HMDA) data to include some limited pricing and other data related to the predatory-lending issue. Community groups had pointed out that HMDA had become increasingly obsolete as mortgage market disparities had moved from a question of access to any loan to one of access to fairly priced credit. They argued for public data on pricing and loan terms that might signal predatory practices, including the presence of loan features like prepayment penalties and balloon payments. The board, however, clearly signaled that it was not likely to add a good deal of data to HMDA, arguing that it did not want to excessively burden lenders. After issuing the original proposal, which only suggested adding a few simple fields, the board received many comments from the lending industry complaining about the costs and burdens that any new data fields would cause.

Community organizations, on the other hand, found the board's proposal far too timid. They had seen the "regulatory burden" argument raised again and again over the years, including in the original debate over HMDA, during the debate over the 1989 Financial Institutions Reform Recovery and Enforcement Act changes to HMDA, and when small business lending data collection was proposed in 1993. Yet, these changes have never been shown to unduly burden an institution or result in significantly reduced credit availability. In fact, as chapter 7 argues, the 1989 HMDA changes were an important tool in boosting lending to lower-income and minority households. The costs of these sorts of data changes are primarily fixed costs that are easily spread over literally millions of loans and over many years. Moreover, given current information technologies, these arguments have become increasingly hard to accept. Community groups argued that the modest, short-term conversion costs were necessary to collect key data that would enable a much better understanding of credit access issues and allow regulators to conduct fair lending, community reinvestment, and consumer compliance examinations much more efficiently.

Banking interests lobbied the board hard to severely limit any changes to HMDA data. In cases of data disclosure laws, financial industry lobbyists tend first to argue to limit data collection by arguing undue burden. Then, as in the case of the 1989 changes to HMDA and the 1995 CRA small business data, when the data become available and are limited in their explanatory power, they argue that the data are of no use to identify potential discrimination or predatory lending.

Edward Gramlich, a member of the FRB, pointed to the need for expanding HMDA in a comprehensive way:

> Other steps may need to be taken, and may be taken, to deal with predatory lending. But we should be able to agree that more information is an important prerequisite to sensible policies in this area. Increased HMDA data collection is the first step in gaining broader understanding of the business practices of subprime lenders and in helping us distinguish appropriate from inappropriate lending practices. (Gramlich 2000)

Gramlich and staff at the board continually argued that predatory lending data was "anecdotal," despite the thousands of documented cases of abusive loans affecting a wide spectrum of subprime lenders. Despite Gramlich's call for more comprehensive data to detail the problem more precisely, when it came to actually proposing HMDA changes, the board was very timid. It proposed only three additions to the fields collected under HMDA: the annual percentage rate (APR) of the loan; whether the loan is classified as high cost under HOEPA; and whether the loan is for a manufactured home.[7]

Unfortunately, these three fields are not at all adequate for making HMDA data the much more powerful tool that it could be in identifying potential predatory-lending practices or discrimination, or in determining the fair lending and Community Reinvestment Act performance of depositories. There are a number fields that are readily accessible to lenders that could easily have been incorporated into HMDA. These include debt burden and credit history information for applicants. Also, because elderly homeowners are disproportionately victimized by predatory lending, and because age is a protected class, it would have been logical for the board to add applicant age into the data.

Perhaps the most glaring omission, however, was that of the up-front points and fees on the loan. These charges are the driving force behind predatory lending. The bulk of what we know about predatory lending indicates that a primary motivation for lending abuses and the resulting high defaults and foreclosures stem from the excessive points and fees financed into the loans. Responsible subprime lenders rely primarily on the interest rate to recover revenues, so that lenders have a greater interest in loan repayment. While the APR theoretically incorporates fees into its value, and high fees do increase the APR, this measure does not give adequate information on fees in a loan.

As an example of why APR alone can obfuscate actual costs to the borrower, consider two thirty-year fixed-rate loans, one at 10.6 percent interest with no points and fees and the other at 9.7 percent interest with 8 percent points and fees. Both will have APRs of 10.6 percent. However, many subprime borrowers prepay (pay off their loan) in two years or less. Over such a period, the first loan costs the borrower 0.9 percent more per year in interest, for a two-year total of 1.8 percent, while the second costs the borrower 8 percent more in fees—or 4.4 times more in costs than the first loan. In fact, by not collecting points and fees data, the board has given lenders a perverse incentive to generate more of their revenue through fees rather than interest, so that their APR is lower. This is precisely the opposite of responsible lending practice.

The board modified its original proposal before issuing the final regulation, but it did not add any new fields (other than the original three).[8] Moreover, it changed the APR reporting to reporting the difference between the APR and current Treasury rates (a useful change) only for those loans with APRs 3 percentage points or more over those of Treasury rates.[9] This was in response to vocal complaints from prime lenders, most of whom will now not have to report pricing information at all. One problem this outcome causes is that it will be difficult to do more sophisticated analyses of loan pricing because only a segment of loans by most subprime lenders will have pricing information. Only their highest-cost loans will include pricing data. Thus, any disparities by race or geography, for example, will be minimized in the reported data. This is especially convenient for banking organizations that own both prime and subprime lending units. The subprime unit will report some pricing data, but the prime unit will report little to none. Thus, it will be difficult to clearly quantify patterns of possible racial steering or related problems within banking organizations. Moreover, lenders may shift revenue to fees to lower their APRs to be just under the 3 percentage-point threshold. Finally, without some credit history data, lenders will dismiss disparities as due primarily to differentials in credit history, without having to offer any evidence in this regard. Again, banks argued against including such data in HMDA, but later they will almost certainly argue that, without such data, the pricing information cannot be interpreted.

The Office of the Comptroller of the Currency and Office of Thrift Supervision Step Up to the Plate for Subprime Lenders

As states like Illinois, New York, and Georgia followed North Carolina and began to pass antipredatory-lending laws in 2001 and 2002, lenders began to push for lender-friendly federal policies that would override state laws. Lenders argued that state laws would create a "patchwork" of regulation across the country that would reduce the efficiency of the banking system by making it difficult for lenders and secondary market firms to operate national lending operations. Advocates of state laws, including governors and legislators, argue that states have a right to protect their citizens, especially when it comes to something as important as defending the ability of residents to retain their homes. Moreover, real estate laws, including foreclosure laws, vary by state. Lending markets have accommodated such differences without causing significant harm to loan availability.[10]

Lenders seeking to challenge state predatory-lending laws pursued a mixed strategy of seeking a federal statute aimed at preempting state laws and, at the same time, trying to get federal bank regulators to preempt state laws.

The first approach would remain difficult as long as Democrats would hold significant power in the Senate and Senator Paul Sarbanes, a supporter of increased predatory-lending regulation, would retain the ranking Democratic seat on the committee. Thus, lenders—particularly banks, thrifts, and bank-owned lenders—also adopted the second strategy. Both thrifts and national banks appealed to their federal regulators (the Office of Thrift Supervision [OTS] and the Office of the Comptroller of the Currency [OCC], respectively) to preempt state predatory-lending regulations. Unfortunately for those on the side of state authority in this area, the regulators have a vested interest in preempting state consumer protection laws. The ability to preempt state law is perhaps the greatest source of value in the federal thrift and national bank charters. As mentioned before, bank regulators are funded by levying fees on the institutions they regulate and often pursue policies that may encourage banks—especially larger ones—to move or remain under their supervision. Even the shift of one large bank can significantly affect an agency's revenues. When Chase Manhattan Bank (now J.P. Morgan Chase) merged with Chemical Bank in 1995 and changed from a national to a state charter, the OCC lost 2 percent of its budget in fees (Rosen 2002).

The more power that a regulator's charter gives an institution, the more likely it is that institutions will want to be chartered under that regulator's authority. In the past, competition between regulators was mostly restricted between the national bank (i.e., OCC) charter and the state charter (i.e., Federal Deposit Insurance Corporation, Federal Reserve, and state regulators). However, as thrifts have been allowed to become much more like commercial banks, and banks have become more involved in mortgage markets, the thrift-bank distinction has become less meaningful. Thus, all of the federal bank regulators, to some degree, compete to retain and attract banks and thrifts under their authority. In 1974, Arthur Burns, chairman of the FRB, expressed concerns that this situation would lead to a possible "competition in laxity" among the regulators (Scott 1977). Since then, there have been repeated concerns that banks "forum shop" to find the most comfortable regulator (Dennis 1978; Matasar and Pavelka 1998). A version of this "race for the bottom" may involve regulators vying to offer banks as much preemption power as they can. Demonstrating the importance of preemption to the value of a charter type, a banking attorney was quoted in the *American Banker* regarding the OCC's preemption actions as asking, "Why would you want a national charter but for the preemption authority?" (Davenport 2003).

The OTS moved first to preempt state banking laws by preempting key provisions of Georgia's predatory lending law in January of 2003, so that federal thrifts were exempted from the law. A week later, the OTS preempted New York State's predatory-lending law. State regulators immediately objected to the OTS moves. Community groups saw the OTS's action—under Bush appointee James Gilleran—as particularly antagonistic, given that the preceding director of the OTS, Clinton appointee Ellen Seidman, had, among federal regulators, voiced some of the strongest concerns over predatory lending (Blackwell 2003).

The OCC was not about to let the thrift charter gain a clear regulatory advantage over the national bank charter. In November of 2002 it issued a letter to national banks asserting its jurisdiction over all state regulators and asked banks to inform it if a state regulator may have asserted its authority over a national bank. In comments to the press after the OTS decision, the OCC pointed out that it needed a request from a bank before it could follow the OTS's preemption move (Blackwell 2003). It was not long before a national bank, National City Bank out of Cleveland, requested that the OCC preempt the Georgia law. Community groups, governors, attorneys general, and state legislatures argued that the OCC should not move to preempt state consumer protection laws. In the summer of 2003, the OCC did preempt the Georgia antipredatory-lending law, even after industry interests had succeeded in getting the law substantially weakened. The agency went on to suggest that it would preempt all similar state laws, and it issued regulations doing so in early 2004. The OCC's move in some ways was a more assertive move in defense of banks to ignore state laws, because its authority under banking statutes to preempt state laws is much less clear. It essentially relied on historical regulatory practice and its own interpretation of such practices, rather than on the more specific statutory authority that the OTS used.

The Power of Community Organizing and the Use of Reputational Risk

Despite the mixed successes in securing substantial consumer protection laws on the predatory-lending issue and the moves of federal regulators to preempt those laws that have been enacted, it is clear that community advocacy on this issue has made a major impact. The FRB, local and state legislatures, and state regulators would not have made the proconsumer moves that they did without the advocacy work done by scores of community groups in neighborhoods across the country nor without the strong research and documentation provided by public interest advocacy groups. But the modes of advocacy have extended beyond the passage of specific laws. When organizers failed to win adequate legal protections from regulators and legislators, they took their advocacy to investors and the general public. In particular, they recognized the impact of spotlighting a lender's predatory-lending behavior on the lender's reputation among regulators, investors, and the public. Banks and regulators have become concerned about predatory lending not just due to the litigation or regulatory sanctions that it might bring about, but also due to the impact that substantial charges and evidence can have on the firm's overall reputation. This effect is especially true for banking organizations, which are dependent on public confidence in their institutions and, to some degree, on their reputations as being socially responsible. Most immediately, this sort of advocacy can impact a bank's CRA evaluation, especially when examiners are evaluating whether a bank's products are "responsive to community credit needs." Perhaps more importantly, if a bank is effectively branded as a predatory financial institution, it stands to lose institutional clients and even some individual customers. Safety and soundness regulators, in turn, worry about reputational risk because it could eventually hurt the bank's earnings and even jeopardize its financial soundness.

There are a number of examples in recent years that illustrate the power of community organizing and research to go beyond impacting specific public policy to create a climate that fosters more responsible lending. One example involves Bank of America and its former affiliate subprime lender, Equicredit. Bank of America owned Equicredit, one of the largest subprime lenders in the country, in the late 1990s. Equicredit operated primarily as a "wholesale" lender, making loans through thousands of independent mortgage brokers across the United States. The lender had been cited by consumer and community groups as a perpetrator of predatory lending, especially in large northern cities such as Philadelphia and Chicago.[11] The Woodstock Institute singled out the bank as having lending patterns that were especially concentrated in black neighborhoods in Chicago, even when compared to other subprime lenders (Immergluck and Wiles 2000b). The institute showed that, in examining refinance lending in the Chicago area, Equicredit's market share among subprime lenders in black neighborhoods was six times its share in white neighborhoods. Its share of *all* refinance loans in black neighborhoods was thirteen times that in white tracts. Meanwhile, Bank of America's prime lenders had market shares in white tracts that were six to eight times the corresponding shares in black tracts. The parent organization, Bank America Corporation, essentially had one high-cost lender for black neighborhoods and another low-cost lender for white neighborhoods. After selling another subprime unit, Nationscredit, in the summer of 2000, Bank of America sold the assets of Equicredit in October 2001 and ceased subprime lending operations. While loan losses may have exceeded expectations to some degree, it was clear that the negative impact of Equicredit on Bank of America's reputation had a significant role in the decision (Boraks 2001).

Another example that demonstrates the power of effective organizing and the role of reputational risk is the highly publicized acquisition of the

ill-reputed subprime lender, the Associates, by Citigroup, which was announced in September 2000. The Associates, which had been sued over abusive lending practices literally hundreds of times, had been singled out by
many as among the worst predatory lenders in the country. Its involvement
in abusive practices received extensive coverage in the media.[12] Led by North
Carolina's Coalition for Responsible Lending, community groups around
the country first asked Citigroup to commit to strong measures to clean up
the Associates. The bank responded by preparing a reform plan, but community groups were largely dissatisfied with the bank's plans, including
Citigroup's proposal to limit fees only to 9 percent of a loan's principal
amount. It also initially refused to stop selling single premium credit life
insurance or to dramatically restructure the Associates' broker network.

The coalition, together with other groups around the country, called on
federal regulators to hold public hearings on the acquisition. They were able
to obtain prominent and repeated press coverage in the *New York Times* that
highlighted troubles with the Associates, questioned the wisdom of the acquisition, and detailed community groups' dissatisfaction with Citigroup's
steps to reform the subprime lender (Oppel and McGeehan 2000). While
federal regulators refused to hold a hearing, New York State regulators agreed
to hold one. Even though the acquisition was approved in fairly short order,
the coalition and others kept the spotlight on Citigroup's management of the
old Associates business and continued to criticize what they saw as inadequate reforms. While some still view Citigroup's performance as inadequate, it is hard to deny that the activism on the Associates acquisition and
the work afterward led to some significant reforms and the loss of a funding source for thousands of former Associates' brokers.[13] Other examples
of how organizing and the use of reputational risk have curtailed predatory
lending include First Union Bank's (now Wachovia) shutdown of the Money
Store, an ill-reputed lender, in 1999, and changes in lending operations at
Household Finance.[14]

Misplaced Theory Versus Evidence on the Effects of State Predatory Lending Laws

The policy debate over predatory lending continues. Consumer advocates
continue to work to pass state lending laws similar to those in North Carolina and New York State to restrict predatory practices on high-cost loans.
Lenders continue to argue that such laws will result in a withdrawal of
lenders from markets and the "drying up" of credit, particularly for lower-
income borrowers. Consumer groups tend to counter these claims with at
least three arguments:

1. Some decline in lending is desirable because many irresponsible loans are being made, and any benefit from these loans does not outweigh the costs and risks that they entail.
2. The regulations will result in many loans being made at more reasonable prices and terms, and this will reduce the costs to many borrowers.
3. The regulated environment will reduce the important negative spillovers of predatory lending, including extremely high foreclosure rates, especially in minority neighborhoods.

The subprime lending industry's arguments are probably best represented by a paper sponsored by the American Bankers Association by Robert Litan, a vice president of the Brookings Institution. He is also cochair of the Shadow Financial Regulatory Committee, which has argued against essentially any sort of predatory-lending regulations.[15] Litan (2003) makes a number of arguments against the sort of regulations passed in North Carolina, including but not limited to three key points:

1. Lenders will restrict lending by causing creditors to "deny an ever larger fraction of would-be borrowers access to formal credit."
2. Some so-called predatory lending practices, including single-premium credit insurance, are in fact beneficial.
3. Governments should not do anything else until the impacts of federal regulators' recent actions against predatory lending are evaluated.

Litan's arguments rely generally on traditional neoclassical economic theory and a framework of well-functioning, perfectly competitive markets. The assumptions of such a framework are not well suited for the subprime market, however. One key assumption is that consumers are "shoppers" who have good information on price and quality of the product. The hundreds of predatory-lending cases detailed in reports and hearings at all levels of government make it very difficult to accept the notion that high-cost loan borrowers are well-informed shoppers in a perfect market of competitive lenders. As described in chapter 6, the subprime market is much better characterized as hypersegmented, so that specific lender groups target specific neighborhoods and borrower types. And the subprime market, especially the higher-risk end, is typified by aggressive "push-marketing." Kim-Sung and Hermanson (2003) found that 56 percent of borrowers with loans originated by mortgage brokers—who dominate subprime markets in many places—reported the contact being initiated by the broker. Stein and Libby (2001) found that over one-third of subprime borrowers reported that the idea to take out a loan secured by their home came through aggressive and targeted marketing efforts by the lender or broker. As William Apgar, former HUD assistant secretary, said in predatory lending hearings in 2000, "Subprime loans are sold, not bought."[16]

Litan also points to usury laws of earlier decades to suggest that the state predatory lending laws will dramatically constrain credit for those who need it. The clear underlying principle of this and other of his arguments is that any reduction in credit supply compared to that offered by a deregulated market necessarily results in a decrease in social welfare. After all, neoclassical economists tend to equate the equilibrium supply of credit in an unregulated market as achieving maximum social welfare. This sort of theory ignores a full cost-benefit or risk-benefit analysis. Perhaps these laws will result in some deserving borrowers being unable to get credit that would benefit them. This may be a cost of such action. However, what if, for every borrower who is not able to get a loan, 100 others get loans without having substantial equity stripped out of their homes? What if, for every deserving borrower not able to receive a loan, one or more homes will not go into foreclosure and be abandoned in a struggling, working-class neighborhood? These are the sorts of questions that Litan's and the subprime industry's criticisms ignore. Yet good policy analysis examines the benefits, costs, and risks of the policy proposal and compares them to the status quo.

The usury law example is also directly misleading. Usury laws are outright bans on charging interest rates above a certain level. The focus of most predatory-lending statutes is to avoid limiting interest rates and to prohibit certain practices and terms with loans priced above certain thresholds. The argument that such thresholds act as "implicit" usury caps is weak. Unlike Federal Reserve HOEPA regulations, which provide few substantive protections to borrowers and rely primarily on additional disclosure forms, the meaningful state laws are more substantive. Loans that exceeded HOEPA thresholds became somewhat stigmatized largely because those familiar with them knew that they contained many abusive features, which were not illegal, and because regulators and others had started looking more closely at them. Their litigation risk increased significantly as the probability of being caught increased.

There is no reason to believe that a lender making a legal, high-cost loan in North Carolina suffers significant stigma for making such loans. In fact, a recent survey of subprime mortgage outlets suggested that regulations may improve customer confidence that the financing they receive is fair (Posner and Meehan 2002). This could bring benefits to the lenders as a result. Will lenders be more careful in offering high-cost loans, and might this have an impact on the lenders' costs in making such loans? The answer is, hopefully, yes, and this will generally be a desirable effect if the new costs are commensurate with the current social costs of such lending. But this does not mean that these increased costs will be passed on to borrowers. The regulations will make it more difficult for lenders to earn extraordinary profits on these loans. If lenders are engaged in high-risk secured home lending, which is more likely to result in people losing their homes and neighborhoods experiencing high rates of foreclosures, they should be subject to more scrutiny. This necessarily entails some modest and mostly one-time costs spread out over millions of loans over many years. Just like many other consumer protection regulations, it is a cost that is worth the resulting benefits.

Litan (2003) also argues that some predatory practices can in fact be beneficial, and that prohibiting them will restrict access to credit. He cites SPCI as one example. He argues that SPCI makes more sense for subprime borrowers because they are more likely to stop paying their life insurance premiums due to financial difficulties. The SPCI supposedly reduces the lender's risk by making it clear that the loan is insured in case of death or disability. This is not a compelling argument. First, mortgage lenders do not typically require borrowers to have life insurance. And because subprime loans tend to be smaller than prime loans, it is among prime loans where such risk is greater. Moreover, these are secured loans and, in the case of higher risk loans, typically very well secured. Subprime lenders normally tolerate lower loan-to-value ratios than prime lenders do. If the borrower dies and the mortgage cannot be repaid, the loan is still secured by the home. Also, SPCI policies rarely extend for more than five to seven years. The risk of the borrower's not repaying the loan due to death or disability increases as the borrower ages, so it seems unlikely that lenders would see much benefit from these sorts of policies. Finally, in testimony made by the Consumer Credit Insurance Association at the FRB hearings on predatory lending, representatives of the association did not make this argument.[17]

In fact, it was the overwhelming arguments against single premium credit insurance that made it nearly impossible for the Federal Reserve to continue to ignore the practice. Lenders often receive 40 percent or more of the SPCI premium as a commission. Frequently there are ownership or close financial ties between the lender and insurer. Credit insurance is a particularly effective revenue-generating tool among less sophisticated borrowers. More than 40 percent of borrowers with credit insurance either thought it was necessary to receive their loan or were unaware that they had the insurance (Baron and Staten 1994). There are more responsible alternatives. One of the largest providers of credit life insurance in the country, an affiliate of the Credit Union National Association, primarily offered monthly premium insurance well before the policy debate over SPCI began.

Finally, Litan argues that state predatory lending laws are unwise because the Federal Reserve took some action:

> There is simply no evidence . . . of how extensive the predatory lending problem remains in the light of the most recent federal initiatives. Thus, asking legislatures to enact a more restrictive regime governing subprime loans is asking them to take on faith the existence of a problem that federal policy makers have recently and aggressively addressed. (Litan 2003)

Of course, those advocating for state laws generally strongly disagree with the notion that federal policymakers have acted "aggressively." This argument is like saying that someone who has worked for significant spousal abuse laws in a state where a law has just been passed to fine abusers ten dollars should wait until the effects of that law are studied before pressing for more serious penalties. The "aggressive" actions, primarily by the Federal Reserve, resembled the status quo much more than what advocates for reform felt needed to be done. While the actions were important to remedy the SPCI problem, they did almost nothing to address the many other predatory lending practices being employed by brokers and lenders.

Litan's arguments depend largely on appeals to economic theory and models of well-functioning markets. He has pointed to a few recent empirical studies on the effect of the North Carolina law. It is worth delving into these empirical studies, as well as some that he did not address. The first study is that of the Center for Responsible Lending (CRL), a leading advocate for predatory lending laws and an affiliate of the North Carolina Coalition for Responsible Lending, which led the fight for the North Carolina law. Using HMDA data, Ernst, Farris, and Stein (2002) tracked lending changes in North Carolina as compared to the rest of the country from 1998 to 2000, the year the law went into full effect. The CRL study found that per capita subprime lending dropped in all states in 2000, due to an overall slowdown in the subprime and prime lending markets. Per-capita subprime lending (loans per resident) fell faster in North Carolina than it did nationally, falling from 54 loans per 10,000 residents in 1999 to 39 per 10,000 residents in 2000, compared to a drop of 42 per 10,000 to 34 per 10,000 for all other states combined. Thus, the percentage drop was certainly larger in North Carolina, but the state's initial level was at a substantially higher level. After the law went into effect, the North Carolina and national lending rates converged significantly, although North Carolina's subprime lending rate remained almost 15 percent higher than that of the rest of the nation. Overall, subprime lending in the state dropped 24 percent in the state compared to 15 percent for all other states; but again, the raw level of subprime lending in the state remained higher than the rest of the country combined.

The high level of lending in North Carolina both before and after the law was adopted is an important point that is missed by many observers, in part because industry-funded studies (e.g., Elliehausen and Staten 2002) have portrayed the percentage drop in subprime lending as a clear signal that the law is causing legitimate credit needs to go unmet. Yet, North Carolina was, prior to the law's being adopted, a particularly active state for subprime lenders. Subprime lenders may have been so active in North Carolina prior to 2000 precisely because the state was underregulated. In fact, the high rate of subprime lending was likely an important reason that the state was the first to take action on the issue. What is key is that the share of home loans made by subprime lenders began at a higher rate in North Carolina in 1998 and 1999 than the rest of the country combined, and remained at a higher rate in 2000. From 1999 to 2000, the state fell only from fifth to sixth among all states when ranked by the percentage of home loans made by subprime lenders.

Contrary to industry claims that the North Carolina law would cause lenders to flee the state, the CRL study found that all of the twenty-one lenders constituting more than 1 percent of the North Carolina subprime market in 1999 originated loans in the state in 2000. Moreover, a 2001 survey by an industry trade publication found that lenders in the state were continuing to offer a full array of loan products. The CRL analysis also showed that the share of subprime loans going to borrowers with incomes of less than $25,000 decreased only slightly from 33.5 percent to 32.9 percent, and that North Carolina still had a higher percentage of the loans than any other state in 2000.

In order to control for the effects of national changes in lending markets and changes in the economic climate in North Carolina, the CRL study used a form of economic shift-share analysis. The authors found that, of the 24.3 percent decline in subprime lending in North Carolina, 17.7 percent was due to national lending market changes and changes in the state's economy. This left a decline of 6.6 percent that is attributed to the predatory lending law.

The Credit Research Center (CRC), an industry funded research center based at Georgetown University, also analyzed changes in lending in North Carolina after the law was passed (Elliehausen and Staten 2002). They compared lending in counties in North Carolina to those in South Carolina, Tennessee, and Virginia. The CRC study found that, after controlling for differences in the credit and debt attributes of residents, subprime originations dropped by 14 percent from the earlier period to the later period in North Carolina. The CRC authors attributed this effect to the predatory lending law. One basic shortcoming of the study is that it compared changes between loans made from January 1997 through September 1999 to the period from October 1999 to June 2000, even though the principal components of the North Carolina law did not take effect until the third quarter of 2000. Thus, the authors measured, at most, only an initial response to the law's adoption, and not its implementation.

The CRC authors found larger declines for low-income borrowers and cited this result as additional evidence that the decline was attributable to the law. This analysis spurred two basic types of responses. The first was a very different conclusion as to the implications of the given results, and the second was a set of methodological concerns. Critics of the CRC study held a different perspective on the predatory lending problem. A 14 percent decline in subprime lending, even if it was due to the law, was certainly not out of line with the expectations of those advocating such laws. The CRC authors argued that these observers "adopt a paternalistic view that high-cost lending is harmful per-se and that high-risk borrowers should not be allowed to obtain mortgage credit in the market" (Elliehausen and Staten 2002).

This characterization of supporters of antipredatory lending distorts the perspective of most advocates, who tend not to hold such views. However, advocates for increased regulation also tend not to accept that any product that an unregulated market delivers must be beneficial. Rather, they tend to see some high-risk lending as inappropriate under any circumstances (e.g., when loan payments exceed 60 percent of the income of an elderly person on Social Security), some as containing abusive terms and pricing, and some as appropriate and fairly priced. Voluminous evidence documenting thousands of abusive loans has been presented at federal, state, and local government hearings and in dozens of studies across the country. Moreover, the estimates of the share of subprime loans that exhibits predatory lending practices are generally well in excess of 14 percent (Stein and Libby 2001; Ernst, Farris, and Stein 2002).

Even though the CRC findings were consistent with the notion that North Carolina law has had generally desirable consequences, there were some key methodological problems with the study. The foremost concern is that the study, while attempting to account for different subprime lending volumes in counties in the four-state region over time, did not account for changes in key demand-side variables over that time period. The demand-side variables used were fundamentally credit-quality and debt-burden variables, as well as a few population and household characteristics. However, there were no exogenous variables to describe changes in the local economies of the counties. At the same time, the researchers used four dummy variables to describe whether the observation is in a specific state before or after the intervention date. The absence of sufficient demand-side county-level controls raises the concern that the decline observed for North Carolina was caused by a change in demand for loans due to some local economy effects. The variables used in the CRC regressions did not control for such variations. For example, if North Carolina's economy slowed compared to the other states, the demand for mortgages of all types might also be expected to slow relative to other states. In fact, Figure 8.1 shows that the average unemployment rate did fall in North Carolina from the pre-intervention period to the post-intervention period, from 3 to 3.3 percent. Meanwhile, the unemployment rate actually dropped significantly in Tennessee and Virginia and remained constant in South Carolina. This means that the variable representing changes in North Carolina after the intervention, which the CRC authors attributed to the law, could very well have been attributed to the decline in the North Carolina economy, relative to the stable or improving economies of the comparison states.

A second methodological problem with the CRC study concerns the data that were used. The authors utilized data that an accounting firm collected from only 9 members of the American Financial Services Association (AFSA), a trade group of finance and mortgage companies, many of which do subprime lending. The authors did not explain how or why only 9 lenders were chosen by the accounting firm from the more than 500 members of the association. The authors of the study suggested that the nine lenders constituted a substantial and representative sample of subprime lending nationally. However, more than 250 subprime lenders were identified by HUD in 1999. The unclear selection mechanisms for the data and the very small number of lenders in the data present serious validity problems for the CRC study.[18] First, these lenders were not randomly selected. The data were collected by PriceWaterhouseCoopers in the summer of 2000 at the direction of AFSA. A number of selection-bias problems may have occurred. First, in order to elicit data favoring its strong advocacy against the North Carolina laws and others like it, AFSA may have chosen certain lenders that were likely to reduce lending in North Carolina because they historically made loans with features that the law considered predatory. Other lenders, who might not make as many loans with such features, might be expected to gain market share after the law was passed and compensate for any lending slowdowns by the nine selected lenders. Even if AFSA didn't "choose" the lenders, the timing of the data collection was such that lenders might have been more likely to supply data if they felt their data would show declines in lending volume.

One area of commonality between the CRC and CRL studies is that the base level of subprime lending in North Carolina was found to be substantially higher than in most other states. The CRC study found much lower initial levels of subprime lending in Virginia and Tennessee in particular. Again, this suggests that subprime lenders may have targeted North Carolina

Figure 8.1 **Changes in Unemployment Over the CRC Study Periods in North Carolina and Adjacent States**

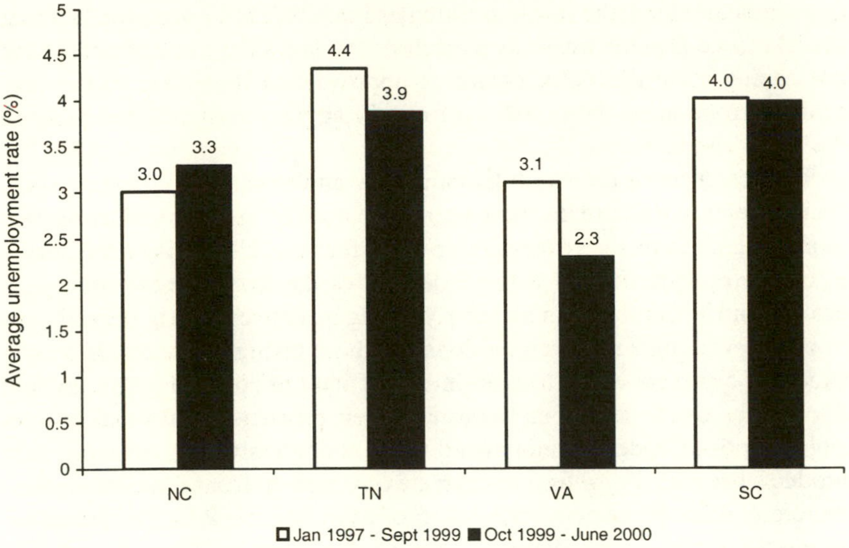

☐ Jan 1997 - Sept 1999   ■ Oct 1999 - June 2000

Source: Bureau of Labor Statistics.

in particular, perhaps due to the presence of a more lax regulatory climate before the antipredatory lending law was enacted.

A third study that attempted to get at the effects of the North Carolina law overcame some of the shortcomings of the CRC study. Harvey and Nigro (2002) examined HMDA data from 1998 to 2000 for five Southeastern states, including North Carolina. They also looked at loan activity before and after the legislation. They found that subprime loans declined significantly—by 14.7 percent—in North Carolina from before to after the legislation, but increased slightly, by 2.5 percent, in the comparison states. This drop was somewhat smaller than that found in the CRL study, but occurred over a somewhat different time period. Importantly, Harvey and Nigro found that subprime applications declined even more (24 percent) in North Carolina. They also found that denial rates did not change after the law was adopted and that the state did not see more of a decline in lenders than the comparison states. Thus, they argue that the decline in subprime lending in the state was due to less aggressive marketing. The authors also measured larger declines in applications among minorities than among whites.

These findings may be interpreted in very different ways. The authors appeared concerned that the decline in marketing to the state, and particularly to minority borrowers, might leave borrowers without access to credit.

However, given the hyperaggressive "push marketing" that is so common among subprime and, especially, predatory lenders, others view this effect as an indication that the law is working as intended. Moreover, the fact that denial rates did not increase as a result of the law suggests that people are not having more difficulty obtaining approvals of loans due to the law, again corroborating the problem of overly aggressive marketing prior to the law's adoption.

The designers of the North Carolina law and similar regulations expect such policies to reduce extremely aggressive marketing because they make it more difficult to finance excessive up-front fees into a loan. With the ability to charge up-front fees of 8 to 10 percent of the loan or more, mortgage brokers and lenders have an extremely strong incentive to push market loans to people who may not even be thinking about taking out loans. If fees in excess of 5 percent of the loan are more difficult to obtain, brokers are less likely to be overly tenacious in pushing their products. Banks and responsible subprime lenders cannot afford to be as aggressive in marketing their products because they refuse to charge exorbitant up-front fees. These fees, therefore, drive the hypersegmentation of mortgage markets. Prime and responsible lenders cannot compete with the extremely aggressive marketing of predatory mortgage brokers, so they choose not to try to serve such markets at all. The deregulationist relying on theories of well-functioning markets will tend to respond that competition will drive down fees to the point where they cover costs. But this theory again presumes a borrower who understands the very complicated pricing of mortgages, who is not under financial duress, and who shops around for the lowest-priced loan. In a large part of the subprime market, this simply does not occur.

Harvey and Nigro (2002) conducted a number of econometric analyses that confirm that subprime lending in North Carolina declined compared to other states. They improved a great deal on the CRC study by controlling for local economic conditions and neighborhood-level environmental factors. Their results indicate that there was an 11.4 percent drop in the odds of a borrower's obtaining a loan at a subprime versus a prime lender due to the North Carolina law. Given that 12 percent of mortgages in North Carolina were subprime in the pre-statute period, the odds against getting a subprime loan at that time were about 7.3 to 1. This means that the law's effect was to reduce the odds of getting a subprime loan from 7.3 to 1 against to 8.3 to 1 against. While significant, this hardly seems like a signal that subprime credit has dried up. Results of another regression in the paper indicate that the North Carolina law reduced the share of loans made by subprime lenders in a typical metropolitan area by about 1.8 percentage points.

Harvey and Nigro (2002) also examined the effect of the law on changes in market shares between bank and nonbank subprime lenders. They did this to test the theory that the law was expected to have a large impact on nonbank subprime lenders because these lenders were more likely to make predatory loans. The results show that the odds of getting a loan from a nonbank versus a bank subprime lender declined by 31 percent due to the North Carolina law. This is a substantial effect and again supports the notion that the law is particularly impacting predatory loans. It lends a great deal of support to the notion that, while the law may have reduced subprime lending by a modest amount, its bigger impact will be to boost the market share of more responsible subprime lenders.

Another study that examined lending patterns before and after the North Carolina law used a very large, established multilender database compiled by a private firm that has been collecting lending data for years. The data are routinely collected and widely used in the lending industry. Quercia, Stegman, and Davis (2003) compared lending in North Carolina to four nearby states and to the entire South. They found that subprime lending declined 17 percent from the pre-statute to post-statute period, while declining only 1.2 percent in the South. This study was a preliminary, descriptive study, however, and did not attempt to control for the effects of other factors that may have reduced lending in North Carolina as some of the other studies do. For example, South Carolina and Tennessee also experienced significant, though smaller, declines in subprime lending, at 8.2 percent and 4.1 percent respectively. The authors also calculated that subprime home purchase loans increased substantially, by 43 percent, compared to rates ranging from 11 to 55 percent in the nearby states and 17 percent for the rest of the South. Thus, the law did not appear to have a negative effect on the volume of home purchase loans in the state. This is consistent with the notion that the law targets predatory loans, since predatory lending generally occurs among refinance loans.

Quercia, Stegman, and Davis (2003) also broke out changes in lending by credit score range. Subprime loans to borrowers with credit scores below 580 (borrowers with clear credit troubles) actually increased substantially, by 31 percent, similar to the increases in the other nearby states, except for Tennessee, which grew at only 19.8 percent. They also found a decline of 28 percent in subprime loans to borrowers with high credit scores, above 660, who should most likely be able to qualify for prime credit. The other states had much smaller declines in loans to high-score borrowers, all under 10 percent.

The data set used by Quercia, Stegman, and Davis allowed them to look at some specific lending practices. Loans with prepayment penalties of three years or more (prepayment penalties of that length are often considered abusive) declined by 72 percent in North Carolina while increasing by at least 23 percent in each of the other states and for the rest of the country.

Loans with balloon payments declined by 53 percent, higher than the national drop of 16 percent. This study was the first to go beyond measuring changes in lending levels to actually look at changes in the terms of loans. Its results suggest that the law has had a desired effect of reducing predatory practices. The fact that the declines in the abusive practices are larger than the aggregate lending amounts also suggests that more responsible lending is substituting for less responsible lending.

A 2002 survey of 280 subprime branch managers and brokers in multiple states by the investment firm Morgan Stanley went beyond North Carolina by comparing the experiences of lending outlets in different states.[19] The authors found that tougher laws were not having a substantial effect on their lending volumes (Posner and Meehan 2002). The study compared subprime growth rates for lending outlets in different states and found that the growth rate for "tough" states was 37 percent compared to 31 percent for "easy" states. They also found that "only 16 percent of subprime branch mangers . . . believe that volume has been negatively affected by regulation or lending practice changes, whereas 30 percent believe the changes have helped their business." The study's conclusions included the following:

> Predatory lending laws do not appear to have dampened the growth outlook. In fact, 84% of our respondents thought changed lending practices were having a neutral to positive impact on volumes . . . our survey respondents indicate that enhanced disclosures are making borrowers feel more comfortable about the lending process. And lower points and less onerous prepayment penalties help make the economic terms more attractive. Even the toughest new laws, in states like North Carolina, for example, do not seem to be affecting branch volumes. . . . As one example, Wells Fargo Financial has reduced the maximum number of points it charges, from 10 to 7. Many lenders are reducing the magnitude or duration of prepayment penalties. (Posner and Meehan 2002)

It is important to look beyond the rhetoric of lobbyists and appeals to overly simplistic economic theory. The empirical evidence concerning changes in lending markets in North Carolina and other states that have enacted substantive laws strongly suggests that concerns that such laws will cause subprime credit to "dry up" are clearly misplaced. Rather, these laws appear to have reduced subprime lending only very modestly, with effects on subprime volumes that are estimated at between 6 and 15 percent of lending volumes. Further, the more detailed studies suggest that the laws' are having the intended consequences of decreasing the prevalence of predatory practices and shifting market share to more responsible lenders. The evidence points to the laws having some very modest negative effects on subprime lending volumes. Given the clearly significant scale of the problem, these modest effects certainly give little cause for concern that policymakers have gone too far by adopting laws like North Carolina's. If anything, these studies overlook the benefits of these laws. They tend to focus much more on the cost of predatory lending laws rather than on the benefits. For example, none of the studies above addressed the benefits of reducing loan defaults and foreclosures caused by predatory lending, or the positive benefits to the neighborhoods in which predatory lending is reduced. More work needs to be done to be able to document the full benefits of such policies.

CHAPTER 9

The Community Reinvestment Act and Fair Lending Policy in the Twenty-first Century

The Community Reinvestment Act's Impact

Since its enactment almost thirty years ago, the Community Reinvestment Act (CRA) has been a controversial law. To advocates of CRA, the law is one of the few policies that appear to work in favor of communities and households that suffer from a whole host of disadvantages in housing and small business credit markets. Deregulationists and some bankers argue that banking is not fundamentally different from any other market and that CRA amounts to unwise intervention in the private marketplace. The deregulationists tend to operate from a highly ideological perspective of rejecting government involvement in banking unless blatant, intentional, and easily detected geographic discrimination occurs. They sometimes add that fair lending laws should be sufficient to deal with what they imply are rare occurrences of such discrimination (Shadow Financial Regulatory Committee 1994). Some banks, typically smaller ones, argue that CRA is an expensive, burdensome regulation, and that their banks are somehow inherently responsive to the credit and service needs in their communities.

As is the case with a good deal of research concerning high-profile policies, the studies that have examined the impact of CRA frequently begin with different assumptions and arrive at different conclusions. In fact, until recently, there had been little rigorous empirical research on the impact of the law. Some of this was due to the unavailability of good data that would provide the sort of detail required in addressing the question of impact. Moreover, CRA is a law that does not have just one sort of impact. It may affect home purchase lending, for example, but have little impact on small business lending. Or it may have a greater impact in some parts of the country where the law is more vigorously enforced, or perhaps only during times when regulators are more vigorously enforcing the law. In fact, even advocates of the law did not generally expect research to find that the law had very substantial measurable impacts up until the late 1980s. This is because the law was so weakly enforced until that time that it was widely considered a "dead letter" (Bush 1999). Staffing at regulatory agencies for consumer issues, including CRA, was cut back dramatically in the early 1980s, in part due to the safety and soundness crises of the period. Moreover, the Reagan administration could hardly have been called a supporter of the law.

As described in chapters 6 and 7, the law became more vigorously enforced in the late 1980s and early 1990s and then again in the middle 1990s, although regulation has never been extremely strong and has never equaled the degree of rigor seen in the early 1990s. Researchers are especially challenged by the fact that CRA is not the only federal policy that may affect bank and lender behavior. On the supportive side, fair lending laws and policies affecting the government-sponsored enterprises (GSEs) have certainly had significant impacts. Thus, attempting to compare banks, which are covered by CRA, to nonbank mortgage companies, which are not, is difficult. This is because increased CRA enforcement has often been accompanied by increased fair lending enforcement, which applies to all lenders. Also, when examining changes over time, it is difficult to separate out any CRA impact from impacts of changing interest rates or other macroeconomic conditions. Finally, some argue that technological change, including the use of credit scoring, has increased lending to lower-income borrowers. While this may be true, it is difficult to isolate this effect. Moreover, policies could impact the use of such technologies and increase their benefits to lower-income communities. For example, when the Department of Justice filed a case against Deposit Guarantee Bank for the use of credit scoring in ways that disadvantaged minorities, it made many lenders review how their scoring systems were used and correct for biases against minorities. Similarly, if regulators were to vigorously inspect automated underwriting systems for disparate impact discrimination, it could improve the effect of these technologies on lower-income families.

While a few academic economists have consistently published articles criticizing CRA—often relying primarily on theoretical arguments—the bulk of the more sophisticated research, especially in the last ten years, increasingly points to the law's having a significant impact on lending flows to lower-income and minority communities.[1] Moreover, while a good deal of evidence has now been compiled on the impact of CRA on mortgage lending, much less has been done concerning impacts where data is much more difficult to come by, including small business lending and community development investments. This deficiency has resulted in overlooking some important impacts of CRA, including the building and strengthening of partnerships between banks and community development organizations and the development of a whole host of new institutions that, but for CRA, would not exist—at least not at anywhere near the scale they exist today. These include what are now called community development financial institutions (CDFIs), which were recognized formally by the federal government in 1994, but have been around at least since the 1970s in significant numbers. CDFIs have grown significantly since CRA was enacted (Corporation for Enterprise Development 2003).

The Effects of the Community Reinvestment Act on Bank and Loan Profitability

One complaint from CRA's critics is that the law is a burdensome regulation that causes banks to lose money. A version of this argument is that the regulation requires a great deal of reporting requirements and paperwork. This claim has been an important political weapon for CRA foes. Much of the evidence on this point seems particularly sensitive to political influences. In the summer of 1999, Senate Banking Committee Chairman Phil Gramm accused federal regulators of grossly underestimating the time it takes banks to comply with CRA, and he pushed for higher estimates (Anason 1999a). Regulators estimated that the industry spent 1.25 million hours a year collecting CRA data. As part of his efforts to exempt small banks from CRA altogether, Gramm argued that small-town bankers each devote upward of 200 hours a year to comply with CRA. This is despite the very limited exams that small banks undergo, especially since the 1995 regulatory changes. Regulators had already increased their estimates of compliance time dramatically, raising the industrywide annual compliance cost estimate from $5.3 million in 1995 to $35.4 million in 1999. Even using the larger figure, compliance costs amount to less than 0.06 percent of estimated annual earnings of the industry (Anason 1999b).

A closely related criticism of CRA is that it causes banks to make many bad loans and lose a good deal of money. A Federal Reserve Board (FRB) study of the profitability of CRA lending attempted to identify profitability through a voluntary survey of the 500 largest banking organizations in the country (Avery, Bostic, and Canner 2000). The survey ended up with 143 respondents. While the study revealed critical information on the performance of lending that is "CRA eligible" as well as "special" CRA programs, there were some research design issues that made it difficult for the survey to avoid serious bias. First, the notion of identifying and isolating the profitability of different sorts of specific lending programs is often problematic. While some institutions track their programs this way, others may not. Moreover, even if they do, such measures may not be completely representative of the financial value of the program to the company. Banks, like other firms, frequently offer products and programs that run at an apparent loss—either for a short time or for an indefinite period—because they have some indirect effect on the company's performance. For example, a company may offer what are essentially "loss leaders" in order to attract customers. Mortgages in general are often not considered a highly profitable area for banks, but they frequently offer them to be able to offer customers all the services that their competitors provide. Another issue that is difficult to get at in a one-time survey is that of life-cycle effects. Banks may lose money, or make very little, on a certain product or customer segment in the short run, but expect to capture a substantial portion of such customers as their earning power increases and they move into more profitable product areas. Thus, any study based on a one-time cross section of customers is likely to underestimate the long-term profitability of lower-income borrowers and programs designed to meet their needs. Finally, from a societal perspective, the profitability of programs to individual banks is hardly a complete measure of the net benefit of a program to society. CRA programs should be evaluated for their long-term effects not only on the individual banks that offer them but also on other banks, borrowers, and entire communities. If a bank subsidizes a home ownership counseling program for first-time home buyers, it is adding human capital—in the form of a better educated consumer—into the mortgage market. This creates efficiencies and produces future responsible borrowers for other banks. If no banks were to offer such programs, fewer people would become successful and sustainable home owners.

Despite some of the limits to the board's study, it did have some interesting results. Avery, Bostic, and Canner (2000) found that, although special CRA single-family loan programs had mean 90-day delinquency rates that were somewhat higher than conventional mortgage programs (1 percent versus 0.78 percent), the median delinquency rate for the special programs was much lower (0.07 percent versus 0.53 percent). This suggests that the typical special CRA program performs much better than banks' conventional mortgages overall. However, for a few institutions, the CRA programs are poorly managed and do not perform well. (As will be discussed below, loan delinquency is not the sole indicator of loan profitability to a bank; other factors, including prepayment risk, play important roles as well.) The study also looked at the profitability of CRA lending overall, including conventional as well as special programs, and found that 77 percent of all CRA-related mortgage lending and 94 percent of home purchase and refinance lending programs were reported to be at least marginally profitable. The authors found that 96 percent of respondents reported that their CRA-related small business lending was profitable or marginally profitable, and 82 percent reported that it was as profitable as their other small business lending. Finally, Avery, Bostic, and Canner (2000) asked banks whether earning a satisfactory or outstanding rating was the motivation for the special mortgage program if they had one. While only 1 percent of institutions cited CRA as the only reason for their programs, about three-quarters of the institutions cited their CRA rating as a contributing factor. Thus, CRA should be viewed as a complementary or contributing force in the development of these programs but not as the sole factor behind them.

Other studies have looked at the loan performance issue. Van Order and Zorn (2001) examined prime mortgages to low-income or minority (LIM) households compared to other mortgages for a large sample of mortgages originated in the 1990s. This study is an improvement on simple delinquency and default studies because it considers another important element of loan profitability—prepayment risk. When mortgage borrowers refinance or sell their homes and prepay their mortgages more quickly, lenders' profits tend to drop. Van Order and Zorn found that, while the loans to LIM borrowers (not just "CRA loans") defaulted at somewhat higher levels, they prepaid at lower levels. This prepayment risk has a cost that is at least on the same order of magnitude as that due to credit risk. Moreover, Van Order and Zorn found that the lower prepayment risk of the LIM loans was of similar magnitude to the default risk and, if anything, the lower prepayment risk was of greater magnitude. Thus, even if a certain segment of loans has somewhat higher delinquencies or defaults, it does not necessarily mean that those loans are less profitable to the lender.

Another challenge is to distinguish between CRA-induced programs and lending to lower-income or minority borrowers of any sort. For example, as explained in chapter 5, many loans to minority borrowers tend to come from subprime lenders. Yet we know that these loans also tend to perform much worse than prime loans. One way of getting at this issue is to examine the special CRA programs of banks, as Avery, Bostic, and Canner (2000) did. Tholin (1993) also took this approach and examined loans made by a set of lenders with specialized community lending programs. She found that the lenders' single-family loans had lower delinquency rates than for the overall single-family loan market. While multifamily delinquency rates were somewhat higher than market comparables, foreclosure rates were not.

One study that avoids some, but not all, of the limitations of the studies focused on particular lending programs examined the relationship between banks' propensity to make lower-income loans and their overall earnings. Canner and Passmore (1997) identified banks that made significant numbers of mortgage loans and examined their lending patterns. They found that banks making more loans to lower-income borrowers were no less profitable than banks that made fewer such loans. They obtained similar results for banks that make more loans to lower-income areas.

The Community Reinvestment Act, Fair Lending, and Access to Credit

Until the Financial Institutions Reform Recovery and Enforcement Act changes to the Home Mortgage Disclosure Act (HMDA) were made, it was difficult to obtain a quantitative sense of CRA's impact on overall lending markets. Improvements to HMDA in 1993 further increased the utility of the data. One of the earliest national studies on CRA lending trends to utilize some of the improved HMDA data was conducted by Federal Reserve Bank of Chicago researchers (Evanoff and Segal 1996). The article examined mortgage loans from 1990 to 1995. The authors found that banks increased lending to low- and moderate-income neighborhoods and focused on measuring the impacts from 1993 to 1994, during the initial discussions of CRA reform. They calculated that lower-income lending increased by 35,000 loans and $2.7 billion in just that one year in U.S. metropolitan areas. This is a particularly significant increase given that average monthly mortgage rates increased from 7.3 percent in 1993 to 8.4 percent in 1994.

Schwartz (1998a) examined the impact of CRA agreements on the lending of banks by comparing banks with agreements to those without in the same metropolitan areas. He found that the presence of an agreement increased the amount of bank lending to low-income and minority households and neighborhoods. He calculated that the market share of banks involved in CRA agreements among low-income borrowers was 92 percent of their overall market share, while the market share of banks not involved in agreements among low-income borrowers was only 78 percent of their overall market share. For blacks, the difference was even greater, with the black market share of banks involved in agreements reaching 112 percent of their overall market share to blacks while banks not involved in agreements reached only 77 percent. In low-income tracts, the banks involved in agreements reached 140 percent of their overall market share, while banks not involved in agreements reached just 90 percent.

To date, the most comprehensive study of CRA's impact on mortgage lending examined the differences in prime lending between banking and nonbanking organizations across the United States (Joint Center for Housing Studies 2002). This study found that 36 percent of the loans of banking organizations (banks and their affiliates) in the banks' assessment areas were

CRA-eligible, compared to just 29.4 percent of the lending of the same organizations outside their assessment areas and 28.7 percent for nonbank organizations. Thus, banks made more loans to lower-income places and people in areas that were scrutinized in CRA evaluations. Moreover, the Joint Center researchers found that the percentage of within-assessment-area loans by banking organizations that were CRA-eligible increased from 31.8 percent to 36 percent from 1993 to 2000, which coincides with the implementation of CRA reform.

Bostic et al. (2002) examined whether banks respond to CRA regulation by improving their lending performance in lower-income communities when they anticipate an upcoming acquisition. For CRA supporters, this would be an anticipated and desirable effect. In examining mergers over 1991–1995, the authors found that CRA lending was an important predictor of future acquisitions. In particular, they found that when a bank moved from the 25th to the 75th percentile in CRA lending activity, its probability of making an acquisition increased by 8 percent. They also found the effect to be driven by relatively larger banks, which are more likely to be scrutinized for CRA performance during a merger process.

Bostic and Robinson (2003a) studied the impact of CRA agreements on changes in mortgage lending at the county level. They looked at agreements over a three-year period and changes in lending during that period. They found that CRA agreements initiated in the second and third years of the period had substantial effects on lending. A CRA agreement initiated in the second year increased CRA-eligible mortgage lending by 20 percent, and an agreement in the third year increased by 14 percent. Moreover, total mortgage lending increased at the same rate, suggesting that the increased CRA lending generally represented new loans that did not displace non-CRA lending.

In another study, Bostic and Robinson (2003b) measured the impact of CRA agreements on the lending activity of the banks involved in the agreements. They found that lenders involved in agreements increased lending as a result of the agreements. The largest increases occurred two to three years after the agreements. They also found that lending increases persisted after the agreements ended, concluding that "CRA agreements have helped lenders find new profitable opportunities in previously overlooked communities."

Very little work has been done on identifying the impact of CRA on small business lending. CRA regulation and enforcement has been much more heavily focused on mortgage lending, so the expectations of finding much effect on commercial lending have been small. Regulators did not even have any systematic data on small business loans until 1996, and the data are still not as complete or robust as HMDA data. Moreover, policy and public attention have traditionally focused more on mortgage lending. Robb and Zinman

(2001) examined small business lending activity in different counties and classified banks based on whether they were subject to a "tough regulator" or not, using data from Thomas (1998). They found evidence that CRA improved access to credit for small firms in places where CRA was more aggressively enforced. However, they did not find evidence that CRA benefited firms in lower-income areas. This is consistent with the failure of regulators to pay substantial attention to the location of banks' small business loans compared to their analysis of housing loans. Rather than focus on geography, regulators have tended to look at the total volume of small business lending and the level of lending to very small firms.

One study, whose lead author has been a repeated critic of CRA, suggests CRA has not been responsible for the gains in lending to lower-income and minority borrowers in the 1990s, and that "market forces" deserve all of the credit (Gunther et al. 1999). There are two fundamental problems with the formulation of this study's assumptions. First, the authors rely on the concept of a market somehow wholly independent of government action. In fact, banking is an industry that benefits greatly from all sorts of government action, including deposit insurance, access to the Federal Reserve discount window, access to the GSEs, and regulation itself. Moreover, mortgage and finance companies are also critically tied into a web of financial infrastructure—including secondary markets, government guarantees, and borrowing from banks—that is heavily dependent on government action and subsidy. A second fundamental problem is that the study portrays a world in which CRA is a force independent of the market. In fact, the premise of CRA is that it complements and encourages private-sector activity, and not that it acts as a separate, competing force. By encouraging banks to take a second look at lower-income communities, CRA has helped open up new markets that banks rarely went near in years past. An example is multifamily lending, which banks were often very reluctant to do in the 1970s and early 1980s. CRA, combined with low-income housing tax credits and other factors, encouraged lending for apartment buildings. In Chicago, for example, multifamily lending increased dramatically in the late 1980s and early 1990s, so that many lenders were making such loans in lower-income areas by the early 1990s (Goldwater and Bush 1995). The availability of credit, in turn, spurred a significant increase in the rehabilitation of apartment buildings throughout the city.

Besides problems with the premises of the Gunther et al. (1999) study, there are other difficulties with many of its specific theoretical and empirical arguments. Gunther and his colleagues first argue on theoretical terms that the barriers to credit that once existed have disappeared and that low-income communities no longer face significant credit access problems. While the nature of some of the credit problems in lower-income communities has changed, it does not follow that disparities and problems no longer exist. Steeped in a conservative deregulationist framework, the authors suggest three barriers to credit access: limited competition, information barriers, and coordination problems. They then argue that the "market" has changed in ways so that each of these barriers has been overcome.

Competition, in the authors' view, makes discrimination and redlining impossible. Lenders who discriminate will simply lose profitable opportunities to those who do not. Limits to competition, they argue, have gone by the wayside as geographic and interest-rate restrictions have fallen. As support for this argument, they point to the growth of the subprime mortgage market as bringing improved access to credit to the underserved. They ignore the severe problems that have accompanied the rise of the subprime market and predatory lending (see chapter 5). While some progress in selected products has been made, it is generally not true that mortgage or banking markets offer more competitively priced credit to those who need it in lower-income communities. Moroever, the mortgage lending industry has become markedly more concentrated in recent decades (Joint Center for Housing Studies 2002).

The role of information technology has been as much a force in the hypersegmentation of mortgage markets as in improving access to credit. Database and other computerized technologies, while bringing some benefits in reducing overt discrimination, have great potential for exacerbating both disparate treatment and disparate impact discrimination, including the targeting of vulnerable populations with high-cost loans. (See chapters 4 and 5.) The last sort of lending problems that Gunther et al. maintain have been largely resolved are what they refer to as "coordination problems." This is when the problems of individual properties spill over and cause lenders to worry about conditions of the entire neighborhood. Here, the authors simultaneously argue that CRA may actually impede cooperative efforts to overcome coordination problems and that such problems have been "reduced substantially." On the first point, they argue that CRA does not give lenders sufficient incentive to coordinate activity. Yet, CRA regulations give banks explicit credit for all sorts of "coordinated" activity, from investing in community development loan funds to seeding community development planning and rehabilitation efforts. In fact, many of the practitioners who "coordinate" community development activity rely critically on CRA in gaining bank support for their work. The private market does not adequately reward cooperative ventures. Without CRA, banks and investors would look more for short-term rewards. Redeveloping communities that have suffered from decades of disinvestment is often a long-term endeavor.

Gunther et al. (1999) attempt to provide some empirical support for their arguments. Unfortunately, the data are not up to the task. Using HMDA data from 1993 to 1997, the authors hope to convince readers that the market alone is responsible for increased lending to lower-income neighborhoods and homebuyers. They compare changes in the home-purchase lending of banks, thrifts, and mortgage companies that are affiliated with banks or thrifts to changes in lending of independent mortgage companies. The authors do not formulate a convincing counterfactual—an estimate of what lending patterns would have looked like without CRA. They imply that independent mortgage lenders are themselves an appropriate comparison, but, in fact, this comparison is problematic. Independent mortgage companies are entirely different creatures from banks. Mortgage companies earn money primarily through mortgage lending, while banks earn income through a variety of means. In recent years, banks have experienced significant pressures to move toward serving more affluent markets. Without CRA, it is likely that banks' share of lending to lower-income neighborhoods and households would look substantially worse. The authors of the Joint Center report on CRA lending make a convincing case that banks, when under CRA, do a better job at serving lower-income communities (Joint Center for Housing Studies 2002).

Another problem with comparing banks to mortgage companies is the fact that fair lending regulations that complement CRA were enforced more vigorously in the early and mid-1990s, and these regulations may have disproportionately affected mortgage companies. As shown in chapter 7, the enforcement of these laws was stepped up in the early 1990s, following significant press coverage of new mortgage data on racial disparities and the 1992 Boston Federal Reserve study. Mortgage companies are regulated for fair lending primarily by the Departments of Justice and Housing and Urban Development, which are both executive branch agencies. On the other hand, the more independent bank regulators play a major role in enforcing fair lending at banks and thrifts. Thus the Clinton administration was able to move more forcefully in expanding fair lending enforcement than in reforming CRA. Gunther et al. (1999) also did not distinguish the nature of lending in different communities. Many of the leading independent mortgage companies that were included in their comparison group are subprime lenders. The frequent problems of subprime and predatory lending are well documented in chapter 5.

Overall, the preponderance of recent evidence on the impacts of CRA suggests that the law has had a substantial positive effect on lending to lower-income people and places. Some of these effects may be the result of CRA and increased fair lending enforcement in the 1990s combined. Much of the evidence points to impacts on mortgage lending, mostly because that is where the data are available to measure impacts. The initial data on small business lending suggest that the effects on *overall* small business lending may be significant, but that there is not a corresponding effect for lower-income neighborhoods. There has been essentially no systematic research on the impacts of CRA in the areas of community development investments and basic financial services. The anecdotal evidence suggests that CRA has been quite important for spurring bank investments, especially since CRA reform gave more explicit credit for such activity. Less is known about impacts on financial services. Since enforcement in this area has been among the most lax areas in CRA exams (see discussion below), measurable impacts would not be expected to be very large.

The Community Reinvestment Act—A Law in Search of Modernization and Enforcement

Notwithstanding the significant impacts of CRA, the law has suffered from persistent problems of weak implementation and enforcement. It rests on the efforts of severely resource-constrained community and public interest groups to prod both regulators and banks to adhere to the law. While some have argued that CRA works via a sort of "regulation from below" by giving community groups significant standing in the regulatory process, changes in recent years have weakened the influence of such groups as well as other aspects of the law. In fact, the true power of community groups has come when they have been able—oftentimes with the important assistance of key elected officials—to mobilize power to compel regulators to enforce the law in more meaningful ways. This may occur through highly organized campaigns that shine the media spotlight on a problem like lending discrimination or predatory lending. Effective community reinvestment activism is as much about advocating for policy change as it is about negotiating with banks. And with banks becoming ever larger and more geographically dispersed, policy advocacy will become even more important. Community groups in any given city will find it ever more difficult to gain the attention of a bank CEO. More action will have to be focused on changing the policies that banks operate within and the enforcement of those policies. At the same time, some attention to continued and increased national-level organizing around the activities of the largest financial institutions will still be required.

Some of the policy changes that are important to preserve or expand the impact of CRA require legislation. In 2001, the National Community Reinvestment Coalition (NCRC), together with many of its members, formulated a comprehensive legislative proposal to address the need for modernizing

CRA, especially given the passage of GLBA in 1999. The bill was sponsored by Representatives Thomas Barrett of Milwaukee and Luis Gutierrez of Chicago and received the endorsement of the U.S. Conference of Mayors and the National League of Cities. The bill, while not successful, was an important articulation of a vision of what community reinvestment advocates viewed as an appropriate, new CRA social contract for the twenty-first century.

At the same time, many of the changes I am suggesting below—a good number of which are contained in the NCRC bill—could be made without legislation, either through revising formal regulations or through changing regulator procedures and attitudes. Many CRA and fair lending successes have come when regulators have exhibited a commitment to enforce the statutes and regulations due to either successful pressure from community groups—manifest through media and congressional attention—or changes in political leadership. I will identify here only some of the changes that I believe should be addressed. I do not claim that this list of changes is comprehensive or somehow sufficient, but it provides a start, I believe, for some of the most important issues.

Expanding the Community Reinvestment Act

Numerous studies have pointed to the shrinking umbrella of CRA relative to the financial services sector (Campen 1998; D'Arista and Schlesinger 1993; Joint Center for Housing Studies 2002). CRA, which covers only banks and thrifts, misses many of the most important providers of credit and financial services, including mortgage and finance companies, insurance companies, securities firms, and credit unions. In 1980, more than 70 percent of mortgages were originated by banks and thrifts (Joint Center for Housing Studies 2002). By 1997, mortgage companies alone had 56 percent of the mortgage market. Beginning in the late 1970s, banks saw assets shift to money market mutual funds. Banks now control a much smaller share of savings dollars and face competition from finance companies in small business and consumer credit markets.

To allow banks to expand into other financial services areas to maintain high profit levels, regulators and Congress have allowed them to increasingly enter new lines of business other than taking deposits and making loans. Regulators began this activity largely in the 1980s, but it accelerated in the 1990s. By the end of the decade, banks were involved in all sorts of securities and other nonbanking activities. While Congress made such changes more comprehensive with the Gramm-Leach-Bliley Financial Services Modernization Act (GLBA) of 1999, regulators had already allowed many of the changes.

What Congress failed to do under GLBA was modernize CRA to keep pace with the myriad changes in financial institutions and financial markets.

Federal policy has facilitated the emergence of financial services industries and even prompted some of them. Convergence has been caused by a mix of technological and policy developments that are difficult, if not impossible, to disentangle. Banking and mortgage markets are not just shaped by entrepreneurs and technology. They remain, as Hoffman (2001) says, the stuff of high politics. This is true of securities and insurance markets as well. Financial markets fundamentally rely on all sorts of government-supported infrastructure, especially regulatory capacity. One only has to think of the importance of the swift legislative response to the Enron and WorldCom collapses, in the form of the Sarbannes-Oxley bill of 2002, to recognize this. This bill was critical to restoring public confidence in financial markets. Deregulationists continue to propose self-regulatory schemes, yet they are either not adopted (as evidenced by banks not opting out of Federal Deposit Insurance Corporation [FDIC] insurance) or are typically failures (as evidenced by the Public Company Accounting Oversight Board's largely self-regulatory predecessor).[2]

Now, as financial industries have reached perhaps their final stage of convergence, the choice must be made between maintaining a policy system that explicitly articulates a social contract concerning lower-income communities on the one hand, and abandoning the social contract on the other. CRA has been that contract for depository institutions. The law has been justified, by advocates as well as regulators, by the benefits that banks receive in the form of federal deposit insurance. Nonbanks, it is argued, receive no such benefit. However, this is certainly not true in the age of convergence. Many nonbanks are affiliates of banks and thus benefit from deposit insurance and the public's confidence in banks. Deposit insurance allows the financial holding companies (FHCs) or bank holding companies (BHCs) to gather low-cost capital, which they can then use to fund mortgages or loans with a cost of funds well below private securities. Moreover, lenders who sell to Fannie Mae and Freddie Mac, including most mortgage companies who are not affiliated with banks as well as bank-affiliated lenders, are relying on two institutions that would not exist but for government action and that continue to receive subsidies and implicit guarantees from government.

The government also provides a regulatory infrastructure that is critical to functioning financial markets and that justifies social contract policies like CRA. These policies provide the confidence that financial firms cannot provide themselves. It is arguable that the larger the explicit and implicit benefits that an industry receives from government action, the larger its obligation under its social contract should be. But it is difficult to argue that any financial services activity does not receive substantial benefits of this sort. Some forms of government benefits, like deposit insurance, may be easier to measure, but this does not mean that the others are any less real or important.

Unfortunately, the political pendulum has recently swung further away from extending the social contract of CRA to the more integrated financial services sector. Regulators appear to be finding more ways to shield banks from CRA review. Under GLBA, for example, the Citigroup acquisition of the Associates in 2000 did not require Federal Reserve Bank approval, because the transaction did not involve the merger of two bank holding companies. Because the Associates owned only what are called "limited purpose" banks, it was not a bank holding company, and the only approvals required were by the Office of the Comptroller of the Currency (OCC) and the FDIC for safety and soundness or antitrust concerns.

The most obvious way to extend CRA would be through a form of "functional" regulation. Any financial institution that makes housing or small business loans should be subject to the act, regardless of its status as a depository. Mortgage companies now make more than half of all mortgages and benefit from a strong history of federal involvement in mortgage markets (see chapter 2) as well as ongoing indirect subsidies and regulation. Consumer protection provided by federal and state regulators gives borrowers confidence in the mortgage marketplace, yielding efficiencies and gains to lenders. The next logical extension of CRA would be in the coverage of institutions competing with banks in offering retail investment and money market account services. Securities markets are federally and state regulated and benefit from such regulation. Large mutual fund and securities firms invest regularly in federal and GSE securities and state and local bonds. They also benefit from the securities market regulatory infrastructure and from implicit "too big to fail" guarantees. Insurance companies benefit from government regulation of the mortgage and real estate markets, in which they are major investors, as well as from state regulation.[3]

Functional CRA regulation would mean that mortgage companies would be evaluated primarily for their lending performance in housing markets, while industrial finance companies would be regulated for their small business lending. Securities firms would be evaluated under something like the current CRA Investment Test. Some have suggested a sort of national reinvestment fund that such firms would invest in, but the more decentralized approach of CRA is likely to be more effective and responsive to local needs. Securities firms would need to have national-level assessment areas, or areas that reflect the distribution of their customer bases.

The natural first step is to extend CRA to mortgage and finance companies and credit unions. These institutions are currently heavily involved in retail credit provision. Credit unions have vigorously fought any efforts to impose even the most minimal "CRA-lite" regulations by the National Credit Union Administration, their regulator. They argue that nonprofit credit unions, by design, serve their communities, and that these communities are designed by the membership of the credit unions themselves. In times when credit unions were clearly restricted to drawing on employees of specific companies or closely related groups of companies, this may have been a reasonable response. However, over the last decade or so, credit unions have been able to expand their "field of membership" to include large geographic areas as the sole basis for membership. As this occurs, the justification for treating credit unions differently from banks diminishes. Their nonprofit status does not justify such exclusion. Credit unions are essentially cooperatives, but they are not charitable organizations. There are various ways that they can exclude lower-income people, either intentionally or unintentionally, from their membership base. Moreover, the federal credit union charter was intended to serve people of modest means. Yet a study in the Chicago area found that, while lower-income households were less likely to have a bank or a credit-union account than middle- and upper-income households, the magnitude of the effect was larger for credit union accounts (Jacob, Bush, and Immergluck 2002). That is, lower-income households were even less likely to hold a credit union account than a bank account, after controlling for a variety of household characteristics.

Current CRA regulations offer banks the best of all possible worlds regarding affiliate activity. Affiliate activity is not considered in the CRA exam of a bank unless the bank chooses to have it included. Moreover, a bank may choose to include affiliate activity only for certain product lines.[4] For example, a bank could choose to include only the small business loans of its affiliates but not the home purchase or home improvement loans. In effect, a bank can cherry-pick those activities that make it look better while avoiding any activities that might detract from its performance. In addition, banks are able to count loans purchased from their own affiliates for consideration under the Lending Test. So, by purchasing only an affiliate's loans made to lower-income borrowers or neighborhoods, a bank can improve its lending test score.[5] So, rather than affiliates' being "covered" under CRA, current regulations actually treat banks more favorably than if affiliate activity were not considered under CRA at all.

Assessment Areas

A critical weakness in current CRA policy is the way in which assessment areas are constructed. Assessment areas define the geographic boundaries of the lending, investment, and service activities that are reviewed in a bank's CRA evaluation. The CRA statute itself says very little about this critical issue. It states that institutions have a "continuing and affirmative obligation to help meet the credit needs of the local communities in which they are chartered to do business." It also states that regulators shall "assess the institution's record of meeting the credit needs of its entire community, including low- and moderate-income neighborhoods."[6] Regulators were given the charge of implementing the statute, including the definitions of community. The legislative history of the act discussed in chapter 6 makes clear that the initial version of the CRA bill did conceive of a notion of community that was quite restrictive to areas near branch office locations. The bill as originally introduced talked about "primary savings service areas," which were the areas in which banks got most of their deposits via their branches. This strictly localized concept of financial intermediation was heavily criticized by CRA opponents in the legislative debate for oversimplifying the financial system. They were largely correct on this point. Secondary markets, including the Federal Home Loan banks and also the emerging Fannie Mae and Freddie Mac, allowed banks to move excess deposits to areas in need of capital for mortgage lending. While some reinvestment advocates were not pleased with the change, Senator Proxmire conceded this argument and agreed to change to a concept of community, rather than savings area. Thus, the legislative history supports the notion that the concept of community should not be restricted to the physical location of branches or deposit holders. In fact, the first CRA regulations that followed the statute also allowed for a much wider definition of community that was not necessarily tied to branch locations.

In 1978, regulators proposed two fairly specific approaches (and left open a much less specific third option) to delineating its community, but also offered a third, much less restricted, option for banks. The two more specific options included:

(1) . . . the use of existing boundaries such as those of standard metropolitan statistical areas (SMSAs) or counties in which the bank's office or offices are located . . . a small bank may delineate those portions of SMSAs or counties it reasonably may be expected to serve.

(2) . . . may use its effective lending territory, which is defined as that local area or areas around each office or group of offices where it makes a substantial portion of its loans and all other areas equidistant from its offices as those areas. . . .

The second option, which was formulated shortly after the regulatory debate, clearly suggests that regulators felt it reasonable for banks to delineate community areas based on where they made loans. The legislative history suggests that a focus on the location of lending as well as the location of branches and deposits was intended after the shift from the original savings area concept.

Again, according to Dennis (1978):

> A rule of reason would dictate that large banks . . . should define community for CRA purposes in terms of the parameters of the metropolitan areas where they market their "retail" activities, seek deposits, are chartered, have their home offices and make most of their loans to individuals. . . . The CRA would impact these institutions most by imposing a legal obligation to meet credit needs in the low and moderate-income neighborhoods within this "community." . . . The concept of community is flexible enough to permit the use of different criteria for the same institutions in different geographic areas.

Yet current CRA regulations specify that assessment areas should be constructed around existing physical branch locations. Regulators have sometimes cited the statute or the legislative history in justifying this restriction. They are apparently not reading the entire history and are relying only on the original bill as introduced or perhaps some of the less specific rhetoric surrounding the legislation. It is clear that designating assessment areas based on the locations of lending as well as deposits and branches is consistent with the statute.

The result of regulators' current formulation of assessment areas is that some very large banks—either in terms of lending or deposit activity—have identified single, sometimes quite small, metropolitan areas as their assessment areas. This leaves the bulk of their lending and/or deposit activities outside the boundaries of serious CRA evaluation. For example, in 2003, the OCC approved a charter for the Charles Schwab Bank, NA, in Reno, Nevada. The bank will offer lending and insured account products to Charles Schwab and Company's 7.8 million account holders around the country. The investment-banking firm has 395 domestic offices in 48 states and branches in Puerto Rico and the Virgin Islands. Yet, the bank will technically have only one office location in Reno. The bank plans to select its CRA assessment area as including only the Reno metropolitan area, and the OCC has implied that it will accept such a designation.[7]

American Express Centurion Bank is an $11 billion credit card bank in Salt Lake City, Utah. American Express issues tens of thousands of small business credit cards throughout the country through the bank. However, the bank designated its assessment area as the Salt Lake City area only, even though it is effectively the largest small business lender in many cities around the country. State Farm Insurance owns a thrift that offers loan and deposit products through its agents located throughout the country, but its assessment area covers only the Bloomington-Normal, Illinois, metropolitan area.[8]

Telebank, which was later acquired by E-Trade bank, was permitted to establish an assessment area that was limited to Arlington, Virginia. Yet E-Trade makes loans throughout the country by telephone and the Internet.

Internet and "branchless banks" that use alternative delivery mechanisms do not fit into the current notion of branch-based assessment areas. One Internet bank, the Atlanta-based NetBank, has set specific lending targets through its CRA strategic plan. These targets are established for ten states in addition to Atlanta, which as a group account for 70 percent of its deposits and 50 percent of its loans ("CRA Rules" 2002). This is at least a step in the right direction, and should serve as a model for how assessment areas can be developed for lenders originating a good deal of business far from branch locations. This is not just an issue for banks that do not have branches. Even when a bank makes some loans via branches, if it makes a substantial portion in metropolitan areas or counties without branches, those places should be included in its assessment area.[9]

Some have argued that branchless banks should be treated like limited purpose or wholesale banks that do little retail lending and are evaluated based only on their investment and community development lending activity (Parry Fox 2003). This argument is not compelling. If these banks are offering retail deposit and lending products, they should be subject to the same regulations as other retail institutions.

Another continuing problem with assessment areas is the ability of banks to designate areas in ways that avoid low- and moderate-income communities. While the current regulations contain language that attempts to prevent this, the ability of banks to choose assessment areas at a scale below a metropolitan area (or county in the rural communities) provides a perverse incentive in the regulations. If a bank is able to select only a portion of a metropolitan area as its assessment area, then it will have a strong incentive to choose a more affluent segment of the region. This creates an implicit CRA advantage to banks located in such areas.

A hypothetical example is useful in illustrating the problem. Let us assume we have two modest sized banks, one located in the lower-income half of the metropolitan area and the other located in the upper-income half. Let us say that 40 percent of all borrowers in the low-income section are low or moderate income, but only 15 percent of borrowers in the upper-income section are low or moderate income. If the first bank made 35 percent of its loans to low and moderate income borrowers and the second made 25 percent, other things being equal, the second bank is likely to perform better on the CRA lending test. The bank is primarily judged against the composition of the assessment area. If both banks were judged against the composition of residents in the entire region, the first bank would perform better. The owners of the first bank may argue that it is harder for them to serve borrowers on the other side of the metro area. However, given the realities of CRA ratings, it will still not be difficult for them to obtain a satisfactory rating. What is more important is that the bank located in an area with more low-income residents should generally not be held to a higher standard due to its location in or near lower-income neighborhoods. This only serves to handicap the bank that chooses to locate a branch in a lower-income area. The simple solution is to more rigorously enforce the standard that regulators have established—that assessment areas should generally constitute entire metropolitan areas or, at the least, entire counties, even for smaller institutions. Very small institutions are not subject to the large-bank evaluation system anyway, so this issue becomes less relevant for them.

Research has documented the problem of assessment areas being skewed away from lower-income communities. Antonakes (2001) examined the selection of assessment areas by banks. He found that the number of banks choosing a community as part of its assessment area, the assets of those banks, and the number of bank offices located in the community all increase with increasing median family income and decline with higher minority population levels. Banks remain quite free to construct assessment areas that avoid lower-income and minority communities.

Basic Banking Services

In the late 1990s, access to basic banking services, including low-cost checking and savings accounts, began to receive increased attention from community groups and policymakers. This reaction was due, in part, to the explosive growth of check-cashing outlets and payday loan operations throughout the country (Caskey 1994; Squires and O'Connor 2001; Stegman and Faris 2003). In the past, community groups had focused primarily on the lending activities of banks, without giving much attention to basic banking services. The one major exception was that community groups had paid a good deal of attention to branch locations and branch closing behavior (Schwartz 1998b). But community and consumer groups began to move beyond simply looking at bank branch locations to more clearly link the lack of access to affordable basic checking and savings accounts in lower-income communities with the growth of check-cashers. The bulk (88 percent) of those using check-cashing outlets do not have any form of bank account (Dunham 2001). Community groups also articulated the notion that a household's experience with mainstream banking reduced its likelihood of borrowing from payday lenders and using other high-cost financial service providers. Recent research confirms this notion. Adults whose parents had a banking relationship are less likely to take out payday loans, other factors held constant (Stegman and Faris 2003).

The growth in community concern on the issue has led to regulators' paying more attention to problems in accessing basic banking services. While national figures show that approximately 9.5 percent of households do not have any form of savings or checking account, the figures in large cities tend to be much higher. In New York City and Los Angeles, where the OCC conducted special surveys, 42 percent and 32 percent of individuals, respectively, did not have transaction accounts (Dunham 2001). When comparing groups with similar incomes, having a bank account is strongly correlated with maintaining some savings. While savings can be held outside of bank accounts, including in cash, gold or jewelry, safety deposit boxes, or retirement accounts, for those unbanked individuals with incomes below $15,000, only 17 percent had savings of any form. However, among banked individuals with incomes below $15,000, 75 percent had some savings (Dunham 2001). Moreover, 40 percent of those at this income level with bank accounts added to their savings regularly, while only 8 percent of low-income individuals without savings did.

The problem of the use of high-cost basic banking services is one that is closely linked to neighborhood location. Rhine et al. (2001) found that, after controlling for race, income, employment status, education, and other characteristics, residents of lower-income neighborhoods were significantly more likely to use a check-cashing outlet than similar households in other neighborhoods. Moreover, these households were also less likely to have a bank account. The two issues are directly linked, in that the lack of a bank account is a predictor of check cashing outlet usage, holding other factors constant. While in some areas, unbanked households are often able to cash checks at low costs at cooperating banks or retailers, in many other places, this is not the case. A family with an income of 18,000 can easily spend $500 per year on check-cashing and related fees (Caskey 2001). In large cities, 20–40 percent of the unbanked pay fees to cash checks regularly, with fees ranging from 2 to 4 percent of the check's face value.

While physical proximity to bank branches may play some role, the presence of branches appears not to be sufficient in reducing the dominance of fringe financial services firms in lower-income and minority neighborhoods. This is partly because the high balance requirements and very punitive penalties for overdrafts that are featured in most bank accounts make these accounts less than useful to many residents of lower-income neighborhoods. Moreover, banks continue to suffer from the reputation—sometimes deserved and sometimes not, depending on the institution—that they discriminate against minority communities.

In the last several years, community groups, public interest organizations, and others have worked with banks to encourage the development of products that suit the needs of lower-income communities. Approximately one-half of the unbanked say they do not use banks because it is not worth it, given their small savings levels (Caskey 2001). However, if the costs of bank accounts were reduced, more would find it worthwhile to open an account. One example of new product development that involved the Chicago CRA Coalition and Bank One has been cited repeatedly as a success. As part of a CRA agreement in 1998, Bank One agreed to work with the coalition to examine the bank's existing deposit products and to study the development of a new, affordable, and accessible basic banking account (Williams 2000). After working with the coalition for approximately six months, the bank agreed to offer a pilot "alternative banking program" in one low- to moderate-income neighborhood on the city's southwest side and soon followed with five more communities. Within the first year, almost 1,000 checking accounts had been established, as well as 500 savings accounts. The average balances on the accounts were higher than anticipated, with an average of almost $600 for checking accounts and $1,300 for savings accounts. The accounts featured very low opening deposits and minimum balances, as well as unlimited check writing and use of the bank's ATMs. The bank also sponsored financial literacy workshops in the communities in which it partnered with local community groups.

Caskey (2001) has recommended that banks open special outlets to provide fee-based check-cashing and money order services, in addition to regular products, especially those geared to low-balance customers. He has suggested that banks offer deposit-secured loan programs to help those with credit problems repair their credit. Forty-two percent of the unbanked report delinquencies on bills. Thus, they have been effectively cut off from prime credit markets and forced to rely on payday lenders, title lenders, and pawnshops.

Notwithstanding the increased attention to the nature of basic banking services by community groups, bank branch locations remain skewed away from low-income and minority neighborhoods. This is a concern not only for access to basic banking services, but also for access to prime mortgage credit and, especially, small business loans. (See chapter 3 for a discussion of the link between branch locations and small business lending.) Nationally, branches per capita increased from 1975 to 1985 due in part to relaxations of intrastate branching laws (Avery et al. 1997). From 1985 to 1995, however, the number of branches per capita declined. Low- and moderate-income zip codes accounted for two-thirds of the 1985–1995 decline, even though they accounted for only one-fifth of branches in 1985.

Avery et al. (1999) examined the impact of mergers on the number of branches in a zip code. Using a national dataset of bank branches by zip code, they found that mergers involving banks with branches in the same zip code (a "within-zip" merger) resulted in less per capita growth in branches than other mergers, due to the actions of the merging banks. Zip codes that contained more bank branches affected by within-zip mergers experienced less growth in branches. Moreover, this negative effect of mergers on branch growth was exacerbated in low-income zip codes. Thus, when banks with branches in the same zip code merged, they tended to reduce branches and to reduce them further when located in lower-income areas. Mergers also reduced branch locations in lower-income neighborhoods when there was no overlap in branches. Even mergers of banks without branches in the same zip code but with a presence in the same metropolitan banking market (within-market-but-not-within-zip mergers) resulted in fewer branches in low-income zip codes (Avery et al. 1999). No such effect was found in higher-income areas.

The result of mergers and acquisitions as well as other restructuring in the industry is that low-income and minority neighborhoods continue to suffer from poorer access to bank branches. Smith (2003) found that, in the Chicago area, low-income zip codes had 0.79 branches per 10,000 residents versus 1.36 in moderate-income zip codes, 2.7 in middle-income zip codes, and 3.7 in upper-income areas. Moreover, middle-income zip codes with mostly minority populations had 2.14 branches per capita versus 2.77 in mostly white middle-income zip codes. Squires and O'Connor (2001, 145) found similar results in the Milwaukee area. In Milwaukee's lower-income city-designated "target area," there were 3.54 branches per 10,000 households versus 7.19 in the rest of Milwaukee County. While bank branches grew from 11 in 1970 to 22 in 1996 in the target area, the increase outside the target area was much larger, from 61 to 224.

Stegman, Cochran, and Faris (2002) critiqued the recent practices and policies of bank regulators in implementing the CRA Services Test. They recommended that examiners more consistently measure the geographic distribution of bank branches against the distribution of households and that they measure the actual delivery of financial services (e.g., number of accounts opened) to low- and moderate-income communities rather than give banks credit for the mere existence of alternative delivery channels, such as ATMs and loan production offices. They called for regulators to analyze the nature of so-called affordable accounts and to compare them with some clear benchmarks. They also urged regulators to examine the geographical distribution of bank accounts by census tract.[10]

Recent CRA exams exhibit a great deal of inconsistency and relatively little depth of analysis in the Service Test section as compared especially to the Lending Test section. Moreover, Stegman, Cochran, and Faris (2002) found that when banks performed "so poorly on the lending and investment tests that they were in danger of receiving a Needs to Improve rating overall . . . their Service Test scores were much higher than would otherwise be expected." The higher Service Test scores often gave banks just enough cumulative points to earn an overall satisfactory rating. Thus, the Service Test appears to be the "fudge factor" that some examiners use to ensure that a bank does not get a needs-to-improve overall CRA rating. This not only indicates the weakness of the Service Test, it also adds a great deal of evidence to the notion that examiners work hard to avoid giving banks overall ratings below the level of satisfactory.

Investments

Under the Investment Test, banks are evaluated for the extent to which they make investments in projects that promote community development. This might include investments in community development financial institutions (CDFIs), small business investment companies (SBICs), low-income housing tax credit projects, municipal revenue bonds of various sorts, and geographically targeted mortgage-backed securities, as well as deposits (including federally insured ones) in low-income credit unions, minority-owned banks, or community development banks.[11] Also included are grants to community organizations, CDFIs, or other nonprofits that primarily benefit low- and moderate-income individuals or communities. The Investment Test, like the Service Test, counts as one-quarter of the overall CRA rating.

CRA reform boosted the importance of bank investments by making investment activity an expectation for banks with more than $250 million in assets. Many banks had been investing in community development activities before 1995, and such activities generally boosted their prospects for better CRA ratings. However, the 1995 formulation of the Lending Test gave investments new importance. It recognized the role of community-based development financing as a key part of the financial infrastructure in lower-income communities. CDFIs, community development corporations, and other actors provide a vehicle to expand credit access and "prime the pump" for mainstream lending and banking. CDFIs, in particular, are able to draw on bank, government, and philanthropic dollars, and blend them in strategic ways, often tying lending to other community development activities.

CDFIs by themselves will never be big enough to solve the capital access problems of lower-income and minority communities. However, they serve as the development finance laboratories for mainstream lenders by being the "first in" for underserved market areas. The classic example is Shorebank in Chicago, which, by financing a new generation of entrepreneurs rehabilitating older apartment buildings, seeded a new housing industry that was later financed by mainstream banks (Taub 1994). Investments in CDFIs enable them to leverage the necessary debt and equity capital to maintain adequate lending capacity and to do so with adequate equity-to-debt ratios. These CDFIs, in turn, are able to meet many credit needs that are unmet by conventional financial institutions. The need for such alternative lenders may be due to discrimination, redlining, or market failures in which private, individual institutions do not have incentives to lend to projects where private returns do not equal the aggregate social return. CDFIs are able to combine the motivations of profit-seekers with those of philanthropic and economic development actors. This can be a great advantage when attempting to make somewhat difficult but catalytic investments in communities that have experienced significant neglect over substantial periods of time.

CDFIs are key beneficiaries of the Investment Test. While CDFIs—particularly community development credit unions—date back to the first half of the twentieth century, their numbers started to grow in the 1960s and 1970s. As of 2003, there were approximately 800 to 1,000 CDFIs in the United States (Corporation for Enterprise Development 2003). Of these, more than 670 were certified as federal CDFIs by the Treasury Department's CDFI Fund, although far fewer receive any funding from the federal program. Moreover, a majority of community development credit unions are not even certified as federal CDFIs.

The two most numerous types of CDFIs are community development credit unions and community development loan funds. In a survey of 512 CDFIs, the Corporation for Enterprise Development (2003) found that, in 2001, the surveyed CDFIs had financed almost 7,500 businesses—including many very small firms—creating more than 15,000 jobs and maintaining another 37,000. The same CDFIs, as a group, directly developed more than 2,600 housing units and renovated more than 5,700 units in 2001. They financed or facilitated the construction and rehabilitation of another 35,000 units. In addition, the surveyed CDFIs closed more than 7,100 mortgages, typically for first-time buyers. The CDFIs also funded 501 nonprofit facilities that served more than 630,000 people. These facilities included day care centers, hospitals, and schools. The 512 surveyed CDFIs together had almost $6 billion in outstanding financing at the time of the survey. In 2001, they provided $2.9 billion in financing and provided training and technical assistance to almost 7,000 businesses and more than 121,000 individuals. Almost three-quarters of CDFI customers were low income, and 63 percent were minorities. Most of the CDFIs had been around for some time, with the average starting year being 1984. CDFIs work in both urban and rural areas. The acceleration in the growth of CDFIs in the 1970s and 1980s is more than coincidentally related to the Community Reinvestment Act. Even though the Investment Test did not begin until 1995, banks received CRA credit for support of CDFIs well before this.

There are a number of ways in which CRA benefits CDFIs (Santiago, Holyoke, and Levi 1998; Immergluck 1998). The most important way is through encouraging banks to make equity or equity-like investments in CDFIs. The 512 CDFIs surveyed by the Corporation for Enterprise Development (2003) reported more than $850 million of their current equity capital came from banks in 2001. The bulk of this amount ($745 million) went to community development loan funds.[12] In fact, banks, thrifts, and credit unions accounted for more than one-third of loan fund capital. Many banks also participate in loan pools or similar vehicles that provide CDFIs with a great deal of lending capacity. These loans are considered under the community development portion of the Lending Test.

Currently, CRA examiners generally do not distinguish between very different types of investment activity to determine the investment test rating. Grants, deposits in eligible institutions, investments in nontargeted SBICs, and other disparate investments are generally summed with no weighting or disaggregation. The sum of investments is sometimes then compared to a bank's own equity capital. This overly simple analysis does not adequately distinguish between lower- and higher-risk investments, or between investments yielding higher or lower private financial returns to the bank. A $100,000 investment in a SBIC that does not target lower-income areas or minority-owned firms and is expected to bring the bank a private rate of return of 20 percent is likely to be given as much weight as a $100,000 long-term, subordinate investment in a nonprofit CDFI that does difficult-to-finance real estate projects in low-income communities and can provide only a modest rate of return to the bank (but may be more likely to yield a higher social return). The regulations require examiners to consider the responsiveness to community needs and the extent to which the private market meets a need, but the extent to which examiners do this varies widely. The regulations should direct examiners to consider community needs more explicitly. Specifically, the current provision that banks will receive credit for investments that are not "routinely provided by the private market" should be taken very seriously during exams. Each category of investment other than grants should be measured relative to a bank's equity capital. Grants should be measured against a bank's recent earnings, a common approach in measuring philanthropic giving by corporations.

Some (Thomas 2003; American Bankers Association 2002) have argued that the Investment Test should be abolished. One argument is that banks should not be expected to make investments, but that if they do, they should be able to get credit for such activity under the Lending Test (American Bankers Association 2002). Bank consultant Kenneth Thomas (2003) argues that investments do not help meet community credit needs and so are inconsistent with the legislative intent of the act. However, the legislative history of CRA clearly indicates that the statute was intended to do more than merely eliminate geographic lending discrimination by individual banks. Legislators recognized that creative approaches to deal with the legacies of discrimination and disinvestment were needed and that banks should support such activities. They wanted banks to find ways to serve lower-income markets that were consistent with safety and soundness requirements, including working with what were then mostly public-sector credit enhancement programs.

Today, with the decline of direct government involvement in community economic development, CDFIs and other nongovernmental investment recipients (e.g., low-income housing tax credit syndications) are often the primary vehicles for pulling together public and philanthropic funds to provide the sort of credit enhancements necessary to be the lead, catalytic investments in somewhat riskier projects. Working with CDFIs allows banks to focus on the more conventional lending needs of the community, or to take senior positions on loans where CDFIs may take somewhat riskier junior positions. Redlining and discriminatory markets have real legacies, and in some particularly troubled markets, efforts to "prime the pump" are required. These efforts are challenging and require substantial specialized skills and resources. CDFIs are designed for this purpose. These are real credit needs, and it was clearly the intention of those drafting the CRA to encourage the involvement of banks in such efforts.

Small Business Lending

In terms of getting the attention of CRA regulators, small business lending has largely been the poor stepsibling of housing lending. This position is based, to some degree, on the lower levels of attention given small business development in lower-income neighborhoods by community groups and public interest organizations. This lack of attention may be due to the greater needs regarding housing in recent decades, the wider distribution of the lending and investment activities in the housing sector, or other factors. An unfortunate product of the lesser scrutiny of small business lending activities by community actors is that regulators have not vigorously implemented CRA for small business lending. This lack of implementation is evident in the regulations themselves as well as in the enforcement through the bank examination process. In the 1993–1995 CRA reform process, for example, rather than carrying through with proposals to collect race and gender data on small business loans at a loan-by-loan level, as is done with the HMDA data, regulators responded to bank pressure and developed regulations that only collect total industry figures of loan activity by census tract. Moreover, the lending reports for each institution do not reveal how much a bank lends in particular neighborhoods.

In terms of the implementation of the regulations, examiners have generally focused much more on the total level of activity of banks' small business lending than on the geographical distribution of the loans. This observation was corroborated by Robb and Zinman (2001), who found that tougher CRA enforcement led to higher levels of small business lending but not to more lending to lower-income neighborhoods. Examiners generally give much more attention to geographic and income-distributional issues in examining mortgage loans. Examiners do give significant attention to the size of small businesses receiving loans, but this is less consistent with the legislative intent of CRA than the geographic analysis.

Predatory Lending, Fair Lending, and the Community Reinvestment Act

Chapter 8 addresses the need for consumer protection laws to reduce predatory lending. However, there are two other areas of regulation than can impact predatory lending: CRA and fair lending policies. Fair lending regulation is critical to identifying disparate pricing and terms of loans between protected and unprotected classes.[13] Unfortunately, little aggressive enforcement in this area has occurred to date. (See chapter 7.) Because many subprime lenders are affiliates of banks through a holding company structure, the one bank regulator that has the greatest potential to identify discriminatory practices across a banking organization (including both bank and nonblank affiliates) is the FRB. The board is the regulator of BHCs and FHCs. As such, it has the ability to examine disparate patterns of lending across different lending units of the holding companies. For example, when the OCC or the FDIC examine a bank for fair lending, they do not have the ability to examine whether the bank focuses its prime lending on predominantly white borrowers while an affiliate focuses subprime lending on predominantly minority borrowers. The board, however, has the ability to do this but has generally chosen not to do so. In a 1999 report on fair lending reviews during large bank mergers, the U.S. General Accounting Office (GAO) recommended that the board conduct such intra–holding company analyses. The GAO commented that FRB is "uniquely situated to monitor the activities of these nonbank mortgage subsidiaries by virtue of its role as the regulator of bank holding companies" (U.S. General Accounting Office 1999). Even after GAO's recommendation, the board continues to ignore fair lending problems of bank affiliates. With the increasing involvement of BHCs and FHCs in subprime lending, but without BHC- and FHC-wide fair lending exams, identifying discrimination will become increasingly difficult.

Another important aspect of fair lending enforcement is the broker-lender relationship. Many lenders, including many subprime lenders, utilize extensive broker networks as their primary retail lending systems. While lenders generally are liable for explicit fair lending violations of the brokers with whom they work, subtler but more systematic decisions vis-à-vis brokers may be significant sources of discrimination. For example, if a lender solicits relationships with brokers primarily located in minority communities for its subprime products but focuses on lenders in other areas for its prime products, examining broker actions will not necessarily reveal disparate treatment or impact. It is often the selection of brokers that is the discriminatory action. Moreover, if a lender establishes tight quality controls for its prime lending via brokers (e.g., reviews of loan performance for different brokers), but is lax with its quality controls for its subprime brokers, less scrupulous subprime brokers will gravitate to it as a source of credit for borrowers vulnerable to predatory lending.

CRA can be used to reduce predatory lending and to encourage responsible, fair subprime lending. A number of consumer groups have recommended much closer scrutiny of the quality of loans to lower-income places and households. While there is some movement in this direction, far more can be done. Fair lending and consumer compliance exams may uncover problems of disparate treatment in lending terms or outright violation of consumer lending laws. However, the CRA exam process should also ensure that institutions that are doing more responsible lending receive more credit than those that are doing less responsible lending. Moreover, lenders that make legal but problematic loans should be penalized under CRA. The regulations should call for an examination of subprime loans for predatory features, including excessive up-front fees (more than 4 percent of the total loan amount), heavy prepayment penalties (more than 2 to 3 percent of the loan's principal amount, or lasting for more than three years from origination), single-premium credit insurance, mandatory arbitration, or debt-to-income ratios above 50 percent. If a lender makes a claim that loans with such features are somehow beneficial to the borrower, the lender should be compelled to demonstrate this with actual cases. Such evaluations will not only penalize lenders who make abusive loans, but also reward those lenders making sound, responsible subprime loans. This would make CRA a more effective tool for encouraging responsible subprime lending.

Loan Purchases Versus Originations

Under current CRA regulations, banks get credit for loans that they originate and for loans that they purchase from other lenders. The argument support-ing this policy is that loan purchases increase the ability of the originators to make the loan by enhancing the liquidity of the financing. This argument makes sense only if the loan is not readily salable to government secondary markets, which are the dominant purchasers of conventional prime loans. Thus, banks should not receive credit for loans that are salable to Fannie Mae or Freddie Mac. Moreover, care must be taken to ensure that CRA credit is not given for purchases of predatory loans. The ability to count loan purchases has also created the opportunity for banks to "game" the CRA evaluation system by allowing banks to purchase loans purely to inflate their reported CRA loans. Some cases have been reported of different lenders "exchanging" loans so as to recycle them through different lenders and gain CRA credit (Joint Center on Housing Studies 2002). The regulations do not permit this, but the activity is difficult to detect.

A related issue that concerns the Investment Test is the ability of banks to receive credit for their investments in mortgage-backed securities that pri-marily contain loans to lower-income borrowers or in lower-income areas. This is cause for substantial concern. These sorts of securities are an impor-tant method of funding subprime lending. Without scrutiny of the loans backing the securities, offering CRA credit for such investments might en-courage the funding of predatory lending operations.

The Community Reinvestment Act and Neighborhood Racial Composition

Federal regulators and the banking industry have frequently argued that CRA was not intended to deal with issues of access to credit by different racial groups. CRA exams today focus only on the distribution of lending, invest-ments, and services across neighborhoods and households of different in-come levels. Race, they argue, is the domain of fair lending laws. There are three fundamental problems with this argument. First, there is nothing keep-ing regulators from addressing a problem using multiple policy tools. Fair lending laws have some advantages over CRA in dealing with issues of ac-cess to credit by minority borrowers. However, CRA has some advantages as well, including a broader, more inclusive process in which community groups have greater access to the evaluation process. Second, CRA is concerned with access to credit across space. As regulators themselves have argued, statutes predating CRA already gave the agencies the authority to examine banks for how well they serve community credit and service needs (see chapter 6). At the minimum, examiners should evaluate banks for lending and service patterns across neighborhoods of different racial and ethnic composition and not just of different income levels.

A third argument against considering either borrower race or neighborhood racial composition under CRA is the statute's language, which specifically mentions low- and moderate-income areas but not race. However, the legislative history, while not using the term "race" per se, is replete with references to "inner-city" neighborhoods. In fact, it is clear from the history that inner-city neighborhoods were the areas of greatest concern to legislators. In 1977, as well as today, the term "inner city" is clearly associated with predominantly minority neighborhoods. Therefore, it is very difficult to argue that legislators were not interested in providing improved access to credit to minority neighborhoods—regardless of their income level. There are numerous middle-income black neighborhoods in central cities, and increasingly in suburbs, throughout the United States. Moreover, many of the lending disparities that have developed in recent years are more pronounced across neighborhood racial composition than across neighborhood income level (Bradford 2002; Calem, Gillen, and Wachter 2002; Immergluck and Wiles 1999).

The Politics of Credit Access and the Rise of the Deregulationists

Access to credit has always been a controversial topic in the United States, from colonial-era arguments about the need for a central bank to current debates over predatory mortgage lending. The nature and specific subjects of the debates have changed, but credit is such a powerful determinant of the economic and social opportunities of individuals and communities that, by their very nature, credit markets and their structure will always be politically contested. Credit means more than access to current resources. It helps to determine future access to primary goods such as income, wealth, and a home. It is a potent signal of one's life chances and the life chances of one's children. As credit history has become increasingly used to determine everything from the price of auto insurance to the ability to rent an apartment or gain employment, it has become a sort of economic opportunity rating. A poor credit rating can restrict one's opportunities in all sorts of markets.

Credit is also the subject of political debate and social construction because its provision is so lucrative to banks, finance companies, and other suppliers. Political decisions regarding financial services regulation have driven the industrial structure of financial markets. At every stage in the historical development of U.S. financial markets, different types of firms have seen the prospects of great gain or great loss in public policy and have waged correspondingly intense lobbying battles. Moreover, the close involvement of government in financial services has greatly benefited the sector. Banking and securities markets were nurtured by state and federal government throughout much of U.S. history because policymakers recognized how important these industries were to local and national economic development and opportunity.

In the last twenty-five years, there has been a deliberate and organized movement, aggressively promoted by the financial services sector, Congress, and many federal regulators, to reduce the public-sector oversight of the financial services sector. This is especially true in the arena of consumer protection and community reinvestment policies. The deregulationists arguing in favor of this shift suggest that such moves result in greater efficiencies. They apply the logic of a market for widgets to the market for home loans or small business credit. The ideology of free-market advocates and a corresponding gospel of deregulation have been accepted even by many who do not have a clear financial interest in a laissez-faire financial system. By the late twentieth century, the typical policymaker at both the federal and the state level had developed what social scientists call "priors" that included strong antiregulatory postures. Regulation is now frequently seen as ineffective and often counterproductive. However, those holding such views rarely rely on evidence for such claims.

For most of the history of the United States, the deregulationist ideology did not dominate policy thinking as it does today. With some exceptions, it is really only in the last decades of the twentieth century that the country began moving aggressively toward a vision of "unfettered" free markets. The current devotion to free markets has helped conceal the highly political nature of banking and credit markets. It has masked the extent to which the nation's economic successes have been derived, in no small part, from a long history of government action and involvement in financial markets. Ignored is the fact that government agencies and actions created, subsidized, and institutionalized most of the fundamental infrastructure of today's credit markets, typically to the benefit of the industry as much as consumers. This infrastructure includes the long-term fully amortizing mortgage; the secondary markets that make mortgages cheaper and more plentiful; the mortgage-backed security, which has enabled the growth of entirely new lending industries; and all sorts of standardization and discipline that have enhanced the stability and growth of the financial services industry.

Acknowledging the special role of government in supporting the development of the U.S. financial systems—not just banking and mortgage lending but industries like securities and insurance—is key to moving beyond the myopic and naive arguments that work in favor of continually deregulating the financial services sector and, in particular, restricting the scope of laws such as CRA. The act represents a social contract between the banking industry and the broader public. Banks owe their existence to a wider financial infrastructure that was—and in most cases still is—operated by or dependent on government in fundamental ways. In the same way, mortgage companies and securities firms depend on regulation and government action for their effective operations. The complexity of the financial system depends on government regulation and owes many of its innovations to government sponsorship and, frequently, to outright subsidy. Just because some of the more explicit subsidies no longer continue does not suggest that the social contract is no longer valid. The U.S. market for financial services is as robust as it is today precisely because government has played a strong role in supporting and regulating its development.

The Persistence of Discrimination and Redlining and the Failures of Federal Regulators

Contrary to assertions commonly made by doctrinaire neoclassical economists, discrimination and redlining are persistent and, in some ways, inherent features of credit markets. Significant progress in reducing some forms of discrimination has been made, particularly as a result of CRA and fair lending laws. However, despite technological changes in mortgage and small business lending, problems of disparate treatment and disparate impact continue to plague these markets. The nature of some problems have changed, but technology has not eliminated or drastically reduced disparities.

The problem of poor access to mortgage loans has been transformed into a problem of poor access to fairly priced credit and one of frequently unsustainable credit promoted by abusive lenders. In small business lending, credit scoring and the decline of relationship lending may bring some benefits to the strongest firms in lower-income neighborhoods. However, these trends make it more difficult for the firms at the margin to obtain credit at advantageous terms. Moreover, the segmentation of bank customers by income, account size, and marginal profitability has moved banks to charge higher fees for holders of small accounts.

One of the principal reasons for ongoing problems in these markets is that bank and financial services regulators have done a poor job of implementing reinvestment and fair lending laws. If not for pressure from community and consumer groups, together with the accompanying media and congressional attention, it is not clear that regulators would provide any meaningful enforcement of these laws at all. In the 1970s, advocates like National People's Action called on regulators to enforce the Fair Housing Act and pushed for the adoption and initial implementation of CRA. Today, the NCRC, with more than 800 organizational members across the country, as well as fair housing groups, local governments, and others, continue fighting regulators' inclinations to render CRA and fair lending laws completely toothless. The National Consumer Law Center, AARP, the Consumer Federation of America, and others have joined with the reinvestment advocates to push for state antipredatory lending laws and to fight federal regulators' moves to preempt such policies.

Notwithstanding the important advocacy work by community and consumer groups, CRA and fair lending laws have been only as successful as regulators have allowed them to be. The effectiveness of CRA was most pronounced from 1989 to about 1992, after Congress chastised regulators for failing to enforce the law and passed important amendments to CRA and HMDA. In the middle to late 1990s, improvements to CRA regulations and more aggressive prosecutions of fair lending violations by the Department of Justice also had some positive impacts. However, by the end of the decade, regulators had generally moved back to a mode of weak enforcement. CRA advocates were forced into a defensive posture by congressional attacks from Senator Phil Gramm and others. Instead of being able to exploit such legislation to enact improvements to CRA, as was done with the savings and loan bailout bill in 1989, advocates had to fight furiously to avoid the effective evisceration of the law.

Community Reinvestment and Fair Lending for a New Century

The need for an updated CRA social contract remains the major challenge. Despite limited enforcement, CRA and fair lending laws have had a positive impact on access to credit in lower-income and minority communities. However, with some "modernization" to keep pace with changes in financial markets and with better enforcement, the laws could be much more effective. The evidence on the effectiveness of the CRA, in particular, has accumulated in recent years and points to positive impacts, particularly on access to home mortgage credit. There is little doubt that the law has had impacts in other areas, especially in the development of community development financial institutions and the prevention of greater numbers of bank branch closures in lower-income neighborhoods.

The limits to CRA and fair lending laws and the vacillating enforcement of the laws by federal regulators mean that these policies have a great deal more promise than provided by their implementation thus far. Much could be done through changes in the administrative rules by regulatory agencies and a renewed political will to enforce the regulations. In some cases, legislative improvements to coverage of CRA is also needed. Until the political environment changes significantly, the prospects for improvements to CRA are not terribly strong. Regulators tend to be more concerned about keeping the banks they currently regulate from changing their charters. Regulators derive their revenues from fees imposed on the banks they regulate, providing a perverse incentive against strong regulation. Congress hardly seems concerned with issues of fair lending. Even with all the attention that the predatory lending issue has received in recent years, Congress appears more prone to preempt state antipredatory lending regulations than to pass any substantive protections of its own.

Reinvestment advocates have not sat still, however. They continue to push for antipredatory lending policies at the state level. They are also working against lender-supported proposals to further advance deregulationist agendas, such as the preemption of state consumer lending laws. Just as importantly, on the predatory lending issue at least, community groups have developed additional tools that do not rely directly on policymakers. Community and public interest organizations have used the power of financial institutions' "reputational risk" as a tool to encourage lenders to reform their lending practices. North Carolina's Coalition for Responsible Lending organized a highly publicized campaign against Citigroup during and after its purchase of the Associates.[14] ACORN, the national organizing network, waged a strong battle against the lending practices of Household Finance. In 2000, both efforts produced demonstrable, if not always entirely satisfying, results. Both lenders pledged to stop offering single-premium credit life insurance, a notoriously predatory loan product. They also made other reforms in controls over broker abuses and other practices. More than the specific gains, these advocacy efforts showed that, even without regulatory support, well-organized community campaigns can influence the behavior of major lenders. With the growing dominance of the top twenty mortgage lenders in the United States, this is an increasingly attractive approach. Community organizers and advocates do not have the resources to wage lending reform campaigns against dozens of lenders. But by taking on the largest and worst of the lenders, these groups can achieve substantial victories and demonstrate that responsible reinvestment is a viable alternative to dual markets and predatory lending.

None of this is to say that policy advocacy efforts are misplaced at this time. In the long run, policy changes are needed to provide sustainable improvements in credit markets. Moreover, political climates are not predictable. As Squires (2003c) has noted, the Fair Housing Act hardly seemed a possibility until the assassination of Martin Luther King Jr. At the same time, given the political climate as this book goes to press, a mixed strategy is needed to provide some tangible prospects for near-term improvements in lending markets while still working on policy issues.

Efforts utilizing reputational risk should be expanded to other areas of reinvestment, including expanding prime mortgage lending activity in minority communities and improving access to small business loans and basic banking services. State and local governments can choose to do business with responsible banks that provide loans to underserved markets, and they can publicize these efforts widely. Local and national community groups need more support to develop "CRA scorecards" that rank lenders on how well they serve local credit and banking needs. Given the complexities of modern financial markets these days, these scorecards need to be carefully constructed to not inadvertently reward predatory financial service providers. The scorecards must use appropriate measures of responsible lending and services to be effective.

There is still much work to do in the area of community reinvestment and fair lending. Current laws, especially as they are being interpreted by regulators, are becoming increasingly outmoded. Most important, the forces that affect the vigor with which regulators implement the law continue to move in favor of the ever more concentrated financial services industry. The challenges for community organizers and reinvestment advocates continue to change and emerge. Resources for such groups will never match the resources of those pushing for even further deregulation and the essential abolition of the social contract between banking and society. Yet this reality makes the need for supporting such efforts even more important. The alternative is to allow the gains that have been made to be reversed and to ignore the problems caused by hypersegmented financial services markets.

Notes

Notes to Chapter 1

1. See Hamilton (2001, 595–96).
2. Community Reinvestment Act Hearings Before the U.S. Senate Committee on Banking, Housing and Urban Affairs, Senate Hearings, 100th Congress, 2nd sess., March 22–23, 1988. Senate Hearing 100-652. Washington, DC: U.S. Government Printing Office, 7.
3. See Cincotta (1999).
4. I borrow the term "deregulationist" from Coggins (1998), who also applied it to financial regulation policy, although not specifically to issues of regulating matters of access to credit and retail financial services.

Notes to Chapter 2

1. Banks are allowed to choose to have regulators consider their affiliates' lending in their Community Reinvestment Act performance evaluations. This does not equate with Community Reinvestment Act affiliates being covered under the Community Reinvestment Act. See chapter 9 for more discussion of this issue.
2. There is a significant revolving door between the Federal Reserve and the deregulationist economics camp. For example, economists such as Gregory Elliehausen, Thomas Durkin, Robert Eisenbeis, and Charles Luckett have worked at the Federal Reserve Board and have served as staff or committee members at the Credit Research Center, a largely antiregulation, industry-funded research group, sometimes simultaneously.
3. Including George Benston, Thomas Cargill, and Thomas Durkin.

Notes to Chapter 3

1. Some of the analysis in this section was previously reported in Immergluck (2002).
2. Community Reinvestment Act data do not include all lending to small firms. In the first year for which the data were released, 1996, the small banks and thrifts that are not required to report these data accounted for approximately 35 percent of the outstanding business loans of $1,000,000 or less reported on the balance sheets of banks and thrifts (Bostic and Canner 1998). However, smaller banks constitute a much smaller portion of the banking market in large urban

areas than in rural and small city markets. Thus, the omitted banks are expected to constitute a much smaller percentage of small business lending in large cities, which are of particular concern here. Data from the 1993 National Survey of Small Business Finances show that commercial banks accounted for 63 percent of outstanding loans to small nonfinancial corporations (Federal Reserve Board of Governors 1997). Finance companies constituted another 18 percent, with other sources accounting for the rest.

3. Ordinary least squares regression of small-area lending flows suffers from problems of spatial autocorrelation, which can result in biased coefficient estimates in ordinary least squares. However, a spatial lag model can be used to account for the spatial autocorrelation present in these data. To account for spatial lag effects, a spatially lagged dependent variable is used in the following specification:

$$l_i = \alpha + \rho \lambda_i + \beta b_i + \gamma z_i$$

where l_i is the number of loans to businesses with $1,000,000 or less in sales in tract i, and b_i is the number of businesses with $1 million or less in sales in tract i. λ is a spatially lagged value of the number of small business loans, l, and ρ is the spatial autoregressive coefficient and expected to be positive. λ measures the lending level of nearby census tracts, with inverse-distance weighting so that the lending in the closest tracts is given the greatest weight. λ measures the extent to which a tract is surrounded by tracts with high or low volumes of lending. Finally, the vector z_i is a set of tract characteristics including the proportion of firms in manufacturing, wholesaling, and retailing sectors; the proportion of firms that are relatively large; tract income; tract population; tract race and ethnicity; and credit quality. The latter is the average Dun and Bradstreet credit score for firms in the tract. See Immergluck (2002) for a more exhaustive discussion of spatial autocorrelation and the spatial lag regression technique employed here.

4. De novos were defined as banks with charters dating between 1990 and 1999 and with assets of less than $500 million in 2001. The few larger banks with recent charters were excluded to guard against new charters representing acquisitions and mergers.

Notes to Chapter 5

1. Lenders, until recently, were not expected to request racial information for loan applications taken via the telephone or Internet.

2. Fortunately, this is one area where policy changes have reacted appropriately to changes in mortgage lending. In 2002, the Federal Reserve Board modified Regulation C, which implements the Home Mortgage Disclosure Act, to require lenders to request race and other data in applications taken via phone or Internet.

3. Census tracts are categorized into four categories, including predominantly white (85 percent or greater non-Hispanic white); mixed-majority (50 percent to 84 percent non-Hispanic white); mixed-minority (greater than 50 percent minority but less than 75 percent black); and predominantly black (75

percent or greater black). These categories were developed in Immergluck and Wiles (1999) and used by the Department of Housing and Urban Development (2000a).

4. All independent variable data are from Claritas Inc. Most are updated estimates of 1990 census data. The household debt figure is based on Claritas's proprietary survey data.

5. Many of the examples of predatory lending listed in Table 5.4 were described by William J. Brennan Jr., director of the Home Defense Program of the Atlanta Legal Aid Society Inc., in his statement before the U.S. Senate Special Committee on Aging on March 16, 1998.

6. See, for example, Rheingold, Fitzpatrick, and Hofeld 2001; Stein and Libby 2001; National Training and Information Center 1999; Department of Treasury and Department of Housing and Urban Development 2000.

7. The exception occurs when inflated, fraudulent appraisals allow for a larger loan than should normally be approved. The inflated appraisal allows for a larger loan while still keeping within the loan-to-value limits of the lender. Such appraisals are typically found in broker-originated loans, when the broker has an "arrangement" with the appraiser. This scheme also allows for equity-stripping in home purchase transactions. In such cases, the practice results in the buyer's paying too much for the house.

8. See www.firstamres.com and www.dataquick.com. One firm that sells pre-foreclosure data, CRS Data Solutions, has labeled its Web site and software, perhaps aptly, "Sharkbait." See www.digitaldeal.com. Sites accessed on May 29, 2003.

9. The Web site, www.mortgagelists.com, accessed on July 14, 2003, lists ethnicity as one of the demographic fields that was available for constructing marketing lists.

Notes to Chapter 6

1. The body of policy that directly or indirectly affects credit access in urban communities includes a number of programs that are of secondary concern here, including Small Business Administration programs, various housing subsidies, and programs of the Economic Development Administration. These programs can be supportive of reinvestment and fair lending, especially when they are used to reduce the uncertainties of lenders that are "first-in" to lending in areas that have seen little lending previously.

2. Even though the Fair Housing Act was not passed for another twenty years, the courts sometimes recognized overt acts of discrimination as being in violation of much earlier civil rights laws. Section 1982 of Title 42 of the United States Code, a section of the Civil Rights Act of 1866, says, "All citizens of the United States shall have the same right, in every State and Territory, as is enjoyed by white citizens thereof to inherit, purchase, lease, hold, and convey real and personal property."

3. See Senate Report No. 589, 94th Congress, 2nd sess., reprinted in the *U.S. Code: Congressional and Administrative News* (1996), 403, 406.

4. Much of the discussion of the Home Mortgage Disclosure Act's legislative history is based on Moskowitz (1987).

5. Moskowitz (1987) raised the question of whether Home Mortgage Disclosure Act and Community Reinvestment Act advocates' testimony in favor of market-driven systems masked a stronger distrust for markets and their effects on lower-income neighborhoods, while representing a politically astute understanding of the dominant ideologies in Congress at the time.

6. U.S. Senate Committee on Banking, Housing, and Urban Affairs, *Hearings on S. 406*, 95th Congress, 1st sess., March 23–25, 1977, 2.

7. First statement from *Congressional Record*, (January 24, 1977): S. 1202. Second from U.S. Senate Committee on Banking, Housing, and Urban Affairs, *Hearings on S. 406*, 95th Congress, 1st sess., March 23–25, 1977, 2.

8. Public Law 94-200, Title III, §§ 302(a), Home Mortgage Disclosure Act.

9. U.S. Senate Committee on Banking, Housing, and Urban Affairs, *Hearings on S. 406*, 95th Congress, 1st sess., March 23–25, 1977, 2.

10. Ibid., 1 and 2.

11. U.S. Senate Committee on Banking, Housing, and Urban Affairs, *Community Credit Needs: Hearings on S. 406*, 95th Congress, 1st sess., March 23–25, 159 (Washington, DC: Government Printing Office, 1977).

12. Transcript of markup session, Tuesday, May 10, 1977, vol. 5, p. 355, cited in Dennis 1978.

13. "Community Reinvestment Act of 1977: Implementation," *Federal Register* 43, no. 198 (October 12, 1978): 47147.

14. Ibid., p. 47510.

15. McClusky cites the Federal Deposit Insurance Corporation's denials of merger applications from Pennsylvania's Dauphin Deposit Bank and Trust Company and New York's Greater New York Savings Bank, and the Office of the Comptroller of the Currency's rejection of a charter change by a bank in Indiana.

16. These figures do not include what were certainly hundreds if not thousands of formal relationships developed between banks and a variety of non-profit intermediaries, community development corporations, and community organizations, largely as a result of the Community Reinvestment Act. These relationships are more narrowly targeted than the Community Reinvestment Act agreements and are not generally thought of as Community Reinvestment Act agreements. Many of these relationships led directly to lending and investments in low- and moderate-income neighborhoods. At the same time, "sunshine" regulations added under the 1999 Gramm-Leach-Bliley Financial Modernization Act do define many such relationships as Community Reinvestment Act agreements under that law.

Notes to Chapter 7

1. "Continental Bank Corporation; On Denying Acquisition of a Bank," *Federal Reserve Bulletin* 75, no. 4 (April 1989): 304–6.

2. Two years later, the Federal Deposit Insurance Corporation Improvement Act required the expansion of the Home Mortgage Disclosure Act to additional, smaller mortgage lenders. This change took effect in the 1993 reporting year. The Federal Deposit Insurance Corporation also gave the Departments of Justice and Housing and Urban Development expanded roles in fair lending enforcement and added some disclosure protections to loan applicants.

3. The steep decline in the Office of the Comptroller of the Currency outstanding ratings is consistent with the findings of Stegman, Cochran, and Faris (2002). When they ran logistic regressions on Community Reinvestment Act ratings, they found that the Office of the Comptroller of the Currency had the lowest ratings controlling for bank size and other bank characteristics.

4. Complete data were not available at the time of this analysis for 2003. However, one large bank, E-Trade Bank, with $14 billion in assets, received a needs-to-improve rating in 2003.

5. Conversation with confidential source.

6. *United States vs. Chevy Chase Federal Savings Bank*, Civil Action no. 94-1824, 1994.

7. See Proposed Rules, Federal Reserve System, 12 CFR Part 202, Equal Credit Opportunity, March 12, 1998, 63 FR 12326-01.

8. Proposed Rules, Federal Reserve System, 12 CFR Part 202, Equal Credit Opportunity, Monday, August 16, 1999, 64 FR 44582-01.

9. Press release titled, "Committee Republicans Urge Federal Reserve to Drop Plan to Collect Data on Credit Applicants." News from the Senate Banking Committee, December 6, 1999. Letter dated December 6, 1999.

10. Fishbein (2003) provides an interesting history of advocacy involving not only Fannie Mae and Freddie Mac but also the Federal Home Loan Bank Board.

11. U.S. Senate Committee on Banking, Housing and Urban Affairs, *Hearings on the Community Reinvestment Act*, 100th Cong., 2nd sess., Senate Hearing 100-652, March 22 and 23, 1988. Washington, DC: U.S. Government Printing Office.

12. The government-sponsored enterprise goals define low- and moderate-income as households with incomes less than 100 percent of the area median income, rather than the 80 percent used for the Community Reinvestment Act purposes.

13. These arguments included comments from the National Consumer Law Center and the Woodstock Institute on Department of Housing and Urban Development's Regulation of the Federal National Mortgage Association (Fannie Mae) and the Federal National Mortgage Corporation (Freddie Mac) Proposed Rule, Docket No. FR-4494-P-01.

14. See www.federalreserve.gov/events/publicmeeting/19980813/ for testimony at the August 13, 1998, Federal Reserve hearing on the Bank One–First Chicago merger. Site accessed on July 12, 2003.

15. Conversation with confidential source.

16. The definition of "community development" is a technical one. According to Community Reinvestment Act regulations, it includes: (1) affordable housing (including multifamily rental housing) for low- or moderate-income individuals; (2) community services targeted to low- or moderate-income individuals; (3) activities that promote economic development by financing businesses or farms that meet Small Business Administration size eligibility standards (contained in 13 CFR 121.802[a][2] and [3]) or have gross annual revenues of $1 million or less; or (4) activities that revitalize or stabilize low- or moderate-income geographies. While many of what are considered community development activities are limited to those that benefit low- and moderate-income places or people, the formal definition includes some activities that are not necessarily so focused, including many activities. The consideration of activities that do not

clearly benefit low- and moderate-income places or people remains a point of controversy among regulators and community reinvestment activists.

17. Loans for multifamily buildings (five or more units) may be counted both as housing loans and as community development loans.

18. The Federal Deposit Insurance Corporation has produced *Community Reinvestment Act: Guide to Developing the Strategic Plan.* This document includes some general information on what a strategic plan should contain. It does not specify how goals should be derived.

19. Lists of wholesale and limited purpose banks are generally available on the regulatory agencies' Web sites.

Notes to Chapter 8

1. One might argue that the Home Ownership and Equity Protection Act facilitated the growth of the subprime market by explicitly recognizing the legitimacy of extremely high-cost lending, including the legitimacy of charging fees of more than 8 percent of the loan amount.

2. Illinois followed the lead of Chicago by issuing regulations modeled on the North Carolina and Chicago laws in April 2001.

3. The following description is based on the author's attendance at the meeting described.

4. Representative James Leach, chairman of the Banking and Financial Services Committee, *Hearings on Predatory Lending Practices,* U.S. House of Representatives, Committee on Banking and Financial Services, May 24, 2000. Available at http://commdocs.house.gov/committees/bank/hba64810.000/hba64810_0.htm (June 2, 2003).

5. Citigroup, Household International, and American General Financial Group all pledged to stop offering single-premium credit insurance in the summer of 2001, prior to the Federal Reserve's finalizing its Home Ownership and Equity Protection Act proposal. *American Banker,* July 23, 2001.

6. Rules and Regulations, Federal Reserve System, 12 CFR, Part 226, "Truth in Lending," *Federal Register* 66 (December 20, 2001): 65604-01.

7. The addition of a data field for manufactured home loans was driven by growing concerns in the late 1990s over abuses by lenders specializing in lending to owners of manufactured homes.

8. The board made a number of other improvements to the Home Mortgage Disclosure Act, including requiring telephone and Internet lenders to request race and gender information from applicants and limiting reporting exemptions to a smaller set of small lenders. However, the board backtracked on a proposal to require institutions to report all home-equity lines of credit, leaving this at the lender's option.

9. Rules and Regulations, Federal Reserve System, 12 CFR, Part 203, "Home Mortgage Disclosure," *Federal Register* 67 (February 15, 2002): 67 FR 7222-01.

10. In fact, at least one company markets software that enables lenders to readily monitor compliance with various state predatory-lending laws. The firm Experity, based in Columbia, South Carolina, markets a product called the "Predatory Lending Monitor." The product interfaces with major loan origination systems. From September 2002 to March 2003, the company had completed nineteen

installations of the product. Press release available at www.experity.com/press_releases/PR_3_19_2003.html (June 23, 2003).

11. Examples of Equicredit's practices being labeled predatory or irresponsible include the following:

1. Gale Cincotta testified before Congress that "the connection between banks and predatory mortgage lenders must also be brought to public attention. Banks are responsible when they have predatory, subprime subsidiaries and affiliates such as First Union's The Money Store and BankAmerica's Equicredit." (Committee on Banking and Financial Services, May 24, 2000). Available at http://financialservices.house.gov/banking/52400cin.htm (June 6, 2003).

2. In congressional testimony, Professor Cathy Lesser Mansfield singled out Equicredit's default experience, which climbed from 5.58 percent in 1996 to 8.27 percent in 1998. See written *Testimony of Professor Cathy Lesser Mansfield Before the Committee on Banking and Financial Services*, U.S. House of Representatives, May 24, 2000. Available at http://financialservices.house.gov/banking152400man.htm (June 6, 2003).

3. The Coalition for Responsible Lending cited Equicredit as one of several lenders that refinanced zero percent interest loans by Habitat for Humanity borrowers into high-cost loans. See comments by Coalition for Responsible Lending on Office of Thrift Supervision's *Responsible Alternative Mortgage Lending Rulemaking*, Docket No. 2000-34, July 5, 2000.

4. Equicredit was involved in numerous predatory lending lawsuits. One example is a case settled in 2002, in which Bank of America agreed to refund 12,000 homeowners $2.5 million for being "duped by aggressive loan brokers into taking out high-cost loans." The press quoted a Philadelphia legal aid attorney as noting "we would get at least one case a week involving an elderly homeowner, usually female and African American, who had gotten a loan with Equicredit, but did not know the terms of the loan or how much it was costing them" (DiStefano 2002).

12. For example, the Associates, then owned by Ford Motor Company, was featured in a twelve-minute segment on ABC's *Prime Time Live* on April 23, 1997.

13. One example of continuing complaints about Citigroup's commitments on subprime lending is that they do not cover all units of the banking organization. One of Citigroup's major subprime lenders is called Travelers Federal Savings Bank, which was not included in Citigroup's pledges regarding subprime lending practices. Consumer groups are concerned that the bank will merely shift lending activity to the Travelers unit, avoiding any commitment on lending practices.

14. For a detailed description of the campaign against Household Finance's lending practices, see Hurd and Kest (2003).

15. The Shadow Financial Services Regulatory Committee's position on predatory-lending law is perhaps best summarized by this statement: "The

Committee believes that existing laws against unfair trade practices and fraud, if effectively enforced, are sufficient to deal with the problem of flipping and other predatory practices." See Statement no. 173, Shadow Financial Services Regulatory Committee, published December 3, 2001; available at www.aei.org/publications/pubID,16349/pub_detail.asp. The committee has also taken the stand that the Community Reinvestment Act should be abolished.

16. Author's personal notes from Chicago hearing of the Department of Housing and Urban Development/Treasury Predatory Lending Task Force, May 25, 2000.

17. The Consumer Credit Insurance Association has argued that offering property-secured insurance made life insurance more available for home owners who could not otherwise qualify for it, an argument for which they have provided no evidence. See testimony of Robert Burfeind, Consumer Credit Insurance Association, at the Federal Reserve Board's Home Ownership and Equity Protection Act hearings on July 27, 2000 in Charlotte, North Carolina. Available at www.federalreserve.gov/events/publichearings/20000727/default.htm (April 21, 2003).

18. This author asked the Credit Research Center study authors if they knew how the nine firms were selected for the survey. They replied that they did not, but simply accepted the data provided to them. Elliehausen and Staten (2002) state that "AFSA commissioned PriceWaterhouseCoopers to collect loan-level data on subprime mortgages from nine AFSA members," implying that American Financial Services Association selected the lenders.

19. This study caused a good deal of concern among industry groups that have been fighting predatory lending laws. Morgan Stanley later submitted a letter at New York City hearings on a proposed predatory lending law stating that the study should not be used to support new predatory lending laws. The letter did not dispute any of the fundamental findings or conclusions of the study, however.

Notes to Chapter 9

1. Three frequent critics of the Community Reinvestment Act are Jonathon Macey (Macey and Miller 1993), George Benston (Benston 1997, 1999), and Keith Hylton (2000). I discuss the more sophisticated and empirically based critique of a fourth critic, Jeffery Gunther, in the main text.

2. The Public Company Accounting Oversight Board was created by the Sarbanes-Oxley bill in 2002 to replace the largely self-regulatory system of the accounting profession.

3. Insurance companies present a challenge in terms of federal policy because they are generally only state regulated. There has been some talk of a federal insurance charter. Without such a charter, it is unclear who might enforce a Community Reinvestment Act for insurers, although this is not a major impediment to policymaking.

4. Technically, the regulators' "Question and Answers," as of June 2003, suggest that examiners will attempt to identify situations in which banks steer loans that are less favorable for Community Reinvestment Act purposes to affiliates while retaining loans that are more favorable. It is unclear how often or how rigorously such tests are performed. The burden is clearly on the regulator to verify such patterns. Federal Financial Institutions Examination Council, "Com-

munity Reinvestment Act, Interagency Questions and Answers Regarding Community Reinvestment," July 12, 2001. Available at www.ffiec.gov/cra/doc/ffiec_qa01.doc (June 22, 2003).

5. The precise language from the Community Reinvestment Act Question and Answers is "an institution can count as a purchase a loan originated by an affiliate that the institution subsequently purchases, or count as an origination a loan later sold to an affiliate, provided the same loans are not sold several times to inflate their value for CRA purposes."

6. 12 U.S. Code 2901, Title VIII of Public Law 95-128, October 12, 1977.

7. See Office of the Comptroller of the Currency, "Decision of the Office of the Comptroller of the Currency on the Application to Charter Charles Schwab Bank, NA, Reno, Nevada," February 4, 2003. The Office of the Comptroller of the Currency is requiring the bank to report some summary data on the bank's lending outside of the Reno metropolitan area. Available at www.occ.treas.gov/foia/foiadocs.htm (February 28, 2004).

8. The former head of the Office of Thrift Supervision, Ellen Seidman, was quoted as saying that the office would "look at" the performance of thrifts that market through nontraditional means far beyond the reach of regular branches ("Thrift Regulator Checks" 1999). It is unclear how this would be done and whether the commitment survived Ms. Seidman's tenure at the agency.

9. The Woodstock Institute and the National Community Reinvestment Coalition have proposed market-share-based tests to determine the inclusion of a metropolitan area or rural county in a bank's assessment area. They recommend that, if a bank makes more than 0.5 percent of all loans of a certain type in a region, then that region should be included in the bank's assessment area. In more competitive markets, 0.5 percent is a significant presence. See Woodstock Institute, "Comments on Advanced Notice of Proposed Rulemaking on Community Reinvestment Act Regulation Review"; available at www.woodstockinst.org/crareg02.html (February 18, 2003).

10. Stegman, Cochran, and Faris (2002) also recommend a change to the 50–25–25 weighting scheme in the current Community Reinvestment Act regulations, so as to allow banks to receive a score based on the Service Test's receiving up to 40 percent of the overall weight.

11. Community development financial institutions include community development loan funds, community development banks, microenterprise loan funds, community development credit unions, and community development venture capital firms. Community development financial institutions can also benefit from community development loans made by banks to community development financial institutions for the purposes of relending. This credit is given under the Lending Test.

12. Other forms of community development financial institutions are less suitable investees for banks. Credit unions have difficulty accepting any form of investments. And banks generally do not invest in other banks. Venture capital funds often require more patient investment than banks are able to provide. Loan funds are able to accept "equity-equivalent" investments, and banks receive explicit Community Reinvestment Act credit for these investments.

13. For a more exhaustive set of recommendations on the mechanics of fair lending examinations and statistical analysis, see Ross and Yinger (2002).

14. Allen Fishbein, an attorney and longtime Community Reinvestment Act advocate, argues that the earlier Citicorp-Travelers merger was a "pivotal experience in the history of the CRA challenge. The outcome [the failure of challenges to stop the merger] serves to illustrate the increasing limits of relying exclusively on the traditional CRA challenge strategy. It suggested that strategies aimed more directly at reputational risk and corporate campaigns may be necessary in future efforts." Conversation with author, September 17, 2003.

Bibliography

AARP. 1997. "Progress in the Housing of Older Persons." Available at http://research.aarp.org/il/d16376_toc.html#Acknol (May 22, 2003).

Abrams, Charles. 1955. *Forbidden Neighbors: A Study of Prejudice in Housing.* New York: Harper.

Abravanel, Martin, and Mary Cunningham. 2002. *How Much Do We Know? Public Awareness of the Nation's Fair Housing Laws.* Washington, DC: U.S. Department of Housing and Urban Development, Office of Policy Development and Research.

Allen, James. 1995. "A Promise of Approval in Minutes, Not Hours." *American Banker,* February 28, 23.

American Bankers Association. 2002. "Community Reinvestment Act," February. Available at www.aba.com/industry+issues/issues_reg_burd_menu.htm (May 25, 2003).

Anason, Dean. 1999a. "Gramm Says Regulators Understate CRA Burden." *American Banker*, August 20.

———.1999b. "Regulators: CRA Data Collection Costs Banks 7 Times Expected Sum." *American Banker*, August 23.

Ando, Faith. 1988. *An Analysis of Access of Bank Credit.* Los Angeles: UCLA Center for Afro-American Studies.

Antonakes, Steven. 2001. "Assessing the Community Reinvestment Act: Impact on Low Income and High Minority Communities." *Journal of Business and Economic Studies* 7: 1–31.

Avery, Robert. 1999. "Access to Credit for Minority-owned Businesses." In *Proceedings of the Business Access to Capital and Credit Conference, March 8–9,* 277–84. Washington, DC: Federal Reserve System Board of Governors.

Avery, Robert, Raphael Bostic, Paul Calem, and Glenn Canner. 1997. "Changes in the Distribution of Banking Offices." *Federal Reserve Bulletin* 83, no. 9: 708–25.

———. 1999. "Consolidation and Bank Branching Patterns." *Journal of Banking and Finance* 23: 497–532.

Avery, Robert, Raphael Bostic, and Glenn Canner. 2000. "CRA Special Lending Programs." *Federal Reserve Bulletin* (November): 711–31

Babcock, Frederick. 1932. *The Valuation of Real Estate.* New York: McGraw.

Bailey, Dawn. 2000. "Fannie Takes Aim at Predatory Lending." *National Mortgage News,* April 17, 3.

Baron, John, and Michael Staten. 1994. *Credit Insurance: Rhetoric and Reality.*

West Lafayette, IN: Credit Research Center, Krannert Graduate School of Management, Purdue University.

Bates, Timothy. 1973. "An Econometric Analysis of Lending to Black Businessmen." *Review of Economics and Statistics* 55: 272–83.

———. 1993. *Banking on Black Enterprise: The Potential of Emerging Firms for Revitalizing Urban Economies.* Washington, DC: Joint Center for Political and Economic Studies.

———. 1997. *Race, Self-employment, and Upward Mobility: An Illusive American Dream.* Washington, DC: Woodrow Wilson Center Press.

———. 1999. "Available Evidence Indicates that Black-owned Firms Are Often Denied Equal Access to Credit." In *Proceedings of the Business Access to Capital and Credit Conference, March 8–9,* 267–76. Washington, DC: Federal Reserve System Board of Governors.

Benston, George. 1997. "Discrimination in Mortgage Lending: Why HMDA and CRA Should Be Repealed." *Journal of Retail Banking Services* (Autumn): 47–57.

———. 1999. "The Community Reinvestment Act: Looking for Discrimination That Isn't There." *Policy Analysis* no. 354, October 6.

Berger, Allen, Seth Bonime, Lawrence Goldberg, and Lawrence White. 2000. The Dynamics of Market Entry: The Effects of Mergers and Acquisitions on De Novo Entry and Small Business Lending in the Banking Industry. Working paper, Federal Reserve Board of Governors.

Bitler, Marianne, Alicia Robb, and John Wolken. 2001. "Financial Services Used by Small Businesses: Evidence from the 1998 Survey of Small Business Finances." *Federal Reserve Bulletin* (April): 183–205.

Blackwell, Rob. 2003. "Second OTS Preemption: Predator Law in N.Y." *American Banker,* January 31.

Blanchflower, Daniel, Phillip Levine, and David Zimmerman. 1998. Discrimination in the Small Business Credit Market. Working paper, National Bureau of Economic Research, Washington, DC.

Boraks, David. 2001. "Why Did B of A Get Out of Subprime?" *American Banker,* August 16.

Bostic, Raphael, and Glenn Canner. 1998. "New Information on Lending to Small Businesses and Small Farms: The 1996 CRA Data." *Federal Reserve Bulletin* (January): 1–21

Bostic, Raphael, and K. Patrick Lampani. 1999. "Racial Differences in Patterns of Small Business Finance." In *Proceedings of the Business Access to Capital and Credit Conference, March 8–9,* 149–79. Washington, DC: Federal Reserve System Board of Governors.

Bostic, Raphael, Hamid Mehran, Anna Paulson, and Marc Saidenberg. 2002. Regulatory Incentives and Consolidation: The Case of Commercial Bank Mergers and the Community Reinvestment Act. Working paper no. 2002-06, Federal Reserve Bank of Chicago.

Bostic, Raphael, and Breck Robinson. 2003a. "Do CRA Agreements Influence Lending Patterns?" *Real Estate Economics* 31 (March): 23–51.

———. 2003b. "What Makes CRA Agreements Work? A Study of Lender Responses to CRA Agreements." Paper presented at *Sustainable Community Development: What Works, What Doesn't and Why,* the Federal Reserve System's

Third Biennial Research Conference, Washington, DC, March 27–28.

Bradbury, Katherine, Karl Case and Constance Dunham. 1989. "Geographic Patterns of Mortgage Lending in Boston, 1982–1987." *New England Economic Review* (September/October): 3–30.

Bradford, Calvin. 1979. "Financing Home Ownership: The Federal Role in Neighborhood Decline." *Urban Affairs Quarterly* 14: 313–35.

———. 1990. *Partnerships for Reinvestment: An Evaluation of the Chicago Neighborhood Lending Programs.* Chicago: National Training and Information Center.

———. 2000. "Statement. Perspectives on Credit Scoring and Fair Mortgage Lending." *Profitwise* 10, no. 3.

———. 2002. *Risk or Race? Racial Disparities in the Subprime Refinance Market.* Washington, DC: Center for Community Change.

Bradford, Calvin, and Gale Cincotta. 1992. "The Legacy, the Promise, and the Unfinished Agenda." In *From Redlining to Reinvestment: Community Responses to Urban Disinvestment,* ed. Gregory Squires, 228–86. Philadelphia: Temple University Press.

Bradford, Calvin, and Dennis Marino. 1977. *Redlining and Disinvestment as a Discriminatory Practice in Residential Mortgage Loans.* Report to the U.S. Department of Housing and Urban Development, Office of Assistant Secretary for Housing and Equal Opportunity. Chicago: University of Illinois Center for Urban Studies.

Brissot de Warville, J.P. 1964. *New Travels in the United States of America,* trans. Mara Soceanu Vamos and Durand Echeverria. Cambridge, MA: Belknap Press of Harvard University Press.

Brooks, Rick. 1999. "Unequal Treatment: Alienating Customers Isn't Always a Bad Idea, Many Firms Discover: Banks, Others Base Service on Whether an Account Is Profitable or a Drain." *Wall Street Journal,* January 7, A1.

Burgess, Ernest W. 1925. "The Growth of the City: An Introduction to a Research Project." In *The City,* ed. Robert E. Park, Ernest W. Burgess, and Roderick D. McKenzie, 37–44. Chicago: University of Chicago Press.

Bush, Malcolm. 1999. "The Recent Role of Community Organizing in the Implementation of the Community Reinvestment Act of the United States." Paper presented at the Association of Research on Nonprofit Organizations and Voluntary Action, Washington, DC, November.

Bush, Malcolm, and Dan Immergluck. 2003. "Research, Advocacy, and Community Reinvestment." In *Organizing Access to Capital: Advocacy and the Democratization of Financial Institutions,* ed. Gregory Squires, 154–68. Philadelphia: Temple University Press.

Calder, Lendol. 1999. *Financing the American Dream: A Cultural History of Consumer Credit.* Princeton, NJ: Princeton University Press.

Calem, Paul, Kevin Gillen, and Susan Wachter. 2002. "The Neighborhood Distribution of Subprime Mortgage Lending." Unpublished manuscript.

Campen, James. 1992. "The Struggle for Community Reinvestment in Boston, 1989–1991." In *From Redlining to Reinvestment: Community Responses to Urban Disinvestment,* ed. Gregory Squires, 38–72. Philadelphia: Temple University Press.

———. 1998. "Neighborhoods, Banks, and Capital Flows: The Transformation of the U.S. Financial System and the Community Reinvestment Movement." *Review of Radical Political Economics* 30, no. 4: 29–59.

Canner, Glenn. 1981. "The Community Reinvestment Act: A Second Progress Report." *Federal Reserve Bulletin* (November).

———. 1982. "The Community Reinvestment Act and Credit Allocation." Unpublished report. Washington, DC: Federal Reserve System.

———. 1999. "Evaluation of CRA Data on Small Business Lending." In *Proceedings of the Business Access to Capital and Credit Conference, March 8–9*, 53–84. Washington, DC: Federal Reserve System Board of Governors.

Canner, Glenn, Thomas Durkin, and Charles Luckett. 1998. "Recent Developments in Home Equity Lending." *Federal Reserve Bulletin* 84 (April): 241–51.

Canner, Glenn, and Wayne Passmore. 1997. "The Community Reinvestment Act and the Profitability of Mortgage-Originated Banks." Finance and Economic Discussion Series, Federal Reserve Board, February.

Canner, Glenn, and Dolores Smith. 1991. "Home Mortgage Disclosure Act: Expanded Data on Residential Lending." *Federal Reserve Bulletin* 77 (November): 863–64.

Carruthers, Bruce G., and Timothy Guinnane. 2002. "Uniform Small Loan Laws in the United States, 1990–1940: A Case Study in the Influence of Foundations." Unpublished manuscript.

Caskey, John. 1994. *Fringe Banking: Check-Cashing Outlets, Pawn Shops, and the Poor.* New York: Russell Sage Foundation.

———. 2001. "Reaching Out to the Unbanked." In *Changing Financial Markets and Community Development: A Federal Reserve System Research Conference,* ed. Jackson Blanton, Sherrie Rhine, and Alicia Williams, 81–92. Richmond, VA: Federal Reserve Bank of Richmond.

Cavalluzzo, Ken, Linda Cavalluzzo, and John Wolken. 1999. "Competition, Small Business Financing, and Discrimination: Evidence From a New Survey." *Proceedings of the Business Access to Capital and Credit Conference, March 8–9,* 180–266. Washington, DC: Federal Reserve System Board of Governors.

Center for Responsive Politics. 2000. "Banking Deregulation," June 1. Available at www.opensecrets.org/news/banks/index.htm (May 14, 2003).

"Chicago Lays Plans for Race Segregation." 1917. *Cleveland Advocate,* April 14, 1.

Chinloy, Peter. 1995. "Public and Conventional Mortgages and Mortgage-Backed Securities." *Journal of Housing Research* 6, no. 2: 173–96.

Christiano, Marilyn Rice. 1995. "The Community Reinvestment Act: The Role of Community Groups in the Formulation and Implementation of a Public Policy," Ph.D. diss., University of Maryland, College Park.

Cincotta, Gale. 1999. "Opportunity in Next Wave of Mergers." *Shelterforce* 108 (November/December).

City of Milwaukee. 2003. "Urban Legends: The Outstanding Purchasing Power of Milwaukee's Central City Neighborhoods and How Top Retail Consultants Overlook It and Use Misleading Urban Stereotypes Instead." Available at www.ci.mil.wi.us/citygov/mis/Presentations/Marketing/marketing001.htm (May 27).

Cole, Rebel, and John D. Wolken. 1996. "Bank and Nonbank Competition for Small Business Credit: Evidence from the 1987 and 1993 National Surveys of Small Business Finances." *Federal Reserve Bulletin* (November): 983–95.

Coggins, Bruce. 1998. *Does Financial Deregulation Work? A Critique of Free Market Approaches*. Northampton, MA: Edward Elgar.

Corporation for Enterprise Development. 2003. "Community Development Financial Institutions: Providing Capital, Building Community, Creating Impact." Available at www.cfed.org (July 5).

Cowell, M.A., Jr., and Monty Hagler. 1992. "The Community Reinvestment Act in the Decade of Bank Consolidation." *Wake Forest Law Review* 27: 83–101.

"CRA Rules Still in Flux for Internet-Only Banks." 2002. *American Banker*, November 18, 23.

Credit Research Center. 2003. "CRC Staff and Organization." Available at www.msb.edu/prog/crc/history.html (May 12).

Crews-Cutts, Amy. 2003. "Mortgage Markets, Home Prices, and Credit Quality." Paper presented at the National Mortgage Servicing Conference and Expo, New Orleans, LA, February 26–28. Available at www.mbaa.org/present/2003/cutts_0226.pdf (May 30).

Curry, Timothy, and Lynn Shibut. 2000. "The Cost of the Savings and Loan Crisis: Truth and Consequences." *FDIC Banking Review* 13, no. 2: 26–35.

Dane, Stephen M. 1993. "Eliminating the Labyrinth: A Proposal to Simplify Federal Mortgage Discrimination Laws." *University of Michigan Journal of Law Reform* (Spring).

D'Arista, Jane, and Tom Schlesinger. 1993. "The Parallel Banking System." In *Transforming the U.S. Financial System: Equity and Efficiency for the 21st Century*, ed. Gary A. Dymski, Gerald Epstein, and Robert Pollin, 157–99. Armonk, NY: M.E. Sharpe.

Davenport, Todd. 2003. "Why OCC May Tread Lightly on Georgia Law." *American Banker*, April 9.

Dedman, William. 1988a. "Atlanta Blacks Losing in Home Loans Scramble: Banks Favor White Areas by 5–1 Margin." *Atlanta Journal/Constitution*, May 1, A1.

———. 1988b. "A Test that Few Banks Fail—In Federal Eyes." *Atlanta Journal/Constitution*, May 3, A1.

———. 1988c. "Federal Study Finds Bias in Lending Across Nation." *Atlanta Journal/Constitution*, July 17, A1.

———. 1989. "Racial Lending Gap Less in South than in Midwest." *Atlanta Journal/Constitution*, January 22, A1.

DeFerrari, Lisa, and David Palmer. 2001. "Supervision of Large Complex Banking Organizations." *Federal Reserve Bulletin* (February).

Dennis, Warren. 1978. The Community Reinvestment Act of 1977: The Legislative History and Its Impact on Applications for Changes in Structure Made by Depository Institutions to the Four Federal Financial Supervisory Agencies. Working paper no. 24, Credit Research Center.

de Senerpont Domis, Olaf. 1998. "San Francisco Weighs Pulling Cash from B of A, Which is Leaving City." *American Banker*, June 15, 1.

DiStefano, Joseph. 2002. "Bank to Refund Fees in Predatory Lending Cases." *Philadelphia Inquirer*, April 26, C1.

DeYoung, Robert, Lawrence Goldberg, and Lawrence White. 1999. "Youth, Adolescence, and Maturity of Banks: Credit Availability to Small Business in an Era of Banking Consolidation." *Journal of Banking and Finance* 23: 463–92.

Drake, St. Clair, and Horace Clayton. 1962. *Black Metropolis*. New York: Harper and Row.

DuBois, W.E.B. 1996. *The Souls of Black Folks*. New York: Penguin Books.

Dunham, Constance R. 2001. "The Role of Banks and Nonbanks in Serving Low- and Moderate-Income Communities." In *Changing Financial Markets and Community Development: A Federal Reserve System Research Conference,* ed. J.L. Blanton, S. L. Rhine, and A. Williams, 31–58. Richmond, VA: Federal Reserve Bank of Richmond.

Durkin, Thomas A., and Michael E. Staten, ed. 2002. *The Impact of Public Policy on Consumer Credit.* Boston: Kluwer Academic. Available at www.msb.edu/prog/crc/ExtendHistory.html (June 15).

Dymski, Gary. 1993. "How to Rebuild the U.S. Financial Structure: Level the Playing Field and Renew the Social Contract." In *Transforming the U.S. Financial System: Equity and Efficiency for the 21st Century,* ed. Gary Dymski, Gerald Epstein, and Robert Polin, 101–32. Armonk, NY: M.E. Sharpe.

———. 1995. "The Theory of Bank Redlining and Discrimination: An Exploration." *Review of Black Political Economy* 23: 37–74.

———. 1999. *The Bank Merger Wave: The Economic Causes and Social Consequences of Financial Consolidation.* Armonk, NY: M.E. Sharpe.

Elliehausen, Gregory, and Michael Staten. 2002. Regulation of Subprime Mortgage Products: An Analysis of North Carolina's Predatory Lending Law. Working paper no. 66, Credit Research Center.

Ernst, Keith, John Farris, and Eric Stein. 2002. *North Carolina's Subprime Home Loan Market and Predatory Lending Reform.* Durham, NC: Center for Responsible Lending

Evanoff, Douglas, and Lewis Segal. 1996. "CRA and Fair Lending Regulations: Resulting Trends in Mortgage Lending." *Federal Reserve Bank of Chicago Economic Perspectives* (November/December): 19–46.

Fannie Mae. 2001. *2001 National Housing Survey.* Washington, DC: Fannie Mae.

Federal Financial Institutions Examination Council. 1999. Interagency Fair Lending Examination Procedures, January.

Federal Reserve Board of Governors. 1978. *Federal Reserve Bulletin* 64 (July): 579.

———. 1980. "Information Statement Re: Community Reinvestment Act." *Federal Reserve Bulletin* (January): 30–32.

———. 1997. *Report to the Congress on the Availability of Credit to Small Businesses.* Washington, DC: Federal Reserve Board of Governors.

Feldman, Ron. 1997. "Credit Scoring and Small Business Loans." *Community Dividend* (Spring): 3–9.

Fenstermaker, Joseph. 1965. *The Development of American Commercial Banking: 1782–1837.* Kent, OH: Kent State University Press.

Fishbein, Allen. 1992. "The Ongoing Experiment with 'Regulation from Below': Expanded Reporting Requirements for HMDA and CRA." *Housing Policy Debate* 3: 601–36.

———. 1993. "The Community Reinvestment Act After Fifteen Years: It Works, but Strengthened Federal Enforcement Is Needed." *Fordham Urban Law Journal* 20, no. 2: 293–310.

———. 2003. "Filling the Half-Empty Glass: The Role of Community Advocacy in Redefining the Public Responsibilities of Government-Sponsored Housing Enterprises." In *Organizing Access to Capital: Advocacy and the Democratization of Financial Institutions,* ed. Gregory Squires, 102–18. Philadelphia: Temple University Press.

Fisher, Robert. 1994. *Let the People Decide: Neighborhood Organizing in America.* Updated ed. New York: Twayne.

Ford, Frank. 1996. *Survey of Small Business Lending in Denver.* Denver: Colorado Center for Community Development, University of Colorado at Denver.

Frame, W. Scott, Michael Padhi, and Lynn Woosley. 2001. The Effect of Credit Scoring on Small Business Lending in Low- and Moderate-Income Areas. Working paper 2001-6, Federal Reserve Bank of Atlanta.

Frame, W. Scott, Aruna Srinivasan, and Lynn Woosley. 2001. "The Effect of Credit Scoring on Small Business Lending." *Journal of Money, Credit, and Banking* 33: 813–826.

Fraser, Katherine. 1999. "CRA Protests Rarely Play Role in Stopping Mergers, Treasury Report Says." *American Banker,* May 12, 2.

Frazier, E. Franklin. 1957a. *Black Bourgeoisie: The Rise of a New Middle Class in the United States.* New York: Collier.

————. 1957b. *The Negro in the United States.* New York: Macmillan.

Freddie Mac. 1996. *Automated Underwriting: Making Mortgage Lending Simpler and Fairer for America's Families.* Washington, DC: Freddie Mac.

"Freddie Mac Expecting 31% Boost in Subprime Business." 2000. *Inside B&C Lending,* May 22.

"Freddie Mac Launches Program of Securitizing Subprime Mortgages." 1997. *American Banker,* June 3, 1.

Gale, Dennis E. 2001. "Subprime and Predatory Mortgage Refinancing: Information Technology, Credit Scoring and Vulnerable Borrowers." Paper presented at the Housing and the New Economy sessions of the American Real Estate and Urban Economics Association Midyear Meeting, Washington, DC, May 31.

Galster, George. 1996. "Future Directions in Mortgage Discrimination Research and Enforcement." In *Mortgage Lending, Racial Discrimination, and Federal Policy,* ed. John Goering and Ron Wienk, 679–716. Washington, DC: Urban Institute Press.

————. 1999. "The Evolving Challenges of Fair Housing Since 1968: Open Housing, Integration, and the Reduction of Ghettoization." *Cityscape* 4: 23–138.

Garver, Rob. 2002. "In Focus: Redlining Inquiry in Illinois Likely to Repeat." *American Banker,* August 19, 1.

Garwood, Griffith, and Dolores Smith. 1993. "The Community Reinvestment Act: Evolution and Current Issues." *Federal Reserve Bulletin* (April): 251–67.

Geisst, Charles. 1990. *Visionary Capitalism: Financial Markets and the American Dream in the Twentieth Century.* New York: Praeger.

Glabere, Michael. 1992. "Milwaukee: A Tale of Three Cities." In *From Redlining to Reinvestment: Community Responses to Urban Disinvestment,* ed. Gregory Squires, 149–69. Philadelphia: Temple University Press.

Goering, John, and Ron Wienk. 1996. *Mortgage Lending, Racial Discrimination, and Federal Policy.* Washington, DC: Urban Institute Press.

Goldwater, Sidra, and Malcolm Bush. 1995. *CRA Boosts Multifamily Housing Loans in Chicago.* Chicago: Woodstock Institute.

Gramlich, Edward. 2000. Speech on Predatory Lending, Federal Reserve Bank of Philadelphia, December 6.

Green, George. 1972. "Louisiana 1804–1861." In *Banking and Economic Development: Some Lessons of History,* ed. Rondo Cameron, 199–231. New York: Oxford University Press.

Greider, William. 1987. *Secrets of the Temple: How the Federal Reserve Runs the Country.* New York: Touchstone.

Greunstein, Deborah, and Christopher Herbert. 2000. *Analyzing Trends in Subprime Originations and Foreclosures: A Case Study of the Atlanta Metro Area.* Cambridge, MA: Abt Associates.

Gries, John, and James Ford. 1932. *Home Finance and Taxation, Reports of the Committees on Finance and Taxation.* Washington, DC: President's Conference on Home Building and Home Ownership.

Gunther, Jefferey, Kelley Klemme, and Kenneth Robinson. 1999. "Redlining or Red Herring?" *Federal Reserve Bank of Dallas Southwest Economy* (May/June): 8–13.

Hallahan, Kirk. 1992. "The Mortgage Lending Controversy: National People's Action Takes on the Lenders and Wins Anti-Discrimination Legislation in Congress." Paper presented at meeting of the Association for Education in Journalism and Mass Communication, Montreal, August.

Hamilton, Alexander. 2001. *Alexander Hamilton: Writings.* New York: Library of America.

Hammond, Bray. 1957. *Banks and Politics in America: From the Revolution to the Civil War.* Princeton, NJ: Princeton University Press.

Harris, Abram. 1936. *The Negro as Capitalist. A Study of Banking and Business Among American Negroes.* Gloucester, MA: Peter Smith.

Harvey, Keith, and Peter Nigro. 2002. "Do Predatory Lending Laws Influence Mortgage Lending? An Analysis of the North Carolina Predatory Lending Law." Unpublished manuscript.

Hays, R. Allen. 1995. *The Federal Government and Urban Housing: Ideology and Change in Public Policy.* Albany: State University of New York Press.

Helper, Rose. 1969. *Racial Policies and Practices of Real Estate Brokers.* Minneapolis: University of Minnesota Press.

Hillier, Amy. 2003a. "Redlining and the Home Owners' Loan Corporation." *Journal of Urban History* 29, no. 4: 394–420.

———. 2003b. "Who Received Loans? Home Owners Loan Corporation Lending and Discrimination in Philadelphia in the 1930s." *Journal of Planning History* 2, no. 1: 3–24.

Hinz, Greg. 2001. "Lobbying Bid Falls Short for Bank One." *Crain's Chicago Business,* November 19.

Hoffman, Susan. 2001. *Politics and Banking: Ideas, Public Policy, and the Creation of Financial Institutions.* Baltimore: Johns Hopkins University Press.

Hope, John. 1899. "The Meaning of Business." In *The Negro in Business,* ed. W.E.B. DuBois. New York: AMS Press.

Horne, David. 1997. "Mortgage Lending, Race, and Model Specification." *Journal of Financial Services Research* 11: 43–68.

Horwitt, Sanford D. 1989. *Let Them Call Me Rebel: Saul Alinsky—His Life and Legacy.* New York: Knopf.

Hoyt, Homer. 1933. *One Hundred Years of Land Values in Chicago.* Chicago: University of Chicago Press.

Hurd, Maud, and Steven Kest. 2003. "Fighting Predatory Lending from the Ground Up: An Issue of Economic Justice." In *Organizing Access to Capital: Advocacy and the Democratization of Financial Institutions,* ed. Gregory D. Squires, 119–34. Philadelphia: Temple University Press.

Hylton, Keith. 2000. "Banks and Inner Cities: Market and Regulatory Obstacles to Development Lending." *Yale Journal on Regulation* 17: 197–251.

Immergluck, Dan. 1997. *Is CRA Reform for Real?* Chicago: Woodstock Institute.

———. 1998. *The Community Reinvestment Act and Community Development Financial Institutions: Qualified Investments, Community Development Lending, and Lessons from the New CRA Performance Evaluations.* Chicago: Woodstock Institute.

———. 2002. "Redlining Redux: Black Neighborhoods, Black-owned Firms, and the Regulatory Cold Shoulder." *Urban Affairs Review* 38: 22–41.

Immergluck, Dan, and Geoff Smith. 2001. *Bigger, Faster. . . . but Better? How Changes in the Financial Services Industry Affect Small Business Lending in Urban Areas.* Washington, DC: Brookings Institution Center on Urban and Metropolitan Policy.

———. 2003. "Measuring Neighborhood Diversity and Stability in Home-Buying: Examining Patterns by Race and Income in a Robust Housing Market." *Journal of Urban Affairs* 25, no. 4: 473–91.

Immergluck, Dan, and Marti Wiles. 1999. *Two Steps Back: Predatory Lending, the Dual Mortgage Market, and the Undoing of Community Development.* Chicago: Woodstock Institute.

———. 2000a. *An Analysis of the 1998 Refinance Lending Patterns of Bank of America Corporation Affiliates in the Chicago Area.* Chicago: Woodstock Institute.

———. 2000b. *Where Banks Do Business: An Analysis of Small Business Lending Patterns from 1996 to 1998 in the Chicago Area.* Chicago: Woodstock Institute.

Interagency Task Force on Fair Lending. 1994. "Policy Statement on Fair Lending." *Federal Register,* April 15, 59 FR 18266-01.

Jackson, Kenneth. 1985. *Crabgrass Frontier: The Suburbanization of the United States.* New York: Oxford University Press.

Jacob, Katy, Malcolm Bush, and Dan Immergluck. 2002. *Rhetoric and Reality: An Analysis of Mainstream Credit Unions' Record of Serving Low-Income People.* Chicago: Woodstock Institute.

Jargowsky, Paul. 1997. *Poverty and Place: Ghettos, Barrios, and the American City.* New York: Russell Sage Foundation.

———. 2003. *Stunning Progress, Hidden Problems: The Dramatic Decline of Concentrated Poverty in the 1990s.* Washington, DC: Brookings Center on Urban and Metropolitan Policy. May.

Joint Center for Housing Studies. 2002. *The 25th Anniversary of the Community Reinvestment Act: Access to Capital in an Evolving Financial Services System.* Cambridge: Harvard University Joint Center for Housing Studies.

Keating, Larry, Lynn Brazen, and Stan Fitterman. 1992. "Reluctant Response to Community Pressure in Atlanta." In *From Redlining to Reinvestment: Commu-*

nity Responses to Urban Disinvestment, ed. Gregory Squires, 170–93. Philadelphia: Temple University Press.

Khademian, Anne M. 1996. *Checking on Banks: Autonomy and Accountability in Three Federal Agencies.* Washington, DC: Brookings Institution Press.

Kim-Sung, Kellie, and Sharon Hermanson. 2003. *Experiences of Older Refinance Mortgage Loan Borrowers: Broker- and Lender-Originated Loans.* Washington, DC: AARP Public Policy Institute.

Klebaner, Bejamin. 1990. *American Commercial Banking: A History.* Boston: Twayne.

Kuttner, Robert. 1998. *Everything for Sale: The Virtues and Limits of Markets.* New York: Knopf.

Lamoreaux, Naomi. 1994. *Insider Lending: Banks, Personal Connections, and Economic Development in Industrial New England.* Cambridge, UK: Cambridge University Press.

Landerman, Elizabeth. 2001. "Subprime Mortgage Lending and the Capital Markets." *FRBSF Economic Letter,* no. 2001-38, December 28.

Lang, William, and Leonard Nakamura. 1993. "A Model of Redlining." *Journal of Urban Economics* 33: 223–34.

Lea, Michael. 1996. "Innovation and the Cost of Mortgage Credit: A Historical Perspective." *Housing Policy Debate* 7, no. 1: 147–74.

Lee, Mathew. 1999. "Inner City Press Community Reinvestment Reporter, Archive Number 2," April–May. Available at www.innercitypress.org/crrep299.html (July 18, 2003).

———. 2003. "Community Reinvestment in a Globalizing World: To Hold Banks Accountable, from the Bronx to Buenos Aires, Beijing, and Basel." In *Organizing Access to Capital: Advocacy and the Democratization of Financial Institutions,* ed. Gregory Squires, 135–53. Philadelphia: Temple University Press.

Lemann, Nicholas. 1992. *The Promised Land: The Great Black Migration and How It Changed America.* New York: Vintage.

Lindsey, Lawrence. 1994. Statement before the Subcommittee on General Oversight, Investigations, and the Resolution of Failed Financial Institutions of the Committee on Banking, Finance, and Urban Affairs, U.S. House of Representatives, February 1, Federal Reserve Board of Governors, Washington, DC.

"Lindsey Continues to Hit Race, Gender Reporting under New CRA Reform Proposal." 1994. *BNA Banking Reporter,* October 10.

Litan, Robert. 2003. *Unintended Consequences: The Risks of Premature State Regulation of Predatory Lending.* Washington, DC: American Bankers Association.

Livermore, George. 2001. "Real Estate Information in a Wired World." *Mortgage Banking* (April): 81–88.

Luttrell, Clifton. 1972. "The Hunt Commission Report: An Economic View." Paper presented to the Management Group of the Federal Reserve Bank of St. Louis, April 14.

Macey, Jonathon, and Geoffrey Miller. 1993. "The Community Reinvestment Act: An Economic Analysis." *Virginia Law Review* 79, no. 2 (March): 291–348.

Manning, Robert. 2000. *Credit Card Nation: The Consequences of America's Addiction to Credit.* New York: Basic Books.

Marantz, Steven. 1989. "Inequities Are Cited in Hub Mortgages: Preliminary Fed Finding Is 'Racial Bias.'" *Boston Globe,* January 11, Metro section, 1.

Marantz, Steven, and Teresa Hanafin. 1989. "Report of Lending Bias Draws Mix of Reactions." *Boston Globe,* January 12, Metro section, 1.

Mariano, Joseph. 2003. "Where the Hell Did Billions of Reinvestment Come From?" In *Organizing Access to Capital: Advocacy and the Democratization of Financial Institutions,* ed. Gregory Squires, 27–42. Philadelphia: Temple University Press.

Massey, Douglas, and Nancy Denton. 1993. *American Apartheid: Segregation and the Making of the Underclass.* Cambridge, MA: Harvard University Press.

Matasar, Ann, and Deborah Pavelka. 1998. "Federal Bank Regulators' Competition in Laxity: Evidence from CRA Audits." *International Advances in Economic Research* 4: 56–69.

Mayer, Martin. 1998. *The Bankers: The Next Generation.* New York: Truman Talley Books.

McCarthy, George, Sharron Van Zandt, and William Rohe. 2001. *The Economic Benefits and Costs of Homeownership: A Critical Assessment of the Research.* Washington, DC: Research Institute for Housing America.

McCluskey, Orin. 1983. "The Community Reinvestment Act: Is It Doing the Job?" *Banking Law Journal* 100, no. 1: 33–57.

McDonald, Heather, 1995. "Secondary Mortgage Markets and Federal Housing Policy." *Journal of Urban Affairs* 17: 53–79.

McLenighan, Valjean, and Malcolm Bush. 1994. *More for Our Money: A Primer on Public Deposit Programs.* Chicago: Woodstock Institute.

Mester, Loretta. 1999. "What's the Point of Credit Scoring?" *Federal Reserve of Philadelphia Business Review* (January/February): 3–16.

Metzger, John. 1992. "The Community Reinvestment Act and Neighborhood Revitalization in Pittsburgh." In *From Redlining to Reinvestment: Community Responses to Urban Disinvestment,* ed. Gregory Squires, 73–108. Philadelphia: Temple University Press.

Moskowitz, Eric. 1987. "Pluralism, Elitism, and the Home Mortgage Disclosure Act." *Political Science Quarterly* 102: 93–112.

Munnell, Alicia, Lynne Brown, James McEneaney, and Geoffrey Tootell. 1992. Mortgage Lending in Boston: Interpreting HMDA Data. Working paper no. 92-7, Federal Reserve Bank of Boston.

———. 1996. "Mortgage Lending in Boston: Interpreting HMDA Data." *American Economic Review* 86, no. 1: 25–53.

Myrdal, Gunnar. 1944. *An American Dilemma: The Negro Problem and Modern Democracy.* New York: Harper and Row.

National Community Reinvestment Coalition. 2002. *CRA Commitments.* Washington, DC: National Community Reinvestment Coalition.

———. 2003. "NCRC and Community Reinvestment: A Mission and Movement for Economic Justice." Unpublished manuscript. Washington, DC: National Community Reinvestment Coalition.

National Conference of State Legislatures. 2003. "Banking and Financial Services: Predatory Mortgage Lending." Available at www.ncsl.org/programs/banking/bankmenu.htm (June 24).

National Training and Information Center. 1999. *Preying on Neighborhoods: Subprime Mortgage Lenders and Chicagoland Foreclosures.* Chicago: National Training and Information Center.

Neighborhood Reinvestment Corporation. 2003. "Chicago's Homeownership Preservation Challenge: Foreclosures on Neighborhood Housing Services (NHS) Neighborhoods." Unpublished manuscript.

Nesiba, Reynold. 1996. "Racial Discrimination in Residential Lending Markets: Why Empirical Researchers Always See It and Economic Theorists Never Do." *Journal of Economic Issues* 30: 51–77.

Nier, Charles L., III. 1999. "Perpetuation of Segregation: Toward a New Historical and Legal Interpretation of Redlining Under the Fair Housing Act." *John Marshall Law Review* (Spring).

Novak, William. 1996. *The People's Welfare: Law and Regulation in Nineteenth-Century America.* Chapel Hill: University of North Carolina Press.

Oppel, Richard, Jr., and Patrick McGeehan. 2000. "Along with a Lender, Is Citigroup Buying Trouble?" *New York Times,* October 22, Section 3, 1.

Orlebeke, Charles. 2000. "The Evolution of Low-Income Housing Policy, 1949 to 1999." *Housing Policy Debate* 11, no. 2: 489–520.

Parks, Daniel. 1999. "Where Gramm Draws the Line." *Congressional Quarterly Weekly,* April 24, 944.

Parry Fox, Carol. 2003. "CRA Rules Should Be Adjusted to Help Branchless Banks." *American Banker,* April 4, 9.

Pawasarat, John, and Lois M. Quinn. 2001. *Exposing Urban Legends: The Real Purchasing Power of Central City Neighborhoods.* Washington, DC: Brookings Institution Center on Urban and Metropolitan Policy.

Pennington-Cross, Anthony, Anthony Yezer, and Joseph Nichols. 2000. Credit Risk and Mortgage Lending: Who Uses Subprime and Why? Working paper 00-03, Research Institute for Housing America, Washington, DC.

Phillips-Patrick, Fred Eric Hirschhorn, Jonathon Jones, and John LaRocca. 2000. "What About Subprime Mortgages?" *Mortgage Market Trends* 4, no. 1 (June).

Pierce, Joseph. 1947. *Negro Business and Education: Their Present and Prospective Development.* New York: Harper.

Pogge, Jean. 1992. "Reinvestment in Chicago Neighborhoods: A Twenty Year Struggle." In *From Redlining to Reinvestment: Community Responses to Urban Disinvestment,* ed. Gregory Squires, 133–48. Philadelphia: Temple University Press.

Posner, Kenneth, and Athina Meehan. 2002. "Channel Check: Surprisingly Strong Subprime Growth." *Morgan Stanley Industry Overview,* August 1. Available at www.butera-andrews.com/legislative-updates/directory/Media/other/MS-SubPrime.pdf (May 14, 2003).

Quercia, Roberto, Michael Stegman, and Walter Davis. 2003. *The Impact of North Carolina's Anti-Predatory Lending Law: A Descriptive Assessment.* Chapel Hill: Center for Community Capitalism, University of North Carolina at Chapel Hill.

Rawls, John. 1971. *A Theory of Justice.* Cambridge, MA: Belknap Press of Harvard University Press.

Rengert, Kristopher. 2002. "The Effect of Minority Ownership of Financial Institutions on Mortgage Lending of Minority and Lower Income Home Seekers: A Cross-Section and Time-Series Analysis." Ph.D. diss., Rutgers University.

Rheingold, Ira, Michael Fitzpatrick, and Al Hofeld, Jr. 2001. "From Redlining to Reverse Redlining: A History of Obstacles for Minority Homeownership in America." *Clearinghouse Review* 34, no. 9/10 (January/February): 642–54.

Rhine, Sherrie, Maude Toussant-Comeau, Jeanne Hogarth, and William H. Greene. 2001. "The Role of Alternative Financial Service Providers in Serving LMI Neighborhoods." In *Changing Financial Markets and Community Development: A Federal Reserve System Research Conference,* ed. Jackson Blanton, Sherrie Rhine, and Alicia Williams, 59–80. Ricmond, VA: Federal Reserve Bank of Richmond.

Rhoades, Stephen. 2000. "Bank Mergers and Banking Structure in the United States, 1980–1998." Staff study 174, Federal Reserve System Board of Governors, Washington, DC.

Robb, Alicia, and Jonathon Zinman. 2001. "Does the Community Reinvestment Act Reduce Small Business Credit Constraints?" Paper presented at the Annual Meeting of the Association for Public Policy Analysis and Management, Washington, DC, November 1.

Rolnick, Arthur, and Warren Weber. 1983. "The Free Banking Era: New Evidence on Laissez-Faire Banking." *American Economic Review* (December): 1080–91.

Rosen, Richard. 2002. "Is Three a Crowd? Competition Among Regulators in Banking." Paper presented at the 2002 Federal Reserve Bank of Chicago Bank Structure Conference, May 8.

Ross, Stephen, and John Yinger. 2002. *The Color of Credit: Mortgage Discrimination, Research Methodology, and Fair Lending Enforcement.* Cambridge, MA: MIT Press.

Rousseau, Peter, and Richard Sylla. 1999. Emerging Financial Markets and Early U.S. Growth. Working paper 7448, National Bureau of Economic Research, Washington, DC.

Samolyk, Karen, and Christopher Richardson, 2001. "The Impact of Bank Consolidation on CRA Small Business Lending." Paper presented at the Annual Meeting of the Association for Public Policy Analysis and Management, Washington, DC, November 1.

Santiago, Nellie, Thomas Holyoke, and Ross Levi. 1998. "Turning David and Goliath into the Odd Couple: How the New Community Reinvestment Act Promotes Community Development Financial Institutions." *Brooklyn Law School's Journal of Law and Policy* 6: 571–651.

Scheessele, Randall. 1999. *1998 HMDA Highlights.* Washington, DC: U.S. Department of Housing and Urban Development.

———. 2002. Black and White Disparities in Subprime Mortgage Refinance Lending. Working paper no. HF-014, U.S. Department of Housing and Urban Development, Office of Policy Development and Research, Washington, DC.

Schwartz, Alex. 1998a. "Bank Lending to Minority and Low-Income Households and Neighborhoods: Do Community Reinvestment Agreements Make a Difference?" *Journal of Urban Affairs* 20: 269–301.

———. 1998b. "From Confrontation to Collaboration? Banks, Community Groups, and the Implementation of Community Reinvestment Agreements." *Housing Policy Debate* 9: 631–62.

Scott, Kenneth. 1977. "The Dual Banking System: Model of Competition in Regulation," *Stanford Law Review* 30: 1–49.

Seiberg, Jaret. 1998. "Nationsbank and B of A Pledge Record $350B to CRA Lending." *American Banker,* May 21, 1.

Shadow Financial Regulatory Committee. 1994. "Proposed Revisions to Community Reinvestment Act Regulations," Statement 105, February 14.

Sidney, Mara. 2003. *Unfair Housing: How National Policy Shapes Community Action.* Lawrence: University Press of Kansas.

Silver, Joshua. 2002. "Statement: Perspectives on Credit Scoring and Fair Mortgage Lending." *Profitwise.*

———. 2003. "Findings from an Analysis of Subprime Lending in Six Cities." Draft results. Washington, DC: National Community Reinvestment Coalition.

Skillern, Peter. 2000. "Comments for the House of Representatives Subcommittee on Capital Markets, Securities and Government-Sponsored Enterprises Hearing, June 15, 2000." Available at http://financialservices.house.gov/banking/61500ski.htm (May 3, 2003).

Smith, Adam. 1976. *An Inquiry into the Nature and Causes of the Wealth of Nations,* ed. R.H. Campbell, A.S. Skinner, and W.B. Todd. Oxford: Clarendon Press.

Smith, Geoff. 2003. *Where Banks Aren't: Despite Growth in Chicago Area Bank Offices, Lower-Income and Minority Communities Remain Underrepresented.* Chicago: Woodstock Institute.

Smith, James F. 1977 "The Equal Credit Opportunity Act of 1974: A Cost-Benefit Analysis." *Journal of Finance* 32: 609–22.

Smith, Shanna, and Cathy Cloud. 1996. "The Role of Private, Nonprofit Fair Housing Enforcement Organizations in Lending Testing." In *Mortgage Lending, Racial Discrimination, and Federal Policy,* ed, John Goering and Ron Wienk, 589–610. Washington, DC: Urban Institute Press.

SMR Research. 2002. "Subprime Customer Markets: Where Subprime Mortgage and Home Equity Customers Are Most and Least Concentrated." Advertisement. Available at www.smrresearch.com/scm02.html (May 15, 2003).

Snowden, Kenneth. 1994. "Mortgage Rates and American Capital Market Development in the Late Nineteenth Century." *Journal of Economic History* 48, no. 3: 671–91.

Squires, Gregory. 1992. *From Redlining to Reinvestment: Community Responses to Urban Disinvestment.* Philadelphia: Temple University Press.

———. 2002. "Comments on Martin D. Abravanel's 'Public Knowledge of Fair Housing Law: Does It Protect Against Housing Discrimination?'—Organize! The Limits of Public Awareness in Ensuring Fair Housing." *Housing Policy Debate* 13, no. 3: 505–14.

———. 2003a. *Organizing Access to Capital: Advocacy and the Democratization of Financial Institutions.* Philadelphia: Temple University Press.

———. 2003b. "The New Redlining: Predatory Lending in an Age of Financial Service Modernization." *Sage Race Relations Abstracts.*

———. 2003c. "No Progress Without Protest." *Shelterforce* 128 (March/April).

Squires, Gregory, and Sally O'Conner. 2001. *Color and Money: Politics and Prospects for Community Reinvestment in Urban America.* Albany: State University of New York Press.

Stegman, Michael, and Robert Faris. 2003. "Payday Lending: A Business Model That Encourages Chronic Borrowing." *Economic Development Quarterly* 17: 8–32.

Stegman, Michael, Kelly Thompson Cochran, and Robert Faris. 2002. "Toward a More Performance-Driven Service Test: Strengthening Basic Banking Services Under the Community Reinvestment Act." *Georgetown Journal of Poverty Law and Policy* (Summer).

Stein, Kevin, and Margaret Libby. 2001. *Stolen Wealth: Inequities in California's Subprime Mortgage Market.* San Francisco: California Reinvestment Committee.

Stock, Richard D. 2001. "Predation in the Subprime Lending Market: Montgomery County." Project 1097. Dayton, OH: Center for Business and Economic Research, University of Dayton.

Stone, Deborah. 2002. *Policy Paradox and Political Reason: The Art of Political Decision-Making.* Rev. ed. New York: Norton.

Sugrue, Thomas. 1996. *The Origins of the Urban Crisis: Race and Inequality in Postwar Detroit.* Princeton, NJ: Princeton University Press.

Sylla, Richard. 1972. "The United States 1863–1913." In *Banking and Economic Development: Some Lessons of History,* ed. Rondo Cameron, 232–62. New York: Oxford University Press.

———. 1998. "U.S. Securities Markets and the Banking System 1790–1840." *Federal Reserve Bank of St. Louis Review* (May/June): 83–98.

Taub, Richard. 1994. *Community Capitalism: The South Shore Bank's Strategy for Neighborhood Revitalization.* Cambridge, MA: Harvard Business School Press.

Taylor, Andrew. 1995. "Banks Primed for Regulatory Relief." *Congressional Quarterly,* April, 29, 1164.

———. 1998. "Sen. Gramm's Maneuvers Temporarily Derail Financial Services Overhaul." *Congressional Quarterly Weekly,* September 5, 2344.

Taylor, John. 1999. Testimony before the Senate Committee on Banking, Housing and Urban Affairs' Hearing, Financial Services Legislation, February 25, National Community Reinvestment Coalition, Washington, DC.

Taylor, John, and Josh Silver. 2003. "The Essential Role of Activism in Community Reinvestment." In *Organizing Access to Capital: Advocacy and the Democratization of Financial Institutions,* ed. Gregory Squires, 169–87. Philadelphia: Temple University Press.

Temkin, Kenneth, Jennifer Johnson, and Diane Levy. 2002. *Subprime Markets, the Role of GSEs, and Risk-Based Pricing.* Washington, DC: U.S. Department of Housing and Urban Development, Office of Policy Development and Research.

Tholin, Kathryn. 1993. *Sound Loans for Communities: An Analysis of the Performance of Community Reinvestment Loans.* Chicago: Woodstock Institute.

Thomas, Kenneth. 1998. *The CRA Handbook.* New York: McGraw Hill.

———. 2003. "Investment and Service Tests Take 'Community' Out of CRA." *American Banker,* January 31, 7.

"Thrift Regulator Checks Lending Compliance Far Beyond Home Base." 1999. *Best Newswire,* June 18.

U.S. Commission on Civil Rights. 1961. *Housing: 1961 Commission on Civil Rights Report, Book 4.* Washington, DC: Government Printing Office.

U.S. Department of Housing and Urban Development. 2000a. *Unequal Burden: Income and Racial Disparities in Subprime Lending in America.* Washington, DC: Department of Housing and Urban Development.

———. 2000b. *Unequal Burden in Baltimore: Income and Racial Disparities in Subprime Lending.* Washington, DC: Department of Housing and Urban Development.

U.S. Department of Justice. 2001. "Fair Lending Enforcement Program," January. Available at www.usdoj.gov/crt/housing/b1101.htm (May 23, 2003).

U.S. Department of Treasury and U.S. Department of Housing and Urban Development. 2000. *Curbing Predatory Home Mortgage Lending*. Washington, DC: Department of Housing and Urban Development.

U.S. General Accounting Office. 1999. "Large Bank Mergers: Fair Lending Review Could Be Enhanced With Better Coordination." Report no. GGD-00-16. Washington, DC: General Accounting Office.

Vandell, Kerry. 1995. "FHA Restructuring Proposals: Alternatives and Implications." *Housing Policy Debate* 6, no. 2: 299–383.

Van Order, Robert, and Peter Zorn. 2001. *Performance of Low-Income and Minority Mortgages*. Cambridge, MA: Harvard University Joint Center for Housing Studies.

Walker, Juliet. 1998. *The History of Black Business in America: Capitalism, Race and Entrepreneurship*. New York: Twayne.

Walter, John R. 1995. "The Fair Lending Laws and Their Enforcement." *Federal Reserve Bank of Richmond Economic Quarterly* 81, no. 4: 61–77.

Walters, Neal and Sharon Hermanson. 2001. "Subprime Mortgage Lending and Older Borrowers." *AARP Data Digest*, no. 57.

White, Eugene. 1998. "Were Banks Special Intermediaries in Late Nineteenth Century America?" *Federal Reserve Bank of St. Louis Review* (May/June): 13–32.

Williams, Marva. 2000. *Community-Bank Partnerships Creating Opportunities for the Unbanked*. Chicago: Woodstock Institute.

Wilson, William Julius. 1996. *When Work Disappears: The World of the New Urban Poor*. New York: Knopf.

Woodstock Institute. 1978. *Implementing the Community Reinvestment Act*. Chicago: Woodstock Institute.

———. 1994. *Saving CRA Reform: Key Performance, Disclosure Measures Threatened*. Chicago: Woodstock Institute.

———. 2002. "MAF Bancorp Investigated for Fair Lending Violations: Woodstock Institute Uncovers History of Poor Lending Performance." Available at www.woodstockinst.org/fairlendingpress.html (August 10, 2003).

"Woodstock Paper Troubled by Weak CRA Enforcement." 1997. *Inside Fair Lending* 8, no. 10: 12.

Wright, Robert. 2001. *Origins of Commercial Banking in America, 1750–1800*. Lantham, MD: Rowman and Littlefield.

Wyly, Elvin, and Steven Holloway. 2002. "The Disappearance of Race in Mortgage Lending." *Economic Geography* 78: 129–69.

Yinger, John. 1995. *Closed Doors, Opportunities Lost: The Continuing Costs of Housing Discrimination*. New York: Russell Sage.

Zielenbach, Sean. 2000. *The Art of Revitalization: Improving Conditions in Distressed Inner City Neighborhoods*. New York: Garland.

Ziorklui, Sam. 1994. "The Performance of Black-owned Commercial Banks: A Comparative Analysis." *The Review of Black Political Economy* 23: 5–23.

Index

A

Abrams, Charles, 87–88, 135
Abt and Associates, 121
A.C. Nielsen, 130
Accommodation loans, 24, 33, 53
Activism. *See* Community activism
Addams, Jane, 139
African Americans. *See* Business
    lending discrimination;
    Mortgage lending
    discrimination; Predatory
    lending; Subprime lending
African Insurance Company
    (Philadelphia), 55
African Society for Mutual Relief
    (New York), 55, 88
African Union Society (Rhode
    Island), 55
Aldrich-Vreeland Act (1908), 30
Alinsky, Saul, 139–40, 141
Allegheny Council to Improve Our
    Neighborhoods-Housing
    (ACTION-Housing)
    (Pittsburgh), 141
Alternative Mortgage Transaction
    Parity Act (AMTPA) (1982), 125
American Banker, 82, 220
American Bankers Association, 145,
    149–50, 173, 204, 224
American Economic Review, 103
American Express, 31
American Express Centurian Bank
    (Utah), 15, 252

American Financial Services
    Association (AFSA), 48, 230
American Institute of Real Estate
    Appraisers, 88, 91
American National Bank of
    Chicago, 166
AmeriTrust (Cleveland), 163
*A Monetary History of the United
    States, 1867–1960* (Friedman &
    Schwartz), 45–46
Amortization, 19, 38, 39
An American Dilemma (Myrdal), 60
Annual percentage rate (APR), 218–19,
    276n.7
Anticipated discrimination, 102
Asian immigrants, 58–59
Asset-backed securities, 126–27,
    128*f*
Associates, 222–23, 249, 269,
    277n.12
Association of Community
    Organizations for Reform
    Now (ACORN), 161–62,
    198, 269
Atlanta Community Reinvestment
    Alliance (ACRA), 168–69
Atlanta Journel/Constitution,
    168–69
Automated underwriting; *see also
    specific institution*
lawsuits, 195
mortgage lending discrimination,
    103, 106
mortgage lending history, 43–44

B

Babcock, Frederick, 90–91, 94–95
Back of the Yards (Chicago), 6, 140
Balloon payments, 122, 123*t*, 234
Bank Act (1935), 30
Bank America Corporation, 222
Bank branch location, 75–77, 81
Bank charters, 20, 22, 23–29, 30
Bank consolidation/mergers. *See*
    Mergers
Bank holding companies (BHCs),
    31–32, 248, 262–63
Bank Holding Company (BHC) Act
    (1956), 31–32, 161–62
Bank-ins, 141–42
Bank of America, 190–91, 214, 222
Bank of Chicago, 142
Bank of Indiana, 161
Bank of North America
    (Philadelphia), 22
Bank One (Illinois), 191, 203–4,
    212–13, 256
Banks, N. P., 55
Barrett, Thomas, 247
Bereuter, Doug, 202
Bills of exchange, 20, 23–24
Bond investment, 30
Boston Globe, 169–70
Boston Redevelopment Authority,
    169–70
Boutte, Alvin, 62
Brookings Institution, 224
Building and loans; *see also* Savings
    and loans (S&Ls)
  commercial banking history, 19–20
  mortgage lending history, 33, 34, 35
Burgess, Ernest W., 89–90, 91, 139–40
Burns, Arthur, 149, 220
Bush, George, 98, 196, 221
Business Banking Board, 83
Business lending discrimination; *see*
    also Mortgage lending
    discrimination

Business lending discrimination
    (*continued*)
  bank branch location
    credit market exclusion,
        75–77, 81
    de novo banks, 81
    government intervention, 76–77
    small business opacity, 76
  historical context
    accommodation loans, 53
    Asian immigrants, 58–59
    black business capacity, 58–59
    black-owned financial
        institutions, 54–58, 59–60,
        61–62, 88–89
    black political power, 64
    black solidarity movement,
        56–57, 61
    business response, 54–62
    Civil War, 55
    compensatory capitalism, 63
    cooperative business
        development, 57–58
    credit market exclusion, 52–66
    economic development, 6,
        53–54, 57–58, 60–61
    economic separatism, 57–58, 61
    employment discrimination,
        56–57, 62
    government intervention, 53–54,
        55–56, 61–64, 65–66
    Great Depression, 59–60
    housing discrimination, 56–57, 62
    military banks, 55–56
    mutual aid societies, 54–55
    post-1960s, 62–66
    pre-1960s, 52–62
    self-help movement, 57–58, 61
    slavery, 53–55
    Small Business Administration
        (SBA) loans, 62, 63–64
    urbanization, 56–57
  lending trends
    bank consolidation, 77–79

Business lending discrimination,
  lending trends (*continued*)
    contemporary status, 52
    credit access, 77–86
    credit cards, 77–78, 85–86
    credit scoring, 81–85
    de novo banks, 79–81, 272n.4
    finance companies, 85
    government intervention, 77–80,
      86
    information externalities, 82–83
    minority-owned firms, 86
    research data, 78–79, 80–81, 82,
      83, 85–86
  overview, 17, 52
  redlining
    credit market exclusion, 67–75
    government intervention,
      68, 70
    information externalities, 67–68
    outcome-based redlining, 68
    process-based redlining,
      68–70
    pure redlining, 68
    research data, 68–75, 272n.3
    statistical redlining, 67
Business necessity test, 106, 139

C

CACI, 130
California
  black-owned financial institutions,
    55, 88, 134–35
  community activism, 143, 191
  predatory lending, 124, 214
Capital City Mortgage, 195
Capital Savings Bank (Washington,
  DC), 56
Carter, Jimmy, 46–47, 145, 146
Carver Federal (Harlem), 134–35
Cash-out loans, 129
Center for Community Change (New
  York), 142, 163, 167, 198

Center for Responsible Lending
  (CRL) (North Carolina), 227–28,
  230–31, 269
Center for Self-Help, 212
Charles Schwab and Company, 252
Charles Schwab Bank (Nevada),
  15, 252
Chase Manhattan Bank, 220
Chemical Bank, 220
Chevy Chase Federal Savings Bank,
  193–94
Chicago Area Fair Housing
  Alliance, 192
Chicago Area Project, 140
Chicago Association for
  Neighborhood Development
  Organizations, 166
Chicago Commission on Race
  Relations (1922), 87
Chicago Rehab Network, 166
Chicago Reinvestment Alliance, 166
Cincotta, Gale, 141–42, 143, 144
Citibank, 191
Citigroup, 16, 204, 214, 222–23,
  249, 269, 277n.13
City, The (Park et al.), 89–90
Civil Rights Act (Title VIII) (1968).
  See Fair Housing Act (FaHA)
  (1968)
Civil rights movement, 133, 134–35
Civil War, 55
Claritas, Inc., 130
Classical deregulationist ideology,
  27–28, 29, 44–45; *see also*
  Neoclassical deregulationist
  ideology
Cleveland Advocate, 87
Clinton, Bill, 49, 174, 221, 245
Colorado, 65
Columbia Bank, 54
Commerce Bankshares, Inc., 161
Commercial banking history
  1781–1832, 22, 23–27
  1832–1913, 22, 27–29

Commercial banking history
(*continued*)
    National Banking Era
        (1864–1913), 29
    1913–1980, 22, 30–32
    1980–present, 22, 32–33
    accommodation loans, 24, 33
    amortized loans, 19
    bank charters, 20
    bank holding companies (BHCs),
        31–32
    bank mergers, 32–33
    bills of exchange, 20, 23–24
    black-owned banks, 55–57, 59–60,
        61–62, 134–35, 140–41
    bond investment, 30
    building and loans, 19–20
    classical deregulationist ideology,
        27–28, 29, 44–45
    commercial paper loan, 24
    community reinvestment, 32
    consumer protection, 30, 31, 32–33
    credit cards, 32
    credit history information, 24, 30–31
    credit unions, 19, 56
    depository-nondepository
        regulation, 32
    economic development role, 22–27
    federally-chartered banks, 20, 23,
        25, 27–28
    free banking, 28, 45
    government intervention, 22–33
        policy-financial services nexus,
            19–22
    growth coalitions, 20
    home mortgages, 33, 35–36, 39, 40
    Industrial Revolution, 31
    insider lending, 24–26
    installment lending, 19
    insured bank deposits, 30, 31
    interstate banking, 32, 43
    intrastate banking, 32–33, 43
    liquidity, 20, 23–24, 33
    managerial capitalism, 31

Commercial banking history
(*continued*)
    margin lending, 30
    money supply, 20, 21, 23, 25, 33
    overview, 17
    real bills doctrine, 20, 29, 30,
        33, 35
    savings banks, 19, 20, 55–56
    scientific management, 31
    secondary markets, 20
    securities market, 30
    small business lending, 26, 31
    standardized financial statements,
        24, 26, 30–31
    state-chartered banks, 20, 22,
        23–29, 30
    stock investment, 30
Commercial paper loan, 24
Commission on Home Building and
    Home Ownership (1932), 93
Commoditization, 38, 41–42, 43–44
Community activism; *see also*
    Community Reinvestment Act
    (CRA) (1977); Fair Housing Act
    (FaHA) (1968); Home Mortgage
    Disclosure Act (HMDA) (1975);
    Predatory lending policy;
    specific initiatives/organizations
    bank-ins, 141–42
    business lending discrimination,
        134–35, 141–43
    civil rights movement, 133, 134–35
    housing discrimination, 134
    mortgage lending discrimina-
        tion, 98
    neighborhood organizing, 139–43
    redlining, 136–37, 140–41, 142,
        143, 150–51, 161–62
    social welfare model, 139–40
    subprime lending, 109
Community Development Block
    Grant (CDBG), 149
Community development credit
    unions, 259–60, 279n.12

Community development financial
institutions (CDFIs), 238,
258–61, 279n.11
Community Development Financial
Institutions Fund, 12
Community development loan funds,
259–60, 279n.12
Community Reinvestment Act (CRA)
(1977)
community activism (1977–1987)
CRA agreements, 165–67,
274n.16
CRA challenges, 161–65
CRA rating system, 159–62,
168–70, 172, 173–74,
176–85, 187, 190
early 1980s, 162–67
legislative history, 145–62
redlining, 150–51, 161–62
community activism (1988–1990s)
CRA agreements, 185–91, 203,
242
fair lending laws, 191–98
fair lending lawsuits, 194–95
financial modernization
legislation, 202–6
government-sponsored
enterprises (GSEs), 196,
198–202, 237
policy changes, 168–74
reform progress, 177–85
reform proposals, 174–77
credit access discrimination, 3–4,
62, 63–64, 67, 70–77, 86,
271n.2
depository-nondepository
regulation, 32, 271n.1
legislation impact, 3–4, 5–6,
236–46
bank/loan profitability, 238–41
credit access, 241–46
criticism of, 4, 238–41, 243–45,
268–69, 278n.1
fair lending, 241–46, 262–63

Community Reinvestment Act (CRA)
(1977), legislation impact
(*continued*)
regulator enforcement, 14–17,
236–37, 242–43, 245–46,
267–68
legislation modernization, 246–65
affiliate activity, 250, 279n.5
assessment areas, 15, 250–54,
279n.9
bank holding companies (BHCs),
248, 262–63
basic banking services, 254–58
business lending discrimination,
261–62
community development
financial institutions
(CDFIs), 258–61, 279n.11
credit unions, 250
financial holding companies
(FHCs), 248, 250, 262–63
financial service expansion,
247–50
functional regulation, 248–49
insurance companies, 249, 278n.3
investments, 258–61
loan purchases versus
originations, 264
mergers, 257
mortgage companies, 249, 250
neighborhood racial
composition, 264–65
political environment, 268–70
predatory lending, 262–64
secondary markets, 251
securities market, 249
legislative history, 145–62, 274n.5
credit allocation, 149, 157–59
enforcement, 149, 157–62,
170–72, 173, 181, 184
implementation, 153–56,
184–85
political environment, 145–46,
187, 190, 202–6

Community Reinvestment Act (CRA)
(1977), legislation history
(*continued*)
    primary savings service area
        (PSSA), 151–53, 154–55
    standard metropolitan statistical
        areas (SMSAs), 154, 251
    terminology dispute, 150–53,
        154–55, 250–52, 265
mortgage lending discrimination,
    98–99, 105–6
rating system, 159–62, 168–70,
    172, 173–74, 176–85, 187,
    190, 203
    Community Development Test,
        177, 210
    composite rating, 177, 209, 210*t*
    Investment Test, 176–77, 207–8,
        249, 258–61, 264
    Lending Test, 176, 207, 250,
        258, 261, 275n.16, 276n.17
    Service Test, 176, 177, 208,
        257–58, 279n.10
    strategic plan option, 204, 209,
        276n.18
    wholesale/limited-purpose
        banks, 177, 210, 276n.19
regulators, 153–62, 169, 170–74,
    176, 178–85
    assessment factors, 155, 156*t*
    Joint Policy Statement, 170–72
    legislation impact, 14–17, 236–
        37, 242–43, 245–46, 267–68
Community Reinvestment
    Association of North
    Carolina, 212
Compensatory capitalism, 63
Confederation Congress, 22, 23
Consumer Bankers Association, 82
Consumer Credit Insurance
    Association, 226, 278n.17
Consumer Federation of America, 268
Consumer Protection Act (1968),
    47–48

Continental Bank (Chicago),
    161, 172
Conventional mortgage, 40, 119
Credit allocation, 149, 157–59
Credit cards
    business lending discrimination, 77,
        85–86
    commercial banking history, 32
    subprime lending, 127, 129
Credit history information
    commercial banking history, 24,
        30–31
    subprime lending, 118
Credit Research Center (CRC)
    (Georgetown University), 48,
        228–31, 278n.18
Credit scoring
    business lending discrimination,
        81–85
    lawsuits, 194, 195
    mortgage lending discrimination,
        106–8
    mortgage lending history, 43–44
    predatory lending, 233
Credit Union National Associa-
    tion, 226
Credit unions, 19, 56, 109, 212,
    226, 250
    community development credit
        unions, 259–60, 279n.12
Cross, Steve, 178–79, 181

D

Daley, Richard J., 214
D'Amato, Alphonse, 190, 203
Data mining, 130–31
DataQuick, 131, 273n.8
Data warehousing, 130–31
Decatur Federal Savings and Loan,
    192–93
Dedman, Bill, 168–70
Delaware, 212
De novo banks, 79–81, 272n.4

Deposit Guaranty National Bank
(Mississippi), 195
Depository Institutions Deregulation
and Monetary Control Act
(DIDMCA) (1980), 22, 42, 43,
50, 125, 150
Negotiable Orders of Withdrawal,
144–45
Regulation Q, 42, 145
Deregulation policy. *See* Classical
deregulationist ideology;
Neoclassical deregulationist
ideology
Diners Club, 32
Discounts, 20
Discover Card, 48
Drexel National Bank, 62
Dual financial market, 96, 119–20,
125, 132
DuBois, W. E. B., 56, 57, 58
Dun and Bradstreet, 72

E

Economic development
business lending discrimination, 6,
53–54, 57–58, 60–61
commercial banking history, 22–27
Economic separatism, 57–58, 61
Economic theory, 4, 227, 234–35
Elderly population. *See* Senior
citizens
Emergency Home Finance Act
(1970), 41
Emergency Opportunity Loan (EOL),
63–64
Employment discrimination,
56–57, 62
Enron, 51, 248
Equal Credit Opportunity Act
(ECOA), 3–4, 14, 64, 65, 77, 86
community activism, 138–39, 191,
192–93, 196–98
legislative history, 138–39

Equal Credit Opportunity Act
(ECOA) (*continued*)
Regulation B, 77, 196–98
terminology, 138–39
Equicredit (Illinois), 214, 222,
227n.11
Equity stripping, 126, 273n.7
E-Trade Bank (Virginia), 15, 253
Evergreen credit, 24
Experian, 48, 130

F

Factors, 24
Fair, Isaac, and Company, Inc., 48, 82
Fair Housing Act (FaHA) (1968), 3–4
agency lawsuits, 138
amendments (1988), 136
community activism, 135–39,
191–93
enforcement, 138
implementation, 137–38
legislative history, 135–36, 273n.2
limitations of, 136–37
mortgage lending discrimination,
96, 98, 135–39
redlining, 136–37
regulators, 137–38
Fannie Mae (Federal National
Mortgage Association), 40, 41,
43, 106, 120, 196, 198–202, 216,
248, 251, 264
Federal Deposit Insurance
Corporation (FDIC)
commercial banking history, 30, 31
Community Reinvestment Act
(CRA) (1977), 152, 153–62,
176, 179, 181, 274n.15
establishment (1933), 30
mortgage lending discrimination, 99
trade areas, 152
Federal Home Loan Bank Act (1932),
36, 37

Federal Home Loan Bank Board,
    37–38, 142
  Community Reinvestment Act
    (CRA) (1977), 151, 152,
    153–62, 163, 170
  Fair Housing Act (FaHA) (1968),
    137–38
Federal Home Loan Bank System
  commercial banking history, 20
  establishment (1932), 20, 36, 92
  mortgage lending history, 36–38,
    40, 41, 92
Federal Housing Administration
    (FHA)
  establishment (1934), 36
  insured loans, 38–40, 92–98
  loan foreclosures, 120
  mortgage lending discrimination
    historical context, 92–98
    redlining, 93–98
  Underwriting Manual, 90–91,
    94–95, 96, 97
Federal Housing Enterprises
  Financial Safety and Soundness
    Act (1992), 199, 201
Federal Housing Finance Agency, 181
Federal housing programs, 50–51, 95
Federal Register, 175
Federal Reserve Act (1913), 30, 35
Federal Reserve Bank of Atlanta, 82,
    127, 168–69
Federal Reserve Bank of Boston,
    169–70, 173
  research study (1992), 103–6, 245
Federal Reserve Bank of
    Chicago, 241
Federal Reserve Bank of St. Louis, 46
Federal Reserve Board (FRB)
  Community Reinvestment Act
    (CRA) (1977), 145, 146, 149,
    153–54, 155, 157, 158–63,
    164f, 167, 169, 170, 172, 173,
    176, 179, 193, 197, 203–4,
    238–40

Federal Reserve Board (FRB)
    (continued)
  credit access discrimination,
    65–66, 82
  Fair Housing Act (FaHA)
    (1968), 138
  Home Mortgage Disclosure Act
    (HMDA) (1975), 144, 216–19,
    276n.8
  legislative authority, 30
  mortgage lending discrimina-
    tion, 99
  predatory lending, 215–16, 220,
    225, 226–27
  Senior Loan Officer Survey, 82
Federal Reserve System
  bank holding companies
    (BHCs), 31
  establishment (1913), 22, 30
  neoclassical deregulationist
    ideology, 45, 46, 47, 271n.2
Federal Reserve Working Paper
    (1992), 103
Federal Trade Commission, 125, 195
Financial holding companies (FHCs),
    32, 248, 250, 262–63
Financial Institutions Reform
    Recovery and Enforcement Act
    (FIRREA) (1989), 43, 172–73,
    178, 184, 187, 198, 206, 217
Financial Services Modernization Act
    (1999), 205
First American Real Estate Solu-
    tions, 131
First Bank of the United States, 19,
    25, 27, 147
First Chicago Corporation, 166
First Chicago NBD, 191, 203–4
First Federal Savings and Loan
    (Toledo), 163
First National Bank of Chicago, 166
First Union Bank, 223
Fleet Mortgage Company, 194
Flipping, 124, 131

Forbidden Neighbors (Abrams),
    87–88, 134
Ford, Gerald, 46
Foreclosures
  mortgage lending discrimination,
    104–5
  mortgage lending history, 37, 92
  predatory lending, 123–24,
    211–12
  subprime lending, 120–21,
    123–24
Fourth Conference for the Study
  of Negro Problems (1899)
  (Atlanta), 57
Freddie Mac (Federal Home Loan
  Mortgage Corporation), 41, 43,
  106, 119, 196, 198–202, 216,
  248, 251, 264
Free banking, 28, 45, 56
Freedom of Information Act, 170
Free Labor Bank (Louisiana), 55
Friedman, Milton, 45–46, 145

G

Garn, Jake, 144, 147
Garn-St. Germain Act (1982), 32, 42,
  43, 50
Garvey, Marcus, 57–58
Gaudette, Tom, 141
General Motors Acceptance
  Corporation, 48
Geodemographic marketing
  tools, 130
Georgia
  Community Reinvestment Act
    (CRA) (1977), 168–69
  predatory lending, 219, 220–21
  subprime lending, 110, 112, 114,
    118, 121
Gilleran, James, 221
Ginnie Mae, 40–41
Glass-Steagall Banking Act (1933),
  10, 30, 31, 46, 49, 202

Government intervention; *see also*
    specific legislation
  commercial banking history, 22–33
  policy-financial services nexus,
    19–22
  mortgage lending discrimination,
    65, 90, 92–98
  mortgage lending history, 33–44,
    92–94
Government-sponsored enterprises
    (GSEs)
  Community Reinvestment Act (CRA)
    (1977), 196, 198–202, 237
  government intervention, 40
  predatory lending, 216
Gramlich, Edward, 215, 217–18
Gramm, Phil, 14–15, 190, 191, 197,
  202–3, 238, 268
Gramm-Leach-Bliley Financial
  Modernization Act (GLBA)
  (1999), 10, 22, 32, 49, 190,
  205–6, 247–48
Great Britain, 23, 34
Great Depression, 29, 37, 59–60, 88
Greater New York Savings Bank, 163
Greenspan, Alan, 197
Growth coalitions, 20
Gryzwinski, Ron, 148
Gutierrez, Luis, 247

H

Hamilton, Alexander, 19, 21, 23, 25,
  27, 45, 147
Harris Trust and Savings Bank
  (Chicago), 166
Hawkes, John D., 49
Heinz, John, 149
Home Mortgage Disclosure Act
  (HMDA) (1975), 3–4
  annual percentage rate (APR),
    218–19, 276n.7
  business lending discrimination,
    196–98

Home Mortgage Disclosure Act
    (HMDA) (1975) (*continued*)
    community activism, 133, 143–45,
        146, 172–73, 176, 191, 192–93,
        194, 196–98, 216–18,
        274n.2
    legislation modernization, 216–19,
        241, 276n.8
    legislative history, 143–45, 146, 148
    mortgage lending discrimination,
        65, 68–69, 98–99
    predatory lending, 216–19, 225
    regulators, 146, 216–19
    subprime lending data, 110, 112,
        113*f*, 115*t*, 116*t*, 272n.2
Home mortgage lending. *See*
    Mortgage lending
    discrimination; Mortgage
    lending history; Predatory
    lending; Subprime lending;
    specific legislation
Home Ownership and Equity
    Protection Act (HOEPA) (1994),
    109, 211, 213, 215–16, 218, 225,
    276n.1
Home Owners Loan Act (HOLA)
    (1933), 37–38, 93
Home Owners Loan Corporation
    (HOLC), 13, 37, 92, 93–94
Hoover, Herbert, 21, 36, 92, 93
Household Finance, 16, 223, 269
Household International, 48
Housing and Community
    Development Act (1977),
    145, 149
Housing discrimination, 56–57, 62,
    96, 134
Housing Training and Information
    Center, 142
Hoyt, Homer, 91
Hull House, 139
Human Relations Commission of
    Chicago (1962), 91
Huntington Mortgage Company, 194

I

Illinois
    basic banking services, 256
    black-owned financial institu-
        tions, 60
    community activism, 140, 141–43,
        165, 166, 191, 196
    credit access discrimination, 64–65,
        77, 81
    mortgage lending discrimination,
        87, 89, 92
    predatory lending, 121–22, 212–14,
        216, 219, 276n.2
    subprime lending, 112, 113*f*,
        114–18, 121, 272n.3, 273n.4
Independence Bank, 62
Independent Community Bankers of
    America, 204
Indiana, 28
Industrial Revolution, 31
Information externalities, 50, 67,
    82–83
Information technology, 129–32, 244
    automated underwriting, 43–44,
        103, 106, 195, 237
    credit scoring, 43–44, 195, 237
    Internet usage, 130,
        131–32, 253
Insource, 130
Installment lending, 19
Insurance companies
    black-owned, 55
    legislation modernization, 249,
        278n.3
    mortgage lending history, 33,
        35–36, 39, 40
Interagency Fair Lending
    Examination Procedures, 195–96
Interagency Task Force on Fair
    Lending (1994), 193
Internet usage, 130, 131–32, 253
Interstate banking, 32, 43, 163
Intrastate banking, 32–33, 43

J

Jackson, Andrew, 22, 27–28, 29, 45
Jefferson, Thomas, 27, 45
Johnson, George, 62
J.P. Morgan Chase, 220

K

Kahn, Alfred, 145
Keynesians, 45, 145
Kuttner, Robert, 143

L

Laissez-faire ideology, 19, 21, 46
Land contract, 91–92, 96
Laufman v. Oakley (1976), 136
Leach, Jim, 215
Lee, Matthew, 181
Lindsey, Lawrence, 167, 176
Liquidity
  commercial banking history, 20,
    23–24, 33
  mortgage lending history, 36–37,
    41, 43
Litan, Robert, 224–25, 226–27
Loan term variations
  mortgage lending discrimination, 95
  mortgage lending history, 35–36,
    37, 38–39, 41, 42
  predatory lending, 122–24
Loan-to-value ratio variations
  mortgage lending discrimination, 95
  mortgage lending history, 35–36,
    37, 39
Long Beach Mortgage, 194–95
Louisiana, 26
Ludwig, Eugene, 175, 178–79

M

Mack, Connie, 202
MAF Bancorp (Chicago), 196

Managerial capitalism, 31
Mapping systems
  mortgage lending discrimination,
    93, 94–95
  policy maps, 47
Margin lending, 30
Marketing/sales, 103, 130, 193–94
  push marketing, 122, 123*t*, 129
Maryland, 53, 88, 118
Massachusetts
  commercial banking history, 23,
    25, 26
  Community Reinvestment Act
    (CRA) (1977), 169–70, 173
  predatory lending, 213
MasterCard, 48
MBNA, 48
McCollum, Bill, 193, 202
McFadden Act (1927), 30, 31
McKenzie, Roderick D., 89–90
McLean, Ken, 143
Memorandum R-49, 42
Mergers
  business lending discrimination,
    77–79
  commercial banking history, 32–33
  predatory lending, 220, 222–23
Metropolitan Area Housing Alliance
    (MAHA) (Chicago), 142
Michigan, 118, 214, 216
Military banks, 55–56
Minnesota, 28
Minority Bank Deposit Program (U.S.
    Department of the Treasury),
    61–62
Minority discrimination. *See*
    Business lending discrimination;
    Mortgage lending
    discrimination; Predatory
    lending; Subprime lending
Monetarism, 45–46
Money Store, 223
Money supply, 20, 21, 23, 25, 33
Moral hazard, 96

Morgan Stanley, 234, 278n.19
Mortgage-backed securities (MBSs),
    40–41, 43
Mortgage Bankers Association of
    America, 119, 193
Mortgage Bankers Association of
    North Carolina, 213
Mortgage bonds, 35
Mortgage brokerage industry
  fair lending initiative, 194, 263
  mortgage lending discrimination,
    100, 102–3
  mortgage lending history, 43
  subprime lending, 129, 132
Mortgage companies
  legislation modernization,
    249, 250
  mortgage lending history, 33, 35,
    39, 40, 41
  subprime lending, 109–10, 126–27
Mortgage Conference of New
    York, 134
Mortgage lending discrimination;
  see also Business lending
  discrimination; Predatory
  lending; Subprime lending
  contemporary context
    anticipated discrimination, 102
    automated underwriting,
      103, 106
    business necessity test, 106, 139
    community activism, 98
    credit scoring, 106–8
    government intervention, 98–99,
      105–6
    lending process, 100–106
    lending trends, 108
    marketing/sales, 103
    mortgage brokerage industry,
      100, 102–3
    neoclassical deregulationist
      ideology, 104–5
    redlining, 103, 105
    research parameters, 99–107

Mortgage lending discrimination
  (continued)
  historical context
    Federal Housing Administration
      (FHA), 92–98
    government intervention, 65, 90,
      92–98
    land contract, 91–92, 96
    real estate industry, 87–88, 89,
      90–92, 94, 96
    redlining, 67–68, 93–98
    research data, 87–88, 89–91, 92,
      94–95, 97
    savings and loans (S&Ls), 91–92
  redlining
    dual financial market, 96
    Federal Housing Administration
      (FHA), 93–98
    historical context, 67–68, 93–98
    lender influence, 105
    mapping systems, 93, 94–95
    marketing/sales, 103
    moral hazard, 96
    pure redlining, 89
    research data, 67–68
    social ecology theory, 89–91
    suburbs, 95, 97
    succession theory, 89–90
Mortgage lending history
  1831–1931, 33, 34–36
  1932–1981, 33, 36–42
  1982–present, 33, 42–44
  amortized loans, 38, 39
  automated underwriting, 43–44
  building and loans, 33, 34, 35
  buyer-holders, 41
  commercial banks, 33, 35–36,
    39, 40
  commoditization, 38, 41–42, 43–44
  conventional mortgage, 40
  credit scoring, 43–44
  Fannie Mae, 40, 41, 43
  Federal Home Loan Banks, 36–38,
    40, 41

Mortgage lending history
   (*continued*)
FHA-insured loans, 38–40
foreclosures, 37, 92
Freddie Mac, 41, 43
Ginnie Mae, 40–41
government intervention, 33–44,
   92–94
government sponsored enterprises
   (GSEs), 40
Home Owners Loan Corporation
   (HOLC), 37, 92, 93–94
individual lenders, 33
insurance companies, 33, 35–36,
   39, 40
liquidity, 36–37, 41, 43
loan term variations, 35–36, 37,
   38–39, 41, 42, 95
loan-to-value ratio variations,
   35–36, 37, 39, 95
Memorandum R-49, 42
mortgage-backed securities (MBSs),
   40–41, 43
mortgage bonds, 35
mortgage brokerage industry, 43
mortgage companies, 33, 35, 39,
   40, 41
overview, 17
risk diversification, 39
savings and loans (S&Ls), 33, 34–39,
   40, 41
   bailout bill, 43
   commercial real estate loans, 42
   federally-chartered, 37–38, 92
   industry collapse, 42–43, 46, 50
   terminating societies, 34
   time deposits, 34
savings banks, 33, 34–36, 39
secondary markets, 36, 37, 38, 39,
   40, 41–42, 43, 46
second mortgages, 36
securitization, 38, 40, 43, 44
standardization, 37–38, 41–42
straight mortgage, 36, 37

Mortgage lending history
   (*continued*)
Veterans Administration (VA) loans,
   39, 40
Multiplier effect, 20
Mutual aid societies, 54–55
Myrdal, Gunnar, 60

N

Nader, Ralph, 145, 163
National Advisory Commission on
   Civil Disorders (Kerner
   Commission), 135
National Association for the
   Advancement of Colored People
   (NAACP), 134–35, 140
National Association of Real Estate
   Boards, 88, 90
National Association of Supervisors
   of State Banks, 29
National Bank Act (1864), 29, 35, 56
National City Bank of Cleveland, 221
National Commission on Consumer
   Finance (NCCF), 47–48, 138,
   271n.3
National Committee Against
   Discrimination in Housing, 144
National Community Reinvestment
   Coalition (NCRC), 165–66, 174,
   187, 203, 204, 246–47, 268,
   274n.16
National Conference of State
   Legislatures (2003), 216
National Consumer Law Center, 268
National Credit Union
   Administrations, 250
National Freedmen's Savings and
   Trust Company, 55–56
National Housing Act (1934), 36, 38
National Housing Conference
   (1972), 142
National Housing Survey (2001)
   (Fannie Mae), 120

National Monetary Commission
    (1908), 30
National Negro Convention (1855)
    (New York), 55
National People's Action (NPA), 142,
    143, 268
National Training and Information
    Center, 142, 166, 198
National Urban League, 137–38
Nationsbank, 190
Nationscredit, 222
Negro World, 58
Neighborhood Housing Services
    (NHS), 6, 141, 165
Neoclassical deregulationist
    ideology, 44–51
  community-individual interests,
      22, 51
  credit policy research, 47–48
  Federal Reserve System, 45, 46, 47,
      271n.2
  monetarism, 45–46
  mortgage lending discrimination,
      104–5
  policy maps, 47
  political environment, 8–12, 236,
      265–67, 271n.4
  predatory lending, 48, 109
  primary economic goods, 9
  progressive perspective, 21–22, 30
  public goods, 21
  quasi-public goods, 21
  spillover effects, 21–22, 49–51
    commercial banking, 50
    federal housing programs, 50–51
    fringe financial institutions, 50
    information externalities, 50
    mortgage lending
        discrimination, 104–5
  utilitarian perspective, 21–22, 30
NetBank (Atlanta), 253
New Deal, 36
New England Economic Review, 170
New Jersey, 216

New Markets Tax Credit, 12
New Mexico, 216
New York
  black-owned financial institutions,
      55, 88
  commercial banking history, 23, 26,
      27, 28, 29
  community activism, 142, 163, 167
  predatory lending, 213, 216, 219,
      220–21, 223
  subprime lending, 114
New York Times, 222
Nixon, Richard, 46, 51, 97
North Carolina, 48, 88
  predatory lending, 212, 213, 216,
      219, 223, 224, 225–26, 227–35
North Carolina Association of
    Mortgage Brokers, 213
North Carolina Fair Housing
    Center, 212
Northern Trust Company
    (Chicago), 166
North Milwaukee State Bank,
    140–41
Northwest Community Organization
    (NCO) (Chicago), 141–42

O

Office of the Comptroller of the
    Currency (OCC)
  bank stock-investment, 30
  community activism, 99, 142
  Community Reinvestment Act (CRA)
      (1977), 153–62, 175, 176,
      178–79, 181, 184, 193, 197
  de novo banks, 79
  establishment (1864), 29
  Fair Housing Act (FaHA) (1968), 138
  Home Mortgage Disclosure Act
      (HMDA) (1975), 143
  mortgage lending discrimination,
      92, 99
  predatory lending, 219–21

Office of Thrift Supervision (OTS)
  Community Reinvestment Act
    (CRA) (1977), 99, 176,
    179, 197
  predatory lending, 219–21
O'Hare Airport (Chicago), 214
Ohio, 118, 214, 216, 221
*One Hundred Years of Land Values in
  Chicago* (Hoyt), 91
Organization for a Better Austin
  (OBA), 141
Organization for the North East
  (O.N.E.) (Chicago), 142–43
Outcome-based redlining, 67–68
Oxford Provident Building
  Association (Philadelphia), 34

P

Panic of 1837, 28
Panic of 1907, 30
Park, Robert E., 89–90, 91, 139–40
Park State Bank (Milwaukee),
  140–41
Pennsylvania
  black-owned financial institutions,
    55, 88
  commercial banking history, 23, 26
  community activism, 141
  mortgage lending history, 23, 26
  predatory lending, 216, 222
  subprime lending, 114, 118
Performance Data, 130
Philadelphia Commission on Human
  Relations (1992), 192
Philadelphia Mortgage Plan, 148
Policy maps, 47
Political environment
  business lending discrimination, 64
  Community Reinvestment Act
    (CRA) (1977)
    legislation modernization, 268–70
    legislative history, 145–46, 187,
      190, 202–6

Political environment (*continued*)
  neoclassical deregulationist
    ideology, 8–12, 236, 265–67,
    271n.4
Powell, Adam Clayton, 134–35
Predatory lending; *see also* Subprime
  lending
characteristics of
    balloon payments, 122, 123*t*, 234
    lending practices, 122–24, 273n.5
    loan flipping, 124, 131
    loan terms, 122–24
    prepayment penalties, 122, 123*t*,
      129, 233
    push marketing, 122, 123*t*, 129,
      224–25
  foreclosures, 123–24, 211–12
  lawsuits, 194–95
  lending increase, 109, 121–22,
    129, 131
  neoclassical deregulationist
    ideology, 48, 109
  overview, 17
Predatory lending policy
  city legislation, 213–14
    state preemption, 214
  community activism
    city-level, 211–12, 213–14
    federal-level, 215–18
    foreclosures, 211–12
    legislation impact, 223–24
    reputational risk strategy,
      221–23, 269–70
    single premium credit insurance
      (SPCI), 214, 215–16,
      226–27, 276n.5
    state-level, 211–13, 219–21
  federal legislation, 211, 213,
    215–16, 218, 225, 276n.1
    annual percentage rate (APR),
      218–19, 276n.7
    modernization of, 216–19
  government-sponsored enterprises
    (GSEs), 216

Predatory lending policy (*continued*)
  mergers, 220, 222–23
  overview, 18
  state legislation, 211–13, 216
    balloon payments, 234
    credit scoring, 233
    economic theory, 227, 234–35
    empirical research, 227–35
    federal preemption, 219–21,
        276n.10
    impact debate, 223–35
    prepayment penalties, 233
    push marketing, 224–25, 232
Prepayment penalties, 122, 123*t*, 129,
    233
President's Commission on Financial
    Structure and Regulation (1971)
    (Hunt Commission), 46
President's Third Annual Report on
    National Housing Goals (1971), 97
Price discrimination, 124
Primary savings service area (PSSA),
    151–53, 154–55
Private banks, 20
Process-based redlining, 68–70
Progressive ideology, 21–22, 30
Proxmire, William
  community activism, 140–41
  Community Reinvestment Act
      (CRA) (1977), 145, 146,
      147–49, 152, 154, 158, 162,
      169, 251
  Home Mortgage Disclosure Act
      (HMDA) (1975), 143–44
Public Company Accounting
    Oversight Board, 248, 278n.2
Pure redlining, 67, 89
Push marketing, 122, 123*t*, 129,
    224–25

R

Reagan, Ronald, 97–98, 237
Real bills doctrine, 20, 29, 30, 33, 35

Real estate industry, 42, 87–88, 89,
    90–92, 94, 96
Redlining. *See* Business lending
    discrimination; Community
    activism; Mortgage lending
    discrimination
Relman, John, 196
Reputational risk strategy, 221–23,
    269–70
Rhode Island, 55
Riegle-Neal Interstate Banking and
    Branching Efficiency Act (1994),
    32–33
Romney, George, 97
Roosevelt, Franklin, 36, 37, 45, 93
Rousselot, John, 144
Rubin, Robert, 204
Russell Sage Foundation, 109
Rust Belt recession (1980s), 98

S

Safety Fund Act (1829) (New York),
    26, 27
Sarbanes, Paul, 153–54, 220
Savings and loans (S&Ls)
  black-owned, 55, 88–89
  mortgage lending discrimination,
      91–92
  mortgage lending history, 33,
      34–39, 40, 41, 42–43, 46, 50
Savings Bank of the Grand Fountain
    United Order of True Reformers
    (Virginia), 56
Savings banks
  black-owned, 55–56
  commercial banking history, 19, 20,
      55–56
  mortgage lending history, 33,
      34–36, 39
Savings Fund and Land Association
    (California), 55, 88
Schultze, Charles, 145
Schwartz, Anna, 45–46

Scientific management, 31
Seaway National Bank, 62
Secondary markets; *see also specific operation*
  commercial banking history, 20
  mortgage lending history, 36, 37, 38, 39, 40, 41–42, 43, 46
  predatory lending, 219
Second Bank of the United States, 22, 27–28, 45
Second mortgages, 36
Securities market
  commercial banking history, 30
  mortgage lending history, 40–41, 43
  subprime lending, 126–27, 128*f*
  tranches, 126–27, 128*f*
Securitization
  mortgage lending history, 38, 40, 43, 44
  subprime lending, 127, 129, 201–2
Seidman, Ellen, 221
Senate Committee on Banking, Housing, and Urban Affairs, 14–15, 143, 151, 190, 191, 197, 202–3, 204, 238
Senior citizens, 126, 129
Shadow Financial Institutions Regulatory Committee, 49, 179, 224, 277n.15
Shaw, Clifford, 140
Shawmut Mortgage Company, 193
Shawmut National Bank, 193
Shawmut National Corporation, 193
Shelby, Richard, 197, 202
Shelley v. Kraemer (1948), 96, 134
Single premium credit insurance (SPCI), 214, 215–16, 226–27, 276n.5
Small Business Administration (SBA) loans, 12, 62, 63–64
Small business investment companies (SBICs), 258, 260
Small business lending. *See* Business lending discrimination

Small business opacity, 76
Smith, Adam, 44–45
Smith, Stephen, 54
SMR Research, 131–32
Social ecology theory, 89–91, 139–40
Social welfare model, 139–40
Solomon Smith Barney, 214
South Brooklyn Against Investment Discrimination, 163
South Carolina, 228–31, 233
South Dakota, 212
South Shore Commission (Chicago), 142
South Shore National Bank (Chicago), 142, 148, 153, 259
St. Germain, Fernand, 144
Standardization
  commercial banking history, 24, 26, 30–31
  mortgage lending history, 37–38, 41–42
Standard metropolitan statistical areas (SMSAs), 154, 251
State Farm Federal Savings Bank, 15
Statistical redlining, 67
Stock investment, 30
Straight mortgage, 36, 37
Subcommittee on Financial Institution Regulation, 144
Subprime lending; *see also* Predatory lending
  community activism, 109
  contemporary status, 132
  credit history information, 118
  defined, 110
  government intervention, 110, 125
  home equity loans
    conventional loans, 119
    dual financial market, 119–20, 125, 132
    hypersegmented market concerns, 119–20
    lending increase, 109, 110, 124–27, 128f, 129

Subprime lending (*continued*)
 hypersegmented market concerns,
  119–24
 lawsuits, 194–95
 lending increase, 109–18
  1994–2001, 110, 111*f*
 lending increase factors, 124–32
  asset-backed securities, 126–27,
   128*f*
  credit cards, 127, 129
  data mining, 130–31
  data warehousing, 130–31
  demand-side, 125–26
  equity stripping, 126, 273n.7
  geodemographic marketing
   tools, 130
  information technology, 129–32
  Internet usage, 130, 131–32
  mortgage brokerage industry,
   129, 132
  mortgage companies, 126–27
  price discrimination, 124
  securitization, 127, 129, 201–2
  security tranches, 126–27, 128*f*
  senior citizens, 126, 129
  supply-side, 125–27
 mortgage companies, 109–10,
  126–27
 overview, 17
 refinance loans
  cash-out purposes, 129
  foreclosures, 120–21, 123–24
  hypersegmented market
   concerns, 119–24
  lending increase, 109–18, 124–32
  1993–1998, 110, 112*t*
  research data, 110–18
Succession theory, 89–90
SunTrust Bank (Atlanta), 168

T

Tax Reform Act (1986), 125
Telebank (Virginia), 252

Tennessee, 88, 228–31, 233
Texas, 118, 141–42, 190–91
Thompson, James, 214
Thrifts. *See* Savings and loans
 (S&Ls)
Toledo Fair Housing Center, 163
Trans Union, 48
Trapp, Shel, 141–42
Travelers Group, The, 191
Travis, Dempsey, 62
Tyco, 51

U

Underwriting. *See* Automated
 underwriting; *specific
 institution*
Universal Negro Improvement
 Association, 57
University of Chicago, 89, 104,
 139–40
Urban Institute, 192
Urbanization, 6–8, 56–57
U.S. Bureau of the Census, 64
U.S. Commission of Civil Rights,
 92, 135
U.S. Department of Energy, 61–62
U.S. Department of Housing and
 Urban Development (HUD)
 business lending
  discrimination, 77
 community activism, 136–37,
  192–93, 196, 199–202
 Fair Housing Act (FaHA) (1968),
  136–37, 192
 government sponsored enterprises
  (GSEs), 199–202
 Home Mortgage Disclosure Act
  (HMDA) (1975), 144
 mortgage lending discrimination,
  97–98
 predatory lending, 215–16
 subprime lending analysis,
  110–18

U.S. Department of Justice
  community activism, 134, 137–38,
    191–96, 197, 198, 268
  Equal Credit Opportunity Act
    (ECOA), 77
  Fair Housing Act (FaHA) (1968),
    137–38, 191
U.S. Department of the Treasury,
    61–62, 215–16
U.S. General Accounting Office
    (GAO), 262–63
U.S. Office of Management and
    Budget (OMB), 137–38
U.S. Supreme Court, 94, 96, 134,
    136, 163
Utilitarian ideology, 21–22, 30

V

Valuation of Real Estate, The
    (Babcock), 90–91
Veterans Administration (VA) loans,
    39, 40

Virginia, 56, 228–31
Visa, 48

W

Warburg, Paul, 30
Washington, Booker T., 57
Washington, George, 19
Wells Fargo Bank, 83
Wells Fargo Financial, 234
Western Union, 32
West Side Coalition (Austin),
    141–42
Wilson, Woodrow, 30
Wisconsin, 28, 118, 130, 140–41
Woodlawn (Chicago), 140
Woodstock Institute (Chicago), 166,
    196, 198, 222
WorldCom, 51, 248
World War II, 7, 21, 39

Y

Yankelovich Partners, 64–65

About the Author

Dan Immergluck is assistant professor in the School of Public and Non-profit Administration at Grand Valley State University in Grand Rapids, Michigan, where he teaches courses in public policy and urban studies. Prior to joining the faculty at Grand Valley, Dr. Immergluck was the Senior Vice President of the Woodstock Institute in Chicago, a nonprofit community development research organization. He has also worked in state government and for a nonprofit community development corporation. In addition to writing on community reinvestment and fair lending topics, Immergluck has published numerous articles and reports on urban policy, community development, housing, and minority business development. Immergluck's research has been covered in the *New York Times*, the *Wall Street Journal*, the *Chicago Tribune*, and numerous other print and broadcast media. He has testified before the U.S. Congress, the Federal Reserve Board of Governors, the Department of Housing and Urban Development, and state and local legislative bodies. He holds a masters in public policy from the University of Michigan and a Ph.D. in public policy analysis from the University of Illinois at Chicago.